AF605886

The Sound of Writing

The Sound of Writing

Edited by
Christopher Cannon
Steven Justice

Johns Hopkins University Press
Baltimore

Printed in the United States of America on acid-free paper
9 8 7 6 5 4 3 2 1

Johns Hopkins University Press
2715 North Charles Street
Baltimore, Maryland 21218
www.press.jhu.edu

Library of Congress Cataloging-in-Publication data is available.

ISBN-13: 978-1-4214-4724-7 (hc)
ISBN-13: 978-1-4214-4725-4 (pbk)
ISBN-13: 978-1-4214-4726-1 (ebook)

A catalog record for this book is available from the British Library.

Contents

Acknowledgments

The editors would like to thank the Krieger School of Arts and Sciences of Johns Hopkins University and the Alexander Grass Humanities Institute, in particular, for funding the conference in which many of the essays of this book were first presented and discussed. We are grateful, too, to Ilene McCoy, who so ably ensured that every aspect of that conference ran smoothly, and to Sharon Achinstein, Jonathan Hsy, Jenna Phillips, William Egginton, Kate McKinley, and Theresa Coletti, who chaired the days' panels with energetic aplomb. Shane Butler, Virginia Jackson, Jeff Dolven, and Eleanor Johnson gave brilliant papers on these days, from which all the conference's attendees benefited greatly, even though, for various reasons, these papers did not become essays here.

It was the faith in this project of Catherine Goldstead, the commissioning editor in the humanities at Johns Hopkins University Press, and Barbara Kline Pope, the press's executive director, that made this volume possible. We are also grateful to Joe Abbott for the exemplary care he took in copyediting this book in its penultimate version.

The Sound of Writing

Introduction

Christopher Cannon and Steven Justice

The catachresis in our title has deep roots in the West's understanding of the senses. Aristotle likened all sensation to the impress of an object into a piece of wax because he thought that whatever we see or hear (or taste or smell), we also touch, since every bodily perception is a mode of "contact" with either an object or a medium.[1] Such a theory necessarily lends itself to noticing other moments or modes in which usually separable senses are conjoined. So, when writing about the parts of animals, Aristotle observed that the "organ of smell" for an elephant is also its hand.[2] Although Aristotle worked hard to separate the senses, the kinds of mash-ups he noticed reappeared in many later aesthetic theories. Herder, for example, thought that sculpture of a certain excellence might "come alive" by transforming "seeing into a form of touching" so that anyone perceiving such a work would be like someone blind from birth whose "eye becomes his hand."[3] What Wagner called the "word-tone-speech" (*Wort-Tonsprache*) of opera addressed itself to "hearing's eye."[4] Even Marx was thinking in such terms when he said that all "human relations to the world—seeing, hearing, smelling, tasting . . . [and] all the organs of . . . individual being" are just differing forms of an "orientation to the object"; that is, all the forms of contact through which we apprehend the physical world are one and the same.[5]

Of course, we were hearing with our eyes long before any of these theories of the senses were devised, if we may assume that each of the many times writing was invented, it was a technology designed to capture speech.[6] Marks on a surface may be part of "oracular and ritual practices," signify "mystic and kabbalistic doctrine," or represent "Gnostic and human belief"—to name only a few nonverbal functions—since there is, as Johanna Drucker has put it in relation to current technologies, no sound "*on* the page."[7] Still, the marks that all known writing systems comprise are a "provocation" for sound (as Drucker also puts it), and we define these marks as writing because their "limited set of shapes" provide an aural map for "the thousands of linguistic noises produced by the specialized organs of the throat and mouth."[8] Jack Goody and Ian Watt thought it required a "stupefying leap of the imagination" to think of "representing sound by a graphic symbol" in this way.[9] Yet we seem to have conjoined sound with the marks we make on surfaces even before such marks became what is normally called "writing" or sought to transcribe the sounds with which they were conjoined.

Pictographic scripts have historically preceded the more simplified form of linear scripts like our own, but, even before glyphs or characters, the images on the walls of the caves of Arcy-sur-Cure in Burgundy, made some twenty-eight thousand years ago, had phonic qualities for their makers.[10] To stand before these representations of animals still familiar to us (a salmon and an ibix, figs. I.1 and I.2), as well as animals long vanished (a mammoth, fig. I.3) is to touch them not just with the eye but with the ear. That is, testing the resonance of this cave (and other paleolithic paintings in similar caves) shows that the most resonant places in these underground spaces are "always decorated or at least marked," as if each such place "calls for a picture."[11] The correspondence is equally strong in the other direction: the images of the salmon, ibix, and mammoth, as well as many others, are all found in particularly resonant parts of the cave, as if every image "required sound."[12] The implication is not, of course, that these images sound like a salmon in the water or an ibix or mammoth moving over the ground. Rather, they reflect back the sounds of breath, of feet disturbing rocks or sliding over dirt, of rubbing folds of clothing, or the clattering of carried objects (stone or metal) as they knock into one another. Because they could only be apprehended by a body capable of making such sounds, these works of art could never have been, nor ever will be, silent. The consequence is that, to hear this art, we do not need to reconstruct the sounds that the Paleolithic man or woman heard twenty-eight thousand years ago because, even now, the images of ibix, salmon, and mammoth produce sounds we can hear.

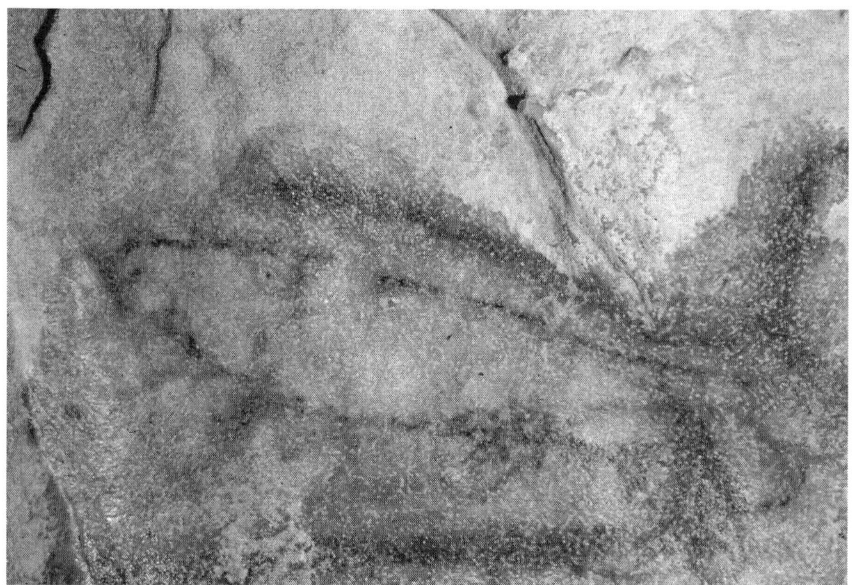

Figure I.1. Salmon (Salle des vagues, Arcy). Collection La Varende. Photo D. Baffier. Used by permission.

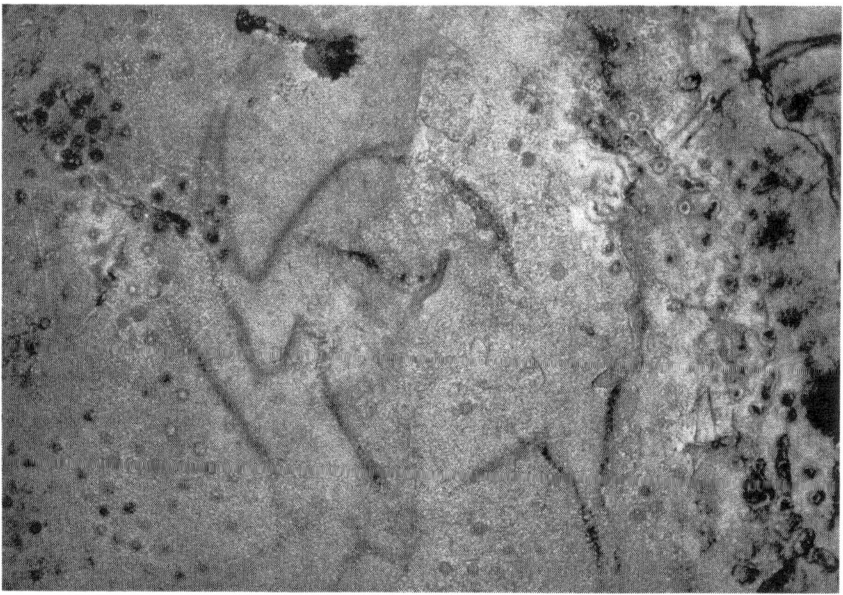

Figure I.2. Ibex (bouquetin) (Salle des vagues, Arcy). Collection La Varende. Photo M. Girard. Used by permission.

Figure I.3. "Diamond-incrusted" mammoth (mammoth "diamante") (Mezzanine, Arcy). Collection La Varende. Photo M. Girard. Used by permission.

Yet, however much and however long sound and marks on surfaces were entwined in human practice, the attunement of our own ears to the sounds of such marks often requires considerable analytic work. Iegor Reznikoff's sense that the drawings in the cave of Arcy-sur-Cure resonated began when he noticed an increased resonance around some paintings, but he could not establish a correlation until he had mapped all the chambers of these painted caves sonically, as he did for many other similar repositories of Paleolithic art. He describes how he walked and crawled through these caves—sometimes in the middle, sometimes near the wall—singing or whistling softly (because the caves were resonant enough to pick up the slightest vibration). When he got the cave to "respond," as he put it, he would use a tuning fork to find the pitch that was producing the resonance but also to establish whether harmonics or overtones of that pitch would also resonate. He tested a variety of orientations for singing and whistling in order to determine which points and angles of origin produced the most vivacious sound, noting the precise location in which this resonance had been created.[13] The result was a number of maps of the chamber called the Salle des Vagues in Arcy-sur-Cure that detailed the relationship of the duration of the resonance (measured in seconds) and

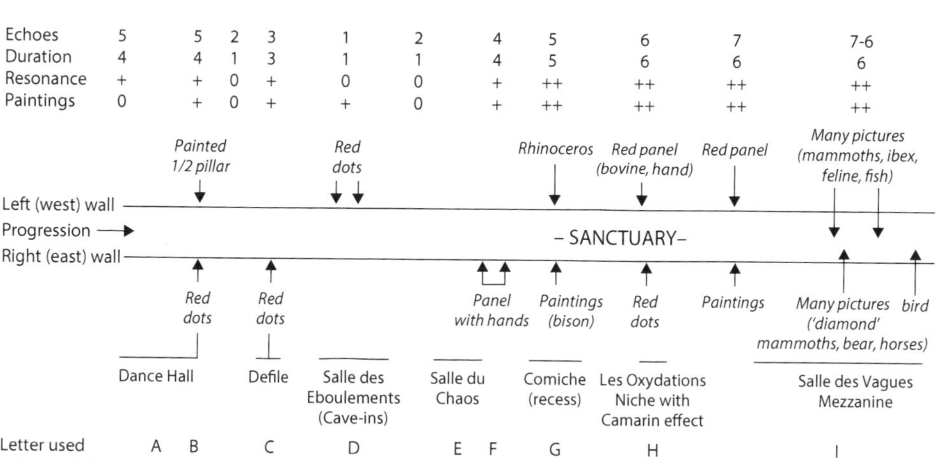

Figure I.4. Sound map of the Salle des Vagues in Arcy-sur-Cure. Iegor Reznikoff, "Prehistoric Paintings, Sound and Rocks," in *Studien zur Musikarchäologie III*, ed. Ellen Hickmann, Anne D. Kilmer, and Ricardo Eichmann (Rhaden/Westfalen: Leidorf, 2002), 47. Used by permission.

the number of audible echoes within that duration to the location of each painting (fig. I.4). These maps show the cave to be most quiet in a blank section of the chamber, or where there were only "red dots," and most sonically alive next to the largest concentration of pictures.

Analytic work has even been required for us to hear the writing before us on pages like this one. Eric Havelock was not unlike Reznikoff in attempting to specify the unique sonic capacities of our own alphabet: although he did not walk through a soundscape, he moved—as if passing through time—through the soundscapes created by known scripts. He thought first about cuneiform writings and Linear B, both "vocalized syllabaries" that broke speech down into the "units of speech as they seem actually to issue from the mouth in what we call 'syllables.'"[14] Since every sign in such a system must contain a vowel, a syllabary signifies by oversupply, providing signs for many more vowels than are meant to be pronounced.[15] The sounds "JAK AND JIL" would have to be represented in a form like the following (where each dyad represents a single sign):

JA KA A NA DA JI LU

In such a system, the number of signs "might run into the hundreds," and so the advance made in the Phoenician "unvocalized syllabary," or North Semitic system (from which Persian, Sanskrit, Aramaic, Arabic, and Hebrew descended), reduced the number of symbols by eliminating the vowels.[16] Because the consequence of this change was to identify single letters with a repeatable element of speech, the Phoenician system is often called the "first alphabet," but this is, in Havelock's view, to get ahead of things, since the simplification came at the cost of the representation of some sounds that had to be filled in by every reader.[17] Jack and Jill could be represented with only six marks, but these marks did not represent the necessary vowels:

J K N D J L

Working through these scripts systematically and across time let Havelock claim that it was the "Greek system" that counted as the "true alphabet."[18] The steps of this analysis revealed that Greek letters create a one-to-one correspondence between defined shapes and particular sounds ("a vibrating column of air which is also started or stopped, or both started and stopped . . . by the action of lips, palate, tongue and, and teeth").[19] It was, in Havelock's view, the Greek alphabet that was "first" because its few letters provided "complete coverage of all possible phonemes."[20]

More recent analysis suggests that Reznikoff and Havelock were wrong about some of the correspondences they claim. Work that tests the acoustics of caves with newer technologies finds weaker (though still significant) correlation between image and resonance than Reznikoff suggested.[21] Havelock's extravagant claims for the tight correlation between the Greek alphabet and new ways of thinking ("the Greeks did not just invent an alphabet; they invented literacy and the literate basis for modern thought") have brought his whole history of scripts into disrepute.[22] These two "sonographies" (to use R. Murray Schafer's term) may not only be inaccurate, but they differ enough from one another that they do not, on their face, suggest how the history of the relationship between sound and writing could be written: Reznikoff proceeds synchronically, coordinating sounds he is making in a present with what he can see on the walls he is standing next to, while Havelock proceeds diachronically, comparing scripts used over several millennia.[23] Yet within these differences, and despite what might be their errors, both Reznikoff and Havelock hear writing by means of a *method*. Beyond the initiating aperçu, they devise a sequence of attuning steps that show that a sonography of writing will not consist of one way of opening one's ears or aligning one's senses perceptually; rather, it needs a variety of investigations, drawing on the modes of analysis of a variety of disciplines.

This book provides more such methods from just such a variety of disciplines and the sounds they reveal, and it insists—both in its presumptions and analyses, collectively and above all—that hearing the sounds of writing *requires* such system. The individual essays here also show that hearing such sounds requires the critique of system. Our insistence on this double imperative reflects the durable effect wrought on all humanistic disciplines by deconstruction half a century ago: only system can permit the rational testing of proposals, but any particular system will also mask the wobbly structures on which its concepts are perched. Thus, as Derrida characteristically insisted, there can be no system of critique, just critique of system in the form of peripheral but vigilant attention to the undecidabilities one finds oneself treating as decided. The essays in this collection have also hoped to exemplify just this imperative—conducting rigorous arguments in the recovery of historical sound while querying the terms necessary for those arguments.

At the same time, such an enterprise can seem a pert snub to lingering deconstructive conventions. The identification of "phonocentrism"—the supposed primacy of voice over writing, which Derrida found to be vessel and symptom of a camouflaged metaphysics and the illusion of meaning securely buttressed—hit literary studies hard. Claiming to hear the "voice" of a literary work came to seem shady and aversive; certainly the present editors, both trained during the years of deconstruction's dominion, felt it in their youth with the force of a taboo. Bliss was it in that dawn to be a graduate student. Derrida gave the study of English writing an occasion to scrap that midcentury hegemon of literary scholarship, the "new criticism," and its habits of argument, which had become ever more untenable. Scrapped, too, was any bluff confidence in hearing the "voices" of poetic and narrative "speakers," as if they were naturally and obviously sounded by the page; the easy recourse to "tone," as if it were a given; and any faith that meaning could be feelingly conveyed by sound. Derrida's criticisms of Saussure and Husserl seemed almost custom-designed against these habits, which multiplication had both discredited and made vapid.

All this was to the good. But we acknowledge this long episode here to say that, in our view, such a critique never did or could discredit the study of written language as evidence of sounded language. The *phōnē* in Derrida's phonocentrism was the "voice" delusively felt to be the true life of language, a speaker's presence in utterance bestowing meaning as if it could be simply "heard"; and his "writing" was the impersonal and unstable reticulation of difference that preceded every utterance and left any fullness of meaning indefinitely deferred. He did not show—was not interested to show, indeed did not seem to think—that the fallacies of phonocentrism meant there could be no reasoning from graphic evidence to sound, no way of making the definitionally vanished sounds of spoken language recorded in writing an object of historical inquiry or of investigating the history of such records.

We began then by comparing the way some of the oldest marks might sound with the way the marks on these pages sound because this book is also interested—again, both collectively and above all—in the way that the history of such sounds and their historical recovery provoke such rigorous and methodical attention. We note Reznikoff's synchronic and Havelock's diachronic mode not to privilege one over the other but to observe that historical understanding impels both; that this, in turn, impels the aspiration to system; and that system both supplies answers to historical queries and must be queried itself. Hearing just how the marks we call letters capture the shape of breaths emerging from mouths and throats makes someone walking through a cave more likely to notice the resonance of marks on a wall; the person who has heard a Paleolithic cave-painting—or learned how sonically active such a painting can be—is more likely to look down at the page on which he or she is recording observations and begin to see how the marks resonate. We need not reach beyond a particular moment to hear how writing sounds or sounded in other times, but our presumption in this volume is that a historical sonography always better attunes our eyes and ears for such hearing.

If history impels us to hear writing more clearly, there is a history *of method* that may inform us, too. Rhetoric as a discipline (from ῥητορικός, or "public speaker") approached the blending of writing and sound as if in diametric opposition to alphabets: initially, "a theory of public speaking" (*ratio dicendi*), it soon became a way of describing the structure of writing, too.[24] Although we are less in touch with this scope when we use the term, Roland Barthes, for one, wanted us to keep in mind that writing is "vocal" even when it is "nothing like speech," that texts are made of "language lined with flesh" to the extent that they always ask us to imagine, through the consonants and vowels we see, the "whole carnal stereophony" by which those letters might be realized—not the sound we might make if we should read the words before us but the sounds that writing captures. When writing began to write about itself in the ancient world, it quickly developed its own vocabulary and technique for pointing to the sound it was capturing. In Quintilian, for example, one term of art for the correspondence was *apta pronuntiatio* (appropriate delivery), and the insistence that the speech or words delivered "be adapted" (*accommodatur*) to the subject about which the rhetor was speaking issued in a more granular set of injunctions describing how such adaptation would occur:

> Given a happy theme the voice flows full unaffected, and with a sort of cheerfulness of its own. In a contentious situation, on the other hand, it is roused in all its strength and strains every nerve. In anger it is fierce, harsh and concentrated, with frequent pauses for breath. . . . In creating animosity, the voice becomes somewhat more hesitant, because only inferiors commonly have recourse to such tactics. In flattery, confession, apology, or request, it is gentle and subdued. Persuasion, warning, promises, and consolations demand a deep voice; fear and shame a restrained one; exhortation needs a strong voice, debate a precise one, compassion one that is flexible, tearful, and deliberately half-muffled.[25]
>
> [Itaque laetis in rebus plena et simplex et ipsa quodam modo hilaris fluit; at in certamine erecta totis viribus et velut omnibus nervis intenditur. Atrox in ira et aspera ac densa et respiratione crebra. . . . Paulum in invidia facienda lentior, quia non fere ad hanc nisi inferiores confugiunt; at in blandiendo fatendo satisfaciendo rogando lenis et summissa. Suadentium et monentium et pollicentium et consolantium gravis: in metu et verecundia contracta, adhortationibus fortis, disputationibus teres miseratione flexa et flebilis et consulto quasi obscurior.]

Such techniques were developed for orations, but just as rhetoric generally came to shape written texts, such injunctions also came to govern writing *as* delivery, mapping these contours of the voice onto the contours of a text.[26] This evolution ensured that writing could be of a particular "kind" (genus) or "form" (forma) or could have in its contours what we have come to call a "style" (12.10.1–2; 5:280–81).[27] Inasmuch as such "style" became something like the recording of a voice, it could be reverse-engineered to play back the sounds of that voice in all its distinctiveness. This is exactly how the historian and rhetor Dionysius of Halicarnassus described the written form of the speeches of Demosthenes, whose "literary style" (λέξις [lexis]), he said, is a technique that "prescribes . . . the kind of delivery that will be required" (διδάσκει . . . μεθ᾽ οἵας αὐτὴν ὑποκρίσεως ἐκφέρεσθαι δεήσει).[28] If readers "take special care to deliver every sentence in the manner intended by the orator" (ἐπιμελῶς . . . παρατηρεῖν, ἵνα τοῦτον ἕκαστα λέγηται τὸν τρόπον, ᾗ ἐκεῖνος ἐβούλετο), they will reproduce the "modulations of the voice" (τὰ πάθη τὰ της φωνης) that had made that writing sound like Demosthenes

Thus, rhetoricians developed ever-finer methods for transforming writing into what Shane Butler has called the "ancient phonograph."[29] In his defense of Archias, the poet, in a trial of 62 BCE, Cicero may be seen to evoke something of the sounds Reznikoff was hearing as he walked through caves when he imagines Homer's singing echoing off the rocks around him: "The very rocks of the wilderness give back a sympathetic echo to the voice; savage beasts have sometimes been charmed into stillness by song; and shall we, who are nurtured upon all that is highest, be deaf to the appeal of poetry?" (Saxa et solitudines voci respondent, bestiae saepe immanes cantu flectuntur atque consistunt: nos instituti rebus optimis non poëtarum voce moveamur.)[30]

For the most part, this correspondence has to be imagined to be heard, and Cicero's style is only briefly matched in sound to his subject (the clause coming to a neat conclusion as "stillness" is described). But the shape of Cicero's declamation was also made audible by a more abstract patterning or recording technique: the prose rhythms called *clausulae*, specific combinations of long and short syllables that were used both to mark and adorn the ends of periods or phrases (in the following passage short syllables are in italics, long syllables are in bold, and the end of each *clausula* is underlined):

> Saxa et so*li*tu*di*<u>**nes**</u> vo**ci** **respond**<u>**ent**</u>**,** bestiae **saepe imma**<u>**nes**</u> can**tu flectun**<u>*tur*</u> **at***que* **consis**<u>**tunt**</u>**:** nos **in***sti***tu**<u>**ti**</u> **re***bus* **op***ti*<u>**mis**</u> **non** *po*ëta<u>**rum**</u> **vo***ce move*a<u>*mur*</u>?[31]

This is not a recording of the cheerfulness or flattery or anger that Quintilian thought an apt delivery could produce, but, just as Reznikoff's "mammoth" does not sound like an animal, these *clausulae* do not sound, nor are they meant to sound, anything like echoes off rocks; they are, rather, an autonomous set of rhythmic patterns playing over the patterns of sense in the words they ornament. In capturing less than the sense of the speaker's words, however, the *clausulae* organize and therefore capture somewhat more of his sound, since their patterns preserve the patterns produced by a vibrating column of air started or stopped by the action of lips, palate, tongue, and teeth. Reading these words out, in other words, would not only produce Cicero's advocacy for Archias but replicate what Barthes would have called the "grain" of his voice; it is "to replay [a] lost soundtrack," as Butler has put it, to hear in the reading or to be in a position to reproduce in reading something of the very sounds Cicero once made.[32]

We now tend to describe the patterns in such a soundtrack in terms of "rhythm," or *rhythmos* (ῥυθμός), and the history of this term could take us back once again to the synaesthesia inherent in Greek theories of the origins of the senses, here as atomists such as Democritus first used "rhythm" to describe not sounds but shapes and patterns perceived with the eyes rather than with the ears,[33] or as Plato applied the term to "choric art," not to describe the speech or song of the chorus but the "order in movement" of their dance.[34] *Meter* is the term of art developed for describing the order or rhythm of the sounds captured by writing, and history is once again a useful method for understanding how this particular sonographic technology works. Here, we could go back to the earliest surviving fragments of Latin literature in Livius Andronicus's translation of the *Odyssey*, or, further still, to the *Odyssey* itself, but since the words on the page before you are English, it is perhaps enough to go back to the oldest poem that survives in what we would call English (though distinct enough from our own speech to call that English "Old"), verses we now call "Caedmon's Hymn." These metrical lines are first noted in the record in the Latin of the *Ecclesiastical History of the English People* (c. 730), where Bede paraphrases the song sung by a man who, he says, miraculously learned to compose such songs late in life. Having retired from a feast just before he was handed the harp with the expectation that he would sing, he falls asleep in a barn, where he dreams about composing a song for the abbess and other "learned men" (*doctiores*) the next day.[35] Bede can only give what he calls the "sense" of this song because, he says, it is "not possible to translate verse . . . literally from one language to another without some loss of beauty and dignity" (ex alia in aliam linguam ad uerbum sine deterimento sui decoris ac dignitatis transferri), and, of course, what he has lost most of all in his detailed rendering is the original poem's sound:

> Nunc laudare debemus auctorem regni caelestis, potentiam Creatoris, et consilium illius, facta Patris gloriae; quomodo ille, cum sit aeternus Deus, omnium miraculorum auctor extitit, qui primo filiis hominum caelum pro culmine tecti, dehinc terram Custos humāni generis omnipotens creauit.
>
> [Now we must praise the Maker of the heavenly kingdom, the power of the Creator and his counsel, the deeds of the Father of glory and how He, since He is the eternal God, was the author of all marvels and first created the heavens as a roof for the children of men and then, the almighty Guardian of the human race, created the earth."] (4.24 [416–17])

So provoking was this loss to many of the English-speaking scribes who copied Bede that in thirteen of the surviving copies of the Latin text they wrote the English they knew next to, or between the lines of, the Latin in front of them, turning an account of an important event in the history of English poetry into a recording of it:

> Nu scylon hergan   hefaenricaes uard
> metudaes maecti   end his mōdgidanc
> uerc uuldurfadur   suē hē uundra gihuaes
> ēci dryctin   ōr āstelidæ

Hē āerist scōp eordu barnum
heben til hrōfe hāleg sceppend
thā middungeard moncynnæs uard
ēci dryctin æfter tīdæ
fīrum foldu frēa allmectig.[36]

Caedmon has been said to have adapted a heroic idiom to Christian themes, using what has been called the "appositive style" (which elaborates a subject through almost-synonymous half-lines), although this aspect of his style survived in Bede's translation.[37] Revivified in these glosses, however, are not only the metrical patterns customary in Old English verse but, in that meter, the grain of Caedmon's voice, muted of course on any number of axes (tone, timbre, volume, pitch) but equally well a full record of the patterns in the language he used.

What was that meter? Because it is the oldest such verse we have, its sound is not easily heard, and another painstaking method was required to detect the sonography Caedmon was employing. What we seemed to know from the end of the nineteenth century is that Old English verse from "Caedmon's Hymn" onward was constructed in half-lines (as the lines are divided above), with a pause or caesura in between them, the contours of which fall into five "types" according to the pattern of stresses, unstressed syllables, and half-stressed or weakly stressed syllables.[38] Over time, such analysis tried harder and harder to attune modern ears to these ancient sounds, for at least one reader found the tempo of such patterns elusive and any attempt to play back its sound "spasmodic" at best: John C. Pope recommended that the five types be allowed to unfold in equal time by adding a "rest" (or brief pause) to the beginning of the shorter line types so that (at least to him) it would sound more "natural."[39] Such attunement continues apace with theories about the kind of rhythm a poet such as Caedmon used still emerging.[40] Later styles of verse in Middle and early Modern English required and so generated new modes of metrical analysis, at first based on classical ideas of "feet" and rhythmic patterns, and these have yielded more recently to "generative" modes of analysis modeled on Noam Chomsky's theories of universal grammar.[41] If these changes in analytic mode—or refinements, as they are usually understood—suggest that we have not been hearing the sounds of writing accurately, their accumulation suggests how we may become more accurate. As if we are adjusting the bass and treble on a stereo (if we have one) or exchanging vinyl for a CD for an mp3, we hear better and more clearly as we elaborate our method.

As closely focused on local questions of language and expression as the essays that follow are, they have these questions of method and theory always at hand: questions about how to refine, extend, combine, and supply new coherence or alertness to hearing the sounds of writing and about how to demonstrate the ways writing has preserved them and questions about what terms, premises, interests, and consequences are called forth by the project and by ways of undertaking it. Two of the essays (those of Meredith Martin and Christopher Hasty) are extensively theoretical in discursive organization, as well as consequence; the others canvass matters methodological and theoretical, working through them while moving at full empirical speed.

The desire to snatch some voice from the lapse of time appears as itself a datum and object of study in the essays that begin the volume and finds itself brought abruptly down to earth by them. The lack of female voices from ancient Greek writing felt by scholars and modern readers appears in Sarah Nooter's essay as a lack already registered in Greek poetry, in epitaphs that create voices for certain women: deceased women mourning their own deaths, female ornaments mourning the deaths of men. The felt lack that this poetry reveals, however, is not the women's thoughts and sensations registered in their own voices; if their composers had been interested in those, they need not have gone far for them. It was the presence of women's voices securing the preservation of men in memory and in family that was wanted and, accordingly, supplied. Nooter shows how the mixing of word and matter, and the mixing of arts, in inscription on stone monuments becomes incorporated into the poems themselves over the course of time and how this incorporation provides one female author material for responding to the expressive structures of memorial verses.

In the essay that follows, Sarah Kay begins with a class of medieval readers who demonstrably faced the need to precipitate from texts the sounds they represented. These readers were scribes copying verse—in this case troubadour verse—and worrying about how to break lines in poems they found written continuously without line breaks and so to display their verse forms. Kay shows that such scribes might not find it a simple task nor have a settled way of going about it: one might be guided, or then one might be misled, by some melody the words had brought to mind. But the mixing of media and of the different senses they address as central is not epiphenomenal. As Kay shows, medieval accounts of the Aristotelian understanding of sense-cognition with which we began here recognized that scanning and associating all the senses was necessary for recognizing the deliverances of each. And poets could use this fact to guide the hearing of their verse once it has lodged silent on the page: an ingenious reading of a Marcabru lyric shows how the poet evokes distinct senses to clarify its sonic organization.

Kay's essay suggests that it's too easy to treat the influence of apparently extrinsic, apparently chance associations on reading and hearing as mere interference, deforming or distracting apprehension by the operation of ideology or vulgar taste or just accident. These associations display a logic, and the logic will sometimes prove solid. Jennifer Richards's essay treats Charles Butler's early seventeenth-century melittological work *The Feminine Monarchie*. Butler, setting out to explain the structure and behavior of hived bees by listening to what he believed to be their songs, transcribed their rhythm and pitch in musical notation and then composed a four-part madrigal (for *human* singers) to narrate the natural history of a swarm. These devices almost beg to be dismissed as unhinged anthropomorphism, fantasizing bees as drawing-room society. But Richards shows that Butler made significant discoveries about bees by these means and that what he misconstrued was "updatable with more accurate information." His musical transcriptions and compositions did not impute human artistry; they gave observed sounds a formalized notation that represented them for others' hearing and made them available for analysis. And she shows that his experiments with phonetic spelling treat human language itself with just such instruments.

In the last generation, the study of Middle English meter, especially that of the period's alliterative long line, has ventured in from the margins of the field to near its center: ambitious, informed by historical grammar, and energetically conceptualized, a tight predictive account has emerged of a meter once thought to be expressive but slovenly. Ian Cornelius extends the logic of this account into territory where it might seem not to apply. Using the example of William Langland's *Piers Plowman,* he asks how a violation of the meter's defining structure (rhythmically asymmetrical half-lines) can be, and can be known to be, deliberate, an effect worked in rhythm rather than its abrogation. Such a judgment is by definition outside meter's predictive competence: metrical schemata cannot even in principle distinguish deliberate violation from mistake. Other critical procedures, in this case text-critical ones, can make it the most probable explanation for one line that is metrically most eccentric. But the explanation in turn raises the question of how medieval readers who were not in a position to collate scribal readings and reason through them might recognize the premeditated effect of such a line. Cornelius shows that Langland trains his readers by a gentle tutorial on meter's liminal possibilities and is aware both of his experiments and of readers' likely difficulties discerning them.

Emily Thornbury's essay catalogues salient features of the British pronunciation of Latin in the earlier Middle Ages. The range of evidence she maneuvers and the conclusions she draws show how much of historical pronunciation remains to be retrieved and leaves evidence for that retrieval; the range of conceptual considerations she raises in doing so demonstrates how intellectually deft and self-aware the work of retrieval can be. In addition to the reconstructed sounds of Anglo-Latin themselves, the essay achieves two brilliant effects. The first is a vivid though implicit riposte to a familiar habit of scholarly discourse. Even now, one can hear medieval Latin—both the language itself and the learned culture for which it stands metonymically—treated as a serenely self-sustaining and self-defining thing over against the welter of local, mutable, mutually incomprehensible or mutually offensive vernaculars. The evidence of Latin dialect differences that she uncovers even within Britain (along with the snide comments she quotes about other people's Latin dialects) makes a bracing antidote to such habits. (And as she points out, such conclusions can in their turn become evidence for political and cultural history.) Second, by such reconstruction and the evidence assembled for it, she is able to uncover what she describes as "experimental" forms of Latin poetry in the early insular centuries.

To the inquiries that surround it in the volume, Meredith Martin poses a question and challenge: when you set out to recover the sound of past writing, what do you think you're looking for? Martin begins by suggesting that the widespread adoption of our now familiar phonetic categorization of consonants ("sibilants, plosives, fricatives, liquids") played a role in silencing arguments in the nineteenth century about pronunciation and about poetic meter at the moment poetry as idea and form was becoming regulated and regularized. Building on the arguments of Virginia Jackson and Yopie Prins, Martin proposes that the installation of these categories for the description of voice—unable truly to *specify* sounds—invites users to assume stable pronunciation (stable over time, stable among and between groups) as the instrument on which the sonic effects of a characterless poetic speaker are played and to assume that poetic meter can be described in patterns shared naturally and uncontroversially among readers, among periods, among classes, among individual speakers. It invites them to imagine as characterless, neutral, unmarked, *natural* precisely the voice whose racial, regional, class, and gendered qualities mark it as normative. On Martin's account, the impetus that disciplined the study of sound in language and in poetry through the last century and a half made invisible (and inaudible) the unregulatable variety of speech and its sounds, as well as the different ways that sonic properties could be selected out for metrical description; it made also invisible the inventive, competing, noncommensurate attempts to mark sound on printed words offered by eighteenth-century lexicographers, orthoepists, and grammarians discussed in the essay's final section.

Martin's question about "the concept of sound in writing" can be usefully put to the essays already discussed, and answers are ready, or readily discoverable, in them; the same can be said of broader questions about abstraction in philological research, about what is selected and excluded for analytical categories, and about what the technical vocabularies of humanities research occlude. The essays that follow all back up a little, in different ways, to put more focus on these larger questions.

Sean Curran's discussion of a thirteenth-century motet does not at first glance seem to "back up" at all: taken at close range, noticing everything, it is an almost-too-close reading (twisting a phrase of D. A. Miller's) of words and music, deploying patiently and precisely the medievalist's technical tools to define what is there to be read and using other of those tools to read it. But these insistently virtuoso interpretations of document and art move in parallel with reflections on the disciplines that produced these tools and their assumption that music as brilliantly complex as *Par une matinee / Mellis stilla / Alleluya* could have been produced only by academics. The reading enabled by those tools shows that the motet itself identifies and responds to that assumption; it suggests a much richer history, and models a more adequate historiography, of the motet form.

Alison Cornish moves lucidly from passage to passage in Dante without announcing larger aims, but her essay assembles as it goes an intricate argument bearing on the feasibility of any written "phonograph." Dante famously writes a treatise advocating the "illustrious vernacular" and then famously abandons the treatise to instantiate his vernacular in the *Comedy*. But, Cornish shows, he recognizes that no written vernacular, however illustrious, can capture or therefore perpetuate and cue the vernacular sounds, simply because vernacular sound is defined as *unfixed* (a term she shares with Martin) in its relation to written language. Correspondingly, the *Comedy* is able to secure (to *fix*) much; but this, its sound, is precisely what it cannot. Dante creates a dynamic in which poetry can emerge from the untutored sounds of the vernacular and can, in turn, act on and refine its reader. It just cannot act sonically. The sound of the illustrious vernacular can be only the sound of its reader.

Christopher Cannon's essay begins by having some fun with the diminutive scale of its object—Chaucer's final *-e*, a single letter that represents either barely a sound or no sound at all—but this object is a persistent embarrassment to Chaucer's readers and has produced a scholarly impasse that has lasted for decades. This was the deadlock of "the metricists" (as Cannon calls them), who insisted that final *-e* must be available as a sounded syllable to preserve that Chaucerian *je ne sais quoi*, and "the grammarians," who insisted brusquely that sounded *-e* was obsolete or obsolescent by Chaucer's time and that facts is facts. Somehow the big feelings of this unresolved debate, once expressed, gave way to a tacit genial agreement that in practice it makes no difference, really. Cannon's argument addresses the logical peculiarities of this deadlock and takes seriously the evidence that, despite it, those on both sides tend to hear that theoretically disputable *-e* in more or less the same way. Cannon concludes by thinking about that desire, mentioned earlier, that spurs the search for past sounds. Yes, such desire charges a debate like this with passion: are we hearing Chaucer's voice or not? But the desire is not only on the side of readers and scholars. Chaucer's art represents Chaucer's choice about how he wished his lines to sound, and Cannon concludes the essay by suggesting that the metrical requirements of each line are all the evidence we need to serve his desire.

The final essay, rangy and meditative, is by Christopher Hasty, who states, untwines, and retwines the following points: the sound of any writing is phenomenologically actual only in an act of *sounding*; that sounding, because it is an act and not merely an event, is susceptible of choice and so also of deliberation, exploration, and experimentation; that soundings, and thus sounds (and thus meanings and connotations as well), are therefore definitionally unfixed, open (his favored word); that such openness is a component of communication, not a drag on it; that poetry and *Kunstprosa* invite readers to slow the sounding, to advert to the deliberation and experimentation it involves; and that, when so slowed, the reader's sounding reveals its similarity and its relation to the soundings to which authors have recourse in the act of composition. These are, we think, the key propositions; but true to the spirit of its inquiry, the essay's exploration of rhythm ("the manner of moving") lives as much by evoking and reflecting on experience, moment to moment, as by achieving conclusions, and by the persistence of its expedition through the "rhythms-events" of a passage from Gertrude Stein.

The phrase "sound of writing" may name many phenomena, and as in any phenomenology, the nature of the description will of necessity shape its object. But this volume embraces such alterations and traffics in their analytic possibilities because it is, above all, an attempt to open this phrase to its descriptive potential and the variety of its meanings. The essays collected here generate that variety, in some part, from their different disciplinary perspectives but, most of all, by moving iteratively across a long temporal axis, sure in the faith that among the most rigorous methods for attuning our ears to writing's sound is historical understanding. In the difference of their archive and approach, all of these phenomenologies are united in their attempts to refine our ability to hear. Like Reznikoff approaching the picture all ears, bending toward the space just in front of the star-studded mammoth the better to capture the overtones or echoes, or Havelock writing out ancient scripts to model how they could capture the sounds of speech, each of the writers in this volume offers a new sonography.

NOTES

1. Aristotle, "On the Soul," in *The Complete Works of Aristotle*, ed. Jonathan Barnes, 2 vols., rev. ed. (Princeton, NJ: Princeton University Press, 1984), 641–92, 424a18–24 and 424b24–34. Aristotle also differentiated between the senses in the details of their function, understanding himself to correct an atomism that "reduced all sensory modalities to touch"; Cynthia Freeland, "Aristotle on the Sense of Touch," in *Essays on Aristotle's "De Anima,"* ed. Martha C. Nussbaum and Amélie Oksenberg Rorty (Oxford: Oxford University Press, 1995), 227–48, 228.

2. Aristotle, "Parts of Animals," in *The Complete Works of Aristotle*, ed. Jonathan Barnes, 2 vols., rev. ed. (Princeton, NJ: Princeton University Press, 1984), 994–1086, 658b29–659a1.

3. Johann Gottfried Herder, *Sculpture: Some Observations on Shape and Form from Pygmalion's Creative Dream*, ed. and trans. Jason Gaiger (Chicago: University of Chicago Press, 2002), 43.

4. Richard Wagner, *Opera and Drama* (Lincoln: University of Nebraska Press, 1995), 273–74, as cited in Mark Payne, "The Understanding Ear: Synaesthesia, Paraesthesia, and Talking Animals," 34–52, in *Synaesthesia and the Ancient Senses*, ed. Shane Butler and Alex C. Purves (London: Routledge, 2013), 44. For the original, see Richard Wagner, *Oper und Drama* (Leipzig: J. J. Weber, 1869), 252.

5. Karl Marx, "Economic and Philosophic Manuscripts of 1844," in Karl Marx and Frederick Engels, *Collected Works*, 50 vols. (New York: International Publishers, 1975), 3:229–346, 299–300, cited in Robert Jütte, *A History of the Senses: From Antiquity to Cyberspace* (Cambridge: Polity Press, 2005), 9.

6. On the "fewer than a dozen instances of the invention of writing . . . recorded in human history," see Johanna Drucker, *The Alphabetic Labyrinth: The Letters in History and Imagination* (London: Thames and Hudson, 1995), 12–13.

7. Drucker, 12 ("oracular . . . mystic . . . Gnostic"); and Johanna Drucker, "Not Sound," 237–48, in *The Sound of Poetry, The Poetry of Sound*, ed. Marjorie Perloff and Craig Dworkin (Chicago: University of Chicago Press, 2009), 239 (*"on"*).

8. Drucker, "Not Sound," 243 ("provocation"); Eric Havelock, "The Oral-Literate Equation: A Formula for the Modern Mind," in *Literacy and Orality*, ed. David R. Olson and Nancy Torrance (Cambridge: Cambridge University Press, 1991), 1–27, 24.

9. Jack Goody and Ian Watt, "The Consequences of Literacy," in *Literacy in Traditional Societies*, ed. Jack Goody (Cambridge: Cambridge University Press, 1968), 27–68, 38.

10. Drucker, *Alphabetic Labyrinth*, 16.

11. Iegor Reznikoff, "Prehistoric Paintings, Sound and Rocks," in *Studien zur Musikarchäologie III*, ed. Ellen Hickmann, Anne D. Kilmer, and Ricardo Eichmann (Rhaden/Westfalen: Leidorf, 2002), 39–56, 43 ("always") and 44 ("calls").

12. Reznikoff, 44.

13. This account summarizes Reznikoff's description in "Prehistoric Paintings," 41–42.

14. Eric A. Havelock, *The Literate Revolution in Greece and Its Cultural Consequences* (Princeton, NJ: Princeton University Press, 1982), 66 ("vocalized") and 68 ("units").

15. Havelock, *Literate Revolution in Greece*, 78.

16. Havelock, 66 ("unvocalized") and 68 ("might").

17. Havelock, 79.

18. Havelock, 65.

19. Havelock, 80.

20. Havelock, 81.

21. See B. M. Fazenda et al., "Cave Acoustics in Prehistory: Exploring the Association of Palaeolithic Visual Motifs and Acoustic Response," *Journal of the Acoustic Society of America* 142 (2017): 1332–49.

22. Havelock, *Literate Revolution in Greece*, 82. For a fuller history of the alphabet, see Drucker, *The Alphabetic Labyrinth*, 10–48; for criticism of the ethnocentrism of Havelock's theories (not all Greeks were literate not least because literacy was "implicated in structures of administrative power") and the extent to which historical claims about the sophistication of the Greek alphabet derive from "the high esteem in which Greeks held literacy," see Sarah Nooter's essay in this volume, esp. 000–000.

23. R. Murray Schafer, *The Tuning of the World* (New York: Knopf, 1977), 7.

24. *Rhetorica ad Herennium*, ed. and trans. Harry Caplan (Cambridge, MA: Harvard University Press, 1954), 2–3 (I.1).

25. Quintilian, *The Orator's Education*, ed. and trans. Donald A. Russell, 5 vols. (Cambridge, MA: Harvard University Press, 2002), 1.11.3.61 (5:116–17). Hereafter, we cite this volume by book and section number, as well as volume and page number, in the text.

26. Quintilian firmly maintained that "speaking and writing well are one and the same thing" (unum atque idem videtur bene dicere ac bene scribere) (12.10.51 [5:308–9]).

27. Russell translates "genus orationis" (kind of oration) here and throughout *The Orator's Education* as "style" (5:280–81).

28. Dionysius of Halicarnassus, "On the Style of Demosthenes," in *Critical Essays*, ed. and trans. Stephen Usher (Cambridge, MA: Harvard University Press, 2014), 1:232–455, 440–43. Hereafter, we cite this volume in the text. We derive this citation and observation from Shane Butler, *The Ancient Phonograph* (New York: Zone, 2015), 188.

29. Butler offers an extended meditation and investigation on what he calls the "vocal claim" (*The Ancient Phonograph*, 25) made by texts.

30. Cicero, "Pro Archia," in *Pro Archia, etc.*, ed. and trans. N. H. Watts (Cambridge, MA: Harvard University Press, 1923), 19:1–42, 26–27. Hereafter, we cite this source by section number as well as volume and page number in the text.

31. We derive this example from Butler (*The Ancient Phonograph*, 169), although we have expanded Butler's markings using Louis Laurand, *Études sur le style des discours de Cicéron*, 2 vols. (Paris: Les Belles Lettres, 1928), 1:214 (from which Butler derived them) to mark syllabic length as well as the end of each clausula.

32. Roland Barthes, "The Grain of the Voice," in *Image, Music, Text* (New York: Hill and Wang, 1970), 179–89; Butler, *The Ancient Phonograph*, 169–70. Butler, here, is also citing John Dugan, "Cicero's Rhetorical Theory," in *The Cambridge Companion to Cicero*, ed. Catherine E. W. Steel (Cambridge: Cambridge University Press, 2013), 25–40, 39.

33. Emile Benveniste, *Problems in General Linguistics*, trans. Mary Elizabeth Meek (Coral Gables, FL: University of Miami Press, 1971; first published in French, 1966), 282.

34. Plato, *Laws*, in *The Collected Dialogues*, ed. Edith Hamilton and Huntington Cairns (Princeton, NJ: Princeton University Press, 1961), 1225–1513, 665a.

35. *Bede's Ecclesiastical History of the English People*, ed and trans. Bertram Colgrave and R. A. B. Mynors (Oxford: Clarendon Press, 1969), 4.24 (416–17). Hereafter, we cite this volume by chapter, section, and page number in the text.

36. Daniel Paul O'Donnell, *Cædmon's Hymn: A Multimedia Study, Archive and Edition* (Cambridge: D. S. Brewer, 2005), 61 (for this edition of the text); for detailed descriptions of the manuscripts of the poem, see O'Donnell, 78–97. We have excluded from our count here manuscripts of the Old English translation of Bede where these verses are not glosses but incorporated into the text.

37. On the poem's use of heroic idioms for Christian themes, see C. L. Wrenn, "The Poetry of Cædmon," *Proceedings of the British Academy* 32 (1946): 277–95; and F. P. Magoun Jr., "Bede's Story of Cædman: The Case History of an Anglo-Saxon Oral Singer," *Speculum* 30 (1955): 49–63. O'Donnell, however, challenges this "critical commonplace" (60 and 60n1). On the formulaic "style," see Fred C. Robinson, *Beowulf and the Appositive Style* (Knoxville: University of Tennessee Press, 1985).

38. For a useful summary of these types, devised by Eduard Sievers, see *Seven Old English Poems*, ed. John C. Pope (New York: Bobbs-Merrill, 1966), 109–16. "Caedmon's Hymn" is analyzed according to Sievers's types in O'Donnell, *Cædmon's Hymn*, 61.

39. John C. Pope, *The Rhythm of Beowulf: An Interpretation of the Normal and Hypermetric Verse-Forms in Old English Poetry* (New Haven, CT: Yale University Press, 1942), 39. On this theory as applied to lines from "Caedmon's Hymn," see Pope, *Seven Old English Poems*, 116–29.

40. Ian Cornelius describes the "paradigm shifts" in the history of Old English meter (including eighteenth- and nineteenth-century theories that preceded Sievers) and Nicolay Yakovlev's more recent claims that morphology rather than stress governs the meter's recurrent patterns. See Ian Cornelius, *Reconstructing Alliterative Verse: The Pursuit of a Medieval Meter* (Cambridge: Cambridge University Press, 2017), 44–66.

41. For a detailed account of these developments in metrical analysis, see Derek Attridge, *The Rhythms of English Poetry* (London: Longman, 1982), 3–55.

CHAPTER ONE

The Sounds and Matter of Women in Ancient Greek Epigrams

Sarah Nooter

> A Grave is a tranquilizing object.
>
> WILLIAM WORDSWORTH, "ESSAYS UPON EPITAPHS" (1810)

Among the unrecoverable items of the vanished ancient Greek world are the sounds of women. In a way, all ancient sounds are now lost to us, but add up all the speeches, plays, poems, and dialogues still preserved, and one can start to sense a kind of cacophony: the clashing field of war, the shrill harangues of the courtroom, the languorous chatter of the symposium. But little can be conjured of the sounds of women; little was said in public, and less was written down. In this formulation, I leave aside the voices of female characters in epic, tragedy, and other fictionalized genres penned by men as overly distant from the sounds, voices, and experiences of actual ancient Greek women. I focus instead on a sort of negative impression of the absence of women in ancient writings: what we might see as the murmurs of the missing. These traces are preserved, I suggest, through efforts toward materializing the sounds of women by material means in epigrams.

In this essay, I seek to tease out the materials and temporalities of female voices in the context of ancient Greek epigrams, in comparison with a few ancient Greek songs. Each of the epigrams I cover aims to offer the voice of a woman and to do so through both poetic sounds and material presence. At times, this material presence is constituted by the actual object on which the writing appeared or a statue that is posed as speaking its words. At other times the materiality is sublimated into the content of the text: stone, dust, or wind is not evident but depicted. In general, we can trace a progression from the use of material (stone, bronze) in the archaic age to the depiction of material in poems in the classical and Hellenistic periods. In every case, however varied the means, we see an attempt to imagine an embodied woman as the source of the sounds written in the text.

Who are these women? They are not constituted through literature—not scripted as characters in epic or tragedy, for example—and thus not smoothed down into narrative teleologies. They are, in this sense, less fictitious than fictive, figures conceived singularly, even sculpturally: merely a voice and a body. Each one shapes its own context. (I write *its*, not *hers*, because these are only figures of the feminine, more neuter than female. They only possess actual voices of women in the most attenuated sense of *of*.) None of the epigrams that I discuss here offers a woman known from myth (although one song that I discuss does). Thus, they are not recurring characters whose pasts are known from stories. Nor are they considered immortal, royal, or otherwise set apart from the run of common humankind. There are no Hecubas, no Electras, no Helens. Yet they are not "realistic," let alone real: these figures are shaped from the stuff of marble and bronze or, conversely, imagined as in dialogue with the wind and other elements in their natural environment. Though they exist as imaginative projections of their authors and observers, they also derive something of their texture from the realities of women in quotidian contexts. Epigrams, in other words, bring us uncommonly close to actual ancient women in an unusually material and unexpectedly sonic formulation.

Various categories come into play in these epigrams: the finality of death, claims to immortality, assertions of presence, invocations and dialectics, maternity and maidenhood, reproductive futurity, queer atemporality. I will suggest that attempts of (male) authors to assert ongoing but abstract temporality—a sort of paradoxically postdeath immortality—are undergirded by the lasting material embodiment of the shapes and voices of women. Such women are portrayed as serving the cause of futurity, whether through memory, motherhood, or a provocative mash-up of the two. What kind of future is being projected here? In the terms of Lee Edelman, it is "the fantasy of meaning's eventual realization" through reproduction. It constitutes, or requires, a constant deferral and even negation of presence.[1] As we move from the archaic period (from the eighth through sixth centuries BCE), through the classical period (the fifth into the fourth century BCE), to the Hellenistic period (late fourth to third centuries BCE), we see a shift from statuary and stone in epitaphs, to images and sounds of wind in song, to the depiction of both stone and wind in literary epigrams. Thus, we follow a path from the construction of physical durability to the written representation of lasting presence. As the materials shift, objecthood and agency change too, alongside the terms of writing and voicing. Ideas and ideals of female embodiment and fantastical futurity move in lockstep with one another. The poems I have chosen to examine here emphasize particularly the role of female voices in the promotion of memory through the continuance of fame, lineage, or both—the promotional work performed by almost all epitaphs.[2]

No text can actually speak itself, except in the voice or mind of a reader,[3] yet each inscribed text contains a fragment of a voice-in-body; each speaking statue and stone promises the written uncanny. We find a grasping for specifically female voices in contexts marked by loss and grief, a desire for the soothing (m)other to negate the finality of death. Only in the final case discussed here, when author as well as speaker is female, do we encounter another answer to the question of impermanence in the face of mortality: a stubborn insistence on remaining in the feeling body and the shifting, shimmering present.

Archaic Epitaphs: Women Speaking from Stone

Epitaphs gain their power through presence in the face of irredeemable absence, coming as they do in the wake of death. In this light, it is not surprising that the authors and patrons of such inscriptions would seek to proclaim and maintain the identity of the deceased. (Many modern gravestones have similar aspirations.) By anchoring the name of the dead either to a particular location or by way of the embodied weight of statuary, epitaphs suggest that they can provide some consolatory permanence through time, a claim to the future rooted in fantasy but also in material heft.[4] Here, for example, is a much-studied inscription that dates from around 540 BCE and was found in Attica near a Parian marble statue of a young woman, to which it was once attached:

> [So says] the sign of Phrasicleia: I will have been called a maiden always,
> having obtained this name in place of marriage from the gods.
> Aristion of Paros made me.[5]

Even a short and apparently simple message like this one conveys an expectation of remembrance into the future and marks out space through the pause of acculturated meaning. The use of *always* to modify the future perfect "I will have been called" (*keklêsomai*) is a particularly pointed way of expressing the anticipation of an ongoing identity that will exist by virtue of being in a specific place, thereby becoming known to future readers of this text. Indeed, the future perfect, which occurs fairly infrequently in Greek, implies that future acknowledgment is already accomplished. Furthermore, the sign, unusually, speaks in two voices: both in the voice of the girl who has died ("*I* will be called") and as the statue who represents her ("Aristion of Paros made *me*"), using a complex act of conflation and ventriloquism to inject not just a marker of identity but an animated presence into the landscape as well.[6]

Yet equally important as these more subtle feats of identity marking is simply the inscription's provision of details and, in particular, of proper names: it is no surprise that the name of the dead woman, Phrasicleia, is present. A name is a *sine qua non* of such an inscription. It is, by contrast, unusual that the name of the artist, and indeed his identifying origin, finds mention too. The inscription thus triangulates itself between specifics: though the word "name" (*onoma*) refers literally to the general title "maiden" (or *kourê*), the proper names allow the epitaph to perform its function of creating cultural specificity from the biologically generic fact of death.

A second example is a hexametric epitaph, attributed to Cleoboulus, which offers a striking example of the use of material, both real and imagined, to project a woman's voice:

I am a maiden of bronze, and I lie on the sign of Midas.
As long as the water flows and the trees grow tall,
remaining on this much-bewailed tomb,
I will report to whoever comes by that Midas is buried here.[7]

Here the statue connected with the inscription is imagined as a brazen maiden who "will report" the identity of the dead man (Midas) for all time, with all time being specifically designated in natural (nondivine) terms—the life span of water and trees. The imagined collaboration of sculpture, writing, and sound creates a character who assumes responsibility for the dead man's future remembrance. The character acts again as a replacement for the fictive collaboration of poet and muse in epic, whereby the former relies on the latter to assure ongoing commemoration. Cleoboulus's epitaphic maiden, whether imagined or real, requires no immortal muse but through its own agency asserts the immortality of its voice, as both statue and maiden, free from the grip of mortality, fragility, or identity.[8] It names no creator and thus does not acknowledge itself to be an *objet d'art*. Furthermore, it refers to the dead only in the third person: *he* is the object.[9] Cleoboulus's epitaph thus creates a fictive woman but infuses her with no animation or characterization, save that she will speak of the deceased. This "maiden of bronze" is more automaton than speaker, silenced by her claim to parrot permanence for all time.

Though many epitaphs simply express grief over the loss of the dead, it is not unusual for some to suggest that their written message can assist in achieving some kind of immortality, a goal often attributed to poetry from Homer onward. In particular, archaic epic promises its heroes a particular kind of glory, known in Greek as *kleos*—the fame that derives from being talked about or sung of by poets. Inscription on stone or metal provides a new method for a mission that is, in some ways, unchanged. As Andrew Ford observes, "It is hardly surprising that some . . . inscriptions borrow commemorative tropes from epic. . . . Because the sense of fame as *kleos*, as repeated oral performance, persisted through the archaic period, the mere fact of song's being inscribed on durable matter might give a powerful new image of lasting fame."[10] And Deborah Steiner emphasizes that, even in Homer, "accounts of the commemoration of the dead . . . regularly harness the two kinds of memorialization to one another . . . no artifact without the speech that disseminates its message, and no verbal renown without some monument to spark it off."[11] Yet epitaphs, removed from the Homeric context, perform differently: they do not typically commemorate the actions of the living but merely the loss of the dead and perhaps lost opportunities for life. Moreover, their texts are performed by "passers-by" one by one, but they do not receive sung or public performance in the manner that songs about heroes are imagined to.

Critically, the function and power of inscribed objects are much greater than in the case of epic performance. Indeed, such objects are imagined as conferring a brand of renown so powerful that death (qua oblivion) cannot entirely prevail, and they are imagined as doing so without the assistance of Homeric muses or, indeed, any god at all.[12] Still more powerful are those epitaphs that come with a statuary body that is positioned to deliver this message of grief and resilience. It seems not accidental that our traces of evidence for such statuary show them to be shaped as *kourai*, or paradigmatic maidens. The sculpted body of a maiden behaves as a sign or substitute for a living woman, reduced to the sole function of expressing remembrance. It performs the function of promoting futurity without the friction of longing for an organic past.

The tradition of epitaphs therefore shows how the technology of writing reinvented the poetic project of preserving sounds through remembrance and reperformance. Simply the use of inscription in a public and enduring context could bolster poetic claims of conferring a death-defying glory, and the conjoining use of ventriloquizing hardware clearly helped. Poetry continued meanwhile to maintain its robust existence in the realm of oral performance, transmitting in real time from god to poet (or performer) to audience. But writing on stone with ventriloquized voicings afforded a new power to the authorship that hid behind these machinations. In these epitaphs, though the muses and other gods are often absent, the use of materials to embody female forms, alongside inscriptions of their supposed sounds, transforms a single instance of dedication into a marker of permanence.[13]

Classical Song: Women Singing into Wind

The matter of attaining the preservation of sound through writing was not unproblematic in the archaic period, and as the numbers of epitaphs increased in the classical period, so too was their status contested. The poet Simonides, though famously an author of epitaphs himself, is also known to have composed this song in complex lyrics:

> Who, trusting in his wits, would praise the dweller of Linos, Cleoboulus,
> who has set against the ever-flowing rivers and the flowers of spring
> and the light of the sun and the golden moon
> and the eddies of the sea the strength of a grave-stone?
> For all of these things are inferior to the gods. As for stone,
> even mortal palms shatter it. This is the counsel
> of a moronic man.[14]

Simonides's critique of Cleoboulus suggests a competition between the movements of nature and the life span of a gravestone. Nature is viewed as equivalent to the divine, and stone (*lithos*) is reduced to a thing both shaped and easily destroyed by men. Indeed, the eternal movements of nature occupy three full lines, accumulating decorous and melodious phrases, while the inscription on stone is dispatched in just two unadorned words: *menos stalas* (strength of *stele*). Moreover, the sounds of nature are riddled with echoes of "always" (*aei*), as the leading phoneme of "everlasting" (*aenaois*) is heard again in "the sun" (*aeliou*): the aural substance of song thus resonates through time. By contrast, the words inscribed in stone are diminished to the state of being unadaptable, static, and soundless.

At the heart of Simonides's critique lies a competition between the movements of nature and the life span of the grave marker. Nature is made equivalent to the divine, and stone (*lithos*) is reduced to a thing both shaped and easily destroyed by men.[15] While Simonides's interpretation is understood to be a reply and reworking of Cleoboulus's inscription, he leaves out the "maiden" altogether and any sense of presence, no matter how artificial, she might be intended to introduce. Her words emphatically connect the inscription to its place, lending it its specificity and location: its *hereness*. Note the emphatic deictic "this here" (*autou têde*) in the penultimate line and the repetition of "here" (*têde*) again in the last.[16] While the lines do not definitely tell us whether the flowing rivers, thriving trees, and rushing sea are close at hand, they do anchor the message—like any spatial deictic—to a place, suggesting that tying the message to its location is part of the service of female embodiment. Simonides's reading of the epitaph separates the stone from both its (female) speaker and its context, steps that were evidently necessary to contend that no voice of stone can be harnessed to project life even into an imagined future.

Is there another way to imagine the preservation of sound and voice? Simonides, I suggest, offers a different path to a similar goal, a path that still threads through the female voice but now as song, sound, and movement. Accordingly, his own song lives in a mode of performance entirely different from inscriptional verse. Simonides's lyric poetry stands apart from the highly patterned verse forms of earlier practitioners of Greek lyric song, such as Alcman and Anacreon. Even the (later) wild, woolly victory songs of Pindar are almost always meted out in patterns of strophe, antistrophe, and epode. By contrast, one of Simonides's most well-preserved poems, the portrait of Danaë and her baby in a chest (fr. 543), has been at least partly saved for us from the wreckage of history by Dionysius of Halicarnassus in the first century BCE merely so that he could note how indecipherable was its metrical arrangement, how like to prose this poetry appeared: "Know well that the rhythm of the song will escape you and you will not be able to infer either strophe, antistrophe or epode, but it will appear to you as one [i.e., continuous] spoken *logos*."[17] Earlier in the passage, Dionysius refers to prose by its common tag, that is, "speech on foot" (*ho pezos logos*), a phrase that is much like our own terms *pedestrian* or *mundane*. One might also translate this phrase as "words that do not leave the ground." Do the sounds of Simonides's song not leave the ground? What would it mean for the song to stay firmly fixed in place?

I would suggest rather that Simonides pushes the envelope on song, implying that voice alone is the true path to future remembrance—particularly in an ethical framework where the voice is that of the devoted mother, serving the path of reproductive futurity. "The Song of Danaë," the poem that Dionysius calls pedestrianly prose-like, invites such a reading of performance as fleeting and yet efficacious. The poem frames a moment in the myth of Danaë, mother of Perseus, after she has been cast into the sea by her father in a chest with the baby Perseus. Though the audience knows they will survive, Danaë does not, and the poem stays with her for just a few minutes, introducing no perspective but her own. She is alone with her sleeping baby, the roaring wind, and rough waves; she is distraught. Much of the extant poem consists of her own words—first to her baby and then, at the very end, to Zeus. Here is what remains of the song:

> When in a chest
> that was inlaid,
> the wind blowing and
> the stirred up water dashed her down
> with fear, not with unwet cheeks
> she cast her loving hand around Perseus
> and said:
>
> O child, such suffering have I.
> But you sleep and, in your babyish
> way, slumber
> in unhappy, bronze-nailed wood,
> in the dark-lit,
> dim gloom, cast out.
> The spray coming from the deep over
> your hair is not a care to you, nor
> is the voice of the wind, lying
> in your purple blanket, lovely faced.
> If the terrible were terrible to you,
> even to my phrases
> you would turn your slender ear.
> But I enjoin: sleep baby
> and let sleep the sea, and let sleep
> unmeasurable evil.
> And may some change of mind appear,
> father Zeus, from you.
>
> For any word I have prayed that is bold
> or apart from justice,
> pardon me.[18]

Danaë's monologue is highly lyrical, rife with imagery and patterning that any poet would be proud to claim. Her imagery plays with the materials of her plight, as she reconfigures the box in which she is trapped, mentioned by the narrator as "an inlaid chest," as "unhappy, bronze-nailed wood." Will it be a sepulcher for her body and baby lost at sea? Does she make of it an epitaph, adding the heft of her substantial and arresting compounds (*chalkeogomphôi, nuktilampei*)? The sounds of the song become most noticeable right when the passage becomes most like a lullaby. It is freighted with rhymes and verbal reverberations that seem particularly well designed for childlike ears to comprehend, starting with the repeating *k/ch* sounds in *k̲eimenos en c̲h̲lanidi, prosôpon k̲alon* and culminating in the repetition of the imperative for "sleep" (*heude . . . / heudetô de . . . heudetô d'a-*). In these lines, the significance of the sounds almost overrides the meaning of the words, particularly if we hear as the addressed child is asked to hear.

It could be suggested that this aural patterning is merely the poetic quality of the whole poem and not of Danaë's voice itself. Yet I contend that Simonides is showing us the beauty of her voice *as* a voice in song but also as a voice that is literally at sea, with no anchor, no placement, no fixity, and thus no power. Her speech is an attempt to animate her baby *as a listener*, but the temporality of the moment—he is sleeping and he is a baby—prevents her from doing so.[19] Her voice, as such, is trapped in this moment of being unheard. In her final words, she turns to Zeus instead and tries to animate him as a listener, but we as readers have no sense of whether he hears her words or not. The only other animated presence in the poem is the wind (*anemos*). It blows (*pneôn*), moves (*kinêtheisa*), and even has a voice itself (*phthonggon*). Indeed, wind is the most basic paradigmatic form of unanchored movement and sound that there is. In the Greek tradition, its blowing is often paralleled with breath, breath with song—the very principle of voice without text and voice as vanishing.[20] Paradoxically, it is the dialogue between helpless mother and evanescent wind that acts as a medium for another form of the same game: the woman's voice ventriloquizing for the cause of (male) futurity.

The embodiment and temporality of these various female configurations exist in tension. The bronze and stone maidens are lasting but nonreproductive; all but anonymous, they are to remain forever in the present, repeating the same message eternally. By contrast, Danaë—a mythic and narrative character—speaks in a fluid, lyrical voice, disembodied, imagined only in song, and intrinsically linked to futurity through reproduction. She is all fragility, drifting in a copper-notched wooden coffin at sea, prey to forces she cannot see; yet she is also fundamentally a mother, an engine of hero-production, whose historical identity is thereby secured and whose forthcoming safe landing is known to the audience. Thus, like the statue that is

Phrasicleia, and Cleoboulus's maiden of bronze, the identity of Danaë is secured by its relationship to the male whose existence she enables. So it goes in archaic and classical Greece, whether on stone or in song.

Hellenistic Epigram: Women Writing Sounds

In the Hellenistic period, another stony (a-stonied? a-stonished?)[21] female voice, this time of a woman named Aretêmias, speaks in the form of epitaph made anew as literary epigrams, fictionalized versions of verses inscribed on stone. Most of these epigrams are understood not to have been actually carved into stone or bronze nor to commemorate the actual dead. Unlike their archaic counterparts that are thought to have existed in service of true monumental commemoration, these epigrams were contrived to play with its formulations and conceits.[22]

Like Danaë, Aretêmias is a ventriloquized mother; like Phrasicleia and the bronze maiden, she is imagined as announcing existence beyond the grave and thus splitting the difference between being an engine of reproduction and a provider of an inorganic fantasy of permanence. Aretêmias's words are written in stone and authored by a man but also understood to speak with a view toward her own remembrance, as opposed to (only) that of a man whom she commemorates. She is not a woman of stone or bronze but (fictionally) a woman of rotting flesh, under "newly dug dirt," whose words are imagined as apiece with stone:

> The dirt is newly dug and on the face of the gravestone
>   half-living wreathes of leaves tremble.
> Deciphering the writing, wayfarer, let us look at the rock,
>   to figure out whose bare bones it tells of:
> "Stranger, I am Aretêmias. My fatherland is Cnidos. I came
>   to marriage with Euphrôn, but was not unlucky in childbirth.
> I gave birth to twins, and left one to attend my husband
>   when he grows old, but one I took as remembrance of him."[23]

This epigram is attributed to the Hellenistic poet Heraclitus[24] (not to be confused with the archaic philosopher and author of gnomic sayings) and is found in the so-called *Greek Anthology*, a lengthy compilation of (mostly) epigrams that covers the classical to the Byzantine era.[25]

Some of the play between words written in stone and a poem meant for circulation in a book is evident in the Hellenistic epigram's trotting out of archaic epitaphic tropes. The address to the "wayfarer" is one; the references to the materiality of the site is another, complete with starkly juxtaposed elements of the organic and the durable: the dirt freshly dug, the leaves of a garland only half alive, the *stele* with its stony face, and the bare, decomposing bones imagined beneath. Not, then, from the crumbling bones but the still stone are we to imagine the voice of Aretêmias arising. After identifying herself by name, country of origin, and husband, she tells of her plight—that she died in childbirth, along with one of her twin infants. In conjunction with her unexpected authorial voice comes a forceful assertion of agency. Her death and the fate of her children are configured very nearly as matters of agency and choice. In the mode of forethought, Aretêmias left a child to attend to her husband and took one for herself to help her remember him. As has often been pointed out, this ending flips the script. It is usually the living who are called upon to recall the dead, but here the dead speaks of her concern to maintain a "remembrance" of the living. Flipped as this script is in that regard, however, the shift is less striking owing to the genders involved: what else should a dead woman do but try to remember her still-living husband?

A more intriguing question attending this epigram is the identity of the speaker of its first half. Who describes the state of the site and stone, addresses the wayfarer, and invites him (us) to "decipher" the words on the stone? There is no good answer to this question: it can scarcely be the poet or the stone itself (much as Phrasicleia speaks *as* stone). The voice is perhaps framed as that of a companion wayfarer, another traveler who enjoins the audience to "decipher," "look," and "figure out" the identity of the decomposing dead through the presumed permanence of the letters chiseled above her.[26] The whole poem is an epigram, but within the fiction of the poem, only the second half of it is an epitaph. The poem thus creates two dissimilar fictive spaces of voicing: one seems to exist ephemerally at a particular moment of encounter with a newly dug grave; the other is able to be conjured eternally through its material inscription on that grave. The voice of Aretêmias, so direct and agential, nonetheless fades into the less vivid and more objectified register. In other words, though the modes of fiction, ventriloquism, and materiality have changed, the mode of female voicing remains subordinated.

Our final text is part of the same tradition as the epigram of Heraclitus, yet it differs in two essential respects from it and the other texts I have considered here. First, its author is a woman; second, it does not explicitly handle the theme of death and thus neither is nor claims (even in the mode of fiction) to be an epitaph. The author is Anyte, credited with writing some twenty-four epigrams. Here is one:

Sit everyone under the lovely, flourishing leaves of the laurel tree,
  and take a sweet drink of the seasonal spring,

so that to your limbs, breathing hard from the labors of the harvest,
you may give rest, beaten by the breeze of West Wind.[27]

Rather than writing in the tradition of epitaphs, Anyte employs the tropes of *locus amoenus* poetry—lush gardens, flowing waters, shady trees, pleasant breezes. It is among the first epigrams to use this mode.[28] This kind of setting had many predecessors in other genres. One early instance is the second fragment of Sappho, the original Greek author of female presence:[29]

Come here to me from Crete to this sacred
temple, where there is a pleasant grove
of apples, and altars fragrant
with incense.

Here, cold water ripples through the branches
of apple-trees, and the whole place is shaded
with roses, and from shimmering leaves
sleep flows down.

Here a meadow, where horses graze, blooms
with spring blossoms, and the breezes
blow gently [
[ ]

There, you arriving, Cyprian one
in golden cups tenderly [pour]
nectar mixed with our festivities
of wine . . .[30]

The pleasant surroundings—the shimmering leaves, the gentle breezes, and cool shade—are evoked in a situation of anticipation: Aphrodite herself is awaited, and the beauty and pleasure of the surroundings seem to bespeak the expectations of her immortal and erotic presence, though the lure here remains *sleep*, signifying and partnering in Greek thought with death. What sort of sleep does one attain in an immortal utopia? It is perhaps the sleep of the immortal if fleeting encounter, the crystalline, midday moment of meetings between the human and the divine.

But in Anyte's epigram, the context is both more earthly and more mortal: the poem addresses itself to an unknown audience, someone whose limbs are tired, perhaps from labors or just from heat, someone who requires respite. The pleasure of the surroundings is enhanced not by expectations of the divine but by juxtaposition with corporeal rigors—work and exhaustion. Even the final phrase, which implies the relief offered by the West Wind, or Zephyr (the most amiable of the winds), envisions the wind as "beating" through the somewhat brutal word *tuptomena*, a word not usually used of gentle sensations, as if the severities of life must be felt even in moments of rest. Against the model of Sappho, then, as well as other archaic exemplars,[31] the beauty of the setting does not especially derive from or suggest immortal visitation, save that of the divinely titled west wind.

Despite the living, breathing quality of the epigram, the potential for death is also present through the shadow of allusion. As Alexander Sens notes, "Here, the relief afforded by the attractive location may be read against the conventional idea that death is a release from pains. . . . The participle ἀσθμαίνοντα (*breathing hard*), a word sometimes used in Homer of dying warriors, is significant: the soothing features of the place restore breath to the fainting traveler."[32] Sens points to a number of phrases that allude uncannily to the plight of warriors in the *Iliad* and other archaic poetry: their weary limbs, their need for rest, the hope for the breeze, the beating rhythm of exhaustion are all reminiscent of this world. The epigram itself addresses strangers in the mode of epitaphs,[33] evoking the cause of memory and permanence, yet makes no request to notice, recall, or decipher. The reader of this poem is not asked to be a vessel of remembrance for future days, only to feel and be in the present day.

As in Danaë's song, the principle of this transient embrace is the wind. As noted above, its very nature is movement; its very effect is affect: the listener or reader is invited to feel the wind, even to hear it pounding in beats. Also as in Danaë's song—and, indeed, in Sappho's second fragment—this one promises rest, albeit not rest as oblivion so much as a mode of atmospheric engulfment, a saturation in this place, in this moment. Here at last is a mortal world that promises nothing more than the present. Here is a female author, unburdened by male triangulation and free of the identity in life-stages meted out by male convenience: maidenhood, motherhood. In fact, there is an unusual lack of framing identification to this voice: no materializing of the body, no classifying of the speaker.[34] Here, too, is an epigram that makes no promises of futurity, neither by reproduction nor by fame. It offers only an instance in the midst of change, captured by verse more than stone, voice more than material. Only the contextual specter of gendered authorship hangs over the whole affair, promising respite from the desperate quest for a forever, fashioned in a female vessel.

I have examined the projections of five written texts from the Greek tradition that claim to preserve the voices and sounds of women. Yet, as we have seen, multiple versions of this ambition existed. The projection of female voices was imagined as speaking through statuary, inscribed in verse, quoted as song, and depicted as rising from an entombed corpse. Each set of material conditions offered new coordinates of temporality: a sculpted embodiment of durable material implied a futurity of unchanging remembrance, while the written sounds of women, separated from materiality, invited the subordination of her individual voice to the ongoing lineage of family. Only the occasion of female authorship, all too rare, allowed for newly conceived temporalities of presence, sounds written to be heard in the framework of ongoing life.

NOTES

1. Lee Edelman, *No Future: Queer Theory and the Death Drive* (Durham, NC: Duke University Press, 2004), 4.

2. I am not suggesting that most epitaphic inscriptions are voiced in the feminine; many, rather, speak in the voice of the neuter, as *sêma*, or inscribed object. See Jasper Svenbro, *Phrasikleia: An Anthology of Reading in Ancient Greece*, trans. J. Lloyd (Ithaca, NY: Cornell University Press, 1993), 29–35. The two archaic examples here are exceptional in attributing their message to an actual or imagined statuary figure of a woman that goes alongside the inscription, instead of simply to the inscription (as object) itself. Yet funerary statues of young women (*kourai*) were not uncommon.

3. This is a meaningful exception, since ancient readers of inscriptions likely read them aloud.

4. Cf. Christiane Sourvinou-Inwood, *"Reading" Greek Death* (Oxford: Clarendon Press, 1995); and Deborah Tarn Steiner, *Images in Mind: Statues in Archaic and Classical Greek Literature and Thought* (Princeton, NJ: Princeton University Press, 2001), 255–59, on the ubiquity of references in epitaphs to their own structure, statuary, or site.

5. The original Greek verse reads:

> Σῆμα Φρασικλείας·κούρη κεκλήσομαι αἰεί
> ἀντὶ γάμου παρὰ θεῶν τοῦτο λαχοῦσ' ὄνομα.
> Ἀριστίων Πάρι[ος μ' ἐπ]ό[η]σε.

Peter A. Hansen, ed., *Carmina epigraphica Graeca*, 2 vols. (Berlin: De Gruyter: 1983–89), 24. All translations of Greek are my own.

For an extended discussion of this inscription and how it relates to the statue with which it was adjoined, see Svenbro, *Phrasikleia*, 9–25. See also Andrew Ford, *The Origins of Criticism: Literary Culture and Poetic Theory in Classical Greece* (Ithaca, NY: Cornell University Press, 2002), 104–5 (primarily on the inscription); and Seth Estrin, "Cold Comfort: Empathy and Memory in an Archaic Funerary Monument from Akraiphia," *Classical Antiquity* 35, no. 2 (2016): 189–214, esp. 207–9. This inscription is frequently an object of study for the very reason given by Svenbro—that is, that we very rarely still have the sculptural monument along with its inscribed base; we usually just have the base (*Phrasikleia*, 9).

6. Gert Vestrheim, "Voice in Sepulchral Epigrams: Some Remarks on the Use of First and Second Person in Sepulchral Epigrams, and a Comparison with Lyric Poetry," in *Archaic and*

Classical Greek Epigram, ed. M. Baumbach, A. Petrovic, and I. Petrovic (Cambridge: Cambridge University Press, 2010), 61–78. Vestrheim speaks to the use of the first person here as "an effective means of adding further force to this rhetoric and thus engaging the reader in the destiny of the dead" (73). Svenbro discusses the personhood of epitaphic inscriptions, noting that the earliest ones we have—from before 550 BCE—tend to refer to themselves (as objects) in the first person (*Phrasikleia*, 26–43). Alternatively, they use the nearest (most first-person-ish) demonstrative *tode* self-referentially. Thomas A. Schmitz looks at personhood in epigrams as against lyric poems from the same period and finds that the variation among voices in the different genres are similar; see Thomas A. Schmitz, "Speaker and Addressee in Early Greek Epigram and Lyric," in *Archaic and Classical Greek Epigram*, ed. M. Baumbach, A. Petrovic, and I. Petrovic (Cambridge: Cambridge University Press, 2010), 25–41. Vestrheim notes, however, that epigrams are far less likely than lyric poems to assert their authors as "individualists" with particularized features or biographies ("Voice in Sepulchral Epigrams," 77).

7. The original inscription as recorded in Gow and Page's *The Greek Anthology* reads:

> Χαλκῆ παρθένος εἰμί, Μίδα δ' ἐπὶ σήματι κεῖμαι.
> ἔστ' ἂν ὕδωρ τε νάῃ καὶ δένδρεα μακρὰ τεθήλῃ,
> αὐτοῦ τῇδε μένουσα πολυκλαύτῳ ἐπὶ τύμβῳ
> ἀγγελέω παριοῦσι, Μίδας ὅτι τῇδε τέθαπται.

Andrew Sydenham Farrar Gow and Denys Lionel Page, eds., *The Greek Anthology: Hellenistic Epigrams* (Cambridge: Cambridge University Press, 1965), *A.P.* 7.153. Other variants include two more lines in the middle. This version is quoted by Socrates in Plato's *Phaedrus* (264c–d). Socrates finds it poorly designed. As Andrej Petrovic notes, the interchangeability (in Socrates's view) of lines 1 and 4 renders the epitaph different from the organized composition of a human body, the model here for a good *logos*. Andrej Petrovic, "Inscribed Epigram in Pre-Hellenistic Literary Sources," in *Brill's Companion to Hellenistic Epigram*, ed. P. Bing and J. S. Bruss (Leiden: Brill, 2007), 49–68, 61.

8. Readers have tried giving the statue an identity, including as a siren or sphinx. See Peter Bing, *The Scroll and the Marble: Studies in Reading and Reception in Hellenistic Poetry* (Ann Arbor: University of Michigan Press, 1995), 118; and Petrovic, "Inscribed Epigram," 62.

9. On the third person as a "non-personne," see É. Benveniste, *Problèmes de linguistique générale* (Paris: Gallimard, 1966), 256.

10. Ford, *Homer*, 99.

11. Steiner, *Images in Mind*, 253. See also Catherine Trümpy, "Observations on the Dedicatory and Sepulchral Epigrams, and Their Early History," in *Archaic and Classical Greek Epigram*, ed. M. Baumbach, A. Petrovic, and I. Petrovic (Cambridge: Cambridge University Press, 2010), 167–79. Trümpy addresses the similarity, writ small, of epitaphs to epic, calling epitaphs "*miniature epics*" (174, Trümpy's italics) and noting that both genres tended to be composed in hexameters, aimed to praise the virtues of their subjects ("depicted as a kind of semi-god") rather than explicitly lament their deaths.

12. See Eva Stehle, *Performance and Gender in Ancient Greece: Nondramatic Poetry in Its Setting* (Princeton, NJ: Princeton University Press, 1997), 209, on the sidelining of muses in the sixth and fifth centuries BCE as "more individualistic ways of positioning the singer developed."

13. See Joseph Day, *Archaic Greek Epigram and Dedication: Representation and Reperformance* (Cambridge: Cambridge University Press, 2010) on the role of dedicatory epigrams in provoking reperformance, another way of conceptualizing permanence. This argument also resembles one that Mary Beard has made about votive inscriptions in a Roman religious context: "Inscribed votive texts enacted that crucial conversion of an *occasional* sacrifice into a *permanent*

relationship." Mary Beard, "Writing and Religion: Ancient Literacy and the Function of the Written Word," in *Literacy in the Roman World*, ed. M. Beard et al. (Ann Arbor: University of Michigan Press, 1991), 35–58, 48 (Beard's italics).

14. Here are the Greek verses:

τίς κεν αἰνήσειε νόωι πίσυνος Λίνδου ναέταν Κλεόβουλον,
ἀεναοῖς ποταμοῖς ἄνθεσί τ' εἰαρινοῖς
ἀελίου τε φλογὶ χρυσέας τε σελάνας
καὶ θαλασσαίαισι δίναις ἀντι<τι>θέντα μένος στάλας;
ἅπαντα γάρ ἐστι θεῶν ἥσσω·λίθον δέ
καὶ βρότεοι παλάμαι θραύοντι·μωροῦ
φωτὸς ἅδε βουλά.

Denys Lionel Page, ed., *Poetae melici Graeci* (hereafter *PMG*) (Oxford: Oxford University Press, 1962), 581.

15. See Ford, *Origins*, 108, who takes Simonides's complaint at face value: "A statue, a burial mound, or any uninscribed artifact had been the silent partner rather than the rival of oral tradition; but once such objects make much of their engraved messages, Simonides attacks their hubristic guarantees of fame"

16. Joseph Day discusses the role of deictics in epigrams, focusing in particular on how they link viewers' encounters with inscriptions on stone to the original ritual acts that presumably underlie them. In his reading, inscriptions can be thought of as provoking performances that are meant to be experienced as reperformances, much as epinician poetry is meant to do. See Joseph Day, "Epigraphic Literacy in Fifth-Century Epinician and Its Audiences," in *Inscriptions and Their Uses in Greek and Latin Literature*, eds. P. Liddel and P. Low (Oxford: Oxford University Press, 2013), 217–30; and Day, *Archaic Greek Epigram.*

17. See *De compositione verborum*, 25: εὖ ἴσθ' ὅτι λήσεταί σε ὁ ῥυθμὸς τῆς ᾠδῆς καὶ οὐχ ἕξεις συμβαλεῖν οὔτε στροφὴν οὔτε ἀντίστροφον οὔτ' ἐπῳδόν, ἀλλὰ φανήσεταί σοι λόγος εἷς εἰρόμενος.

18. Here are the Greek verses:

ὅτε λάρνακι
ἐν δαιδαλέαι
ἄνεμός τε †μηνʼ† πνέων
κινηθεῖσά τε λίμνα δείματι
ἔρειπεν, οὐκ ἀδιάντοισι παρειαῖς
ἀμφί τε Περσέι βάλλε φίλαν χέρα
εἶπέν τ'

ὦ τέκος οἷον ἔχω πόνον
σὺ δ' ἀωτεῖς, γαλαθηνῶι
δ' ἤθεϊ κνοώσσεις
ἐν ἀτερπέι δούρατι χαλκεογόμφωι
<τῶι>δε νυκτιλαμπεῖ,
κυανέωι δνόφωι ταθείς
ἄχναν δ' ὕπερθε τεᾶν κομᾶν
βαθεῖαν παριόντος
κύματος οὐκ ἀλέγεις, οὐδ' ἀνέμου
φθόγγον, πορφυρέαι
κείμενος ἐν χλανίδι, πρόσωπον καλόν.
εἰ τις τοι δεινὸτιστό γε δεινὸν τις

καί κεν ἐμῶν ῥημάτων
λεπτὸν ὑπεῖχες οὖας.
κέλομαι δ', εὖδε βρέφος
εὑδέτω δὲ πόντος, εὑδέτω δ' ἄμετρον κακόν
μετατιτιςία δέ τις φανείη,
Ζεῦ πάτερ, ἐκ σέο

ὅττι δὲ θαρσαλέον ἔπος εὔχομαι
ἢ νόσφι δίκας,
σύγγνωθί μοι. (*PMG* 543)

19. On the animating work of poetry addressed to lost fetuses or babies, see Barbara Johnson, "Apostrophe, Animation, and Abortion," *diacritics* 16, no. 1 (1986): 29–47.

20. See Sarah Nooter, *The Mortal Voice in the Tragedies of Aeschylus* (Cambridge: Cambridge University Press, 2017), 11, 15–17.

21. See Jack Halberstam, *Wild Things: The Disorder of Desire* (Durham, NC: Duke University Press, 2020), 67, on the original meaning of *astonished* as "knocked out by a stone," though this derivation remains controversial. Still more a-stoned is she who is shaped from the stuff in the first place.

22. Yet Peter Bing notes that it remains "hard to distinguish inscribed epigram from quasi-inscriptional. . . . Starting in the Hellenistic age, this genre will not stay put" (*The Scroll and the Marble*, 207). Richard Hunter has written provocatively of the genre: "Perhaps no literary genre makes such a direct appeal to the reader's powers of intellectual reconstruction, to the *need* to interpret, as does that of the epigram; the demand for concision makes 'narrative silences' an almost constitutive part of the genre. In these circumstances, the refusal to speculate amounts to no less than a refusal to read." Richard Hunter, "Callimachus and Heraclitus," *Materiali e discussioni per l'analisi dei testi classici* 28 (1992): 113–23, 114.

23. Here are the Greek lines:

Ἁ κόνις ἀρτίσκαπτος, ἐπὶ στάλας δὲ μετώπῳ
σείονται φύλλων ἡμιθαλεῖς στέφανοι.
γράμμα διακρίναντες, ὁδοιπόρε, πέτρον ἴδωμεν,
λευρὰ περιστέλλειν ὀστέα φατὶ τίνος.
"ξεῖν', Ἀρετημιάς εἰμι· πάτρα Κνίδος· Εὔφρονος ἦλθον
ἐς λέχος· ὠδίνων οὐκ ἄμορος γενόμαν,
δισσὰ δ' ὁμοῦ τίκτουσα τὸ μὲν λίπον ἀνδρὶ ποδαγὸν
γήρως, ἓν δ' ἀπάγω μναμόσυνον πόσιος." (*A.P.* 7.465)

24. This is the only epigram attributed to Heraclitus, but it is possible that he is the poet commemorated by Callimachus in *A.P.* 7.80. Here Callimachus mourns the death of Heraclitus but is consoled by the idea that his "nightingales"—his poems, many think—will live on. The dubbing of the poems as birds, or (metonymically) the songs of birds, suggests another rubric for thinking of the (female) voices of the dead that are ventriloquized through them.

25. These derive in turn from two collections that are referred to here by their abbreviations: the *Palatine Anthology* (*A.P.*) and the *Planudean Anthology* (*A.Pl.*), which is also found in Gow and Page, *The Greek Anthology*.

26. Hunter considers and rejects the reading of this voice as that of a "fellow-traveller," finding it less obviously gestured to than in other epigrams. His solution is that the voice is that of the poet. In his view, "the strategy of the first half of the epigram is, therefore, to focus attention upon the conventions of the funerary epigram and upon the role of the poet in both creating and being constrained by those conventions" ("Callimachus and Heraclitus," 115). If

this interpretation is correct, the reader's recognition of the poet breaks the fictive frame and temporality of the epigram so as to highlight the literary process of its creation. See also Kathryn Gutzwiller, *Poetic Garlands: Hellenistic Epigrams in Context* (Berkeley: University of California Press, 1998), 251, on the poem as potentially a "text in process of composition"; and Doris Meyer, "The Act of Reading and the Act of Writing in Hellenistic Epigram," in *Brill's Companion to Hellenistic Epigram*, ed. P. Bing and J. S. Bruss (Leiden: Brill, 2007), 187–210, on it as a "dramatiz[ing] of the shared realization, viz. bringing-into-being, of a literary text by the combined effort of author and reader" (206). In this way, she writes, "epigrams constitute their audience" (210).

27. Here are the Greek lines:

Ἵζευ ἅπας ὑπὸ καλὰ δάφνας εὐθαλέα φύλλα
    ὡραίου τ' ἄρυσαι νάματος ἁδὺ πόμα,
ὄφρα τοι ἀσθμαίνοντα πόνοις θέρεος φίλα γυῖα
    ἀμπαύσῃς πνοιᾷ τυπτόμενα Ζεφύρου. (*A.P.* 9.313)

28. See Alexander Sens, "Epigram at the Margins of Pastoral," in *Brill's Companion to Greek and Latin Pastoral*, ed. M. Fantuzzi and T. D. Papanghelis (Leiden: Brill, 2007), 147–65, for the dating of this epigram relative to a few others that portray a *locus amoenus*, as well as for the possibility that Anyte's poetry preceded, and thus influenced, the bucolic poems of Theocritus (161–62). See, as well, Karl-Heinz Stanzel, "Bucolic Epigram," in *Brill's Companion to Hellenistic Epigram*, ed. P. Bing and J. S. Bruss (Leiden: Brill, 2007), 333–52, on how Anyte's poems "extend . . . the generic boundaries in interesting ways" (336), mixing the tropes of dedication, commemoration, and bucolic poetry in experimental ways. See also *A.P.* 9.314 and *A.Pl.* 228. On the "high likelihood" that Anyte's epigrams appeared in books, despite the bucolic setting of several of them, see Gutzwiller, *Poetic Garlands*, 71.

29. As J. Murray and J. M. Rowland point out, Sappho is one of our very few conduits to an "authentic female subjectivity" in the Greek world. J. Murray and J. M. Rowland, "Gendered Voices in Hellenistic Epigram," in *Brill's Companion to Hellenistic Epigram*, ed. P. Bing and J. S. Bruss (Leiden: Brill, 2007), 211–32, 211. See Stehle, *Performance and Gender*, on the limitations of such subjectivity, given the patriarchal limits of performative contexts. In the world of Hellenistic epigram, there were several other female poets as well, such as Erinna and Nossis.

30. Here are the Greek verses:

δεῦρύ μ' ἐκ Κρήτας ἐπ[ὶ τόνδ]ε ναῦον
ἄγνον, ὄππ[ᾳ τοι] χάριεν μὲν ἄλσος
μαλί[αν], βῶμοι δὲ τεθυμιάμε-
νοι [λι]βανώτῳ·

ἐν δ' ὔδωρ ψῦχρον κελάδει δι' ὔσδων
μαλίνων, βρόδοισι δὲ παῖς ὁ χῶρος
ἐσκίαστ', αἰθυσσομένων δὲ φύλλων
κῶμα κατέρρει

ἐν δὲ λείμων ἰππόβοτος τέθαλεν
ἠρίνοισιν ἄνθεσιν, αἰ δ' ἄηται
μέλλιχα πνέοισιν [
[ ]

ἔνθα δὴ σὺ . . . ἔλοισα Κύπρι
χρυσίαισιν ἐν κυλίκεσσιν ἄβρως

ὀμμεμείχμενον θαλίαισι νέκταρ
οἰνοχόαισον.

(Edgar Lobel and Denys Lionel Page, *Poetarum Lesbiorum fragmenta*, corr. edn. (Oxford: Oxford University Press, 1963), *Fr.* 2)

31. See, e.g., the *Odyssey* 5.65–75, where Hermes marvels at the beauty of Calypso's island, and the *Homeric Hymn to Pan* (*HH* 19). See also Anyte *A.P.* 9.144, which handles the influence of Cypris on a place—a more ambiguous tribute.

32. Alexander Sens, ed., *Hellenistic Epigrams: A Selection* (Cambridge: Cambridge University Press, 2020), 64. Anyte's use of Homeric tropes is often discussed in the context of the "gendering" of her voice as a mix of "masculine and feminine perspectives" (Murray and Rowland, "Gendered Voices," 230). For other treatments of Anyte's poems, in terms of gender and genre, see Jane McIntosh Snyder, *The Woman and the Lyre: Women Writers in Classical Greece and Rome* (Carbondale: Southern Illinois University Press, 1989), 67–77; and Ellen Greene, "Playing with Tradition: Gender and Innovation in the Epigrams of Anyte," *Helios* 27, no. 1(2000): 15–32. Both see Anyte as being located in a "middle ground" (Greene 15) between traditionally masculine and feminine tropes and concerns. Both also link her particularly unconventional gender identity with her innovative use of form and genre.

33. Sens, *Hellenistic Epigrams*, 64.

34. So Stanzel, "Bucolic Epigram," 338: "In the absence of a clear identity for the speaker the reader might be justified in equating the voice with that of the poetess." Kathryn Gutzwiller, "Anyte's Epigram Book," *Syllecta Classica* 4 (1993): 71–89, looks at Anyte's poetic persona as formed by the composite of her epigrams, noting that "while this traditional epigrammatist appears at first glance to be characterized by having no characteristics at all, that impression is in fact false. . . . Anyte, by her dominating interest in women, children, and animals and by the attention she paid to the landscape, defined her literary self by her deviation from the standard imposed upon the traditional epigrammatist, that of celebrating upper-class, masculine achievements and values" (72–73).

CHAPTER TWO

Reading Impressions

The Sound of the Sight of Occitan Verse

Sarah Kay

Reading with One's Ears

French philosopher François Noudelmann exhorts us to "read with our ears."[1] Although at times he concedes that a text's sonority may be inaudible, except in the reader's imagination, he says little about how readers access (or create?) imaginary sounds. The process whereby seeing a page of writing can translate into an auditory experience seems, in general, to have been little studied, as compared with the related one of translating the sight of a visual image or artifact into speech that the notion of ekphrasis has made familiar. This essay, by contrast, addresses the challenge of inferring the sonic qualities of medieval songs from the visible, graphic traces we have of them. Specifically, it explores to what extent readers attentive to scribal effort, metrical possibilities, and potential textual implications might be led to conjecture means of hearing these songs even in the near silent environment of the page.

Noudelmann's call to read with one's ears is striking today, but I doubt it would have greatly surprised medieval readers. Innovations in manuscript production from at least as early as the Carolingian period placed a premium on using visible means to place sound within the reach of readers' ears. Techniques for notating music were developed, along with other visual prompts to auditory reception, including punctuation, illumination, and page layout. Writing has probably always conveyed sound, but the Middle Ages pioneered means of soliciting and shaping readers' hearing that are still operative, even if modern ears have tended to close off from them. Medieval texts are, moreover, typically orchestrated by implied voices that, as well as being actualized aloud in performance, are likely to have been heard at least mentally in reading too.[2] Historical research has responded to the solicitations of such voices by investigating possible modes of live performance, especially of dramatic or musical works.

It is not obvious, however, how one should perform the majority of troubadour lyrics, given that 90 percent of them are transmitted without musical notation. Manuscript users might sometimes have recognized a song as having—or as fitting—a melody they were able to recall. But in this corpus of some twenty-five hundred songs that manifest a huge variety of stanza forms, memory can hardly have been a failsafe recourse, the more so as texts could be copied two centuries or more after they were composed, often far from their Occitanian origins. Rather than being able to sing the songs, readers may simply have recognized them as singable or as somehow songlike. Asking how sonic effects arise means treating manuscripts, in Shane Butler's term, as a type of "phonograph" on which recorded voices might—even if sometimes dimly and with distortion—be played.[3]

The definition of a phonograph on a popular science internet site describes its mechanism in ways that chime with both manuscript production and premodern accounts of hearing: "Sound is collected by a horn that is attached to a diaphragm. The sound causes vibrations in the air that travel down the horn causing the diaphragm to vibrate. The diaphragm is connected to a stylus and pressed into a cylinder covered in wax (or alternatively a thin layer of tin foil)."[4] Some of this description is relevant to writing, a horn being also the reservoir for the scribe's ink, the pen a stylus, and parchment a diaphragm.[5] Not surprisingly, it echoes medieval theories of hearing, too, since the tympanum of the ear is also a diaphragm, and the traces left by sound are made, according to Aristotle, as if on wax (though not tinfoil). That such traces are, consequently, *impressions* made by one body *pressing into* another is an essential feature common to recordings performed by a phonograph, a pen, or the sense organs of animate creatures.

Medieval manuscripts record Occitan songs in a variety of formats. Mostly, but not exclusively, troubadour songs are compiled in lyric anthologies that are called songbooks even when they contain no music. A few early texts that predate these dedicated compilations have *neums*, a form of musical notation in which pitches and melodic contours are represented only in approximate and relational terms. The subsequent development of what musicologists call "square notation," whereby notes are positioned on staves whose pitch is fixed by a clef sign, is attested in only four troubadour songbooks out of thirty or more, two of them primarily collections of Northern French lyric (W, X), the staves in the other two being often (G) or preponderantly (R) blank.[6] In the great majority of troubadour texts, copied without any musical notation, the most salient sonorous feature is the versification, and it is this that most manuscripts foreground in one of two ways. Songs are written line by line in a few, mainly late, manuscripts, where the end of each line may, additionally, be marked by a punctum, the medieval equivalent of a full stop. The commonest layout, however, presents each stanza as a unit of prose, divided internally by a series of puncta that are usually understood as delimiting metrical lines.

While these two common ways of recording songs invite reading with one's ears, it cannot be said they facilitate it. Prosody's potential soundtrack will inevitably be heard, imagined, or performed by readers in varying—and varyingly approximate—ways, according to their level of musical knowledge, metrical competence, and poetic sensibility. In what follows, I analyze potential soundings of two poetic examples, my aim being less to show how their realizations might differ than to explore how these differences arise, how they can be theorized within a medieval framework of thought, and how they are represented in the poems themselves.

The common thread through this discussion is *impression*. A pen may press on parchment, versification on the ear, and both on the senses; such impressions, I will argue, make it possible to hear, or to imagine hearing, sounds in the songs that one sees. The capacity to impress is clear from the tactile (often percussive) terms used from antiquity onward to describe structures of language, poetry, and melody. Beat, stress, ictus, pulse—all designate forms of pressure exerted by the articulation of syllables in declamation, verse, and song.[7] Rhyme and assonance result in some syllables also impressing with a like sonority. As with all instances of past sound, however, the sonic qualities involved are elusive and subject to fluctuation across time as languages, poetic conventions, and performance styles change.

"Sancta Maria, | Vergen Gloriosa"

The early thirteenth-century Occitan Marian hymn "Sancta Maria" offers opportunities for diverse auditory impressions, in part because of the seemingly inconsistent—or experimental?—quality of the sole copy, found in a collection of Occitan religious lyrics in Wolfenbüttel, Herzog August Bibliothek MS Cod. Guelf Extrav. 268, fols. 36r–37r (see figs. 2.1, 2.2, and 2.3).[8] The pages' strange appearance,

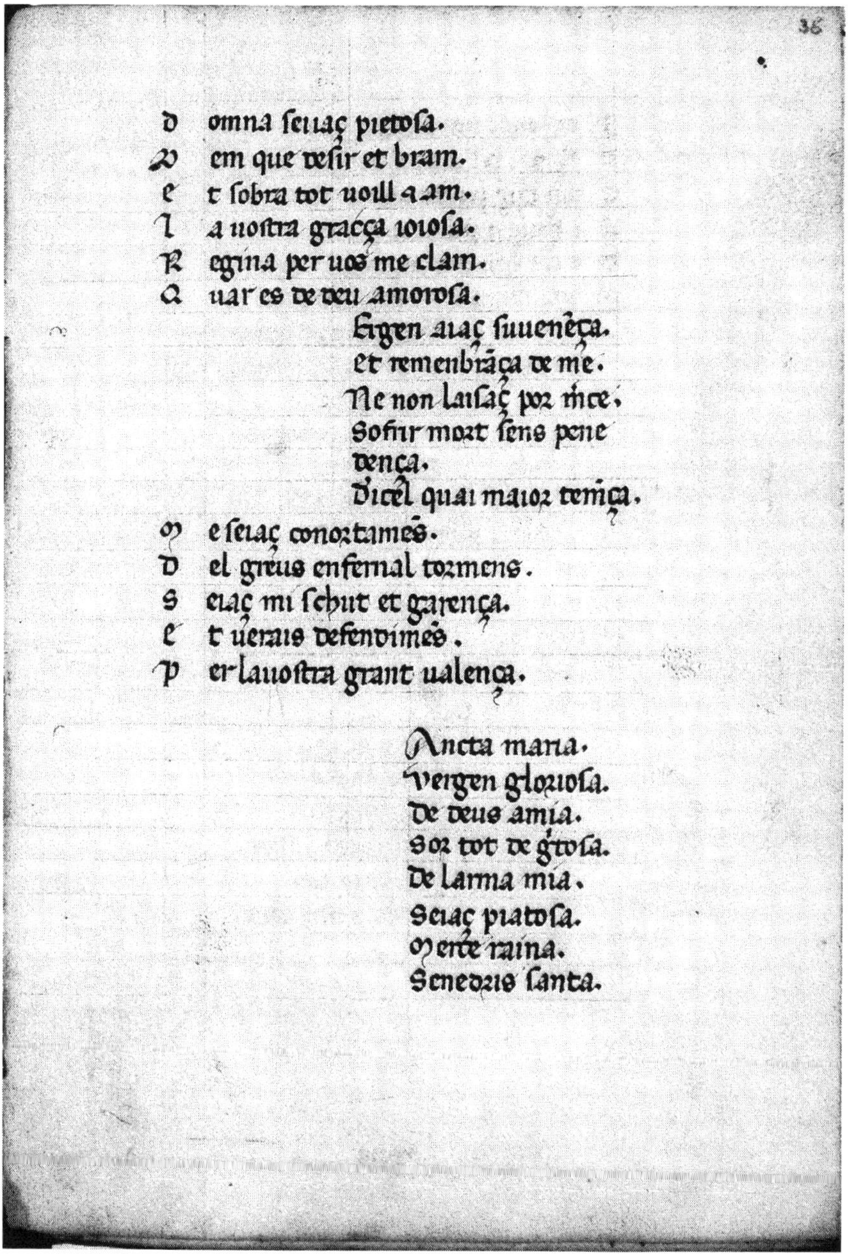

D omna seiaç pietosa.
M em que desir et bram.
E t sobra tot uoill q'am.
L a nostra graçça ioiosa.
R egina per uos me clam.
Q uar es de deu amorosa.
Sigen aiaç suuenença.
et remenbrança de me.
Ne non laisaç por merce,
Sofrir mort sens pene
dença.
Dicel quai maior temença.
M e seiaç conortamens.
D el greus enfernal tormens.
S eiaç mi schut et garença.
E t ueraiis defendimens.
P er la uostra grant ualença.

Sancta maria.
Vergen gloriosa.
De deus amia.
Sor tot de gratiosa.
De larma mia.
Seiaç piatosa.
Mente raina.
Senedris santa.

Figure 2.1. Beginning of anonymous Marian hymn, *incipit* "Sancta Maria." Wolfenbüttel Herzog August Bibliothek, Cod. Guelf. Extrav. 268, fol. 36r.

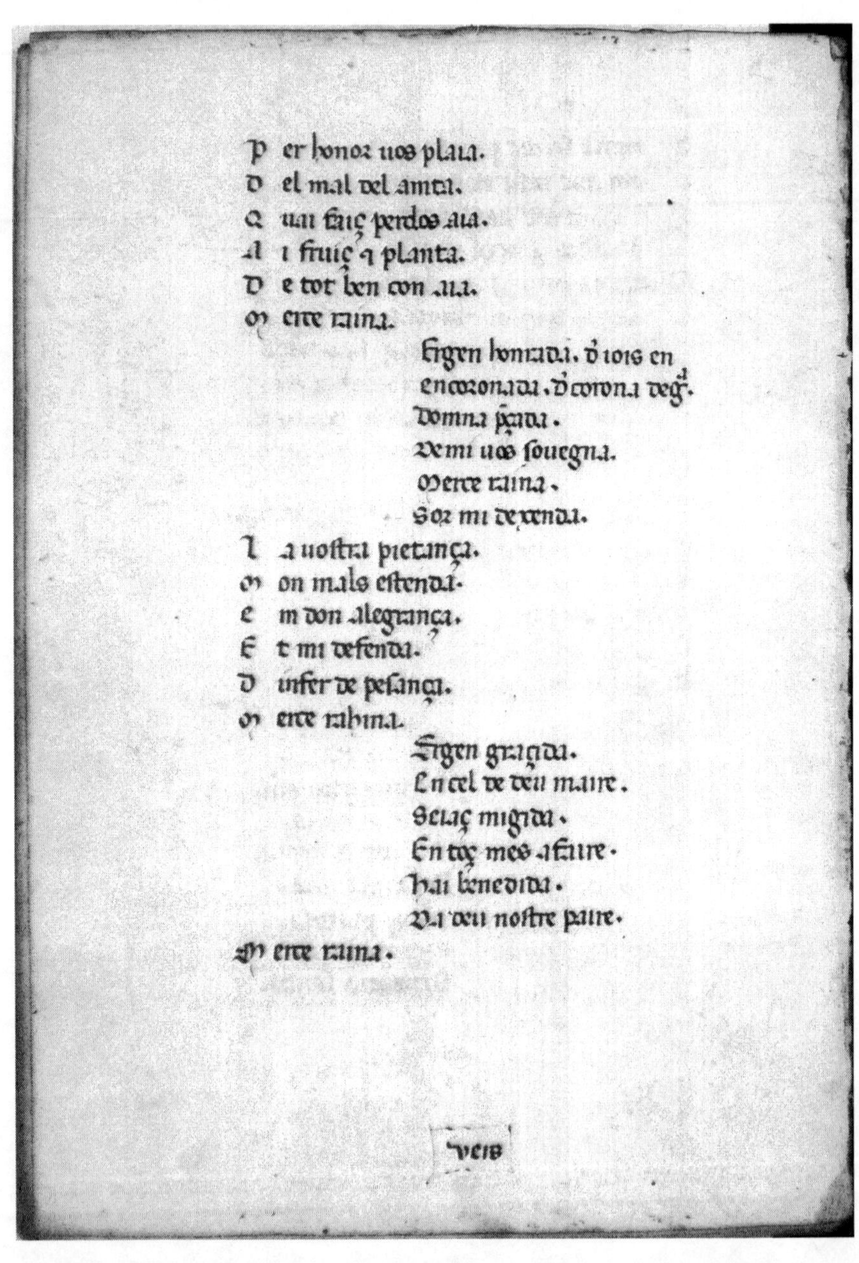

P er honor uos plaia.
D el mal del arma.
Q uan faiç perdos aia.
A i fruiç q planta.
D e tot ben con aia.
M erce raina.
Eigen bontada. d ioia en
encoronada. d corona deg.
Domna pciada.
De mi uos souegna.
Merce raina.
Sor mi dexenda.
L a uostra pietança.
M on mals estenda.
E m don alegrança.
E t mi defenda.
D infer de pesança.
M erce rahina.
Eigen graciada.
En cel de deu maire.
Selaç migrada.
En toç mes afaire.
Hai benedida.
Da deu nostre paire.
Merce raina.

veis

Figure 2.2. "Sancta Maria," continued. Wolfenbüttel Herzog August Bibliothek, Cod. Guelf. Extrav. 268, fol. 36v.

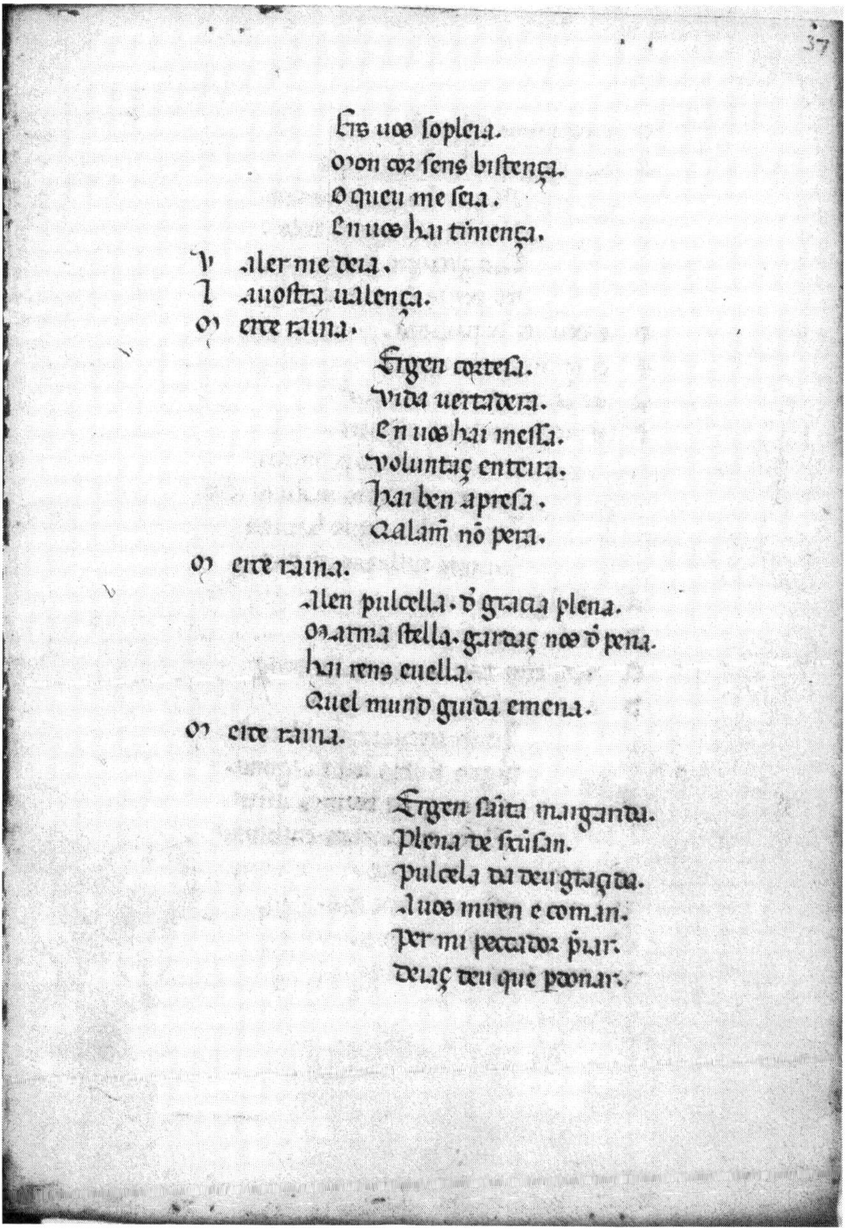

Figure 2.3. End of "Sancta Maria." Wolfenbüttel Herzog August Bibliothek, Cod. Guelf. Extrav. 268, fol. 37r.

with passages of text alternately ranged left and indented, arises from their being unfinished. The large, blank, square spaces were left for decorative initials that were never executed; I supply the missing letters in square brackets in my transcriptions.

Lacking musical notation, the line-by-line layout of the hymn's opening, reinforced by the emphatic scale of the anticipated initial and the use of a punctum at the end of every line, focuses attention on how the text is configured (fig. 2.1). In Occitan verse, the length of a metrical line is reckoned by counting the syllables up to the last stressed syllable, which, in rhymed verse, is also the one containing the main rhyme vowel. By "stressed," I mean both a syllable capable of bearing lexical stress and, if the line is read or declaimed as verse, often the only syllable in the line to carry metrical stress; when sung, however, although the rhyme will typically sound prominently, the rhythmic qualities of the melody displace those of the text. When the rhyme extends over two syllables of which the first is stressed and the second not, it is "feminine." Reading the text on this page as regular Occitan verses, then, will sound out eight four- and five-syllable lines with feminine rhymes. The first six alternate between the rhymes *í-a* and *ós-a*; the seventh introduces a new ending *ín-a*, which, on turning the page, will be revealed as a refrain line whose form is constant and which does not rhyme with any other line (medieval Occitan poetic treatises call this a *rima esparsa*). At the foot of the page, the eighth line introduces a different rhyme again, soon recognizable as marking the onset of a second stanza and a new series of six lines with alternating rhymes. In short, we infer a stanza outline 4′a 5′b 4′a 5′b 4′a 5′b 4′C,[9] as transcribed here:

[S]ancta María,	Holy Mary,
vergen glorióssa,	glorious Virgin,
de Deus amía,	beloved of God,
sor tot degnitósa,	worthy above all,
de l'arma mía	on my soul
seiaç piatósa.	take pity.
Merce, raína!	Have mercy, Queen!

This is the form followed by Emile Levy, one of the hymn's editors, and its plausibility is confirmed by the existence of analogues in troubadour songs also addressed to the Virgin.[10]

Immanuel Bekker, the hymn's first editor, heard the stanza differently, however, printing it thus:

[S]ancta Maria, vergen gloriosa,
de Deus amia, sor tot degnitosa,
de l'arma mia seiaç piatosa
Merce, raina.

His decision draws support from the layout, on fol. 37r, of the hymn's final stanza (see fig. 2.3). Here the scribe has run on lines 1 and 2, and 3 and 4, before setting out lines 5, 6, and 7 line by line (lines 5 and 6 together contain too many letters to fit on one line; the refrain line is always copied on its own). The rhyme scheme and refrain are still the same as in stanza 1, but the renewal of the *a* and *b* rhyme syllables stanza by stanza (in Occitan, *coblas singulars*) is confirmed. This final stanza seems to have determined Bekker's layout of choice for the whole hymn:

[V]alen pulcela, de gratia plena,
marina stella gardaç nos de pena.
Hai! rens e vella que.l mund guida e mena,
merce raina.

[Worthy maiden, full of grace,
star of the sea, protect us from harm.
Ah! oar and sail that steers and drives the world,
have mercy Queen.]

We can still hear the same overall number of syllables as in the seven-line format, but now they are grouped in three lines of nine syllables with internal rhyme, followed by the same, four-syllable refrain. (I count nine syllables because an unstressed vowel at the caesura is often discounted metrically, a phenomenon modern scholars call "epic caesura.") Like rhyme, caesura normally falls on a syllable where lexical and metrical stress coincide, so the number and position of stresses may also feel unchanged. Yet this strophic form does feel slower-paced and statelier than the seven-line one. It also opens the possibility of hearing the longer lines as decasyllabic, with the unstressed *-a* at the end of the first hemistich of each line counted as a full syllable metrically ("lyric caesura").

But Bekker did not choose this form because he heard the longer lines as containing either nine or ten syllables. Instead, he perceived the stanza as Sapphic; and perhaps the scribe of Guelf Extrav. 268 did so, too, by the time he got to the end of the hymn.[11] In Latin prosody, a Sapphic stanza's long lines measure eleven syllables. Hearing all eleven in the Occitan text means according syllabic value to the unstressed vowels in both the internal and the end rhymes, resulting in hemistichs of five and six syllables respectively, the final, refrain line also having five. With its versification estranged from vernacular norms, the hymn now appears as a Latin calque where language and meter are to some extent in tension, although the scribe's frequent orthographic Latinisms help edge its language toward Latinity, too.

Given that Sapphic stanzas are widely used in Medieval Latin hymns, a reader of the Wolfenbüttel lyric might read "Sancta Maria" not only as a Latinate calque but as a contrafactum (a song that reprises the meter and melody of an earlier one) and mentally intone it to the music of a Latin model. When sung, each long line would sound out eleven syllables, since unstressed syllables in Occitan are not usually sung any differently from stressed ones. Singing, then, would minimize the tension between form and language that speaking would expose.

A possible model for the imagined or actual performance of "Sancta Maria" is "Ut queant laxis," whose text the editor of the *Analecta Hymnica* prints thus:

Ut queant laxis resonare fibris
Mira gestorum famuli tuorum,
Solve pollute labii reatum,
  Sancte Johannes.[12]

[So that, their voices loosened,
your servants may be able to ring out the wonder of your works,
cleanse the guilt from our soiled lips,
  Saint John.]

Each of the eleven-syllable lines of this hymn is composed of two hemistichs, one of five and one of six syllables, exactly like the Sapphic sound-shape proposed by Bekker for "Sancta Maria." Initially, "Ut queant" underlines the division into hemistichs by means of internal rhymes, and these lend it, alternatively, to being heard as a series of short lines beginning with rhyming couplets: "Ut queant laxis | resonare fibris," and so forth. This latter option is supported by the fact that the opening syllables of the resulting lines create a mnemonic of the musical scale, *ut—re—me—fa—sol—la*. Imagining the Sapphic stanza as a seven-line stanza rather than a quatrain enables us, in turn, to hear the opening stanza of "Sancta Maria," laid out over seven lines on fol. 36v, as Latinate and Sapphic, not, as I did at first, as a standard Occitan verse form.

A more learned reader might experience different impressions again if they were able to hear, in these strophes, the quantitative Sapphic verses of Horace or

Catullus.[13] But educated eyes and ears, even if unfamiliar with these classical models, might have encountered medieval imitations such as that by the eleventh-century master Theobaldus in his verse *Physiologus*. Theobaldus boasts of using different meters for each beast, choosing Sapphics for the Serpent:

Jām sĕnēx sērpēns nŏvūs ēssĕ gāudĕt
ātquĕ jējūnāns măcĭē pĕrhōrrĕt, . . .

[Now the old serpent delights to be new,
and is scaly and wasted through fasting, . . .][14]

I believe this Latin arts text may well have influenced some of the more educated troubadours.[15] Its oldest known manuscript is an eleventh-century school compilation from southern France, now London, British Library, MS Harley 3093. A medieval Occitan scribe or reader might well hear "Sancta Maria" as an echo of school texts like this.

As his editor points out, however, Theobaldus was not able to maintain this meter consistently all through his poem on the serpent.[16] He also left medieval copyists perplexed; they transcribed these stanzas of his bestiary in any number of ways. Faced with what might be the same meter in "Sancta Maria," the scribe of the Wolfenbüttel manuscript was seemingly equally stumped. Over the three pages on which they appear, the hymn's strophes are set out in multiple formats, in visual units of varying lengths. The most egregious case is stanza 3, on fol. 36v (fig. 2.2), which starts by abandoning the line-by-line layout in favor of running on the text and marking units solely with the punctum; before long, an omission causes the text to come completely adrift. Here is a narrow transcription of what is written in the manuscript:

[V]ergen honrada . de jois en
coronada . de corona degna .
domna preçada .
mi uos sovegna .
merce raina .

Levy identifies a lacuna after *jois* in the first line of the copy:

[V]ergen honrada,
de jois . . . . . .
encoronada
de corona degna, . . .

[Honored Virgin,
. . . . . with joy,
crowned
with a crown of worth, . . .]

His solution is better than Bekker's, which reorders the lines to place the lacuna after *encoronada*, thereby making the first hemistich of the second metrical line hypermetric:

[V]ergen honrada, de corona degna,
d'jois encoronada, ... (+1, or even, restoring *de jois*, +2)

[Honored Virgin, worthy of a crown,
crowned with joy, ...]

Neither solution can disguise the fact that the scribe's hearing here was "off," which in turn makes the text impossible for the reader to hear. Indeed, irregularities proliferate throughout the copy. The refrain is not always recognized as marking a stanza boundary; consequently, the stanza is not always recognized as a unit—the first two are run together, as are stanzas 3 and 4; stanzas 5, 6, and 7 are all copied separately but differently from one another; even though almost every missing initial is the same, *V*, the spaces left for it have differing dimensions. The hymn's impressions, written and sounded, are thus elusive and potentially cacophonous.

My point here is not to criticize the scribe. If sound is hard to hear in writing, it is equally hard to put *into* writing. The phonic realization of medieval verse is controversial. The categories of lexical stress, metrical ictus, and musical rhythm are hard to identify and do not necessarily coincide; without musical notation, we can barely even speculate how a sung text might sound. A slow reading of "Sancta Maria" helps identify the reasons for the plurality and plasticity of its impressions, seen and heard. Under prolonged scrutiny, line length, the measure of Occitan verse, proves alarmingly elastic. I have counted metrical lines of four, five, six, nine, ten, and eleven syllables, as stanzas pull now into one shape, now another. Along with these variations, rhyme position fluctuates between line final and internal, and metrical stresses migrate. The sounds of language and form shift as they draw toward or away from different kinds of Latin usage.

Time is crucial in apprehending this plasticity. The Wolfenbüttel scribe seems to have needed time to grasp the sonic structure of the work he was copying. Perhaps he understood it only when he reached the end, after running the gamut of options. His readers find themselves in the same temporal play as they advance, hesitating, through what he has put before them. Depending on their different prior experiences, they may also reach back through earlier times and linguistic experiences as they figure, from conflicting remembered or half-remembered models, how best to construe these verses, according to vernacular practice or the norms of Latin metrical or quantitative prosody.

The complex perceptual processes involved in reading sound in writing lead me, in the next section, to look to the medieval philosophy of perception enshrined in *De anima* texts, which describe how hearing relates to touch, time, and vision. I conclude with a discussion of how the troubadour Marcabru knowingly inhabits, represents, and exploits this perceptual world.

Sound Impressions

It is not easy to unpack what medieval writers thought was at stake in imagining sound, given the privilege they everywhere accord to vision. Yet the Latin *De anima* tradition describes how the animal soul—as distinct from the rational and vegetative souls—receives, warehouses, and puts to use sensory information in the form not of pictures, exactly, but of *species*, the shapes or forms of things, and of *signa*—"impressions" or "imprints"—like that of a seal on wax. A crucial passage, already broached in the introduction to this volume, articulates these important terms together:

> Generally, about all perception, we can say that a sense is what has the power of receiving into itself the sensible forms of things without the matter [*susceptivum sensibilium specierum sine materia*], in the way in which a piece of wax takes on the impression [*signum*] of a signet-ring without the iron or gold. It receives an impression [*signum*] of bronze or gold, but not qua bronze or gold. In a similar way the sense [*sensus*] is affected by what has color or flavor or sound, but not insofar as each is said to be so, but according to its quality and its informing principle [*sed in quantum huiusmodi est et secundum rationem*]. (Aristotle, *De anima*, 2.11.12, 424a17–23)[17]

This account goes from physically imprinting an outline or form to communicating something of the rational or essential character of a thing, a move that subsequent thinkers clearly found challenging. Their comments address two main questions: What are the relationships between the various senses? And how do they lead to cognition? Their voluminous writings on these topics fortunately concern us only as they relate to the inquiry pursued here: how can we understand the sound of verse as heard when it is conjured from writing?

Aristotle's account of perception as imprinting like a signet ring, where what is transferred onto the wax is the outline or impress of the seal but not the material out of which the seal is made, implies that the nature of sense data is not determined by the physical manner of sensation. Rather, a sound or a sight leaves impressions in the same way, just as gold or iron does, even if each sensation makes an impression particular to it. The philosopher's guiding metaphor favors convergences between the senses and underlines the fundamental role among them of touch. An imprint comes into being through touching—impressing—and through process—over time—before it can be perceived across space; so it can coordinate sensations that are more time-based, like hearing, with those that are more spatial, like sight. This potential triangulation of touch, hearing, and sight recalls the earlier analogy of the phonograph with writing and hearing, and it offers promising terrain for reflecting how song inscribed on the page might be read as sound.

The same three senses—hearing, touch, and vision—come together in Aristotle's earlier account of sound, which concludes by summarizing the processes involved:

> What is it that sounds, the striking body or the one that is struck [*verberatur aut verberans*]? Or both, but in a different way? For sound is the movement that can be set in motion in this way from smooth surfaces [*lenibus*], when someone strikes them [*percutiat*]. Therefore, as has been said, not everything sounds when it strikes or is struck [*verberatur et verberans*], e.g., if a needle is struck against another needle [*obiciatur acus acui*]; but what is struck needs to be even [*regulare*]. And the differences between sounding things are manifested in the act of sounding. Just as without light, colors cannot be seen, similarly without sound one cannot tell sharp/high [*acutum*] from flat/low [*grave*]. These words are used metaphorically, from [the realm of] things that are touched. Something that is sharp [*acute*] moves the sense a lot in a short time, whereas what is flat [*grave*] moves the sense little in a long time. Not that what is sharp [*acutus*] is fast, however, or what is flat [*grave*], slow; but it results from the speed of [the touch of] the one and the slowness of [that of] the other. There seems to be a similarity with what is sharp [*acuto*] or blunt [*hebeti*] to the touch. What is sharp [*acutum*] as it were stabs, while what is blunt [*hebes*] pushes, the one producing its effect in a short, the other in a long time, so that the one is quick, the other slow. (Aristotle, *De anima*, trans. James of Venice, 2.8, 420a19–b2)

The text is clear: sound is primarily an effect of touch in its relationship with time, but the sight of color provides a valuable point of comparison. Touch is conveyed by multiple verbs denoting physical impact (*verberare*, *percutere*, *obicere*; striking, beating, clashing together); additionally, tactile qualities are necessary for objects to be capable of sounding, such as being smooth or even to the touch. Touch, furthermore, offers a way of understanding pitch. The difference between a sharp or high sound and a low or flat one is like that between being struck, respectively, by a sharp object or a blunt one. Their impact is felt over time rather than in space. One might think a sharp object would concentrate its impact on the small area of the body which it strikes, but Aristotle's point is rather that it produces its maximal effect quickly. Conversely, low sounds or blunt objects have an effect that seems more protracted. Significantly, the Latin vocabulary of sharp/high and flat/low in this passage applies with particular aptness to hearing medieval song, because the same terms are found distinguishing high from low pitch in music treatises and masculine or feminine rhyme in poetics.

The further point here, that pitch is to hearing what color is to vision, is one of many affinities Aristotle sees between these two senses. For example, he compares an echo with a reflection, specifying that smooth objects like those made of bronze reflect light, much as they reflect sound (*De anima* 419b25–34). A reason for the similarity emerges in book 3 of *De anima*, when the analogy between sense impressions and a signet ring is elaborated with reference to the interactions between the five external senses. Everything that can be touched can also be perceived by other senses (424b24). And everything that can be sensed by a particular medium can be sensed by organs that function in that medium; for example, both color and sound are sensed through the air (424b34).

Aquinas later explains and expands discussion of these interconnections, again focusing on the interplay between hearing and sight: "For the senses perceive each other's special objects indirectly, as sight that of hearing, and vice versa. Sight does not perceive the audible as such, nor hearing the visible as such (for the eye takes no impression from the audible, nor the ear from the visible) but both objects are perceived by each sense only insofar as 'one sense,' i.e., one actual sensation so to say, bears upon an object that contains both" (Aquinas, *In Aristotelis "Librum de anima" commentarium*, sec. 581 [at 425a27–b4]).[18] Aquinas is here pointing to the obvious fact that impressions combine: we rarely rely on one sense in isolation. Aristotle's Latin translators use the term *secundum accidens* for this fact of evoking something indirectly, or "incidentally," with one sense while relying mainly on another, so that if we register with sight that bile is yellow, we also know *secundum accidens* that it is bitter, because taste registers it as such (*De anima* 425b2). Other kinds of information, originally gleaned by the senses but subsequently processed through cognition, also incidentally supplement sense perception, as when we glimpse something colored and know that it is a particular person (425a25). Interplay between the senses accounts for the possibility of coordinating impressions with one another, resulting in what Aristotle's medieval adapters call "the common sensibles" (*communia sensibilia*): physical properties like movement and rest, shape and size, or number and unity, which are essential to perception but cannot be imprinted by any one sense alone. Indeed, perception so far exceeds the direct action of an object on any individual sense that what is called "the common sense" (*sensus communis*) is crucially important for mediating between the individual external senses and cognition.[19] This understanding of common sense is fundamental to grasping how writing could be thought of as heard, given that hearing alone cannot make out a written song nor sight alone register how it might sound.

How might physically unheard sound be heard mentally? Aristotle discusses the means whereby the animal soul manipulates sense impressions in the absence of the objects that caused them in *De anima* book 3, under the headings of memory and imagination (427b14–429a9). Imagination, he says, is distinct from, and intermediary between, sensation and belief or judgment. It cannot exist without the senses, which never err, but like judgment, it is fallible; imagination is freely exercised whereas judgment is constrained by criteria of truthfulness (427b18–21). Concluding, he identifies imagination as moved by the senses and puts them into action (whereas the senses themselves are passive); it is dominated by sight as the most developed of the five external senses; nonhuman animals are completely led by imagination, humans only when their reason is somehow impaired.

Aristotle's commentators develop his conception of the common sense to construct a taxonomy of "internal senses" that act partly as the mental counterparts of the external ones but that also combine and manipulate impressions received from them to form imaginations, memories, creative projects, and the beginnings of cognition and judgment. Spurred by Aristotle's affirmation that these inner senses are common to many animals, Avicenna works to distinguish some of the inner senses of humans from those of other animals, a move later systematized by Albert the Great. But the common sense, Avicenna maintains, is found across species other than humans. The foundation and center of sensation and perception, only it can explain the complexity of animate behavior.[20]

The account assembled here might explain the complex behavior involved in hearing a written text such as "Sancta Maria." Readers would coordinate, via the common sense, their visual impressions (*signa*) of the imprints left by the scribe on the writing surface, together with their warehouse of auditory impressions. The common sensibles would be necessary to register, and make available, such qualities as unity, size, number, sameness, and difference, without which one could not form impressions of the complex sonorities of meter, stress, rhyme, and syllable count, of melodic gestures and cadences. Sometimes readers might retrieve impressions from memory, but often they would rely on imagination to figure how stanza forms might sound. The processes involved would both take time and range across time, turning the space of the page into an arena of evolving actions.

Although "Sancta Maria" does not seem particularly interested in the way perception is lodged in the animal soul and generalized across the animal world, the fact that humans are not alone in recognizing pulse or rhythm clearly matters to other troubadours, notably the important mid-twelfth-century poet Marcabru. Framing blistering satire and obscene humor with metrical virtuosity, his songs are both rousing and perplexing to hear.

Marcabru, "D'aiso laus Dieu"

I have chosen to analyze the song "D'aiso laus Dieu" because scholastic views of sensation not only inform how we might read it but are also represented in it, to the point where the song itself proposes how it might be heard.[21]

"D'aiso laus Dieu" survives in six mainstream songbooks that set it out as prose units stanza by stanza with puncta marking rhymes or line endings; images and transcriptions of all six copies, and the texts of major editions, are consultable online.[22] Editors print the song in six-line stanzas, 4a 4a 8b 4c 4c 8b;[23] the *b* rhyme of the octosyllables, in *-ir*, is constant through all stanzas, but the *a* rhyme changes stanza by stanza (*coblas singulars*). In manuscript, the most visible formal irregularities implying varying sound outlines are variations in the order and number of stanzas, and instances of strophic recomposition. A striking example of the latter comes when songbooks *C* and *E* suppress the last three lines of stanza 4 and add the remaining three to the end of stanza 3. The resulting, anomalous nine-line stanza points to the basic compositional unit of the song as four + four + eight syllables, a unit equally audible as an octosyllabic distich with internal rhyme in one of its lines.[24] Like the Sapphic stanza, this metrical cell directly imitates Medieval Latin models:[25] its *aab ccb ddb* . . . rhyme scheme is a form of tail-rhyme also found in Latin liturgical verse.[26] The song's opening lines, "For this, I praise God | and St. Andrew" ("D'aiso laus Dieu | e Saint Andreu"), suggest that Marcabru may indeed be contrafacting a Latin St. Andrew's day hymn. The versification also recalls Mozarabic poetic forms where rhymes particular to each strophe alternate with a rhyme that recurs throughout the song.[27] All these formal associations contribute audible strands from different registers, languages, and epochs, similar to what we heard in the Marian hymn.

But unlike "Sancta Maria," "D'aiso laus Dieu" is parodic, its text aggressively at odds both with Latin liturgical hymns and Arabic love songs. Its first-person voice goes from vaunting the singer's superior judgment (stanzas 1 and 2), to bragging he can outsmart his neighbors (stanzas 3–8), to promoting (or mocking) the singer's poetic expertise (11). Regarding his neighbors, he claims to have unhindered access to their sexual partners while securely guarding his own. These claims, couched in metaphors of eating, fighting, hunting, and land ownership, between them evoke physical domains of appetite, violence, animality, and domination. Marcabru's parodic target was identified by Aurelio Roncaglia as the "lesser troubadours" whom Marcabru castigates in other songs. Self-presentation as a boasting poem (or *gap*, in Occitan) suggests he may also be mocking earlier *gaps* by the first known troubadour, Guilhem IX. Two other scurrilous songs with the same versification, exchanged between Marcabru and his patron Audric, share the themes of wealth, food, and song, if not sex, to define hierarchies between the two men. Even more than them, "D'aiso laus Dieu" is an obnoxious, if tongue-in-cheek, exercise in one-upmanship.

Parody, literally "singing beside" another text, is as audible a literary device as a contrafactum, but although it has dominated critical readings of this song, my own approach will be different. I understand "D'aiso laus Dieu" as an attempt to sing about sensation, the common sense, and imagination from their perspective and not from that of reason. The limitations of rationality are a constant theme of this troubadour. In "D'aiso laus Dieu," however, rather than lamenting reason's failings, Marcabru takes the bolder step of positioning his voice outside it, in the thick of impressions and imaginings. Although the song repeatedly invokes a rational frame, from the brash "no one has better judgment | than I do" of stanza 1 (3–4, "c'om non es de maior albir | qu'ieu soi") to the poet's claims to rhetorical control in stanza 9, this frame is conjured only to be undone. Adopting, instead, the voice of the exterior and interior senses, the song directs audience and readers to respond to it with theirs, too.

This is clearest in stanza 6, which describes combat in terms that recall accounts of sound:

6 D'estonc breto
e de basto

no sap hom plus, ni d'escremir,
qu'ieu fier autrui
e·m gart de lui,
e no·s sap del mieu colp cubrir.

[Of Breton jabbing,
stick fighting
and fencing no one knows more than I do,
for I strike another man
and protect myself from him,
and he doesn't know how to cover himself from my blow.]

Not only does the impact of striking recall metaphors of sounding and hearing, but the rhythm described in lines 31–33, two short blows with different kinds of cudgel and one long thrust of a blade, captures the sequence of two short lines and one longer one that defines their meter. The mimicry of form by content in these lines continues in the next three, with the singer's rapid jab and parry in the two short lines and successful lunge in the long one.

The same rhythm passes from the language of touch to that of sight and sound in the following stanza, as two small hounds rush forward baying, and a third, larger, one strains back before attacking:

7 En l'autrui brueill
cas cora·m vueill,
e fauc mos dos canetz glatir,
e·l ters saüz
eis de raüs,
bautz e aficatz per ferir.

[I hunt at will
in another man's wood,
and make my two little dogs bay,
and the third St. Hubert hound
comes out backwards,
keen and eager to pounce.]

The configuration these lines describe is probably a metaphor for male sex organs; it animalizes and sexualizes not only the banging and thrusting of the previous stanza but also the verse form. Concomitantly, on the level of sound imagined *secundum accidens*, the noise of blows raining down is transposed into canine yelping. Between stanzas 6 and 7, then, we hear the song's meter as impressions laid down in time by (violent) touch and aggressive animal cries. These groups of two shorts and a long, or two smalls and a large, also call to mind fundamental units of versification (long and short syllables in classical Latin, stress groups in later Latin and the vernaculars) and those, too, of musical notation, also initially combining notes known in the Middle Ages as "longs" and "shorts." Although nowhere notated *for singing*, the song is, as it were, notated *for writing and imaginary listening*.

There is another evocation of animal sound in the song's closing lines, where the troubadour presents himself as "the bird | that has [his] own chicks brought up | by starlings":

11 qu'ieu soi l'auzels
c'als estornels
fauc los mieus auzeletz noirir.

The singer can only be claiming here to be a cuckoo, whose confident, noisy, repetitive, and basically silly call is widely mocked. Starlings, meanwhile, are known for noisily imitating other birds. Is the derision aimed at the repetitiveness of the song's tirelessly reiterated 4a 4a 8b cell? Or is it targeting future silly repetitions of the singer's own repetitive and silly song? Most modern critics have not interpreted the cuckoo reference as self-denigrating but as boasting of the singer's ability to cuckold others, an interpretation that stems, I think, from a misguided willingness to accept at face value the claims to superior cleverness made elsewhere in the song, of which I will consider just two.

In stanza 3, the word *sens* introduces an equivocation familiar in Romance between the rational and sensory meanings of "sense":

3 De ginhos *sens*
soi si manens
que molt sui greus az escarnir.

[I am so rich
in cunning *sense*
that it's very hard to make a mockery of me.]

The singer can certainly be credited with wit and low cunning, which would be one possible meaning of *ginhos sens*. But the phrase also inaugurates a parade of sense-perceptions, each presented maneuvering in its own sphere of activity in its own little imaginary vignette: each sense would then be crafty in its particular reach. In the stanza order adopted by the editors, these vignettes begin with taste and maybe smell (the other's warm bread in stanzas 3–4), then touch, hearing, and sight (the fighting and hunting dogs in stanzas 6–7), and conclude with color in stanza 9.

Stanza 9 is another instance in which the song gestures toward a rational frame—although without, in my view, seeking to occupy it:

9 De pluzors *sens*
soi ples e prens,
de cent colors per meils cauzir;
foc porte sai
et aigua lai
ab que sai la flam'escantir.

[I am pregnant
and teeming with numerous *signs*,
with a hundred colors the better to discern;[28]
I bear fire here,
and water there,
with which I know how to quench the flame.]

In conjunction with *cauzir* in line 51, the term *color*—with its association with the *colores rhetorici*, or rhetorical figures—implies the singer's familiarity with rhetoric as a means to hone argument.[29] But the abundance of *sens*, which appears to ground his confidence (49–50), does not here evoke, as it usually does, a wealth of whichever of reason or the senses (<SENSUS) is more appropriate to the context. The spelling represents the word *senh(s)*, from SIGNA, required for the rhyme with *prenhs* (50, here spelled *prens*), which means "pregnant, with child." *Signum* is, we recall, the term used by Latin translators of Aristotle to designate the imprint or impression made by objects on the senses. This rhetorician's voice emanates not from sense but from a body teeming with impressions, as if about to give birth. In another metaphor, in the second half of this stanza, these impressions blaze away in an internal conflagration that the singer himself has ignited by bringing "fire here"—even if he alternately douses it with "water there."

Sense impressions, whatever the originating external sense, imprint the mind, so it is not surprising that the sense of touch is felt not only in the stanza about beating but throughout the song in metaphors of eating, penetration (or its warding off), and burning or drenching. Impressions form when sensations press into a surface. Although the singer adopts an aggressive policy of penetrating others' wives' bodies while warding off others' incursions, and laying eggs in others' nests, he nevertheless ends up pregnant with impressions, the exact opposite of the impregnable territory he claims (in stanza 8) to be. It is from this blazing warehouse of impressions, this inferno of the common sense, that he draws the *colors* of his song: a rich assembly of patterned sounds and sights, of varying scales of magnitude, and diverse forms of touch, which proliferate through dramatic vignettes and over time. Not only is the song furnished with the contents of the troubadour's imagination; it also represents in its lexis and the situating of its voice how the senses and their impressions work together to produce them.

Earlier in this essay, I compared a manuscript with a phonograph, a comparison that is apt to the Wolfenbüttel copy of "Sancta Maria," where the visual impressions of ink, arranged around blank spaces, are capable of proliferating impressions of sound. In "D'aiso laus Dieu," however, the effect of writing is more like cinema. The units on the page certainly correspond with the poem's formal, sonic structure, but now sound is an element in a 3-D world invigorated by pulse, color, and energy, where the voices of nonhuman animals mingle with the voice of the singer. In both examples, in the absence of musical notation, reading with one's ears is grounded in verse. But as medieval faculty psychology elaborates, and "D'aiso laus Dieu" manifests, its sound is not as much acousmatic as integrated to a polysensory, phantasmatic inner world, a cinematic world whose literally spectacular functioning Marcabru knowingly exploits.[30]

NOTES

1. François Noudelmann, *Lire avec les oreilles* (Paris: Max Milo, 2019); François Noudelmann, "What Is an Acousmatic Reading?" *Paragraph* 41, no. 1 (2017): 110–24.

2. Joyce Coleman, *Public Reading and the Reading Public in Late Medieval England and France* (Cambridge: Cambridge University Press, 1996).

3. Shane Butler, *The Ancient Phonograph* (New York: Zone Books, 2015).

4. "Rough Science: Explore the Challenges," PBS, www.pbs.org/weta/roughscience/series2/challenges/sound/page3.html#.

5. I understand *diaphragm* in sense 4c of the word as defined in the OED: "A membrane stretched in or on a frame; a vibrating membrane." *The Oxford English Dictionary*, ed. J. A. Simpson and E. S. C. Weiner, 2nd ed. 20 vols. (Oxford: Clarendon Press, 1989), s.v. "diaphragm, n."

6. For *sigla* and corresponding shelfmarks of troubadour songbooks, see https://trobaretz.wordpress.com, which provides links to online scans.

7. See Margot E. Fassler, "Accent, Meter, and Rhythm in Medieval Treatises 'De rithmis,'" *Journal of Musicology* 5, no. 2 (1987): 164–90.

8. See Zeno Lorenza Verlato, "Occitania periferica: Il canzoniere religioso di Wolfenbüttel." *Rivista di studi testuali* 4 (2002); the manuscript is dated 1254 in a colophon. Editions: Immanuel Bekker, *Geistliche Lieder des dreizehnten Jahrhunderts: Provenzalisch; aus einer Wolfenbüttler Handschrift (Extravag. 268)* (Berlin: Abhandlungen der historisch-philolog. Klasse der Königl. Preuss. Academie der Wissenschaften, 1844), 13; Emile Levy, "Poésies religieuses provençales et françaises du manuscrit Extravag. 268 de Wolfenbuettel," *Revue des langues romanes* 31 (1887): 246–47. Translations of "Sancta Maria" are mine.

9. István Frank, *Répertoire métrique de la poésie des troubadours*, 2 vols. (Paris: Champion, 1953–57), 1:48, lists it as #268.2. In this standard method of recording stanza structure, which recurs later in this essay, numerals represent the syllable count of each line; a following prime symbol indicates a final, additional "feminine" syllable; lower-case letters designate the rhyme pattern; and upper-case letters identify refrain rhymes.

10. The same rhyme scheme is found with decasyllabic lines in Peire d'Espanha's religious *alba*, PC 342.1; Frank, *Repertoire*, 1:48, #268.1; and an anonymous prayer to the Virgin (no PC number).

11. Bekker's view was adopted by Karl Bartsch and Eduard Koschwitz in their *Chrestomathie provençale (Xe-XVe siècles)* (Marburg: Elwert, 1904), 305–6; and by Georges Lote in his *Histoire du vers français*, vol. 1, *Les origines du vers français* (Paris: Boivin, 1949), 148–49n88.

12. *Analecta hymnica medii aevi*, ed. Guido Maria Dreves and Clemens Blume (Leipzig: Fues, 1886–1922), 2:50, hymn #52. The melody survives in ten sources; see https://cantus.uwaterloo.ca/chant/159469. For its influence on vernacular verse, see Lote, *Histoire du vers français*, 1:98n50.

13. Edgar H. Sturtevant, "Horace, Carm. 3.30.10–14, and the Sapphic Stanza," *Transactions and Proceedings of the American Philological Association* 70 (1939): 295–302.

14. *Theobaldi "Physiologus,"* ed. and trans. P. T. Eden (Leiden: Brill, 1972), 32–33, with Eden's translation and my proposed scansion.

15. Sarah Kay, "Rigaut de Berbezilh, the *Physiologus Theobaldi*, and the Opening of Animal Inspiration," *Reinardus* 28 (2016): 81–99.

16. *Theobaldi "Physiologus,"* 33.

17. This is my translation of James of Venice's mid-twelfth-century Latin version of Aristotle's text, with key Latin terms in brackets (in his later translation, William of Moerbeke uses the identical terms); text is from the Aristoteles Latinus Database (Turnhout: Brepols, 2009-). My translation of *rationem* in the final phrase follows Aquinas's gloss, "secundum rationem, idest secundum formam," in Thomas Aquinas, *In Aristotelis "Librum de anima" commentarium*, ed. P. F. Angeli and M. Pirotta (Turin: Marietti, 1959), *lectio* 24, sec. 554, p. 138. Kenelm Foster, *Aristotle's "De anima" in the Version of William of Moerbeke and the Commentary of St. Thomas Aquinas* (New Haven, CT: Yale University Press, 1951), 340, translates "as having this or that 'informing principle' or form."

18. Foster, trans., *Aristotle's "De anima,"* 355.

19. Daniel Heller-Roazen, "Common Sense: Greek, Arabic, Latin," in *Rethinking the Medieval Senses: Heritage, Fascinations, Frames*, ed. Stephen G. Nichols, Andreas Kablitz, and Alison Calhoun (Baltimore: Johns Hopkins University Press, 2008), 34–35; see also Pavel Gregoric, *Aristotle on the Common Sense* (Oxford: Oxford University Press, 2007).

20. Heller-Roazen, "Common Sense," 40–42.

21. Simon Gaunt, Ruth Harvey, and Linda Paterson, *Marcabru: A Critical Edition* (Woodbridge, UK: D. S. Brewer, 2000), song 16, 209–24; their translation, with significant changes noted.

22. See Medieval Romance Lyric, https://letteraturaeuropea.let.uniroma1.it/?q=laboratorio/tradizione-manoscritta-80.

23. See note 9 above for an explanation of this way of noting the syllable count and rhyme scheme of Occitan verse.

24. See Gaunt, Harvey, and Paterson, *Marcabru*, 210; François Pirot, *Recherches sur les connaissances littéraires des troubadours occitans et catalans des XIIe et XIIIe siècles* (Barcelona: Real Academia de Buenas Letras, 1972), 97–100. Michel Burger, *Recherches sur la structure et l'origine des vers romans* (Geneva: Droz, 1957), 51, notes that short lines in vernacular verse often result from the breaking up of longer ones by means of internal rhyme.

25. Burger, *Recherches*, 50–53. For a detailed study of this verse form, Latin and vernacular, see Pirot, *Recherches*, 96–108.

26. Aurelio Roncaglia, "Il gap di Marcabruno," *Studi Medievali* 17 (1951): 46–70, 62, compares Marcabru's text with a stanza of an early Occitan hymn; see also Catherine Léglu, *Between Sequence and Sirventes: Aspects of Parody in the Troubadour Lyric* (Oxford: Legenda, 2000), 34–35; and Maria-Luisa Meneghetti, "Aldric, Marcabru e il poemetto 'Eu aor Damrideu,'" in *L'ornato parlare: Studi di filologia e letterature romanze per Furio Brugnolo*, ed. Gianfelice Peron (Padua: Esedra, 2007), 3–20.

27. See Otto Zwartjes, *Love Songs from Al-Andalus: History, Structure and Meaning of the Kharja* (Leiden: Brill, 1997).

28. The *Marcabru* editors translate "I am loaded" and "choose."

29. Linda Paterson, *Troubadours and Eloquence* (Cambridge: Cambridge University Press, 1975), 26.

30. The second and final parts of this essay share common ground with chapter 6 of my *Medieval Song from Aristotle to Opera* (Ithaca, NY: Cornell University Press, 2022). "D'aisso [*sic*] laus Dieu" is sung to the melody of a Saint Andrew's day hymn by Christopher Preston Thompson on the companion website at https://cornellpress.manifoldapp.org/projects/medieval-song/resource-collection/1-recordings/resource/6-1-1-recording-of-marcabru-d-aisso-laus-dieu-contrafact-5-11.

CHAPTER THREE

Voices and Bees

The Evolution of Charles Butler's Acoustic Book

Jennifer Richards

Charles Butler (1560–1647), clergyman, chorister, and teacher of grammar and rhetoric, is best remembered for the manual he created for beekeepers, *The Feminine Monarchie, or a Treatise Concerning Bees and the Due Ordering of Them* (1609; new editions 1623, 1634).[1] In addition to providing practical advice on how to look after bee stocks to harvest more honey, he also established the sex of the ruling bee and reimagined the hive as a model society led by females, an idea that may have been palatable to him because he "had lived through the reign of Queen Elizabeth I."[2] Butler gathered his knowledge, as he states on the title page, through the "experience and diligent observation" of bees.[3] Or as Jonathan Woolfson puts it, he studied "in an apicultural rather than a laboratory context."[4] Ancient authorities Aristotle and Pliny learned about bees from books, Butler explains in the preface to the 1609 edition.[5] He read books, too. Indeed, he likely kept a commonplace book to aid composition, with material collected from reading organized under headings to facilitate its easy retrieval, a standard humanist practice learned in the schoolroom.[6] But unlike his contemporaries, he cites classical authorities mainly to ornament his style because he is also out in the field. Crucially, he listened attentively as well. What he heard, and how he wanted his readers to engage with that, is communicated through the "scores" he created for them in his three print editions: first, of the piping of queen bees in 1609, then of the same piping now blended with human voices in a bee song with four vocal parts in 1623 and 1634, and, finally, also in 1634, the presentation of the written text in a phonetic script representing the human "voice."[7]

This essay explores Butler's three editions to understand what we might learn from his evolving acoustic experiment in print. An inquiry like this is not without its challenges; Butler is known about but little studied today. There is no scholarly edition of his writings and, at the time of this writing, no transcription of any of his works on *Early English Books Online* and no translation of his most successful work, *Rameae rhetoricae libri duo* (1597).[8] The excellent studies we do have of *The Feminine Monarchie* are usually from the perspective of a single discipline, with musicologists having the most to say about Butler's work.[9] He is not thought to have anything original to say about the areas in which he published—grammar, rhetoric, music. Nor is *The Feminine Monarchie* of interest to entomologists today. While Butler did identify the sex of the "queen bee," and achieved other advances in knowledge, so much so that the biologist Frederick R. Prete praises *The Feminine Monarchie* as "the first *scientific* book about honey bees and beekeeping," he also made mistakes, including, arguably, by attributing *voices* and *emotions* to virgin queen bees.[10] Yet, as this essay will argue, by thinking across the three fields I am calling "acoustic humanities" to foreground the shared emphasis on sound that connects them—grammar, rhetoric, music—Butler did have something important to tell us about the meaningful sound of bees and how those sounds might be represented for and experienced by readers. This enables us to imagine *The Feminine Monarchie* as a lively hive that we enter and join to gain understanding of its inner workings, as the image facing the title pages in 1623 and 1634 seems to encourage us to do (fig. 3.1), which shows busy worker bees, with two (lazy) drones being removed from the hive.

I say "sounds," but Butler himself describes what he hears as "voices," and here we encounter a problem that might limit our interest in what he has to say about bees: the risk of anthropomorphism.[11] Bees do not possess a voice box, nor do they have ears. Instead, they have wings that beat "at more than 200 times per second," creating a buzzing sound, and an extraordinary sensitivity to vibration.[12] It was the invention of the apidictor—an instrument that measures and records the sound in a beehive—by the BBC sound engineer Edward Farrington Woods that "established

Figure 3.1. (*Opposite*) Charles Butler, *The feminin' monarchi', or the histori' of bee's* (1634), frontispiece (verso). Wellcome Collection. Public Domain Mark.

Quatuor Apum ordines.

Princeps.

Duces.

Plebs.

Inertes fuci.

Miraris Arte conditas mirâ domos,
Opesque regales in his reconditas?
SOLERTIA ET LABORE *fiunt omnia.*

Đeſʻ cur'ous buildings fraugt witʻ riceſt treaſurʻ,
Not witout Caus, to ſoom dooʻ Woonders ſeemʻ:
But dey, wit greater Caus, đoſʻ Woonders Cauſes,
[Bææ's WIT and INDUSTRI] may Woonders deemʻ:
Đeſʻ dooʻ makʻ đoſʻ noʻ Woonders in reſpect:
For wat wil not INDUSTR'US WIT effect?

C.B.

that the workers and the drones have different wing-beat frequencies, and hum at 250 HZ (or B below middle C) and 190 HZ (or flattish G below middle C) respectively."[13] Only in fables and children's books are bees given a voice (or rather speech). In one of Aesop's *Fables*, a very reasonable bee prays to the god Jupiter "in this manere": "God almyghty I pray the[e] that thow wylt gyve to me and graunte / that who so ever shal come for to take awey my hony / yf I pryke hym / he may sodenly deye."[14] Yet, granting this request comes with a nasty stinger in the tail and a useful reminder to readers that this is a moral tale. Jupiter insists that a stinging bee must die, too. Bees are also often given a voice in contemporary children's books like *The Honeybee* (2018), although this time they also share scientific understanding as well. What do the friendly, helpful bees of *The Honeybee* say to each other? "Where are the flowers you found today?" "Dance for us Foragers! Show us the way!"[15]

At the start of this essay, then, I acknowledge this particular challenge, recognizing what Butler gets wrong. I do so, however, to clear space so that we can also acknowledge what he gets right. After all, Butler did not attribute *speech* to bees. Nor was he trying to find meaning in the buzzing of bees. It is the "piping" of the virgin queens that he privileges, focusing on the very sound that entomologists and beekeepers alike recognize as meaningful communication, and he uses the metaphor of "voice" to signify this but also to enable readers to use their own voices to experience it. Butler uses a very different set of skills from those of a modern scientist, then, to record and interpret this sound of piping, drawing on his training in acoustic humanities. This training, practiced in the humanist schoolroom, the music room, and the church, equipped him to explore the communication he heard in the hive out in the field and to think about how that might be communicated in turn. As this essay will suggest in its brief conclusion, and as its author is already exploring with a team of bioenvironmental scientists, literary scholars, musicologists, and software engineers, it is an experiment that is eminently updatable with new information today.

I divide this essay into two parts. In the first part, "Representing the Sound of Bees," I seek to understand what it is that Butler heard, how he presented it on the page, and why we might want to listen. In the second part, "Acoustic Humanities," I examine Butler's work on grammar and rhetoric to explain why the meaning of *The Feminine Monarchie* resides in its performance rather than silent reading, and I attempt to embed the idea that printed books of this period were already imagined as "soundable." I note not just Butler's interest in spelling reform, and his creation of a phonetic alphabet to notate the speaking voice, but also his early training in rhetoric and his production of a slim book in Latin to teach boys how to convey emotion through variations in vocal tone. Here, meaning is found not on the page but off it, in its actual or imagined performance. Butler's experiments with the printed book are unusual, but they can still reveal much that was taken for granted about Renaissance print and its soundability. His books invite us to recognize the sound of marks on a page and to explore the contribution that acoustic humanities can make to both "cultural entomology" and interdisciplinary conversations today.[16]

Representing the Sound of Bees

Butler's decision to give bees a voice is the theme of this section. In giving bees a voice, he knowingly departs from his classical sources. "Voice (φωνή)," Aristotle writes in *History of Animals* (ca. 350 BCE), "differs from sound (ψόφος), and speech (διάλεκτον) from both." The voice is produced with the pharynx, while speech is the articulation of the voice with a tongue. Animals that have neither lungs nor tongue can produce "neither voice nor speech," though they "may be able to produce sounds by other parts of the body." Insects, for example, can "produce a sound by their internal *pneuma* (not externally emitted *pneuma*, for none of them breathes), but some of them buzz, *e.g.*, the bee and other winged insects, and some sing as the saying is, *e.g.*, the cicada."[17] Butler acknowledges his departure from Aristotle when, in a chapter describing the bodies of bees, he presumes (wrongly) that they can hear. "Their heareing and feeling," he explains, "are very quicke. If you touch their hives but lightly, they presentlie perceiving it, make a generall noise." Aristotle, he acknowledges, may "doubt whether they heare, or not," but he adds, "if they did not heare, to what purpose is that musicke made in the hives, before the swarming?"[18] If bees can make music, he reasons, then they must hear. To extend Butler's reasoning a little further: to make music, bees also, presumably, need a "voice" of sorts.

The term *voice* carries the significance of meaningful communication for Butler. Listening to the "voices" of honeybees, for example, leads him to emphasize the social differences among them. For example, a male bee or drone is distinguishable from a female honeybee by what he looks like and wears (so to speak)—"his round velvet cappe, his side gown, his great paunch"—and also by what he sounds like: he has a "lowder voice" like the males of "other living things."[19] Butler has little to say about the voice of the drone, though, probably because he believes he is like an "idle person" who lives "by the sweat of others brows."[20] (A drone's only role, which Butler did not fully understand, is to mate with the queen, at which point he dies.)[21] Butler has much more to say, however, about the voices of the (female) worker bees, and the queen bee and her daughters (the prince or princess bees). "If she [the queen] goe forth to solace her selfe," he explains, the worker bees "attend upon her, garding her person before and behind"; they also make "withall an extraordinarie noise, as if they spake the language of the knight Marshalls men, & so away they fly together." In addition, he observes the effect of the queen's "voice" on her worker bees, when she issues instructions to them: "If by hir voice she bid them goe, they swarme; if being abroad she dislike the weather, or lighting place, they quickly returne home againe; while she cheereth them to battaile they fight, when she is silent they cease."[22]

Butler's interest in the "voices" of queen bees comes to the fore in chapter 5 of his treatise, which focuses on swarming, the process whereby a hive splits into two or more colonies. Swarming is a natural process by which honeybees protect and grow their communities. It usually begins in the early summer—May, June, sometimes July—as the hive fills up and food outside becomes readily available. Nobody knows the exact catalyst for swarming, but, the entomologist Thomas Seeley explains, we do understand how it happens. The first step is that a colony rears ten or more queens, "all daughters of the mother queen." While they are developing, the queen undergoes a change. She is "fed less and less by the workers," who "begin to show mild hostility . . . shaking, pushing, and lightly biting her." "These bouts of rough handling," as Seeley calls them, "force the queen to keep walking about the nest." Thus, the "mother queen," who is "usually too large and heavy to fly, is put into flying trim."[23] The queen is slimmed down; the worker bees are fattened up. Meanwhile the scout bees search for new "dwelling places." When the weather is right, and "the developing queens have reached the pupal stage," the scout bees prepare the worker bees for flight by pressing their thorax against their bodies and activating the flight muscles; this produces a piping sound.[24] This sound begins faintly, building up gradually to blast out the message, "Time to warm up!," and then, a little later, "Time to go!" "And go they do!" declares Seeley. Left behind in the hive are "a few thousand worker bees" and "a dozen or more queen cells, many thousand cells of worker brood, and much food." At this stage, a different piping sound is heard. The first virgin queen to emerge from her cell announces her presence by pressing her thorax against a comb, producing a tooting sound; the queens still in their cells "pipe in response, producing lower-pitched 'quacks' that are somewhat longer than the first virgin queen's 'toots,' " and these sounds let the first virgin queen roaming the hive know "that she has lethal rivals." She will either leave, relinquishing the food resources in the hive, or remain—a riskier path for her to take because she will need "to kill all her deadly serious competitors."[25]

Butler's interest is in the sound of the virgin queens communicating with each other. He hears the same piping as Seeley, and he registers the changes in pitch. So important did he think this is that he notated it with the help of a wind instrument.[26] The 1609 edition includes three four-line staves representing the piping sound in "triple time" or triple meter. The first two staves represent the princess petitioning, at two different pitches; the third stave represents the lower pitch, or "deeper voice," of the queen mother.[27]

Butler uses different tools than did Seeley to explore the sounds in the hive, but as Simon Jackson and Simone Kotva explain, he is remarkably accurate in notating what he hears.[28] He does, however, make errors in interpretation. It is clear from the narrative account that he has misidentified the vocalists. He thinks he hears a "princess" bee petitioning her mother to leave the hive to form a new colony. Once the first swarm has left, he explains, "the next prince [virgin queen], when she perceiveth a competent number to be fledge and ready, beginneth the musick in a begging tune, as if she did pray hir queen-mother to let them go: whereunto if she yeeld consent by hir answering (as to the petition of hir second daughter she seldome saith nay, though sometime shee consent not in two or three daies) then looke for a swarme."[29] In fact, the queen has already left with the first swarm. What Butler is actually hearing is a roving virgin queen announcing her arrival and the challenge of her "deadly serious competitors" in their cells.

Butler's explanation of swarming, and the mistakes he makes in interpreting what he hears, develops in the second edition of *The Feminine Monarchie* (1623), where he adds more detail to the description of the emotional exchange he thinks he hears. In 1609, the princess bee sings in a begging tone; in the 1623 edition, she sings in a mournful and begging "note." Butler thinks we are hearing a daughter both petitioning *and* saying a final farewell to her mother. In the 1623 edition, the mother's response is described in much more detail: "Unto which voice if the Queene vouchsafe to reply, tuning hir *Base* to the young Princes *Treble*, (as commonly she doth, though scarcely intreated in a day or two) then doth she consent. . . . And as the Queenes voice is a grant, so hir silence is a flat deniall."[30] This story is told again in a new musical composition: "Melissomelos" ("song of the bees"), printed in the manner of a table or part book, scored for four human voices—mean (soprano), contratenor, tenor, and bass—with pairs of singers sitting on either side of a table. The music is accompanied by lyrics that retell the story, with the virgin queens cast as Amazonian warriors:

> When so increased is this prudent Nation,
> That their owne limits cannot them suffice;

To seeke new Cities, for new habitation,
They send abroad their num'rous Colonies:
Antiope the prime Prince gone,
Orithya soone
Of hir Queene-mother, making mone,
Begs the like boone:
That with hir traine hir fortune she may seeke:
And this she sings in measures mournfull sweete.[31]

Butler not only retells the story of swarming with an allegorical narrative of Amazon queens; he also incorporates the staves of 1609 in the new bee song (figs. 3.2 and 3.3), recording the piping of four bees. Alongside this, he offers more detail on what we are listening to. As Jackson and Kotva explain: Butler "records that the Queen will 'sing' between middle C and F a perfect fourth above, and that the Princess (and the other bees that join in) sing between G and C above, making a complete octave. Together the bees produce chords—major thirds, perfect fifths and octaves—all in a repeated triple-time rhythm." First, there is "a solo wordless piping" by the daughter named Orithyia, who "is hoping to lead a secondary swarm to establish a new colony"; after a pause, where the queen mother "remains silent" before granting the request, "other bees join in to make up a four-part texture."[32]

The changes in pitch that Butler records are meaningful to him. The distinctiveness of the sound of the mother queen, as he believes her to be, is key. "Sometime a third Princesse" enters into song, "imitating the Queenes voice in time, though differing haply in tune" in order to "incite" the hive to swarm so her turn comes soon. She does not imitate the queen's pitch, though, which would be "treason." Butler hears a concert of voices, and a collective rallying of the hive: "With these various and harmonious notes, answering one an other, and some pawses betweene, they goe solemnly round about the Hive, so to give warning unto all the company."[33]

This blending of human and bee voices in 1623 seems like a deepening of Butler's anthropomorphism. But before we dismiss this experiment too hastily, it is worth comparing Butler's representation of the hive community with that of his contemporary, the clergyman and naturalist Edward Topsell. Just a year before the first edition of *The Feminine Monarchie* was printed, Topsell saw into print *Historie of Serpents* (1608), which includes two chapters on bees. There was a long tradition of anthropomorphizing honeybees, comparing the hive led by a king bee to the political state of a monarchy in order to reflect on human governance.[34] Topsell is part of this tradition. He compares the hive to an elective monarchy: "Bees are governed and doe live under a Monarchy, and not under a tyrannicall state," he explains, "admitting and receiving their King, not by succession or casting of lots, but by respective advise, considerate judgement, and prudent election."[35] This is a happy, well-functioning hive, a "miniature apiarian kingdom," as Linda Phyllis Austern calls it, with a king in charge and the worker bees going about their work accompanied by "pipers and horn-blowers," a scene that recalls how Topsell's contemporaries described "the musical pastimes of the human watchmen and manual laborers."[36] Topsell's bees are given a voice in two respects, then: first, they can communicate, entertain, and make political decisions together; second, they have a vote.[37] What does Topsell make of the piping sound of the (queen) bees that Butler heard in the hive at the time of swarming? He describes swarming as a kind of revolution, when a decision is made to abandon a tyrant and "seeke some other dwelling places." Just as they ready themselves to leave, "there will be heard a solitary, mournfull, and peculiar kinde of voyce, as it were of some trumpet."[38]

There are clear differences between Topsell and Butler that will help us to understand what is distinctive about the acoustic experiment of *The Feminine Monarchie* and why Butler's anthropomorphism is different, based on trained listening and not only on the silent study of authorities, enabling him to look at honeybees in new ways at a time when Renaissance zoology lagged behind Renaissance botany as a discipline, just as the study of its history still does today.[39] We need only compare the two authors' different habits of citation: "some Bees are descended of the kingly race, and borne of the bloud Royall," writes Topsell confidently, identifying Aristotle as the source for this observation.[40] In the preface to the 1609 edition, Butler is far more cautious, explaining why his use of citation is sparing: "But in al their writings they seeme unto me to say little out of experience, and to rely more upon the relation of others than anie certaine knowledge of their owne. Notwithstanding in some of them, specially in *Aristotle & Plinie*, are scatered many true and good observations; which, being found agreeable to experience, I have here and there, as occasion required, for authority and ornament interlaced."[41]

Butler's knowledge comes from experience, as well as from books, and this allows him to disagree fundamentally with his sources on the sex of the "queen." It

Figures 3.2 and 3.3. (*Overleaf*) Charles Butler, *The feminin' monarchi', or the histori' of bee's* (1634), sig. L3v (verso) and sig. L4r (recto). Wellcome Collection. Public Domain Mark.

CONTRATENOR. 1.

S of all stat's the Monarchi' is best; So of all Monarchi's that Fe- mi- nin',
They woork in common for the common weal: Their labour's restles to maintain their stat':

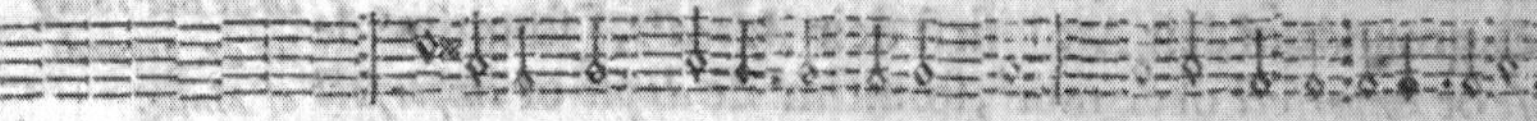

Famous Amazons excels the rest That on this earthy Spher' hav' ever bin.
eir Hexagoni- a no Be- za- leel, for cur'ous Art, may pas or imitat'.

of little harts in weaker sex (so great in field) No pouer of the might'st Mal's can mak' to yeeld:
Sov'raign, & but on', commands this people loyall, The great Marpes' with plenty blest of issu' roi- all:

hey living ay, most' sober and most' chast', Their pain-got goods, in pleasur' scorn to wast'.
An- ti- o- pe and Ori- thy- ji fair, With o- ther Princes hir In- fantas ar.

Soon thousands strong
This Armi royall gallantly
Dooth march along.
Hark, hark, mee thinks, I hear in Not's of choic',
This fairest Ladi's sweetest moornfull voic'.

MEAN. 1

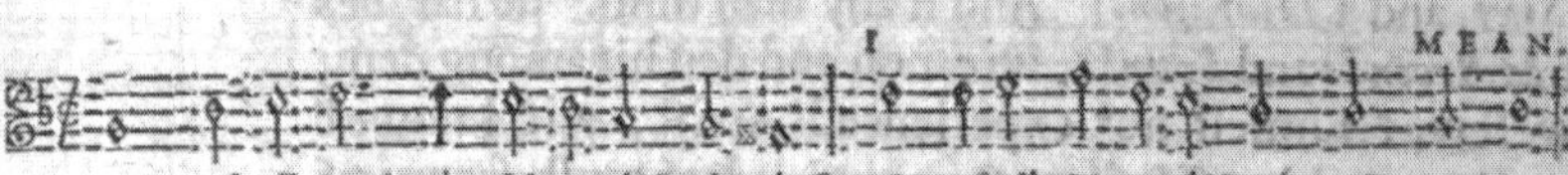

AS of all Stat's the Monarchi' is best; So of all Monarchi's that Fe- m- nin',
They woork in common for the common weal: Their labour's restles to maintain their stat'

Of famous Amazons excels the rest, That on this earthy Spher' hav' ever bin.
Their Hexa- go- ni- a no Be- za- leell, for cur'ous Art, may pas or imitat'.

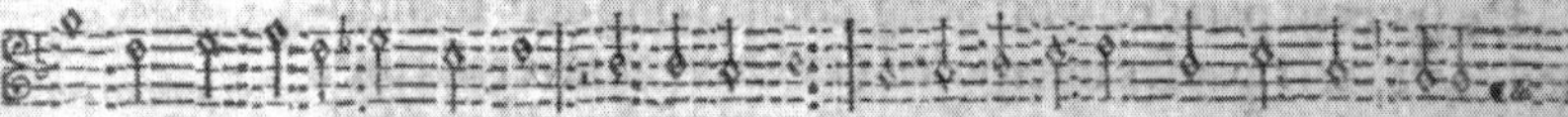

Whos' little harts in weaker, sex (so great in field) No pouer of the might'est Mal's can mak' to
On' Sov'raign, & but on', commands this people loyall, the great Marpes' with plenty blest of issu' r

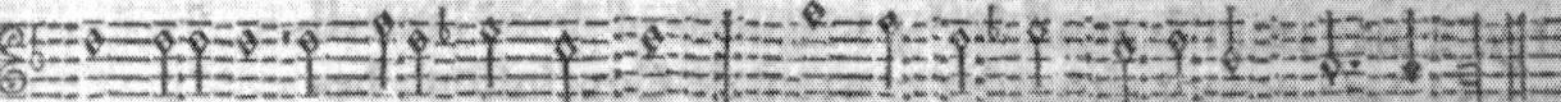

They living ay, most' sober and most' chast', Their pain-got goods, in pleasur' scorn to wast'.
An- ti- o- pe, and Ori- thy- ji fair, With o- ther Princes, hir In- fantas ar.

When so encreased is this prudent Nation,
That their own limits cannot them suffic';
To seek' nu' Cittis, for nu' habitation,
They send abroad their num'rous Coloni's:
Antiope the prim' Princ' gon,

Orithya soon'
Of hir Qeen'-mother, making mon',
Begs the lik' boon';
That with hir train hir fortun' shee may seek':
And this shee sings in mesur's moornfull sweet'

BASSUS.

As of all stat^c^s the monarchi^c^ is best; So of all Monarchi^c^s that Fe-mi[illegible]^c^,
They woork in common for the common-weal : Their labour's restles to maintain their stat^c^ :

Of famous Amazons excels the rest, That on this earthy spher^c^ hav^c^ ever bin.
Their Hexa- gonia no Be- za- leel, for cur'ous Art may pas or imi- tate.

Whos^c^ little harts in weaker sex (so great in field) No pouer of the might'st Mal^c^s can mak^c^ to yee[ld:]
On^c^ Sov'raign,& but on^c^,commands this people loyall, The great Marpes^c^ with plenty blest of issu^c^ roy-[all;]

They living ay, most^c^ sober and most chast^c^, Their pain-got goods in pleasur^c^ scorn to wast^c^.
An- ti- o- pe, and Ori- thy- ja fair, With o- ther Princes, hir In- fan- tas ar.

When so encreased is this prudent Nation,
That their own limits cannot them suffic^c^;
To seek^c^ nu^c^ Cittis, for nu^c^ habitation,
They send abroad their num'rous Coloni^c^s :
Antiope the prim^c^ Princ^c^gon,

Orithya soon^c^.
Of hir Qeen^c^-mother, making mon^c^,
Begs the lik^c^ boon^c^ :
That with hir train hir fortun^c^ shee may seek^c^ :
And this shee sings in mesur^c^s moornfull sweet^c^.

TENOR.

I

[A]s of all stat^c^s the Monarchi^c^ is best; So of all Monarchi^c^s that Fe- mi- nin^c^,
They woork in common for the common weal : Their labour's restles to maintain their stat^c^ :

[O]f famous Amazons excels the rest, That on this earthy Spher^c^ hav^c^ ever bin.
[T]heir Hexa- gonia no Beza- leel, for cur'ous Art, may pas or imitat^c^,

[W]hos^c^ little harts in weaker sex (so great in field) No pouer of the might'est Mal^c^s Can mak^c^ to yeeld:
[On]^c^ Sov'raign,& but on^c^,commands this people loyall, The great Marpes^c^ with plenty blest of issu^c^ roy- all;

[T]hey living ay, most^c^ sober and most^c^ chast^c^, The'r pain-got goods in pleasur^c^ scorn to wast^c^.
[A]n- ti- o- pe,and O- ri-thy- ja fair, With o- ther Princes, hir In- fan- tas ar.

[...] whos^c^ grav^c^ accents if her Princ^c^ly Grac^c^
[vou]chsafe, with Trine Aspect, reply to make,
[Her] sweetest Treble tuning sweeter Base,
[Hi]s moornfull tuit a joyfu'l ende dooth take:
And then, when fit time they espy,

Soom thousands strong,
This Armie royall gallantly
Dooth march along.
Hark, hark, mee thinks, I hear in Notes of choice,
This fairest Ladies sweetest moornfull voice,

also allows him to disagree with his sources and contemporaries on the meaning he attributes to the sound he hears; here, once again, he parts company with Topsell. Although Butler, like Topsell, understands the hive conventionally as a political community, albeit a feminine monarchy, he is not giving bees a version of a *human* voice.[42] Instead, he gives them a musical voice.[43] Quite simply, Butler uses the technologies he has at hand—a wind instrument and his ear—to record the meaningful sounds he hears. His bee song distinguishes between human and bee "voices" and between the singing of lyrics and the piping of queen bees. Butler also distinguishes between the general background buzzing in the hive, which he calls a "confused noise," and the piping.[44] As a result, he shifts attention to the interaction between the queens and their emotions, and he gets closer to what he thinks is going on. And, by creating a score for readers to animate the piping of queens with their own voices, he creates the experience of being inside a hive, the inner workings of which, Frederick R. Prete notes, "are virtually impossible to see."[45]

What about Butler's interpretation of this interaction and the emphasis he places on emotions? To be sure, he gets details wrong, but how could it be otherwise when Renaissance writers "knew nothing of pheremones [*sic*], waggle dances, the role of electromagnetic fields in navigation, or pollination."[46] For scientists who see insects as more like "sophisticated robots" than "little people," Butler's ascription of emotions to them is naive to say the least.[47] But the study of animals, including insects, is changing, as bioenvironmental scientists become increasingly interested in the cognitive biases of animals, who cannot report on their subjectivity or, indeed, their emotion-like states. The ethologist Melissa Bateson contributed more than a decade ago to burgeoning work in this area, focusing on the pessimistic cognitive biases of honeybees. Her team first trained the honeybees to extend their mouthparts to an odor mixture predicting reward and to withhold their mouthparts from a mixture predicting punishment. The team then tested the bees' response by simulating an attack through sustained shaking. They observed the results and measured the chemicals produced: octopamine, the neurotransmitter that functions during reward learning, and dopamine, or serotonin, which mediates the ability to learn to associate odors with punishment. While they were not able to make any claims about the subjective "feelings" of the honeybees in the experiment, they were able to call into question how we identify emotions in any nonhuman animal.[48] The groundbreaking nature of studies like this one, which mark a significant departure from the mechanical understanding of animal behavior, cannot be overemphasized. Calling into question how we identify emotions in invertebrates is a breakthrough in its own right. Yet the cautious, emotionless (or objective) prose of scientific reporting on the possible "emotion-like" states of honeybees seems a million miles from the tradition, familiar to humanities researchers, that acknowledges the role bees play in the human imagination, helping us to understand in a different way our relationship to the natural world and to other animals, as well as our impact on both of them.

Is there a way to bring together these two different explorations of the natural world four hundred years apart without compromising either? Bioenvironmental scientists who explore the emotion-like states of animals keep their emotional distance from their object of study; humanists like Butler enable understanding by creating an emotional connection with theirs. But a conversation between these two polarized positions is possible if we recognize that it is the form of Butler's work that is especially innovative. His engagement with bees is updatable with more accurate information, and this could be a valuable undertaking. After all, emotions are more than chemical changes in bodies; they are part of our experience, and they play a role in how we form relationships with others, including with animals. There are many ways to communicate emotions to be sure—through gesture, facial expressions, smell, and touch. But sound, and changes in pitch, are especially communicative.[49] Attending to voice enabled Butler to recognize that "states" akin to what we would call feelings are being communicated by bees and to create an emotional connection by blending, not blurring, human and animal sounds. It gave him a different "view" of the interactions of bees from his contemporaries, and it enabled him, in turn, to take his readers into a virtual hive. Butler's choice of a table-book form to share his insights is especially apt for this purpose. As Richard Wistreich argues, the "activity of singing music and words from a set of partbooks" is "quintessentially sociable, embodying the egalitarian ideas of civil conversation," producing a pleasing sound and understanding "through coordinated endeavour."[50] By creating a bee song, he is attempting to help his readers understand the behavior of queen bees during swarming in an interactive and connected way.

In this section, I have emphasized the importance of experience to Butler: he gains knowledge of bees by working in the field and by listening to them. But although he clearly preferred the field to the study chamber, the skills he used to record what he heard, and to represent it on the page, were developed in the schoolroom. Butler is a product of what I have been calling *acoustic* humanities. Grammar and rhetoric, as well as music, were taught and learned "off" as well as "on" the page. In the next section, I explore this training further to ascertain how we might want to *listen* to, as well as *look* at, voice-aware printed books such as Butler's differently as a result.

Acoustic Humanities

Print is a usually silent medium for us today, so "soundability" will seem a strikingly novel feature of Butler's print imagination, although, as I am proposing, he was realizing and visualizing on the page the insights of his humanist training and teaching practice. From the 1960s, a series of ambitious studies set out to interpret the impact of the invention of print in the Renaissance on Western societies, making this medium responsible for the spread of literacy, the Reformation, the birth of modern science, even changes in human consciousness.[51] Many of these claims have been challenged in the last few decades, so, for example, we now have a much more nuanced view of the transition from manuscript to print. But one idea, that the "sight-dominance" of writing was finalized with print, has been harder to shift.[52] It is only in the last decade that there has been a concerted effort to explore the way in which printed books are "mere breaths away from utterance."[53] This can mean drawing attention to the ways in which readers conjecture sound "in the near silent environment of the page," as Sarah Kay argues in this volume. It can also mean challenging the influence of (silencing) literary studies in musicology or recovering the importance of the voice to reading and the soundscapes of shared reading.[54] Butler should be part of this work of recovery.

Indeed, Butler is an especially good example through which to explore the potential for the kind of "turn" to the *sound of writing* and print that this volume explores. Educated at Magdalen Hall, Oxford from 1579, where he took his BA in 1584 and his MA in 1587, he then went into the ministry. He was appointed rector of Nately Squires near Basingstoke in 1593, and, two years later, a schoolmaster at the Holy Ghost School in Basingstoke. In 1600, he was appointed vicar of Wootton St. Lawrence, where he remained until his death in 1647. With a secure sinecure at Wootton St. Lawrence, he had the time, sufficient funds, and, clearly, the right contacts in the print world to experiment. This may explain why from 1609 to 1634 he returned repeatedly to *The Feminine Monarchie*, updating its content and "look" to unite the reader's eye, tongue, and ear. As I noted at the start of this essay, in the 1623 and 1634 editions, he invites the reader into a lively, animated hive (fig. 3.1). Both editions include the bee song that blends human and bee "voices." But music is not the only art that Butler drew on to listen to and interpret the sound of bees. In the 1634 edition, *The Feminin' Monarchi'*, he added a new acoustic feature, this time notating the human voice, introducing the phonetic spelling he developed to help the readers of his *English Grammar* (1633, 1634), which he reused in *The Principles of Musik* (1636): Saxon letters are used for double consonants (for example, *ch*, *th*), and apostrophes are used to mark the place of omitted mute vowels. None of this would have been possible without Butler's training in acoustic humanities, and the relationship between his books of the 1630s, on grammar and music and *The Feminin' Monarchi'*, is clear.[55]

Butler was eighty-seven years old when he died. His life span, from 1560 to 1647, makes him one of a small number of people educated in a Tudor schoolroom during the reign of Elizabeth I to have seen the English civil war; this inevitably shaped the content of *The Feminine Monarchie*—for example, its interest in female rule, as I suggested earlier, as well as its methods of analysis. In the 1630s, Butler revisited the experiments of late-Tudor humanists, many of them teachers of grammar like himself, who sought to align eye, tongue, and ear on the page; this group includes Richard Mulcaster (ca. 1531/32–1611) and John Hart (died 1574), who used print to *paint* the speaking voice with a new phonetic alphabet so that the written word could be written and animated again more readily, and, coming a century later, the master of Magdalen College School Owen Price, who reimagined the human body as a musical instrument. Unlike John Hart, Owen Price did not change the letters of the alphabet in *The Vocal Organ* (1665). Instead, he reorganized their order according to the "*Instruments of Pronunciation*," the lips, teeth, tongue, palate, or throat, so they could be (he claimed) remembered more easily. His alphabet begins with the letters "b. f. m. p. ph. w.," which are grouped together because they are pronounced at the front of the mouth.[56]

There was another acoustic "art," however, that shaped Butler's methods and the importance he placed on the voice for meaning-making: rhetoric. Here I turn to the first book he saw into print in 1597, *Rameae rhetoricae libri duo*, a schoolroom textbook, based on Omer Talon's very popular *Rhetorica* (1545), which Butler prepared while a "Tudor" schoolmaster at the Holy Ghost School.[57] Rhetoric was the catalyst for Butler's understanding of the relationship not just between sound and writing but also between voice and emotion. Rhetoric was a staple of the school curriculum in the sixteenth century, and its teaching shaped, and was shaped by, reading and writing. To date, much of our study of the teaching of rhetoric has focused on the canon of *inventio*, that is, the discovery of material for writing, gathered from one's reading, and the aid that supported this process, the commonplace book.[58] Many commonplace books survive, giving unique insight into how individuals organized their reading, as well as the relationship between their reading and writing.[59] For writers whose commonplace books do not survive, like Edward Topsell, it is probably possible to recreate them from the citations in their writing. At the very least, it is not hard to imagine the kind of entry Topsell likely had in his commonplace book under the heading BEES. (Topsell in turn provided content for many other commonplace books.)[60] The same is true of Butler, who clearly had sources at hand when writing *The Feminine Monarchie*. But Butler, unlike Topsell, did not simply repeat what he had read. Instead, he tested the wisdom of the ancients he had gathered against what he saw and heard in the field. More to the point, the innovation of *The Feminine Monarchie* depends not only on *inventio*—and Butler's use of a commonplace book—but *pronuntiatio*, or delivery. This is the fifth skill or canon of rhetoric,[61] and it is often overlooked in our histories of rhetoric because evidence for it is lost in the moment of its practice, and perhaps also because we have not known how to read and animate the schoolbooks that teach it.[62] Butler's interest in this skill is evident from his earliest and, apparently, most successful work, his "book of *tropes and figures*," *Rameae rhetoricae libri duo*,[63] which helps schoolboys explore the expression of emotion by pairing *elocutio* with delivery or *pronuntiatio*. This book can help us to understand not just the meaning that Butler attached to the changes in pitch he heard in the hive but also his belief that a printed book can be animated with the voice.

I am making big claims for a canon of rhetoric—delivery—that Walter J. Ong influentially dismissed, saying it "amounts to almost nothing."[64] The idea that *pronuntiatio* fell out of favor in the Renaissance is itself now something of a commonplace, with the result that it is rarely questioned: Brian Vickers recovered the emotional meaningfulness of the figures of speech, *elocutio*, in his groundbreaking *In Defence of Rhetoric* (1988) but argued that Renaissance rhetoric did not include *pronuntiatio*; similarly, Quentin Skinner argued in 1996 that delivery fell away in a world dominated by the written word.[65] Even Katrin Ettenhuber, who was attentive to delivery in an essay outlining future directions for rhetoric in 2015, including some excellent literary examples to illustrate its importance, still called for "more sustained attention to rhetoric as an art of argument."[66] Yet Talon's schoolbook should make us think again. This slim volume has two parts: the first offers an abbreviated list of figures of speech with examples (*elocutio*); the shorter second part explores voice and gesture (*pronuntiatio*). Not only are these two parts integrated—as Talon explains, "Pronunciatio est apta elocutionis enunciatio" (delivery is a fitting expression of the devices of eloquence)—but the book as a whole provides a prompt to the reader to match figure to vocal tone to experience and perform emotions.[67] I have space for only one example, the figure of *exclamatio*, whereby we stir up a variety of feelings: admiration, despair, hope, indignation, derision, misery, pity.[68] The figure is described in the first part of *Rhetorica*. When we turn to the second part, we learn which qualities of voice will express which emotion in performance: if we want to express pity (*miseratio*), for example, we need a voice that is yielding, full, broken, mournful (*flexibilis, plena, interrupta, flebilis*); anger (*iracundia*) needs a voice that is sharp, fast, interrupted (*acuta, incitata, crebro incidens*); and fear (*metus*) a terse and hesitant (*contractus* and *haesitans*) voice.[69]

Butler was likely taught rhetorical delivery with this book in this way at grammar school; he almost certainly taught it in this way at Holy Ghost School because his *Rameae rhetoricae libri duo* is a nearly identical version of *Rhetorica*. I say "nearly identical" because he does make some revealing changes, one of which is his decision to replace the noun *pronuntiatio* with *prolatio*, "prolation" in English, which connotes time, rhythm, and melody in early music, as well as the act of uttering: "Partes pronuntiationis duae sunt: vox, unde prolatio (quae communi nomine pronuntiatio dicitur), & gestus, unde actio" (delivery has two parts: voice, from which prolation springs [which is called delivery to use the common name], and gesture, from which action springs).[70] This easy-to-miss change emphasizes that, in Butler's mind, rhetoric and music are connected through their shared focus on sound, and it points to where his interests would lead him: to the study of the meaningfulness of sonic variation, on the page and off it, including among bees communicating in a hive, and the humans who aim to understand them.

This essay has focused on the life of a single work, *The Feminine Monarchie*, exploring how its author, Charles Butler, refined his understanding both of its topic—honeybees—and its medium, a printed book that appeared in three editions. I have proposed that *The Feminine Monarchie* is an exceptional example to explore the possibilities of the relationship between inscription on a page and sound. I have also argued that Butler's conception of the potential of the printed book to hold or record sounds, and to enable interpretation of their meaning, was the product of his routine training in acoustic humanities: grammar, rhetoric, music. The same skills he relied on were, of course, also available to his peer Edward Topsell, but unlike Butler, Topsell chose to stay in the study chamber. What might we learn, I wonder, if literary scholars today realized the meaning-making potential of sound and if we formed alliances with our colleagues in the performing arts to revive a version of acoustic humanities? What new collaborations might Butler inspire us to form with musicians, musicologists, bioenvironmental scientists, and beekeepers to explore new ways of communicating across subjects and species and spaces: the library, the lab, the field. Butler's experiment, I propose, is relevant to the interdisciplinary conversations we might have today; indeed, a new project, *Bee-ing Human*, funded by The Leverhulme Trust in the UK, is exploring this further: I am collaborating with colleagues in the UK and the US—literary scholars and digital humanists, musicologists, musicians, and composers, bioenvironmental scientists, evolutionary biologists and software engineers—to explore just this possibility.[71]

NOTES

1. A. H. Bullen and Karl Showler, "Butler, Charles (1560–1647)," *Oxford Dictionary of National Biography*, https://doi.org/10.1093/ref:odnb/4178.

2. Jonathan Woolfson, "The Renaissance of Bees," *Renaissance Studies* 24, no. 2 (2010): 281–300, 299. Other advances in knowledge he achieved include the insight that the queen bee "seems to know the gender of [an] egg in advance of laying it, as male and female eggs are laid in cells of different sizes, a phenomenon which has not been accounted for conclusively even today," and that drones (male bees) were "tolerated in the hive only during the breeding season," while their absence "leads to a smaller colony" (299).

3. Charles Butler, *The Feminine Monarchie, or a Treatise Concerning Bees and the Due Ordering of Them* (Oxford: Joseph Barnes, 1609), title page.

4. Woolfson. "The Renaissance of Bees," 298.

5. Butler, *Feminine Monarchie* (1609), a2v–a3r.

6. On this method see Ann Blair, "Humanist Methods in Natural Philosophy: The Commonplace Book," *Journal of the History of Ideas* 53, no. 4 (1992): 541–51; Peter Mack, "Rhetoric, Ethics and Reading in the Renaissance," *Renaissance Studies* 19, no. 1 (2005): 1–21.

7. Charles Butler, *The Feminin' Monarchi', or the Histori of Bee's* (Oxford: William Turner, 1634).

8. Charles Butler's other works include *Rameae rhetoricae libri duo* (Oxford: Joseph Barnes, 1597), of which there were twelve editions; *The English Grammar, or the Institution of Letters, Syllables, and Words, in the English Tongue* (Oxford: William Turner, 1633, repr. 1634); and *The Principles of Musik, in Singing and Setting with the Two-Fold Use Thereof, Ecclesiasticall and Civil* (London: Printed by John Haviland, 1636).

9. I am grateful to Simon Jackson and Simone Kotva for sharing their unpublished work with me. See Jackson and Kotva, "Writing Animal Song: The Case of Charles Butler's 'Melissomelos, or Bees' Madrigall' " (1624), Cambridge Interdisciplinary Song Seminar, Emmanuel College, Cambridge, Feb. 22, 2017; and Simon Jackson, "Sound in Early Modern England: Shakespeare, Whythorne, Butler and Bacon," in *Literature and the Senses: Oxford Twenty-First Century Approaches to Literature*, ed. Annette Kern-Stähler and Elizabeth Robertson (Oxford: Oxford University Press, forthcoming). See also Gerald R. Hayes, "Charles Butler and the Music of Bees," *Musical Times* 66, no. 988 (1925): 512–15; James Pruett, "Charles Butler: Musician, Grammarian, Apiarist," *Musical Quarterly* 49, no. 4 (1963): 498–509; Linda Phyllis Austern, "Nature, Culture, Myth, and the Musician in Early Modern England," *Journal of the American Musicological Society* 51, no. 1 (1998): 1–47.

10. Frederick R. Prete, "Can Females Rule the Hive? The Controversy over Honey Bee Gender Roles in British Beekeeping Texts of the Sixteenth–Eighteenth Centuries," *Journal of the History of Biology* 24, no. 1 (1991): 113–44, 127.

11. See John S. Kennedy, *The New Anthropomorphism* (Cambridge: Cambridge University Press, 1992), 3–5. It has taken "many centuries," Kennedy argues, "to achieve the present measure of emancipation from vitalism and anthropomorphism," and he laments that it is making a return in science.

12. Claire Preston, *Bee* (London: Reaktion, 2006), 111.

13. Preston, 111–12.

14. Aesop, *The Book of the Subtyl Historyes and Fables of Esope* (London: William Caxton, 1484), N7r.

15. Kirsten Hall and Isabelle Arsenault, *The Honeybee* (New York: Atheneum, 2018), n.p.

16. On Butler's value to cultural entomologists see Prete, "Can Females Rule the Hive?"

17. Aristotle, *The History of Animals*, 4.9 (535a–b), ed. A. L. Peck (Cambridge, MA: Harvard University Press, 1970), 72–75.

18. Butler, *Feminine Monarchie* (1609), B1v.

19. Butler, D5r, E3r.

20. Butler, D5r.

21. Prete, "Can Females Rule the Hive?," 129.

22. Butler, *Feminine Monarchie* (1609), A2r-v.

23. Thomas D. Seeley, *Honeybee Democracy* (Princeton, NJ: Princeton University Press, 2010), 35–37.

24. Seeley, 39.

25. Seeley, 39–42.

26. Butler, *Feminine Monarchie* (1609), F1r.

27. Butler, F1r. For an image of these staves, and commentary on them, see "The 'Piping' and 'Quacking' of Queen Bees," National Library of Scotland, Moir Rare Book Collection, https://digital.nls.uk/moir/piping.html.

28. See Jackson and Kotva, "Writing Animal Song."

29. Butler, *Feminine Monarchie* (1609), E8v–F1r.

30. Charles Butler, *The Feminine Monarchie: Or The Historie of Bees* (London: John Haviland, 1623), K3r-v.

31. Butler, *Feminine Monarchie* (1623), K4v. Figure 3.2 shows the same text in the 1634 edition, albeit in Butler's phonetic spelling.

32. Jackson and Kotva, "Writing Animal Song," n.p. We can hear Simon Jackson's interpretation of Butler's "Melissomelos" performed by the Parish Choir of Little St. Mary's, Cambridge, on YouTube: www.youtube.com/watch?v=p2eonteQEps. The recording was made with support from the Leverhulme Trust by Eastwood Records.

33. Butler, *Feminine Monarchie* (1623), K3v–4r.

34. See Woolfson, "The Renaissance of Bees," 282. See also Timothy Raylor, "Samuel Hartlib and the Commonwealth of Bees," in *Culture and Cultivation in Early Modern England: Writing and the Land*, ed. Michael Leslie and Timothy Raylor (Leicester: Leicester University Press, 1992), 91–129.

35. Edward Topsell, *Historie of Serpents* (London: William Jaggard, 1608), G3v.

36. Austern, "Nature, Culture, Myth," 8; Topsell, *Historie of Serpents*, G4v.

37. See *Oxford English Dictionary*, s.v. "voice (n.)," I.3.a.

38. Topsell, *Historie of Serpents*, G5r.

39. Woolfson, "The Renaissance of Bees," 282; see also Brian Ogilvie, *The Science of Describing: Natural History in Renaissance Europe* (Chicago: University of Chicago Press, 2006), 23–24.

40. Topsell, *Historie of Serpents*, G3r.

41. Butler, *Feminine Monarchie* (1609), a2v–3r.

42. By "voice" I mean a sound "produced by the vocal organs of humans or animals and usually uttered through the mouth or nose; *esp.* sound formed in the human larynx in speaking, singing, or other utterance; vocal sound as a means of human utterance or expression." *Oxford English Dictionary*, s.v. "voice (n.)," I.1.

43. Voice is also the "vocal part in a piece of music; the sequence of notes to be sung by a particular person or group of people. In later use more generally: each of the constituent melodic

lines in a piece of music, whether vocal or instrumental." *Oxford English Dictionary*, s.v. "voice (n.)," I.6.b. See also Austern, "Nature, Culture, Myth."

44. Butler, *Feminine Monarchie* (1623), K4r.

45. Prete, "Can Females Rule the Hive?," 129.

46. Woolfson, "The Renaissance of Bees," 300.

47. Shelley Anne Adamo, "Do Insects Feel Pain? A Question at the Intersection of Animal Behaviour, Philosophy and Robotics," *Animal Behaviour* 118 (2016): 75–79, 76–77.

48. Melissa Bateson, Suzanne Desire, Sarah E. Gartside, and Geraldine A. Wright, "Agitated Honeybees Exhibit Pessimistic Cognitive Biases," *Current Biology* 21, no. 12 (2011): 1070–73, https://doi.org/10.1016/j.cub.2011.05.017. For a more recent contribution to this field of inquiry, see Lars Chittka, *The Mind of a Bee* (Princeton, NJ: Princeton University Press, 2022).

49. See Quintilian, *The Orator's Education* [*Institutio oratoria*], trans. Donald A. Russell (Cambridge, MA: Harvard University Press, 2001), 11.3.62–63: "The voice, acting as intermediary, will then convey to the judges' minds the attitude it has acquired from ours. It is in fact the indicator of the mind, and has all the mind's variations."

50. Richard Wistreich, "Music Books and Sociability," *Il Saggiatore Musicale* 18, no. 1/2 (2011): 230–44, 244.

51. See Walter J. Ong, *Orality and Literacy: The Technologizing of the Word* (London: Methuen, 1982). See also Lucien Febvre and Henri-Jean Martin, *The Coming of the Book* (*L'apparition du livre* [Paris: A. Michel, 1958; London: Verso, 1976, repr. 2010]); and Marshall McLuhan, *The Gutenberg Galaxy: The Making of Typographic Man* (Toronto: University of Toronto Press, 1962, repr. 2011).

52. Ong, *Orality and Literacy*, 121, 124.

53. Christopher Cannon and Matthew Rubery, "Introduction to 'Aurality and Literacy,' " *PMLA* 135 no. 2 (2020): 350–56, 352.

54. See herein Sarah Kay, "Reading Impressions: The Sound of the Sight of Occitan Verse." See also Richard Wistreich, " 'Inclosed in This Tabernacle of Flesh': Body, Soul, and the Singing Voice," *Journal of the Northern Renaissance* 8 (2017): https://doi.org/10.24379/RCM.00000124; Jennifer Richards and Richard Wistreich, "Introduction: Voicing Text, 1500–1700," *Huntington Library Quarterly* 82, no. 1 (2019): 3–16, 11–15; Elspeth Jajdelska, *Speech, Print and Decorum in Britain, 1600–1750: Studies in Social Rank and Communication* (London: Routledge, 2016), xii; Jennifer Richards, *Voices and Books in the English Renaissance: A New History of Reading* (Oxford: Oxford University Press, 2019); Matthew Rubery, *The Untold Story of the Talking Book* (Cambridge, MA: Harvard University Press, 2016); Anne Snaith, ed., *Sound and Literature* (Cambridge: Cambridge University Press, 2020); and Abigail Williams, *The Social Life of Books: Reading Together in the Eighteenth Century* (New Haven, CT: Yale University Press, 2017).

55. On the importance of singing, see Pruett, "Charles Butler," 504.

56. Owen Price, *The Vocal Organ, or A New Art of Teaching the English Orthographie* (Oxford: William Hall, 1665), B1v.

57. With 115 editions, Talon's *Rhetorica* rivaled the classical manuals in popularity; see Peter Mack, *A History of Renaissance Rhetoric, 1380–1620* (Oxford: Oxford University Press, 2011), 30.

58. There has long been a concern to foreground rhetoric as argument; see Quentin Skinner, *Reason and Rhetoric in the Philosophy of Hobbes* (Cambridge: Cambridge University Press, 1996).

59. Victoria E. Burke, "Recent Studies in Commonplace Books," *English Literary Renaissance* 43, no. 1 (2013): 153–77.

60. Burke, 171.

61. The canons of rhetoric are invention (*inventio*), arrangement (*dispositio*), style (*elocutia*), memory (*memoria*), and delivery (*actio* or *pronuntiatio*).

62. See Richards, *Voices and Books*, 88–97.

63. Butler, *Feminine Monarchie* (1609), a4r: "I am out of doubt that this book of *Bees* wil in his infancy lie hidden in obscurity, as the book of *tropes and figures* did for a while go unregarded. . . . But as that did by litle & litle insinuat it selfe into the love & liking of many schooles, yea of the University it selfe, where it hath been both privatly and publikely read . . . so this will in time travaile . . . and be entertained of al sorts, both learned and unlearned."

64. Walter J. Ong, *Ramus, Method and the Decay of Dialogue: From the Art of Discourse to the Art of Reason* (Chicago: University of Chicago Press, 1958, repr. 2004), 273. His view has been widely accepted. See, for instance, Skinner, *Reason and Rhetoric*, 45–46; and Quentin Skinner, *Forensic Shakespeare* (Oxford: Oxford University Press, 2014, repr. 2018), 12–13. Skinner also thinks it significant that Quintilian's "sceptical" treatment of delivery and memory is left until the penultimate book of *Institutio oratoria* (book 11). This is used to explain his focus on only two parts of rhetoric, *inventio* and *dispositio*, in his discussion of Shakespeare's plays.

65. Brian Vickers, *In Defence of Rhetoric* (Oxford: Oxford University Press, 1988), 254–93; Skinner, *Reason and Rhetoric*, 55–58, 110. Lawrence D. Green has provided a comprehensive survey of Renaissance treatments of *pronuntiatio* in "Rhetoricall Daunsinge: *Pronunciatio* and *Actio* in Renaissance Rhetoric," in *Rhetorical Arguments: Essays in Honour of Lucia Caboli Montefusco*, ed. Maria Silvana Celentano, Pierre Chiron, and Peter Mack (Hildesheim: George Olms, 2015), 353–62.

66. Katrin Ettenhuber, "How to Do Things with Rhetoric in Early Modern English Writing," *Oxford Handbook Topics in Literature* (Oxford: Oxford University Press, 2015), https://doi.org/10.1093/oxfordhb/9780199935338.013.13.

67. Omer Talon, *Audomari Talaei rhetorica* (Cambridge: John Legate, 1592), C6r.

68. Talon, B11v–B12r.

69. Talon, C8v–C9r.

70. Charles Butler, *Rameae rhetoricae libri duo in usum scholarum* (Oxford: Joseph Barnes, 1597), E1r. Compare Butler's sentence with Talon, *Rhetorica*, sig. C4v: "Partes pronunciationis duae sunt: vox, unde pronuntiatio: & gestus, unde actio dictur."

71. *Bee-ing Human*, funded by the Leverhulme Trust, is creating a digital edition of Charles Butler's *The Feminine Monarchie*. Thanks to the team at Newcastle who are contributing to this project: James Cummings, Balamurali Gopalakrishnan Nair Sreelatha, Bennett Hogg, Vivek Nityananda, Candy Rowe, Olivia Smith, Tiago Sousa Garcia, and Magnus Williamson.

CHAPTER FOUR

Prosodic Protocols and Interruptions of Them in *Piers Plowman*

Ian Cornelius

Communications Protocols

Within the general context of alphabetic systems of writing, inquiry into relations between writing and sound customarily focuses on the capacity of letters to represent the sounds of speech. Yet, while an alphabet may encode approximately the constituent segments of speech (vowels and consonants), prosodic or suprasegmental attributes (duration, pitch, and stress) are usually entrusted to the implicit knowledge of the reader, not to marks on the page. Indeed, a rough shorthand definition of *prosody* might be "those qualities of speech-sound that are not written" or "qualities written by special supplementary notation."[1] The prosodic dimension of speech illustrates neatly that alphabetic writing is only ever a series of cues; activation of them requires the performer to know rather more than the sound-values of individual written letters. If writing was nevertheless able to function as a phonographic instrument in the cultural spheres of Greek and Roman antiquity, as Shane Butler argues, and throughout the Middle Ages and early modernity, it did so on account of protocols additional to and other than alphabetic literacy.[2] One of those protocols of sound-transmission goes again by the name *prosody*, though now in a sense different from the one I have employed in previous sentences. Beside linguistic prosody, there is artificial prosody, or the design of verse and rhythmical prose.[3] Prior to Thomas Edison's wax cylinders, artificial prosody supplied what we may term an encoding protocol for the transmission of sound in writing.

To appreciate Butler's claim for the phonographic capacities of ancient writing, we need to acknowledge that modern recording technologies have altered, perhaps irreversibly, the standards by which we might judge two semiotic vocal performances to be "exactly alike." This point is among the subtler implications of the audio recordings of Serbo-Croatian singers made in the 1930s and 1950s by Milman Parry and Albert Bates Lord. The singers describe their successive recitations of the same narrative poem as "exactly alike," "word for word and line for line."[4] Modern recording equipment—engraved aluminum plates and magnetized spools of steel wire—exposed variants between the recitations and thereby supplied Lord with the evidentiary basis for his celebrated theorizations of oral-traditional poetics. Lord's focus was always resolutely on nonliterate poetry, a fact that perhaps makes his work an unlikely reference in the present context, yet his recording equipment has implications for a historical assessment of literate as well as nonliterate poetics. The wax cylinder and its successors changed forever what it means for a vocal performance to be reproduced; rewind the tape of history to an earlier era, and the situation is not that vocal performances were irreproducible but that reproduction meant something different. Writing has served often as a medium for the reproduction of vocal performances, and artificial prosodies have been among the protocols of vocal reproducibility, in conjunction with writing or not. This function helps to explain the prominence of verse and rhythmical prose in premodern literary cultures.

In telecommunications and networked computing, a protocol is "a standardized set of rules allowing different machines . . . to communicate with each other."[5] The prefix *http* in web addresses stands for *Hypertext Transfer Protocol* and forms an upper layer in a stack of protocols that enable you to load a website to your computer. The term derives from late antique documentary culture, in which a *prōtokollon* was the first leaf of a papyrus roll, which may be inscribed to identify or authenticate the contents of the roll or date its manufacture. The same term is applied to the first text element of an official pronouncement of a medieval chancery, recording the names of the person or persons on whose authority a pronouncement is issued and to whom it is addressed.[6] Unlike the protocols of either networked computing or diplomatics, prosodic protocols can function without being defined anywhere. Many definitional efforts have been made, from antiquity forward, in studies and instructional manuals, but prosodic protocols are a matter of human cognitive processing, and they can be absorbed from example and in practice, much like the structures of natural languages.[7] Like natural languages, artificial prosodies operate within communities. Writing can help to preserve and standardize the linguistic products of communities and extend them across time and space. Artificial prosodies supply a set of community rules that, among other things, serve to enhance the vocal component of written language.

The present essay is an inquiry into the prosodic protocols that help writing to encode sound, especially the effects that may be derived from midstream interruption, modification, or blending of protocols. These take many forms. Prosimetrum and classical Greek tragedy are genres that enact multiple prosodic protocols within the compass of a single work. Lyric collections may do so as well, since each new poem may employ a prosodic protocol different from the last. Virgil's fragmentary lines in the *Aeneid* are probably an artifact of the unfinished state of that poem, but they supplied an influential precedent to early modern English poets, for whom a fragmentary line became a device for creating meaningful silence.[8] Silence, in this instance, is created by withholding the full complement of linguistic material stipulated by the protocol. The stream of discourse terminates early and the unfilled slots are transmitted empty. As this example shows, one of the chief operations of a prosodic protocol is the segmentation of discourse into what M. L. Gasparov terms "commensurable and equivalent" units.[9] In modern English literary criticism, the usual name for commensurable and equivalent units of metrical discourse is a "line."

Lines and Half-Lines

Packet or even *chunk* might be better than *line* as a name for the constituent units of verse.[10] As Steven Justice has pointed out to me, the problem with *line* is that it designates its referent by a spatial figure; the word thereby invites a misapprehension that prose and verse could be distinguished by the ways they occupy space on a page. Prose is usually made to flow across the full width of a writing column. Verse is usually lineated: each commensurable and equivalent unit is set on its own line of script or type.[11] Yet prose may be cut at syntactic joints and displayed on the page *per cola et commata*, "by phrases," to facilitate recognition of sense-groups. That presentation is employed in some early copies of Jerome's Latin Bible and in some modern printed editions of the text.[12] Likewise, we know that verse may be written unlineated. The most famous examples are perhaps manuscript copies of the earliest Germanic verse, subsequently termed *alliterative*.[13] The chunking or packetizing operation is essential to prosodic forms. Lineation is an optional graphic notation of the prosodic chunks—a form of punctuation or scansion.[14]

We need still to distinguish between verse and rhythmical prose. Gasparov, in a passage already quoted, locates the difference in the role of syntax. If prose is chunked into equivalent and commensurable segments, this is done at syntactic joints; in verse, the chunking operation is performed "independent of syntax."[15] It follows that nonalignment of prosodic and syntactic segments, termed *enjambment*, is a possibility inherent in verse. Moreover, the segmentation of verse is not only independent of syntax but also arbitrary, a matter of artifice and convention. Verse forms depend on certain features of linguistic prosody—vocalic quantity or stress accent, for instance—but they are not derivable from or redundant with the linguistic features on which they depend. Nonredundancy is what enables verse form to enrich the encoding of sound and meaning.

If the fundamental operation of prosodic protocols in verse is to chunk discourse into equivalent and commensurable units independent of syntax, the next step is, often, to run the chunking operation again. The result is a bipartite line structure, composed of two metrical cola. Bipartite line structures are employed in many verse forms, including the poetic portions of the Hebrew Bible, most forms of classical Arabic verse, archaic Irish verse, ancient Greek and Latin dactylic hexameter, medieval Latin Goliardic verse, the classical French Alexandrine, English septenaries, and Germanic alliterative verse. The last of these forms will occupy my attention in the remainder of this essay.

Recognition of the half-line units of alliterative verse was an accomplishment of nineteenth-century philology. The earliest printed editions of Old English verse employed continuous format, imitating the presentation of the manuscripts. The verse was later lineated in short lines, one half-line per line.[16] Jakob and Wilhelm Grimm introduced *kurze Zeile* and *lange Zeile* into the critical vocabulary ("long line" means a pair of half-lines or "short lines"; for analogous alternatives in the construction of troubadour verse forms, see Sarah Kay's contribution to this volume, 46–51). The Grimms adopted a long-line format for their edition of the *Hildebrandslied* (1812), and they offered arguments in support of that representation of verse structure.[17] Rasmus Rask's counterargument initially prevailed, with the result that the short-line format remained the preferred one among British and Scandinavian scholars in the middle decades of the nineteenth century.[18] In 1868, Walter W. Skeat moved nimbly between the two presentations.[19] He made the short-line format the basis for initial remarks, in deference to the *mise en page* of Old English verse in recent English editions, yet his experience with manuscripts of

Middle English led him to favor the long-line presentation, even for Old English verse. Skeat also saw, though imprecisely, what would become the decisive argument in favor of the long-line presentation: the short-line "couplets" of alliterative verse, linked by alliteration, do not have the same prosodic status as an end-rhymed couplet. Whereas the constituent members of an end-rhymed couplet are equivalent and commensurable, the paired short lines of alliterative verse are asymmetrical, differentiated from one another with respect to weight and rhythmical pattern. That perception had not yet been available to the Grimms. Eduard Sievers formulated the argument precisely: since the first half-line is rhythmically freer than the second, admitting a wider range of configurations, a coherent prosodic unit (*Einheit*) is accomplished only in the long line.[20] This is the rationale that underlies the *mise en page* of alliterative verse in modern editions. By convention, the first half-line is termed the on-verse or a-verse, the second the off-verse or b-verse.[21]

When the transmitted text of an alliterative poem fails to divide into paired half-lines, editors and textual critics usually suspect that something has gone wrong in transmission.[22] A half-line can be omitted by accident. Eyeskip on a half-line-ending word can result in accidental fusion of an a-verse with the b-verse of a subsequent line, omitting intervening material. A half-line that is unusually short might have suffered a textual omission. Relineations and other metrical emendations aim to construct whole and well-formed lines from fragmentary or deficient ones. This endeavor is inherently justifiable, for prosodic protocols are a component of a poet's usage, always a basic criterion in establishing the text of a poetic work.[23] It is also possible, however, for poets deliberately to interrupt, suspend, or vary the protocols that elsewhere organize their writing. Usage is hard to define.

Doing Different Voices at the Feast of Conscience

In a recent study, Ralph Hanna proposes that William Langland's prosodic usage has been defined much too restrictively.[24] Langland is known to modern readers as the author of *Piers Plowman*, a long personification allegory and vision poem in English alliterative verse, with inset Latin and French, composed ca. 1365–90.[25] The poem is transmitted in more than fifty manuscript copies, generally taken to represent three authorial versions, the lifework of its poet. It is in many respects an atypical alliterative poem. Hanna suggests that Langland broke the standard alliterative long line into unpaired half-lines and that his motive was to better express the sound of his poem's competing voices.

Hanna's argument takes the form of a local textual suggestion regarding an episode at a dinner party hosted by Conscience.[26] Wille, the poet's fictional avatar, is a disruptive low-table guest at the party; he is engaged in baiting a friar who is Conscience's guest of honor, and his attack is interrupted by the poet himself, apparently speaking *in propria persona*. I present the lines as they are printed in the recent semicritical edition of the B version of *Piers Plowman*, edited by John Burrow and Thorlac Turville-Petre.[27] Middle points in the English text represent metrical punctuation of the half-line boundary in good early manuscripts:

Holywrit bit men be war · I wil nouȝt write it here
On englisch an auenture · it sholde be reherced to ofte
And greue þere-with þat good men ben · ac gramarienes shul rede
Vnusquisque a fratre se custodiat · quia vt dicitur periculum est in falsis fratribus
Ac I wist neuere freke þat as a frere ȝede · bifor men on englissh
Taken it for her teme · and telle it with-outen glosynge (Bx 13.76–81)

[Scripture urges men to be on guard. I do not wish to write it here in English, lest it be repeated too often and the saying of it harm men who are good. Yet the literate should read *Let everyone protect himself from his brother, for, as the saying goes, there is danger in false brothers*. Yet I have never seen any man—I mean those who go about like friars/brothers—publicly take this as the theme of his sermon and preach it in English without evasion.]

As a report of the received text of *Piers Plowman* B, Burrow and Turville-Petre's text is uncontroversial. The manuscripts that transmit this passage are unanimous with respect to the general shape of its English lines. There are few variants in wording. (The Latin quotation is split over two lines in several copies.) Moreover, while Burrow and Turville-Petre aim only to present the text of the archetype of surviving copies of *Piers Plowman* B, not the text as intended by the poet, the archetypal lineation of this passage is credited and approved by critical editors.[28] Hanna, however, relineates and repunctuates to emphasize dramatic action and abrupt shifts in voice.

"Holy writ bit men be war —"
I wol noȝt write it here in englissh,
On auenture it sholde be reherced to ofte
And greue þerwiþ þat goode men ben, ac gramariens shul rede:
Vnusquisque a fratre se custodiat, quia vt dicitur, periculum est in falsis fratribus.
"— Ac I wiste neuere
Freke þat as a frere yede bifore men on englissh
Taken it for his teme and telle it wiþouten glosyng"

In verse 76b of the archetypal text, the poet interrupts the ranting of his fictional avatar, the dreamer; in 80a the dreamer resumes his rant.[29] As relineated, these segments—"Holy writ bit men be war" and "Ac I wiste neuere"—form the corresponding halves of a single line, spoken by the dreamer and united by alliteration on /w/. The constituent parts of this /w/-alliterating line are separated, in Hanna's proposal, by four intruded lines in the voice of the poet. Hanna states that he offers the relineation for the sake of argument: what concerns him is the play of voices in this passage. Yet he also offers some text-critical support for the conjecture. He observes that the relineation removes an enjambment, *write it here / On englissh*, at lines 76–77 of the archetypal text; and he speculates "that an authorial version like the one I have constructed" could have been "assimilated in transmission to the long lines that represent the usual manuscript presentation of Langland's poetry."[30] The claim is that relineation restores a poetic device that was misunderstood and suppressed by the poem's first scribe.

I read Hanna's relineation as a provocation to thought, and I linger over it because I wish to separate the textual suggestion itself (which I reject) from an underlying insight that I wish to amplify. Evaluation of the textual suggestion must, as usual, take account of the usage and patterns of behavior of both the poet and the poet's scribes. To begin with scribal usage, one might observe that Hanna's relineation is suspect in its simplicity: elsewhere in the textual tradition of *Piers Plowman*, where scribes attempt to regularize a line that they perceive to be incomplete, they may shift the place of the line-breaks, but they also often add words, padding the lines out. This scribal behavior will be illustrated later in my argument. The form of the archetypal lines in this passage may indeed be peculiar in some respects, but the lines do not have the appearance of being padded out, and they are not implausible as Langland's writing.

To judge that the archetypal lines are not implausible is to turn from the usage of scribes to the usage of the poet—both what is customary and what is possible within his craft. Evaluations of the prosodic usage of Middle English alliterative poets tend to focus especially on patterns of alliteration and on the accentual contours of second half-lines. Both criteria can be helpful in particular situations, but neither is as helpful in application to *Piers Plowman* as in application to certain other fourteenth-century alliterative poems, for one must make allowances for Langland's wider range of expression and greater permissiveness in prosodic usage.[31] With regard to the half-line boundary, too, Langland's usage is distinctive: he makes some half-line divisions that are never made by, for instance, the *Gawain* poet. Yet Macklin Smith's argument for Langland's "unruly caesura" misses the mark.[32] In what follows, I give primacy to the half-line unit, as the basic building block of Langland's verse. The half-line structure of Langland's verse will serve as a test of the credibility of the archetypal lines and Hanna's relineation of them.

The central peculiarity of the archetypal lines, as I read them, is that the half-line "On englisch an auenture" (77a) is composed from a pair of stranded prepositional phrases, the first belonging to the clause in 76b, the second to the clause in 77b. I cannot think of a precise analogue for that verse structure in *Piers Plowman*, yet the individual enjambments are well supported. With "write it here / On englissh," one may compare the poet's later statement that during the assault of the Antichrist, a remnant of faithful prefer "to deye þan to lyue / Lengore" (to dye than to live longer) (Bx 20.62–63).[33] Turning to the second enjambment, I observe that adverbial "on auenture" appears most often at the head of the line, as in Hanna's relineation.[34] Yet the construction in the archetypal text is paralleled in, for example, the line "Nym it nauȝte an auenture · [þow] mowe it nauȝte deserue" (Don't take it, lest perhaps you not deserve it) (Bx 6.43). The enjambments in Bx 13.76–77 require interpretation, not emendation; they create an effect of a halting authorial voice, very different from Wille's headlong rant in preceding lines. That is, the dramatic effects that Hanna would express by means of relineation and modern punctuation are already expressed in the archetypal text, which deserves to be recognized as the poet's work.

Tests of usage should also be applied to the new lines and half-lines created by Hanna's relineation. At the end of the passage, Hanna creates a new half-line "Ac I wiste neuere," splitting this segment off from the following line. The conjectured half-line is plausible: compare "for I borwe neuere" (for I never borrow) (Bx 19.489b). One should note, too, that the finite verb *wiste* is prosodically flexible: it may participate in alliteration, as it does in Hanna's relineation, or not. (For non-alliterating *wiste*, compare Bx 14.115a: "I wist neuere renke þat riche was" [I never knew a man who was rich].) The test of usage hits a snag, however, in the relineated string "I wol noȝt write it here in englissh, / On auenture it sholde be reherced to ofte." As relineated, this string fails to chunk into half-lines, and this failure must be the principal objection to Hanna's textual suggestion. One could perhaps divide the second line after the auxiliary *sholde*, on the model of lines like "Of þis matere I myȝte · mamely ful longe" (I could ramble on about this for a long time) (Bx 5.22).[35] Yet "I wol noȝt write it here in englissh" offers no point at which it could divide into alliterative half-lines. It reads as prose, or else as iambic tetrameter, not alliterative verse.

On this analysis, we can reject Hanna's conjectural relineation: it produces an unacceptable text and overlooks the effect of the enjambments in the archetypal text. Readers will notice that I take issue with the prosodic shape of the two full lines crafted by Hanna, not with Hanna's contention that Langland could have written unpaired half-lines. In what follows I argue that an unpaired half-line is plausible as a poetic innovation and has precedent within the tradition of alliterative verse. Once recognized as a device available to Langland, the unpaired half-line supplies a way of registering the difficulty of certain lines that switch from English into Latin. There is, finally, at least one passage elsewhere in *Piers Plowman* B in which scribal variants point toward an unpaired half-line, comparable to Hanna's conjectured "for I wiste neuere." I take these points in sequence.

The Independent Careers of Half-Lines

Wherever there is a bipartite line structure, there is latent possibility for the half-line unit to develop an independent career. The first half-line of a dactylic hexameter is doubled to form the so-called pentameter line of the ancient Greek and Latin elegiac couplet.[36] In ancient Greek drama, *stichomythia*, in which speakers alternate full lines in dialogue, could be varied into *antilabē*, in which the metrical line is split between two speakers.[37] At first the change in voices was made to coincide with the medial caesura, mapping onto and emphasizing the bipartite structure of the iambic trimeter line. (The division then became freer, anticipating and supplying precedent for the multiform split lines of dialogue in Shakespeare's plays.) In alliterative verse a precedent for autonomous half-lines is set by the Old Norse *ljóðaháttr* stanza.[38] In this verse form, lines composed of paired half-lines of the traditional type, or nearly that, alternate with shorter lines that may be read as independent half-lines. Among the Old English poems, single half-lines appear in *Wulf and Eadwacer* and sporadically elsewhere, perhaps especially in metrical charms and gnomic verse.[39] The Old Norse *ljóðaháttr* may have been an influence, yet the basic formal innovation could be expected to arise independently at several points. Single half-lines continue to appear in texts of early Middle English alliterative verse: for instance, in the prologue to Lawman's *Brut* and sporadically in alliterative portions of the *Physiologus*.[40] In the fourteenth century, single half-lines appear as regular constituents of a new stanzaic form. In this stanza, an octave of long lines is followed by a five-line bob and wheel. The lines of the wheel usually scan as alliterative half-lines.[41] I quote an example from *A Pistel of Susan* (before ca. 1400):

And tolde
How heor wikkednes comes

Of þe wrongwys domes
Þat þei haue gyue to gomes,
Þis juges of olde.[42]

[And [the Lord] said how their wickedness comes from the unjust judgments that they have given to men—these judges from long ago.]

Here, a one-lift bob is followed by three lines composed in the form of the poet's usual a-verses; the stanza is capped by a b-verse. The alliterative long line has been disassembled and its parts reused as short lines within a new stanzaic form. There were several variations on this form in the fifteenth century.

Langland's Polyglot Prosody

Returning to *Piers Plowman*, one observes that the poem's Latin quotations can have the function of catalysts, binding with the line and splitting it into half-line constituents. *Piers Plowman* is an alliterative poem but also a polyglot collage. In the archetype of *Piers Plowman* B, as edited by Burrow and Turville-Petre, fifty-three lines switch from English to Latin at the half-line boundary.[43] The switches take several forms and deliver a wide range of sonic effects. Often the Latin segment can be read as an ordinary alliterative b-verse incidentally composed of Latin, with no break in protocol:

A proude pryker of Fraunce · *prynceps huius mundi* (Bx 9.8)

[A proud French knight, *prince of this world*]

Here the Latin segment is the right length for an alliterative b-verse, and it continues the pattern of alliteration established in the coordinate a-verse. The Latin segment also has the paroxytone ending (*múndi*) expected from Langland's English lines. A switch between languages does not necessarily entail a switch out of alliterative verse. In a variation on this line type, a short English phrase or single English word may stand just after the half-line boundary, governing the Latin quotation that follows:

I drowe me in þat derkenesse · to *de[s]cendit ad inferna* (Bx 18.115)

[I betook myself in that darkness to [the passage] *he went down to hell*][44]

In the archetype of *Piers Plowman* B, I find about thirty-five lines with this second disposition of languages. The English meter again retains both constituent half-lines; the second half-line just happens to be composed mostly of Latin material.

Whether the switch to Latin occurs at the half-line boundary or just after, the effect is a domestication and vernacularization of Latin. This is especially appropriate when, as often, the Latin is a snippet of the liturgy or catechism or a much-used passage of the Bible. In Bx 18.115, the Latin is a clause of the Apostle's Creed, an authoritative formula of Christian belief and "irreducible core" of Christian religious education, from the Carolingian reforms forward.[45] The clauses of the Creed were integrated into a lifeworld as familiar objects and organic components of a multilingual sensorium. The assimilation of Latin words and phrases into the protocols of alliterative verse is an underexplored element of Langland's usage.[46] Yet my present argument directs attention to another set of multilingual lines, where the Latin element enacts a break with protocols.

When we read a long poem in a stichic verse form, our encounter with each new line is framed and conditioned by the protocols that we have assimilated in prior experience of that form. If a new line of *Piers Plowman* begins in English, we are well justified in assuming that the line is alliterative verse, and we are primed to apply the protocols of alliterative verse to whatever string of linguistic material follows, even if the string switches out of English. Sometimes, however, Langland writes lines in which the protocols operative at the beginning become untenable at the end. When the Paraclete descends in *passus* 19, Conscience commands the dreamer to kneel and sing:

> Welcome hym & worshipe hym · with *veni creator spiritus* (Bx 19.215)
>
> [Welcome him and worship him with *Come, Creator Spirit*]

Veni creator spiritus is the title verse of a hymn used throughout the year in or before Mass and at terce on Pentecost Sunday.[47] The hymn is in accentual octosyllabics, and most lines, including the first, end in a proparoxytone word (*spíritus*), yielding a line-ending contour unmetrical in the formal corpus of Middle English alliterative verse and usually also avoided by Langland. The proparoxytone ending could be described as an incidental violation of alliterative protocols; it seems preferable to recognize that the Latin hymn instances a prosodic protocol of its own and that Langland has switched protocols midline. Such lines may legitimately be termed polymetrical. There are not many. Langland twice splices the title verse *Gloria in excelsis deo* into a line that begins in alliterative verse (Bx 3.335; Bx 12.167). Two other lines switch at midline into Latin dactylic hexameter:[48]

> Catoun and canonistres · conseilleth vs to leue
> To sette sadnesse in songewarie · for *sompnia ne cures* (Bx 7.164–65)

[Cato and canon lawyers counsel us to stop granting authority to dream interpretation, for *Do not concern yourself with dreams.*]

Catoun acordeth þere-with · *nemo sine crimine viuit* (Bx 11.423)

[Cato agrees with that: *No one lives without fault.*]

The hexameter fragments are from the *Distichs of Cato*, a basic school-text.[49] The fragments participate in the alliterative pattern established in the conjoined a-verses (/s/ and /k/, respectively), and they end in a paroxytone word, as expected in alliterative verse. In Bx 11.423, Langland cleverly splices the two verse forms together at their respective caesuras; the final paroxytone, *víuit*, is the ending required by both the Latin and English meters. The distribution and quality of weak syllables in *nemo sine crimine viuit* would be irregular as a b-verse in the formal corpus of Middle English alliterative verse, though acceptable in *Piers Plowman*. In Bx 7.165, the hexameter fragment scans as a regular alliterative b-verse, yet the effect is of polymetrical collage, activating two metrical systems at once.

Another, different collage-effect is produced when an a-verse has, as its complement, a Latin quotation that is just too long to be parsed as an alliterative b-verse:

And þanne had pacience a pitaunce [·] *pro hac orabit omnis sanctus in tempore oportuno* (Bx 13.59)

[And then Patience had a little bit, *For this [forgiveness] everyone holy will pray to you in a seasonable time* (Psalms 31:6)]

Here the a-verse is well-formed, and the quotation from the penitential Psalms functions as an appositive variation of *a pitaunce*.[50] Yet this Latin *pitaunce* is oversized, incommensurate with the poem's English half-lines. The English meter has been suspended at the half-line boundary and a longish quotation inserted in the place of an expected alliterative b-verse. I find seven other instances of this configuration in the B archetype of *Piers Plowman*. With two exceptions, all are in *passus* 13–15. In a few cases I quote the preceding line or two for context:

(1) Þanne hent hope an horne · of *deus tu conuersus viuificabis [nos]* (Bx 5.525)

[Then hope took a horn of *God, you will turn and bring us to life*. (Psalms 84:7)]

(2) [Bx 13.59, quoted above]

(3) Haued nouȝt [Marie] Magdeleigne more · for a boxe of salue
Þan zacheus for he seide · *dimidium bonorum meorum do pauperibus*
(Bx 13.205–6)

[Did not Mary Magdalene receive more for a box of ointment than Zacheus for saying *I give half of my goods to the poor?* (Luke 19:8)]

(4) As dauid seith in þe sauter · *et quorum tecta sunt peccata* (Bx 14.103)

[As David says in the Psalter: *And whose sins are covered.* (Psalms 13:1)]

(5) And whan he deyeth ben disalowed · as dauid seith in þe sauter
Dormierunt & nichil inuenerunt
And in an other stede also · *velud sompnum surgencium domine in ciuitate tua & ad nichilum rediges* (Bx 14.140–42)

[And he is dispraised when he dies, as David says in the Psalter: *They slept and found nothing* (cf. Psalm 75:6). And in another place also: *As in a dream of one waking, Lord, so in your city, and you will reduce [their image] to nothing.* (cf. Psalm 72:20)]

(6) For-þi seith seneca · *paupertas est absque solicitudine semita* (Bx 14.331)

[Therefore Seneca says *Poverty is a road without anxiety.*]

(7) And sitthen þat þe sarasenes · and also þe iewes
Konne þe firste clause of owre bileue · *credo in deum patrem omnipotentem*
(Bx 15.638–39)

[And since the Saracens and also the Jews know the first clause of our Creed, *I believe in God the Father, Omnipotent.*]

(8) The berdes þo songe · *Saul interfecit mille · et dauid decem milia* (Bx 19.137)

[The ladies then sang *Saul killed a thousand and David ten thousand.* (cf. 1 Kings 18:7)]

In (1) the switch to Latin occurs just after the half-line boundary; compare Bx 18.115 and Bx 19.215, quoted above. The English preposition *of* identifies the Psalm as the very *horne* grasped by Hope in the a-verse.[51] A similar construction is adopted in (2) in several copies, in place of the appositive construction given in the archetypal text. Line (7) also places the Latin quotation in apposition with an element in the

English a-verse. In each of the other lines the Latin quotation is the object of a verb of utterance.[52] There are two basic patterns: in (3–6) the English portions adduce an *auctoritas* in running exposition; (8) quotes speech in diegesis. In each case the a-verse has the function of a speech tag, or lexical marker of direct discourse, and those in (3) and (6) are suspiciously light. These two lines could be read as entirely unmetered—that is, as Latin quotations introduced with a bit of connective English.[53] If we are dealing with gradient variation around a set of prototypical line types, a type "a-verse + long Latin quotation" seems the unavoidable interpretation of at least (1), (2), and (7). That each of these lines opens with an alliterative a-verse seems clear. It is also clear that the segments after the half-line boundary are not alliterative b-verses. There is a basic incommensurability between constituent parts.

The line type "a-verse + long Latin quotation" seems to be an innovation in the B version of *Piers Plowman*. Hope's *horne* does not appear in *Piers Plowman* A, and the other lines with this pattern occur after the A version breaks off. In the C version, four of the eight lines are retained in the form of the B archetype.[54] Critical editors of the B version have accepted the line type. With one exception, the Athlone edition prints each of the eight lines in the form given above. The exception is (5), where Kane and Donaldson judge the English portion of Bx 14.142 to be a scribal intrusion and suppress it. Schmidt retains the English portion of that line but divides the Latin quotation over two lines, evidently to create chunks of text more nearly commensurate with Langland's English lines. Schmidt also divides the Latin quotation in (2), for the same effect. Yet the imbalance between English a-verse and Latin quotation seems to be deliberate, and its effect should be respected. If a line like "I drowe me in þat derkenesse · to *de[s]cendit ad inferna*" has the effect of vernacularizing and assimilating Latin elements, examples 1–8 hold the Latin element apart from the English poem and exempt it from the chunking operation basic to verse. The English poem is, as it were, made to wait on a quotative voice that exercises an authority to speak for as long as needed.

The Responses of Scribes

Scribes responded to midline interruptions of protocol in two basic ways. First, where a line ends in a Latin quotation, the length of the quotation may vary: scribes may extend the quotation or truncate it, and they may enter an *et cetera* after whatever portion they have written. An example is supplied by Anima's catechism at the close of *passus* 15 of the B version. In the previous section, I quoted one line from this passage, as (7). The passage joins the feast of Conscience as the two densest clusters of interrupted alliterative lines in *Piers Plowman*. It is printed as follows in the edition by Burrow and Turville-Petre:

> And sitthen þat þe sarasenes · and also þe iewes
> Konne þe firste clause of owre bileue · *credo in deum patrem omnipotentem*
> Prelates of crystene prouynces · shulde preue if þei myȝte
> Lere hem litlum & lytlum [·] *& in ihesum cristum filium*
> Tyl þei couthe speke and spelle · *et in spiritum sanctum*
> And re[d]en it & recorden it · with *remissionem peccatorum*
> *Carnis resurreccionem · et vitam eternam amen* · (Bx 15.638–41)

> [And since the Saracens and also the Jews know the first clause of our Creed, *I believe in God the Father, Almighty*, prelates of Christian provinces should try if they might teach them little by little *and in Jesus Christ, his Son* till they could speak and spell *and in the Holy Ghost*, commit it to memory and repeat it with *forgiveness of sins, the resurrection of the body and life everlasting. Amen.*]

Alliterative a-verses alternate with unmetered clauses of the Apostle's Creed. There is some variation in the amount of Latin supplied by scribes. In one copy (Oxford, Oriel College, MS 79; sigil O), the first Latin quotation is given as *credo in deum patrem & cetera*, omitting *omnipotentem*.[55] In another copy (San Marino, Huntington Library, MS 128; sigil Hm), the scribe writes the first clause of the Creed as printed above but adds an *& cetera* after it, as if inviting readers to supply the continuation, *creatorem celi et terre*, for themselves. Placed at the end of whatever stretch of Latin the scribe had copied, the notation *& cetera* directs readers to supply the remainder from memory.

As a feature of the presentation of Latin in *Piers Plowman*, line-terminal *& cetera* supports John Alford's contention that biblical quotations often imply their continuations.[56] A line-terminal *& cetera* also confirms the authority of the poem's quotative voices, noted above, and it raises an awkward question for a metrical reading of Langland's verse: where, in such cases, does the line end? This is not a question that should arise in verse; the fact that it does arise is another indication that the prosodic chunking operation has been suspended and the English meter interrupted midline. The scribes who supply or transmit *& cetera* at the end of Latin quotations demonstrate their evident acceptance of this complex line type.

Yet the line type was not accepted in every case and by all scribes. Variant read-

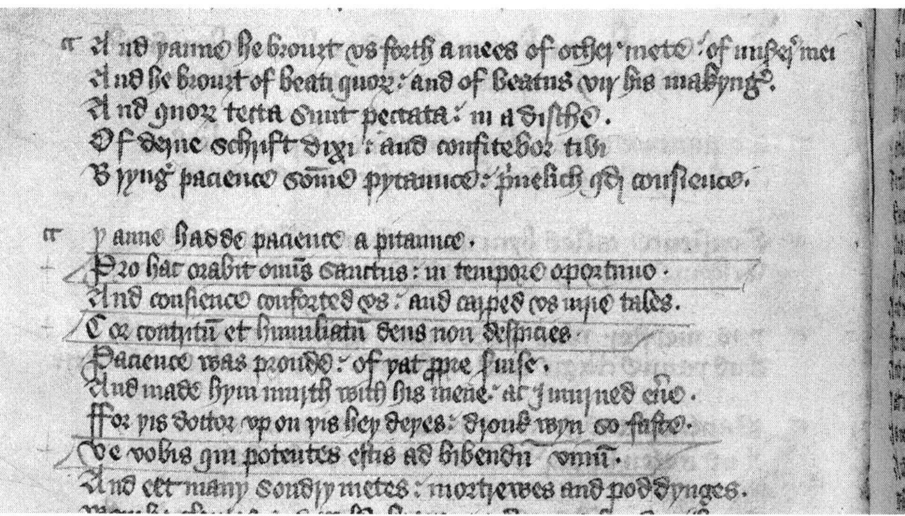

Figure 4.1. Oxford, Bodleian Library, MS Rawlinson poet. 38, fol. 59v (detail). A copy of the B version of William Langland's *Piers Plowman* (sigil R), showing lines corresponding to Bx 13.54–66. Note the presentation of Bx 13.59a as a lone halfline; the quotation from Psalm 31 follows on the next line. Courtesy of the Bodleian Library, University of Oxford. Creative Commons license CC-BY-NC 4.0.

ings in the English portion of the relevant lines sometimes exhibit a scribe's discomfort with the text they encountered in their exemplar. An example is supplied by Bx 13.59, quoted in the previous section in the form printed by Burrow and Turville-Petre. That textual form is well supported in the beta family, the more numerous of the two great families of B-version copies. In the alpha family, one copy (Oxford, Bodleian Library, MS Rawlinson Poetry 38; sigil R) has the English and the Latin on separate lines (fig. 4.1). That may have been the original reading of the alpha family, for there is some indication that the copyist of the alpha hyparchetype preferred to place a singleton a-verse on its own line, with the coordinated Latin quotation shunted off to the line below.[57] So presented, the unpaired a-verse was vulnerable to misinterpretation as a deficient long line, which is what happened in the other alpha-family copy (Oxford, Corpus Christi College, MS 201; sigil F). The redactor responsible for F padded out the received a-verse, creating a full line with acceptable metrical shape: "& þan was brouht to pacyence · þis pytance ful soone." The F-redactor's response is paralleled by one other copyist, for the beta4 group of manuscripts all have a version of the line, "And thanne come to pacience · a pitaunce ybroughte."[58] The scribal revisions in F and beta4 are independent, yet they share a single motive: to turn "And þanne had pacience a pitaunce" into a full line of alliterative verse. I draw the following conclusion: in *Piers Plowman*, an alliterative half-line does not invariably require another alliterative half-line as its complement, but lines that depart from the norm were vulnerable to "correction" and regularization, much as Hanna remarks in defense of his relineation of Bx 13.76–81. I now bring this conclusion to bear on a difficult passage that probably included an empty half-line.

An Empty Tomb and an Empty Half-Line

Late in *Piers Plowman*, Conscience instructs the dreamer on the life of Jesus. The lines that recount the resurrection are printed as follows by Burrow and Turville-Petre:

> The knyȝtes þat kepten it · biknewe[n] hem-seluen
> Þat angeles & archangeles · ar þe day spronge
> Come knelynge [·] to þe corps & songen
> [*Cristus resurgens* · and he ros after]
> Verrey man bifor hem alle · & forth with hem ȝede (Bx 19.151–55)

> [The knights who guarded it testified that angels and archangels, before the day dawned, came kneeling to the corpse and sang *Christ rising again* and afterwards he rose, truly a man before them all, and he went forth with them.]

The *knyȝtes* (151) are the Roman guards of Matthew 27:65, stationed at the grotto to prevent the followers of Jesus from stealing his corpse (*it* 151). The B-version archetype, as presented by Burrow and Turville-Petre, differs from the critical editions only in a pair of readings in the mixed-language line 154.[59] For *Cristus resurgens*, the Athlone edition prints *Cristus [rex] resurgens*, importing *rex* from C-version manuscripts, where this word is a minority variant. For *he ros*, Schmidt and the Athlone editors print *it aroos*, the reading of the C-version archetype. These are plausible restorations of the poet's work.[60] Yet I doubt that any editor has done more than smooth out the underlying metrical difficulties.

Reanalysis may begin with the bracketed punctus in 153. B-version manuscripts uniformly punctuate after *corps*. Burrow and Turville-Petre shift the metrical punctuation, evidently to produce a credible b-verse. This repunctuation is inconsistent with the editors' general practice and unjustifiable. In the editors' base manuscript (Oxford, Bodleian Library MS Laud misc. 581; sigil L), the line reads as follows, with the Latin quotation spliced onto the end of the line: "Come knelynge to þe corps · & songen *cristus resurgens*." The line structure has close parallels earlier in the poem:

And saracenes for þat siȝte · shulle synge *gloria in excelsis &c* (Bx 3.335)

[And Saracens, on account of that sight, will sing *Glory in the highest*.]

He sette a soure lof to-for vs · and seyde *agite penitenciam* (Bx 13.50)

[He set a sour loaf before us and said *Do penance*.]

In these two lines and L's version of Bx 19.153, an alliterative a-verse is paired with a Latin quotation; in each case the Latin quotation is governed by an English verb of utterance that stands after the half-line boundary. At Bx 19.153, L probably transmits the original reading of the beta hyparchetype. The alpha hyparchetype evidently placed the Latin on the subsequent line. Unfortunately, R has lost a quire at this point, so the alpha family is represented only by the eccentric and meddlesome F (virgules in the following quotation have the same function as middle points in earlier quotations):

Comen knelynge to þat corps / & konyngly sunge.
Cristus resurgens a mortuis / & a-noon he roos after.

F's *konyngly*, *a mortuis*, and *a-noon* are padding. They have been inserted to fill out the lines. Yet F's *he ros after* does seem to be necessary to the sense of the passage, as editors emphasize. It reports the resurrection. Beta copies uniformly lack this important clause, but firm textual support comes from the C version, where the clause is transmitted by all copies, with negligible variants, in the form *and hit aroos after*. Burrow and Turville-Petre describe *and he ros after* as a "detached b-verse" (Bx 19.153n), and that is how I would present it:

Come knelynge to þe corps · & songen *Cristus [rex] resurgens*
* * * [· and it aros after]
Verrey man bifor hem alle · & forth with hem ȝede

Editorial asterisks would normally indicate a textual deficiency, yet the sense of this passage is complete; and a detached b-verse, if original, would be vulnerable to precisely the regularizations seen in the manuscripts. Those scribal variants are the evidence from which we may infer an original state of the poem with an omitted a-verse. I hesitate to offer interpretation, but it seems right to acknowledge puzzlement at discovery of a space unexpectedly empty. Moreover, the effect is almost the opposite of the Virgilian type of line fragment. In the *Aeneid* and its tradition, fragmentary lines begin well and abruptly go silent. By contrast, the line "   · and it aros after" observes an interval of silence before resuming speech to state plainly a central miracle of Christianity.

The B version of *Piers Plowman* has a small number of lines that switch conspicuously out of English alliterative meter midline. In most cases the switch is from English verse to Latin prose. In a few cases the switch is into Latin verse—either an accentual hymn or a fragment of dactylic hexameter. These switches are part of the formal artistry and multilingual facility of *Piers Plowman*. They also express Langland's basic recognition that his English meter is bipartite, analyzable into constituent parts, and that the parts can be put to independent use. My textual proposal for Conscience's narrative of the resurrection must remain hypothetical, but I hope to have demonstrated that this passage does not fall neatly into standard alliterative lines. The variant readings point instead toward an unpaired half-line. Precedents can be found in other alliterative poems; possibility was always latent in the form itself, yet Langland's use of independent half-lines remained unsystematic and experimental, encoding a great range of sound and some silence.[61]

NOTES

1. See, e.g., W. Sidney Allen, *Accent and Rhythm: Prosodic Features of Latin and Greek: A Study in Theory and Reconstruction* (Cambridge: Cambridge University Press, 1973), 3–12. Allen observes that in Hellenistic grammatical theory the term *prosody* came to be extended from melodic accent "to certain other features which, like the accent, were not accounted for by the segmental analysis of speech into vowel and consonant phonemes (στοιχεῖα)" (3), or again, that prosody encompassed "relevant features . . . not indicated in the segmental orthography of vowels and consonants—in fact anything which necessitated 'marking the text' (στίζειν τὰς γραφάς)" (10). Hence the close association between prosody and punctuation in ancient and medieval literary culture, as observed by M. B. Parkes, *Pause and Effect: An Introduction to the History of Punctuation in the West* (Berkeley: University of California Press, 1993).

2. Shane Butler, *The Ancient Phonograph* (New York: Zone, 2015). See also the introduction to this volume, esp. 19–20.

3. Allen, *Accent and Rhythm*, 5, traces this usage to fifteenth-century English grammar schools.

4. Albert Bates Lord, *The Singer of Tales*, ed. Stephen A. Mitchell and Gregory Nagy, 2nd ed. (Cambridge, MA: Harvard University Press, 2000), 28.

5. Ann Blair et al., eds., *Information: A Historical Companion* (Princeton, NJ: Princeton University Press, 2021), 838.

6. See Thomas Frenz, *Papsturkunden des Mittelalters und der Neuzeit* (Stuttgart: Franz Steiner Verlag Wiesbaden GMBH, 1986), 10.

7. See Nicholas Myklebust, "Rhythmic Cognition in Late Medieval Lyrics: BL MS Harley 2253," in *The Palgrave Handbook of Affect Studies and Textual Criticism*, ed. Donald R. Wehrs and Thomas Blake (Cham: Springer International / Palgrave Macmillan, 2017), 577–608, 593–95, a general discussion of "metrical puzzles and the cognitive neuroscience of their resolution."

8. Henry Power, "Half Lines," in *The Virgil Encyclopedia*, ed. Richard F. Thomas and Jan M. Ziolkowski, 3 vols. (Chichester, West Sussex, UK: Wiley-Blackwell, 2014), 2:585.

9. M. L. Gasparov, *A History of European Versification*, ed. G. S. Smith and Leofranc Holford-Strevens, trans. G. S. Smith and Marina Tarlinskaja (Oxford: Clarendon Press, 1996), 97.

10. The term *chunk* is used in experimental psychology in studies of memory and pattern recognition. See W. J. Dowling, "Rhythmic Groups and Subjective Chunks in Memory for Melodies," *Perception & Psychophysics* 14, no. 1 (1973): 37–40; and, in application to verse, Nicholas Myklebust, "Misreading English Meter: 1400–1514" (PhD diss., University of Texas at Austin, 2012), 208–16.

11. Parkes, *Pause and Effect*, 97–101, surveys conventions of lineation of verse in West European contexts.

12. See Parkes, 15–16 and plate 10. A modern example of this format is the Latin Vulgate Bible printed by the Württemberg Bible Society.

13. See Daniel Donoghue, *How the Anglo-Saxons Read Their Poems* (Philadelphia: University of Pennsylvania Press, 2018).

14. Similarly, T. V. W. Brogan reasons that "visual display" of verse lines is "epiphenomenal—a function of the medium of presentation—not inherent to the nature of the thing itself." See T. V. F. Brogan, "Line," in *The New Princeton Encyclopedia of Poetry and Poetics*, ed. Alex Preminger and T. V. F. Brogan (Princeton, NJ: Princeton University Press, 1993), 694–97, 696. Brogan's thinking is stimulated by considerations of text encoding; this passage is suppressed in the fourth edition.

15. Gasparov, *History of European Versification*, 97.

16. Compare the presentation of verse in Franciscus Junius, ed., *Cædmonis monachi paraphrasis poetica, Genesios ac præcipuarum sacræ paginæ historiarum* (Amsterdam, 1655); and the appendix to Christopher Rawlinson, ed., *An[icii] Manl[ii] Sever[ini] Boethi[i] consolationis philosophiæ libri V Anglo-saxonice redditi ab Alfredo, inclyto Anglo-saxonum rege* (Oxford, 1698). For commentary see Danielle Cunniff Plumer, "The Construction of Structure in the Earliest Editions of Old English Poetry," in *The Recovery of Old English: Anglo-Saxon Studies in the Sixteenth and Seventeenth Centuries*, ed. Timothy Graham (Kalamazoo: Medieval Institute Publications, Western Michigan University, 2000), 243–79; and Ian Cornelius, *Reconstructing Alliterative Verse: The Pursuit of a Medieval Meter* (Cambridge: Cambridge University Press, 2017), 46.

17. Wilhelm Grimm and Jacob Grimm, eds., *Das Lied von Hildebrand und Hadubrand und das Weissenbrunner Gebet* (Kassel: Thurneisen, 1812), 37–39. For commentary see Jürgen B. Kühnel, *Untersuchungen zum germanischen Stabreimvers* (Göppingen: Kümmerle, 1978), 259–64.

18. See R[asmus] K. Rask, *Angelsaksisk Sproglære tilligemed en kort Læsebog* (Stockholm, 1817), 119–22; Erasmus Rask, *A Grammar of the Anglo-Saxon Tongue, with a Praxis*, trans. B[enjamin] Thorpe, 2nd ed. (Copenhagen, 1830), 149–53.

19. W. W. Skeat, "An Essay on Alliterative Poetry," in *Bishop Percy's Folio Manuscript: Ballads and Romances*, ed. John W. Hales and Frederick J. Furnivall, 3 vols. (London, 1868), 3:xi–xxxix, xiii, xvi, xxiv–xxv.

20. Eduard Sievers, *Altgermanische Metrik* (Halle: M. Niemeyer, 1893), 24–25.

21. Exemplary recent studies of English verse forms are Thomas Cable, *The English Alliterative Tradition* (Philadelphia: University of Pennsylvania Press, 1991); and Geoffrey Russom, *The Evolution of Verse Structure in Old and Middle English Poetry: From the Earliest Alliterative Poems to Iambic Pentameter* (Cambridge: Cambridge University Press, 2017).

22. See R. D. Fulk, "Textual Criticism," in *A Beowulf Handbook*, ed. Robert E. Bjork and John D. Niles (Lincoln: University of Nebraska Press, 1997), 35–53; and Ad Putter, "Metre and the Editing of Middle English Verse: Prospects for Tail-Rhyme Romance, Alliterative Poetry, and Chaucer," *Poetica (Tokyo)* 71 (2008): 29–47. Both discuss the uses of metrical criteria in establishing the text of poems in English alliterative verse.

23. For the criterion of usage, designated *usus scribendi*, see George Kane and E. Talbot Donaldson, eds., *Piers Plowman: The B Version. Will's Visions of Piers Plowman, Do-Well, Do-Better and Do-Best. An Edition in the Form of Trinity College Cambridge MS B.15.17, Corrected and Restored from the Known Evidence, with Variant Readings*, rev. ed., Piers Plowman: The Three Versions (London and Berkeley: Athlone Press and University of California Press, 1988), 130–31. Unfortunately, Kane and Donaldson's account of Langland's verse form has proved especially inadequate.

24. See Ralph Hanna, *Patient Reading/Reading Patience: Oxford Essays on Medieval English Literature* (Liverpool: Liverpool University Press, 2017), 283–84.

25. See, for general orientation, Ralph Hanna, *William Langland* (Aldershot: Variorum, 1993); and George Kane, "Langland, William (ca. 1325–ca. 1390)," in *Oxford Dictionary of National Biography* (Oxford: Oxford University Press, 2004).

26. See, on this episode, Traugott Lawler, *The Penn Commentary on "Piers Plowman,"* vol. 4, *C Passūs 15–19; B Passūs 13–17* (Philadelphia: University of Pennsylvania Press, 2018), 7–10, with references.

27. John A. Burrow and Thorlac Turville-Petre, eds., *Piers Plowman: The B-Version Archetype (Bx)*, XML version 2.0, PPEA Print Series 1 (Raleigh, NC: Society for Early English and Norse Electronic Texts, 2018). Quotations from this edition are cited parenthetically with the prefix "Bx" (e.g., "Bx 13.76"). The first edition (XML version 1.0, published in 2014) is available online at https://piers.chass.ncsu.edu/texts/Bx. For comment on punctuation in this edition and in manuscripts of the poem, see Burrow and Turville-Petre, *The B-Version Archetype*, 28–29; and J. A. Burrow, "Punctuation in the B Version of *Piers Plowman*," in *"Truthe is the beste": A Festschrift in Honour of A. V. C. Schmidt*, ed. Nicolas Jacobs and Gerald Morgan (Frankfurt am Main: Peter Lang, 2014), 5–15. In a departure from Burrow and Turville-Petre's edition, I print Latin in italic type. On scribal presentation of Latin, see Burrow and Turville-Petre, 24; and Judith A. Jefferson, "Scribal Responses to Latin in the Manuscripts of the B-Version of *Piers Plowman*," in *Multilingualism in Medieval Britain (c. 1066–1520): Sources and Analysis*, ed. Judith A. Jefferson and Ad Putter (Turnhout: Brepols, 2013), 195–210.

28. See Kane and Donaldson, *Piers Plowman: B Version*, lines 13.71–75; and A. V. C. Schmidt, ed., *Piers Plowman: A Parallel-Text Edition of the A, B, C and Z Versions*, 2nd and rev. ed., 2 vols. (Kalamazoo: Medieval Institute Publications, Western Michigan University, 2011), B version, lines 13.71–75.

29. The Athlone editors and A. V. C. Schmidt assign the whole passage Bx 13.76a–83b to the poet's voice. This is indeed likely.

30. Hanna, *Patient Reading/Reading Patience*, 284.

31. I offer an introduction to Langland's verse form as usually understood in Cornelius, *Reconstructing Alliterative Verse*, 7–17. For some complexities see 126–29 in that book; and my essay "It's Complicated: Some Irregular Line-ending Morphosyllabic Sequences in *Piers Plowman* B," *Chaucer Review* 58, no. 2 (2023): 259–82.

32. See Macklin Smith, "Langland's Unruly Caesura," *Yearbook of Langland Studies* 22 (2008): 57–101; and Cornelius, *Reconstructing Alliterative Verse*, 183n15.

33. Compare Bx 11.316–17; and Eric Weiskott, "The End of the Line? Alliterative Meter, Macaronic Style, and *Piers Plowman*," *Studies in Philology* 117, no. 2 (2020): 225–39, 230n17 (reporting enjambments between lines in Prol.-9 of the C version).

34. See Joseph S. Wittig, *Piers Plowman: Concordance. A Lemmatized Analysis of the English Vocabulary of the A, B, and C Versions as Presented in the Athlone Editions, with Supplementary Concordances of the Latin and French Macaronics*, Piers Plowman: The Three Versions (London: Athlone Press, 2001), s.v. "auenture, n."

35. Compare also Bx P.89, Bx 10.152, and Bx 15.95. The *Gawain* poet does not write lines in which an auxiliary verb is divided from an immediately following infinitive.

36. See D. S. Raven, *Latin Metre* (1965; repr., London: Bristol Classical Press, 1998), 103–4.

37. Bernd Seidensticker, "Die Stichomythie," in *Die Bauformen der griechischen Tragödie*, ed. Walter Jens (Munich: W. Fink, 1971), 183–220, 201–3.

38. Russell Poole, "Metre and Metrics," in *A Companion to Old Norse-Icelandic Literature and Culture*, ed. Rory McTurk (Malden: Blackwell, 2005), 265–84, 268–69.

39. A. J. Bliss, "Single Half-Lines in Old English Poetry," *Notes and Queries* 18, no. 12 (1971): 442–49; John Miles Foley, "Hybrid Prosody and Single Half-Lines in Old English and Serbo-Croatian Poetry," *Neophilologus* 64, no. 2 (1980): 284–89.

40. See G. L. Brook and R. F. Leslie, eds., *Laȝamon: Brut. Edited from British Museum Ms. Cotton Caligula A. IX and British Museum Ms. Cotton Otho C. XIII*, EETS, o.s., 250, 277 (Oxford: Oxford University Press, 1963–78), lines 20 and 30 in the Caligula manuscript; and Hanneke Wirtjes, ed., *The Middle English "Physiologus,"* EETS, o.s., 299 (Oxford: Oxford University Press, 1991), lines 23, 129, 132, and 161.

41. Karl Luick, "Englische Metrik: Geschichte der heimischen Versarten," in *Grundriss der germanischen Philologie*, ed. Hermann Paul, 2nd ed., vol. 2.2 (Strassburg: Karl J. Trübner, 1905), 141–80, 168–69; Ad Putter, "Adventures in the Bob-and-Wheel Tradition: Narratives and Manuscripts," in *Medieval Romance and Material Culture*, ed. Nicholas Perkins (Woodbridge, UK: D. S. Brewer, 2015), 147–63, 160–61.

42. Thorlac Turville-Petre, ed., *Alliterative Poetry of the Later Middle Ages: An Anthology* (Washington, DC: Catholic University of America Press, 1989), 124, lines 35–39.

43. My study corpus is Burrow and Turville-Petre's 2014 web edition of Bx (XML version 1.0). I follow the editors' XML tagging of language identity, except that in Bx 15.580 I record *metropolitanus* as Latin (cf. Bx 15.43, where the same word is tagged correctly). Individual lines are checked against the editors' 2018 printed edition, which incorporates some corrections.

44. Helena Halmari and Robert Adams, "On the Grammar and Rhetoric of Language Mixing in *Piers Plowman*," *Neuphilologische Mitteilungen* 103, no. 1 (2002): 33–50, 48, interpret English *to* in this line as an infinitive-marker and express surprise that the following Latin verb has a finite inflection. *To* is a preposition and *descendit ad inferna* functions as the noun-phrase complement. Compare Halmari and Adams's earlier analysis of code-switches at the preposition/object boundary (45–46).

45. Quoting Eamon Duffy, *The Stripping of the Altars: Traditional Religion in England, c. 1400–c. 1580*, 2nd ed. (New Haven, CT: Yale University Press, 2005), 53.

46. See Weiskott, "The End of the Line?," criticizing editorial treatment of lines corresponding to Bx 13.19 and Bx 15.73, with instructive general comment on Langland's multilingual prosody. Of related interest is Christopher M. Cain, "Phonology and Meter in the Old English Macaronic Verses," *Studies in Philology* 98, no. 3 (2001): 273–91.

47. Stephen A. Barney, *The Penn Commentary on "Piers Plowman,"* vol. 5, *C Passūs 20–22; B Passūs 18–20* (Philadelphia: University of Pennsylvania Press, 2006), 131–32. John A. Alford,

"Piers Plowman": A Guide to the Quotations (Binghamton: Medieval & Renaissance Texts & Studies, 1992), 29n61, lists quotations from hymns and antiphons.

48. More frequently, Latin hexameters appear in the poem as freestanding lines. For those, see Traugott Lawler, "Langland Versificator," *Yearbook of Langland Studies* 25 (2011): 37–76.

49. The standard edition is Marcus Boas and Hendrik Johan Botschuyver, eds., *Disticha Catonis* (Amsterdam: North-Holland Publishing, 1952). Langland quotes from 2.31 and 1.5. See, for general discussion, Jill Mann, "'He Knew Nat Catoun': Medieval School-Texts and Middle English Literature," in *The Text in the Community: Essays on Medieval Works, Manuscripts, Authors, and Readers*, ed. Jill Mann and Maura Nolan (Notre Dame, IN: University of Notre Dame Press, 2006), 41–74.

50. This construction is analyzed in Halmari and Adams, "On the Grammar and Rhetoric," 43–44.

51. The construction may be termed a genitive of definition. Compare Tauno F. Mustanoja, *A Middle English Syntax. Part I: Parts of Speech* (Helsinki: Société Néophilologique, 1960), 81–82.

52. In (5) the verb occurs two lines above, in 140b. For discussion of lexical markers of direct speech in written Middle English, see Colette Moore, *Quoting Speech in Early English* (Cambridge: Cambridge University Press, 2011), 43–61.

53. Elsewhere, a minimal English speech tag *And seyde / seith* may introduce a line of freestanding Latin prose: Bx 7.129, Bx 8.21, Bx 9.43, Bx 11.3, Bx 12.300, and Bx 15.57. Weiskott, "The End of the Line?," 239, lists some instances in the C version. A freestanding Latin *auctoritas* may also be adduced with *For* or *Þat is*: Bx 3.337, Bx 3.357, Bx 10.396, Bx 12.313, and Bx 15.73. The implication is that a single English word or short English phrase may introduce an unmetered Latin quotation either at the beginning of a line or after the first half-line.

54. Bx 13.206 and Bx 14.103 are within passages dropped in the C version. See Lawler, *The Penn Commentary*, 54–55, 92. The English portions of Bx 14.142 and Bx 14.331 are omitted in the cognate C-version lines. The first of these, C 15.306, also truncates the Latin quotation. In the second, C 16.143, the C-version archetype simply entered the name *Seneca* before the quotation, omitting the B version's speech tag. The C archetype also truncates the Latin quotation in C 17.316 (cognate to Bx 15.639), omitting *omnipotentem*. References to the C version of *Piers Plowman* are to George Russell and George Kane, eds., *Piers Plowman: The C Version. Will's Visions of Piers Plowman, Do-Well, Do-Better and Do-Best. An Edition in the Form of Huntington Library MS HM 143, Corrected and Restored from the Known Evidence, with Variant Readings*, Piers Plowman: The Three Versions (London and Berkeley: Athlone Press and University of California Press, 1997).

55. I quote manuscript readings from Hoyt N. Duggan, gen. ed., *The Piers Plowman Electronic Archive*, vols. 1–8, Society for Early English and Norse Electronic Texts (SEENET) series A.1, 2, 5–7, 9–11 (2000–2014; web edition, 2014), http://piers.chass.ncsu.edu.

56. John A. Alford, "The Role of the Quotations in *Piers Plowman*," *Speculum* 52, no. 1 (1977): 80–99, 82, 86–88.

57. Other examples of this presentation are Bx 19.153–54 (discussed below) and Bx 15.639, where the two alpha-family copies treat the English portion as a full alliterative line (these two copies punctuate after *clause*, an inferior metrical division).

58. Beta4 is composed of the group of manuscripts with the sigla GYOC^{2}CBmBoCot. See Burrow and Turville-Petre, *The B-Version Archetype*, 4.

59. The exception is 153 *þe corps*, for which Schmidt prints *þat corps*, in agreement with F and the C-version archetype.

60. See Barney, *The Penn Commentary*, 123; and Russell and Kane, *C Version*, 124.

61. For questions, criticism, and suggestions that improved my argument I thank Sarah

Nooter and other participants in the Baltimore conference, participants in the Chicago Seminar on Medieval Culture and Intellect, Eric Weiskott, peer reviewers, and especially the volume editors. I have sole responsibility for deficiencies. For additional discussion of Bx 19.152–153, see my article "Some Corrections to the Notation of Verse Structure in Two Recent Editions of Middle English Alliterative Poems," forthcoming in *Filologia Germanica* 15.

CHAPTER FIVE

Latin Verse in Old English Accents

Emily V. Thornbury

> Ther was also a Nonne, a Prioresse, . . .
> Ful weel she soong the service dyvyne,
> Entuned in hir nose ful semely;
> And Frenssh she spak ful faire and fetisly,
> After the scole of Stratford atte Bowe,
> For Frenssh of Parys was to hire unknowe.
>
> CHAUCER, "GENERAL PROLOGUE" TO *THE CANTERBURY TALES*

In the fourteenth century, Madame Eglentyne's London-accented French would likely have marked her as provincial, especially to international travelers like her inventor, Geoffrey Chaucer. But to modern scholars, the peculiarities of Anglo-French are interesting in their own right: this provincial dialect offers us an insight into the complex refractions of national and personal identity at a time when both "English" and "French" were ideas in flux. The Anglo-French that the Prioress's real-world counterparts learned in childhood, and spoke and wrote thereafter, complicates simplistic ideas about vernacularity and national languages. So, too, does the Latin that everyone—from those vowed to religious orders like the Prioress to ordinary laymen and -women—would have heard, memorized, and recited regularly.[1] Chaucer's ambiguous praise of the Prioress's manner of singing and intoning suggests that her spoken Latin, too, might have sounded like an East Ender's; and if a relatively well-educated gentlewoman's version of the Divine Office came off, to cosmopolitan ears, as not quite quite, one can only imagine how the Paternosters and Ave Marias of laypeople in Devonshire or Cumberland would have sounded.

Five hundred or so years earlier, Latin stood alone as the prestige language of England and, indeed, of all Britain.[2] But in one way, the Anglo-Latin of the early

Middle Ages was in a situation closer to that of Anglo-French than to fourteenth-century Anglo-Latin: it was possible to visit places where people spoke (or considered themselves to speak) the language natively. The Romance dialects of Gaul, Spain, and Italy were, by the seventh and eighth centuries—when the English began learning the language—no longer Latin. But they were also not entirely *not* Latin, and they were certainly much closer to it than the various dialects of English.[3] Moreover, the Christian peoples whose native languages were Brythonic and Irish also had long traditions of teaching and speaking Latin.[4]

The Prioress's eighth-century ancestor might thus have pronounced Latin according to the school of Canterbury or York—or Faremoutiers, or Bangor, or Mayo, or indeed even that of Rome.[5] But these early English clerics must have pronounced Latin somehow or other. And it matters how their Latin sounded, not only because the development of Anglo-Latin helps illuminate the trajectory of prestige dialects. Variations in pronunciation could potentially help us understand many features of England's early cultural history that are otherwise difficult to ascertain—including the influence of foreign scholars; differences across time and space in the affiliations between various regions of England and cultural centers abroad; and perhaps even the development of local schools, whose idiosyncrasies might help us date and localize texts, and in so doing clarify the literary history of the Dark Ages. This essay offers only a sketchy line or two toward a dialect map of early Anglo-Latin, but such a map is still perhaps possible, and it would teach us a great deal about the early English kingdoms' relations to each other and to the wider world.

My immediate goals are much more limited: first, to identify some diagnostic markers of Anglo-Latin phonology that might help securely identify texts as of English origin, even if they cannot (yet) be more precisely localized, and to use these patterns of pronunciation to better understand the meter of rhythmic Anglo-Latin verse—and vice versa. A diverse range of evidence, most of it internal to the poetry, suggests that there was indeed a distinctive "Anglo-Latin accent," whose features can help us see how profoundly intertwined Latin and the vernacular were during the Old English period and reveal hitherto unsuspected forms of experimental verse.

We cannot begin with any a priori assumptions about Anglo-Latin pronunciation; too many possible models were available. We know, for instance, that English speakers were in contact with clerics who learned Latin in a number of Romance-speaking areas and that many English ecclesiastics themselves studied overseas. Early missionaries and teachers in Anglophone Britain came from Italy, Francia, and North Africa and made their way across the island, although their influence was particularly strong in Kent and the other southern and eastern kingdoms. During the seventh century—the crucial formative period for early Anglo-Latin—the Latin of native Romance speakers was heard by people across Anglophone Britain.[6] So, too, was the Latin of native Celtic speakers. Irish missionaries evangelized much of the north of England, and many English speakers traveled to Ireland to learn Latin, as well as monastic discipline.[7] Evidence is less clear for the individual impact of native Brythonic speakers, but as it now seems likely that the British church had some influence on its neighbors, especially the West Saxons, Cambro-Latin may also have left its mark in this region.[8]

Moreover, in addition to finding possible models for pronunciation in the quasi-native Latin of Romance speakers and the established academic Latin traditions of Celtic speakers, the early English might have innovated their own rules, either extrapolating from the example of classical poetry or the late antique grammars that circulated throughout the early period or basing pronunciation on that of their native language.[9] To further complicate matters, it is even possible that Anglo-Latin pronunciations were defined against those of other dialects, as suggested by a remarkable passage in the preface to Ælfric's *Grammar*:

> Miror ualde, quare multi corripiunt sillabas in prosa, quae in metro breues sunt, cum prosa absoluta sit a lege metri; sicut pronuntiant *pater* brittonice, et *malus* et similia, quae in metro habentur breues. Mihi tamen uidetur melius inuocare deum patrem honorifice producta sillaba, quam brittonice corripere, quia nec deus arti grammaticae subiciendus est.[10]
>
> [I am especially astonished that many people cut short syllables in prose, which are metrically short, since prose ought to be free of metrical constraint; thus they pronounce *pater* in the British way, and *malus* and so forth, which in meter have short syllables. It seems to me better to address God the Father with a syllable prolonged in honor, than to cut it short in the British manner, since God ought not be subject to grammatical art.]

This comment contains many fascinating dimensions, several of which Melinda Menzer has discussed, including the distinction Ælfric draws between pronunciations appropriate to verse or to prose, and the indication that the Welsh used classical vowel quantities, distinguishing in their own pronunciation the long and short vowels that structured classical Latin verse.[11] This would have set Welsh Latin speakers apart not only from (evidently) the English but from Continental Romance speakers of the time, who no longer differentiated vowels by length: it is perhaps noteworthy that Ælfric does not describe his preferred pronunciation as like that of the Franks but as unlike that of the Welsh or Cornish.[12] Disaffiliation might be a more powerful motivation than affiliation, in other words; and the theological justification given for *pater*'s long initial vowel indicates that pronunciations of a learned dialect like Latin might have reasons behind them, rather than the evolutionary histories of vernacular phonology.

One possible indication that English speakers may even have consciously distinguished their Latin pronunciations from the sound of their native language appears in Abbo of Fleury's *Quaestiones grammaticales*, which he wrote while living in England, at the Fenland monastery of Ramsey, during the late tenth century.[13] In chapters 23 through 25, Abbo takes up the question of pronunciation, denouncing *isti* (those idiots) who refuse to palatalize the consonants in the syllables *ce* and *ci*, instead pronouncing them with a hard (velar) consonant.[14] To him, these syllables sounded like *que* and *qui*—leading to unnecessary confusion (and showing incidentally that Abbo's dialect pronounced <qu> as /k/).[15] Abbo does not specifically address this section to the *Angli*, so it is possible that he had someone other than his hosts in mind. But since the palatalization of <c> and <g> before the front vowels /i/ and /e/ was required in Old English, using a velar consonant in that position would have effectively distinguished the sound of Latin from that of English, emphatically marking such words as foreign.

During the period of the Benedictine reform, when Abbo and Ælfric were writing, Latin was being reconfigured to bear the load of ecclesiastical reform; as it assumed more complex and highly wrought forms, it served to distinguish the monastic intellectual elite not only from illiterate laymen but also from secular clerics who used Latin in more pragmatic guises.[16] What role pronunciation may have played in this linguistic drama is not yet fully clear, though judging from the remarks of these two grammarians, Latin's sound seems to have been a site of active controversy, even when the written forms were stable. It may be that the reform of Anglo-Latin pronunciation was also a way of distinguishing it from the vernacular during the mid to late tenth century and of further differentiating *literate* Latin from the speech of those who had learned the language colloquially rather than from books.

Earlier in the period, however, there is evidence that the sounds of Old English exerted direct pressure on those of Latin and that this pressure resulted in a distinctive Anglo-Latin soundscape that is still perceptible in the form of early rhythmic verse. While sometimes ambiguous, the patterns that emerge from these poems allow us to extrapolate some rules for pronunciation that, in turn, help illuminate the form of poems that might otherwise seem formless.

The first witness to the sound of Anglo-Latin is Aldhelm, abbot of Malmesbury and bishop of Sherborne, who died in 709 after a successful literary as well as ecclesiastical career.[17] In addition to the first substantive works of Latin prose and quantitative verse by an English-speaking author, Aldhelm composed a poem—describing a near-disaster that he and his companions experienced during a journey through Devon and Cornwall—in a rhythmic meter whose adaptation to narrative is apparently of his own device.[18] This meter consists of rhyming octosyllabic couplets with regular proparoxytonic stress: 8pp + 8pp, in Dag Norberg's standard notation.[19] In addition to the predictability of the stress, Aldhelm's poem incorporates another device that makes it extremely valuable for understanding its soundscape: frequent alliteration. While not as strictly rule-governed as Old English verse, alliteration in the *Carmen rhythmicum* is frequent enough that, cumulatively, it provides valuable evidence about sounds considered equivalent and about the stress contours applied to Latin words.

Perhaps the most distinctive pattern to emerge is the alliterative equivalence of *f* and *v*, as we see in this passage:

Horum **a**rchon, **a**trociter
Fumam **v**errens, **f**erociter
Furibundus cum **f**lamine
Veniebat a cardine,
Unde **T**itanis **t**orrida
Labuntur **l**uminaria;
Cumque **f**latus **v**ictoriae
Non **f**urerunt ingloriae,
Tremebat **t**ellus **t**urbida
Atque <u>eruta</u> **r**obora
Cadebant **c**um verticibus
Simul **r**uptis **r**adicibus.[20]

[Their warlord, fiercely driving mists before him, savagely maddened by the gale, came from the quarter whence the burning lights of Titan slip down; and as the winds did not rage without their victory, the distraught earth trembled, and uprooted oaks fell with their crowns as broken as their roots.]

As this passage demonstrates, Aldhelm's alliteration is both intense and variable: sometimes confined to a single verse, sometimes uniting a couplet or even several couplets.[21] But while any individual pairing of word-initial *f* and *v* could perhaps be due to chance, the two letters occur together so often that their alliterative equivalence in the *Carmen rhythmicum* seems impossible to doubt.[22] This feature is particularly interesting because it is not a Romance pronunciation. Initial *f* and *v* were phonemically distinguished in late Latin and its successors; classical consonantal <*u*> became a fricative (usually /v/) or even a stop (most often /b/) in Vulgar Latin relatively early on.[23] Many minimal pairs demonstrate a phonemic distinction between initial *f* and *v*: *filia* (daughter) but *vilia* (refuse); *ficus* (fig tree), but *vicus* (village); *viam* (path) versus *fiam* (I shall become), and so forth. This distinction is maintained in the modern Romance languages as well.[24]

So the alliterative equivalence of *f* and *v* was not something that Aldhelm could have learned from contemporary Italians, Spaniards, or Gauls. But two non-Romance sources for such a pronunciation would have been near at hand. One of these was Old English, in which /v/ and /f/, the voiced and unvoiced forms of the labiodental fricative, occurred in a complementary distribution. The voiced consonant /v/ occurred between vowels but was not phonemically distinguished from unvoiced /f/; as /v/ apparently never occurred word-initially in Old English, it is very plausible that Old English speakers would have devoiced this sound at the beginning of Latin words.[25] But there is also strong evidence that contemporary Irish speakers devoiced initial *v* in Latin words.[26] Aldhelm is thought to have had an Irish teacher or teachers, and he certainly came into contact with Irish Latin speakers.[27] It is possible, then, that Hiberno-Latin was the origin of Aldhelm's phonological conflation of initial *f* and *v*, which was then reinforced by the tendencies of Old English—in which case, the alliterative equivalence of *f* and *v* is most accurately described as Insular.

Aldhelm's placement of word stress is more complicated to establish. He certainly obeyed some common rules for Latin pronunciation; indeed, the meter of his poem effectively depends on the rule that a word of three or more syllables with a light penult is regularly stressed on the antepenultimate syllable.[28] His treatment of words with prefixes is more ambiguous. In Old English, prefixes are normally unstressed, as confirmed (and reinforced) by the alliteration in verse; this tendency is almost invariable for verbs and for several common nominal prefixes.[29] Classical and late Latin, however, permitted stress to fall on verbal prefixes, especially when required by the language's relatively strict tendency to place stress on the penultimate or (if the penultimate syllable is short) the antepenultimate.[30] Line 42 of the *Carmen rhythmicum*, quoted above, would suggest that Aldhelm treated Latin verbal prefixes as unstressed: *eruta* alliterates—fittingly—on its root syllable, although the syllable is short. Elsewhere in the poem, however, his practices are less clear, as we see in this passage:

Attamen **fl**agrant **f**ulmina
Late per **c**aeli **c**ulmina,
Quando **p**allentem **p**endula
Flammam **v**omunt **f**astigia,
Quorum **n**atura **n**ubibus
Pro**c**edit **c**onlidentibus,
Necnon marina **c**erula
Glomerantur in **gl**area,
Qua **i**n**r**uit **i**n**r**uptio
Ventorum ac cor**r**eptio.[31]

[Suddenly lightning flamed across the entire sky when the looming heights spit pallid fires (which proceed naturally from the collision of clouds); and the sea's blue depths piled up upon the shore where the onslaught and attack of the winds rushed in.]

In line 98, alliteration would seem to indicate stress on the root of *procedit* but on the prefix of *conlidentibus*; since the root of *procēdere* is long, both pronunciations would have been orthodox in spoken Latin. In line 101, the prefixes *and* roots alliterate, which is a fancy trick but provides no help in indicating how *irruit* ought to be stressed. Both pronunciations are potentially justifiable: *IRruit* would obey the antepenultimate rule, while *irRUit* would lay emphasis on the root. The double alliteration seems to leave both options viable.

The *Carmen rhythmicum* has thus provided some useful, if sometimes ambiguous, evidence for early Anglo-Latin pronunciations. The treatment of *f* and *v* as alliterative equivalents suggests that Insular Latin had some distinctive phonological tendencies that set it apart from the Latin of Romance speakers; further research on this point might help us recognize more easily the works of English or Irish speakers, even those whose writings survive only on the Continent. It is possible that the devoicing of initial *v* may have been more common in Anglo-Latin than Hiberno-Latin. While early medieval Latin verse from Ireland like the *Hisperica Famina* makes extensive use of alliteration, it is difficult to detect a consistent pattern of equivalence between *f* and *v* in these poems, such as we see in Aldhelm's poem and in a number of other early Anglo-Latin works.[32] Possibly, Irish poets preferred to maintain an academic distinction that did not match their pronunciation, rather like writers of quantitative verse elsewhere. In any event, the *f*/*v* equivalence may serve as a rough rule of thumb for Latin works of unknown authorship, suggesting likely Insular and possibly English origin.

Aldhelm's treatment of word stress is more equivocal. Generally, the alliteration of the *Carmen rhythmicum* suggests he expected verbal prefixes to be unstressed, as in Old English. But in the case of words like *inruit*, he seems to have allowed for the possibility of alternative pronunciations. Such fluidity complicates our understanding of the form of Anglo-Latin rhythmic poetry. In the early medieval period, rhythmic Latin verse was understood as an impressionistic version of quantitative poetry.[33] In many cases, this account seems to track with actual practice; a number of popular rhythmic forms do seem to have been directly based on quantitative models.[34] This translation created problems, however, since forms based on regular patterns of vowel quantities could appear chaotically unpredictable when scanned according to word or phrasal stress. When combined with the possibility of actual uncertainty, or major regional variations, in the placement of stress, the internal dynamics of early rhythmic verse can seem impenetrable.

Allowing for the likelihood of ambiguity or variation does not mean, however, that we must abandon all hope of understanding individual poems or schools of poetry. The scansion of one anonymous, but almost certainly English, hymn reveals the possibility of striking regularities—regularities that may in turn suggest both a relatively standardized set of rules for pronunciation and even an intended performance context.

Magnus miles mirabilis is a hymn to St. Cuthbert that circulated relatively widely; it is preserved in several hymnals and in the cult book for St. Cuthbert given by King Athelstan to Chester-le-Street.[35] In stanza 4, *f* and *v* seem to alliterate, which tracks with the probable English origin of this hymn to an English saint. As nothing connects this poem to Aldhelm's influence, the feature would thus appear to reflect a common pronunciation. While the hymn's precise date and place of origin are unknown, all surviving witnesses are from southern England, and its inclusion in Cambridge, Corpus Christi College 183, the Cuthbert cult book, provides a *terminus ad quem*.[36] It is written in rhythmic Ambrosian stanzas, and alliterates extensively:

1. Magnus miles mirabilis	1. A great wonder-working soldier
multis effulgens meritis	shining with many merits,
Cuthberhtus nunc cum domino	Cuthbert now with the Lord
gaudet perenni premio.	rejoices in his eternal reward.

2. Carnis terens incendia
corde credidit domino
caduca cuncta contemnens
caritatis officio.

2. Treading down the flesh's fires
he entrusted his heart to the Lord
scorning all ephemeral things
in his works of love.

3. Legis mandata domini
laetus implevit opere;
largus, libens, lucifluus
laudabatur in meritis.

3. Joyfully he fulfilled all
duties of the Lord's law;
generous, joyous, a source of light
for his merits he won praise.

4. Fecit manare flumina
fontis signi perpetui,
ubi nulla vestigia
videbantur fonticuli.

4. He caused the waters of a spring
to rise as a perpetual sign,
where no least trace of dews
had before been seen.

5. Linguam resolvit vinculis
longo tempore retentam.
Petrosa terra segetem
parvo produxit tempore.

5. He broke the chains that long time
had bound a silent tongue.
Rocky ground brought forth wheat
in little time.

6. Illius nos auxilium
deprecæmur perpetuum,
ut mereamur dicere
sine fine cum gaudio:

6. Upon ourselves we beseech
his perpetual aid,
so that we may deserve to say
eternally with joy:

7. Gloria patri ingenito,
gloria unigenito
una cum sancto spiritu
in semipterna secula.[37]

7. Glory to the unbegotten Father,
glory to the only begotten Son
one with the Holy Spirit
forever world without end.

Rhythmic Ambrosian stanzas were based on the iambic dimeter hymns of Ambrose of Milan, which were incorporated into most versions of the Divine Office and thus familiar across Latin Christendom.[38] Without the quantitative structure that shaped Ambrose's compositions, the form was stretched and adapted in a variety of ways, defined only by a basic stanzaic template of four roughly eight-syllable lines.[39] Within this, however, many medieval poets devised more stringent rules for themselves; rhyme schemes—sometimes quite elaborate ones—and fixed rhythmic patterns were perhaps the most common choices.[40]

Magnus miles seems at first to resist the common medieval tendency toward ornate internal structure. Its rhymes are monosyllabic, except for the homeoteleuton in the final stanza, and conform to no fixed or recurring pattern. While its syllable count is strictly regular—taking into account the likely elision in the first line of stanza 7—scansion according to standard ecclesiastical Latin pronunciation results in a varied and unpredictable soundscape, with seven different melodic contours across the poem and no two stanzas rhythmically identical. Such variation would make *Magnus miles* difficult to sing, so it is surprising that it appears to have been a relatively popular hymn. Two aspects of the text, however, introduce a suspicious regularity into the apparent chaos: a strong but not invariable tendency toward line-final stress on the antepenultimate syllable and insistent alliteration, which does not always align with standard word stress. If we allow this alliteration—together with Aldhelm's treatment of line-final stress—to guide the poem's scansion, the result is a pattern of startling simplicity and clarity.

Within the poem, the rhythm appears to be defined by two rules: (1) stress falls on the first syllable of phrasally stressed words of three syllables or fewer; (2) stress falls on the first and penultimate syllable of words having four or more syllables unless the penultimate is light, in which case stress falls on the antepenultimate. The result of these rules is a restricted set of three rhythmic contours:

A: /x/xx/xx
B: /xx/x/xx
C: x/x/x/xx

Magnus miles would thus scan:

Stanzas 1 and 2: AABA
Stanzas 3 and 4: AAAA
Stanza 5: AABA
Stanza 6: BBCA
Stanza 7: BBBC

The melodic patterns implied or generated by these lines' stress contours trace, and make audible, the hymn's internal structure, hinting at how this hymn might have sounded in performance. Repeated stanza shapes unite the first five stanzas, which narrate Cuthbert's miracles. The hymn's mode then shifts to prayer in stanza 6, and a doxology in the final stanza. While much of the musical culture of pre-Conquest England has been lost to us, it is possible that the set of paired stanzas in *Magnus miles* implies the use of a double or divided choir; other texts—including Aldhelm's *Carmen rhythmicum*—may allude to such a performance practice, and perhaps we see a trace of it in the rhythms of this hymn.[41]

The sung or chanted Latin of *Magnus miles* would likely have sounded both familiar and foreign to an Old English–attuned ear. The strong initial stress of most words would have echoed the typical pattern of Old English; though the frequent stress on prefixes would have been anomalous in the vernacular, it may indicate that the Latin words were produced and interpreted as wholes rather than habitually parsed into stems and prefixes. Conversely, Old English has exceedingly few polysyllabic words with antepenultimate stress, and these must have sounded distinctively Latinate. While stress and alliteration closely coincide in *Magnus miles*, they are most likely to part ways in words like *fonticuli*: a subtle reminder, perhaps, that Latin's sound was expected to be a little foreign to an English-speaker's ear.

It is not clear how widespread the accentual rules used by the author of *Magnus miles* actually were. Though Aldhelm's word-stress practices are, as we have seen, sometimes ambiguous, his practice seems to have been closer to that of standard ecclesiastical Latin. Patterns of word stress, then, may prove to be useful in finding, describing, and perhaps localizing subdialects of Anglo-Latin. As it happens, the rules for word stress that structure *Magnus miles* do in fact clarify the meter of some unique acrostic verses on folio 52r–v of Cambridge, Corpus Christi College MS 307.[42] The book to which these remarkable poems form a coda is a late ninth- or early tenth-century manuscript of Felix of Crowland's *Vita S. Guthlaci*.[43] Although the first of the poems is a scribal colophon, it is almost certainly not a holograph; not only does it include at least one obvious textual error, but the hand in which all three poems are written is different and probably later than that of the main text of Felix's *Vita Guthlaci*.[44] The other two poems—which the scribe has not clearly separated—also contain textual problems. These are particularly severe in the case of the second poem, which probably originally spelled the name GUDLAC in telestich (i.e., with the final letters of each verse) as well as CALDUG (i.e., GUDLAC backward) in acrostic. As it now stands in CCCC 307, the poem has MUDEAA in its right margin, though not all the words even end with these letters.[45] This unfortunate poem appears to be written in quantitative dactylic hexameters, which may originally even have been relatively correct, although the textual damage—stemming perhaps from damage to the right margin of an earlier copy—makes it difficult to be certain on that point.

It is clear, however, that the poems that precede and follow the CALDUG acrostic are based on fundamentally different metrical principles. The third poem, which reads BEATUSGUDLAC in acrostic and BARTHOLOMEUS in telestich, is described by M. R. James as composed of "lines [that] contain fragments of hexameters but cannot themselves be called hexameters."[46] James's epistemological problem is caused, I believe, by the occasional and deceptive likeness between quantitative and rhythmic Latin meters. Unlike its companion, from which it follows directly on, the final poem scans only as rhythmic verse and incorporates rules for stress very similar to those seen in *Magnus miles*.[47] Here are the first five lines, with their proposed scansion:

/ x x / x x / x / x x / x x / x
Benigne natus in orbe deus ex semine IacoB
/ x / x / x x / x / x x / x
Electosque suos ad alma uocabat regnA
/ x x / x / x x / x / x x / x
Aeternus fulgens dominus qui est iustorum rectoR:
/ x x / x / x / x x / x x / x
Tumulus iste pulchre sacrata membra includiT,
(x) / x x / x / x / x x / x x / x
Ut cunctis per orbem mira fulserunt munera IosepH.[48]

[God was graciously born in the world from the seed of Jacob and has called his chosen ones to the holy kingdom, the eternal shining lord who is the ruler of the just; that vile tomb enclosed the holy limbs, so that Joseph's wonderful reward could shine forth for everyone across the world.]

The shapes of the hexameter's feet have been mapped onto words, with dactyls generally filled by trisyllables or by disyllables followed by a preposition or other function word, and spondees represented by any disyllable; the long first syllable that begins any foot in a heroic line is now represented by a stress. The result is a meter that is fundamentally different from a quantitative hexameter while still clearly modeled on it. Some important features of the heroic line—particularly, caesurae and the complex interplay of metrical ictus and phrasal stress—are impossible in this rhythmic form. What is gained, however, is a more transparent meter. Instead of the years of study necessary to learn no-longer-audible classical vowel lengths, anyone who could pronounce Latin according to the two rules posited above would be able to scan, read aloud—and compose—hexameters like these. Within these parameters, the only structural fault in this poem is the apparently extrametrical conjunction *Ut* that begins line 5, if we allow the *in* of *includit* (line 4) to scan as a preposition.[49]

Benigne natus is a formally ingenious poem, then, but the poet's skill is only perceptible if one pronounces the Latin in a way that would have sounded bafflingly foreign to Continental Latin speakers of any era. This is even more true of the first acrostic in CCCC 307's series, whose form would have been incomprehensible to any but bilingual speakers of Old English and Latin. Fittingly, it is essentially a local and personal poem:

Ego licet uilis uernaculus Xr*isti* **I**;
Adiuuatus gratia iusta depingen **S**;
D*omino* donante digne quae feci **T**;
Vota gud uenimus adsumm **A**
Voluminis istius fuerunt quip **P**';
Addecembri falendas dies putat **I**;
Lucide uiginti uos deprecor exi **N**; /52v
Delere u[*d*] dignetur debitare **X**;
Viventi preces fundere patr **I**;
Semper in*saecu*la cui gl*or*ia mane **T**;[50]

[I, though an unworthy servant of Christ, was aided by grace, by God's gift fittingly writing down those righteous things which Guthlac's vows accomplished. We came to the end of this book: indeed there were clearly reckoned twenty days before the first of December. I beg all of you to make erasures in it—so that the King may see fit [to erase] sins—and to pour forth prayers to the living Father, to whom remains glory forever and ever.]

The acrostic/telestich reads "Eadwaldus ista pinxit" (Eadwald painted them). As I noted earlier, this cannot be Eadwald's own copy; besides the nonsense word *falendas*, a likely misreading of *kalendas* in a Hybrid minuscule exemplar, the abbreviated *nomen sacrum* in the first line (*Christi*, written Xrī i) doubles the telestich letter, and the page break spoils the visual integrity of acrostic and telestich.[51] Despite this, however, an English reader of CCCC 307 might still be able to appreciate Eadwald's ingenuity. Here is an emended text, with a proposed scansion:[52]

x x x x S x   S x x x   S   x
1 Ego, licet **u**ilis   **u**ernaculus Christ   I,
- Sr   x S x   S x x S x
2 Ad**i**uuatus **g**ratia,   **i**usta depingen   S
Sr x S S x   S x x S x
3 **D**omino **d**onante   **d**igne quae feci   T
S x S Sx   Sr x x S   x
4 **V**ota Gud*laci*.   **V**enimus ad summ   A

Sr x x S x Sr x S x
Voluminis istius: **f**uerunt quip P'

\- Sr x Sr x Sx Sr x
Ad **D**ecembri kalendas **d**ies putat I

S x x S(r?) x S - S x Sr
Lucide **u**iginti. **V**os deprecor exi N

S x x x S x x S x x S
Delere, u*t* **d**ignetur **d**ebita re X,

S x x S x S x x S x
Viventi ***p***reces fundere ***P***atr I

S x x S x x x x S x Sr
Semper in **s**aecula, cui gloria mane T.

This is not a Latin meter, rhythmic or otherwise; it is Old English alliterative verse. It is in general reasonably correct. The alliteration is distorted at lines 7 and 10—normally, it should connect the two parts of the line by falling on the first stressed syllable of the a- and b-verses—but Eadwald's treatment of *f* and *v* as alliterative equivalents is, as we have seen, quite correct for an Anglophone, and the alliteration of consonantal *i* with *g* in line 2 is also correct in Old English. Eadwald seems to have allowed two unstressed syllables at the end of a-verses, which is normally not permitted, so he may have been foiled by the dactylic rhythms that Aldhelm exploited. Or perhaps not: one of the chief difficulties here is with resolution, which is as important to Old English meter as it is to quantitative Latin verse, though handled slightly differently. Here, I have applied the Old English rules, which allow a stressed light syllable (i.e., with a short vowel, and not closed by a consonant) to resolve with a following unstressed syllable of any weight within the same word. The precise manifestation of resolution, however, depends on knowing what Eadwald believed the quantity of Latin vowels to be. It is possible, for instance, that he presumed the first syllable of *uiginti* (7) was light and scanned it as (Sr x). The same may be true of *donante* (3), *saecula* (10), and even *vota* (4); if so, then the only line that a speaker of Old English could find serious fault with would be line 8—and line 8 may contain a metrical joke.[53]

Cynewulf, whose runic "signatures" embedded in four poems have attracted critical scrutiny for generations, is thus not the only Old English poet to have worked his name into a colophon.[54] Unfortunately, Eadwald's life and canon are as opaque to us as those of the better-known poet: Eadwald was a common name, November 11 comes around every year, and it is impossible to say even whether

Eadwald composed the other two acrostics in CCCC 307. What we *can* be sure of, though, is that he was part of a culture in which the sound of Latin was fundamentally shaped by that of English, to a degree that renders the distinction between vernacular and "prestige language" very blurry indeed.[55] While this might have appalled a pre-Conquest Chaucer, the distinctive Anglo-Latin accent seen in *Magnus miles* and two of the CCCC 307 acrostics may provide a clue to the origin of other texts written in the same dialect, and perhaps may also help us identify the features of yet other dialects of medieval Latin. In the form of rhythmic verse, we can hear the Old English accent that shaped these remarkable poems; and if we continue to listen, we undoubtedly will hear yet other voices from other times and places, still audible in their Latin verse.[56]

NOTES

1. Over the last two decades, scholars have demonstrated that spoken Anglo-French was a far more varied, complex, and long-lived phenomenon than had previously been recognized: for a wide-ranging sample of this scholarship, see the essays in Jocelyn Wogan-Browne et al., eds., *Language and Culture in Medieval Britain: The French of England,* c. *1100*–c. *1500* (Woodbridge, UK: York Medieval Press, 2009). For the teaching as well as the speaking of French in Chaucer's England, see Ardis Butterfield, *The Familiar Enemy: Chaucer, Language and Nation in the Hundred Years' War* (Oxford: Oxford University Press, 2009), esp. 66–101, 308–49.

2. On the dynamics of prestige languages, see Henry Kahane, "A Typology of the Prestige Language," *Language* 62, no. 3 (1986): 495–508.

3. As many scholars have demonstrated, the transition from Latin to Romance was a complex one, in which shifts in speakers' self-conceptions were as important as changes to syntax and phonology: for a concise, compelling exploration of this, see József Herman, "Spoken and Written Latin in the Last Centuries of the Roman Empire: A Contribution to the Linguistic History of the Western Provinces," in *Latin and the Romance Languages in the Early Middle Ages*, ed. Roger Wright (New York: Routledge, 1991), 29–43. Wright has argued that the Northumbrian scholar Alcuin, through his work to reform the textual apparatus of the Carolingian church and his drive to standardize the way those books were read aloud, was in large part the architect of medieval Latin in Europe: see Roger Wright, *Late Latin and Early Romance in Spain and Carolingian France* (Liverpool: Francis Cairns, 1982), esp. 45–144.

4. For an excellent overview of the complexities of learning Latin in early medieval Europe, with a focus on the British Isles, see Carin Ruff, "Latin as an Acquired Language," in *The Oxford Handbook of Medieval Latin Literature*, ed. Ralph J. Hexter and David Townsend (Oxford: Oxford University Press, 2012), 47–62.

5. For an overview of how and where eighth-century Englishwomen acquired Latin learning, see Helene Scheck and Virginia Blanton, "Women," in *A Handbook of Anglo-Saxon Studies*, ed. Jacqueline Stodnick and Renée R. Trilling (Chichester: Wiley-Blackwell, 2012), 265–79.

6. Merovingian and Italian priests were involved in the conversion of Kent, the establishment of a cathedral and monastery at Canterbury, and missions to the surrounding Saxon and southeastern Anglian kingdoms: see Bede, *Historia ecclesiastica gentis anglorum* [henceforth

HE]: Bertram Colgrave and R. A. B. Mynors, eds., *Bede's Ecclesiastical History of the English People* (Oxford: Clarendon, 1969), I.25, 29; II.3; and Ian Wood, "The Mission of Augustine of Canterbury to the English," *Speculum* 69 (1994): 1–17. The Italian Paulinus accompanied a second group of missionaries and went north to evangelize the Northumbrians and become the first archbishop of York: see Bede, *HE* I.29, II.9, 16. Felix, the first bishop of Dunwich in East Anglia, was a Burgundian: Bede, *HE* II.15. In the later seventh century, Theodore of Tarsus was consecrated archbishop of Canterbury and was accompanied to England by the North African monk Hadrian, who became abbot at the monastery of SS Peter and Paul (St. Augustine's); together they provided their English students with advanced training in Latin, as well as the other academic disciplines of the day, and many of Hadrian and Theodore's scholars went on to abbacies and bishoprics across Britain: Bede, *HE* IV.1–2. Around the same time, Wilfrid, later archbishop of York, studied in Lyons for three years: Eddius Stephanus (Stephen of Ripon), *The Life of Bishop Wilfrid*, ed. Bertram Colgrave (Cambridge: Cambridge University Press, 1927), §6, 12. Somewhat later, Benedict Biscop, founder of the monasteries of Wearmouth and Jarrow in Northumbria, imported a cantor from Rome: Bede, *HE* IV.18. English nuns, especially those of high status, often went to Francia or Gaul for education: see Bede, *HE* III.8, IV.23.

7. Much of Mercia, Northumbria, and East Anglia were converted by a series of Irish missionaries: see Bede, *HE* III.3–5, 15–17, 19, 21, 24, 26. For English scholars in Ireland (and Irish-speaking dependencies like Iona), see Bede, *HE* III.27, IV.4, V.22; Aldhelm, *Epistola ad Ehfridum* (Letter 5, to Heahfrith), in Rudolf Ehwald, ed., *Aldhelmi Opera*, MGH Auctores Antiquissimi 15 (Berlin: Weidmann, 1919), 486–94.

8. For the piecemeal survival of British Christian communities, see Richard Sharpe, "Martyrs and Local Saints in Late Antique Britain," in *Local Saints and Local Churches in the Late Antique West*, ed. Alan Thacker and Richard Sharpe (Oxford: Oxford University Press, 2002), 75–154, esp. 102–30; and for the likelihood that British documentary practices shaped those of early Wessex, see Amy W. Clark, "The West Saxon Boundary Clause in Context," *Early Medieval Europe* 31, no. 1 (2023), 69–94. In *Writing the Welsh Borderlands in Anglo-Saxon England* (Manchester: Manchester University Press, 2018), Lindy Brady has argued that constant interchange rendered the Anglo-Welsh border regions a distinctive cultural zone in the pre-Conquest period; the Latin of such frontier zones merits further investigation.

9. Vivien Law, *Grammar and Grammarians in the Early Middle Ages* (New York: Longman, 1997), esp. 54–123.

10. Julius Zupitza, ed., *Ælfrics Grammatik und Glossar* (Berlin: Weidmann, 1880), 2.

11. Melinda J. Menzer, "Speaking *brittonice*: Vowel Quantities and Musical Length in Ælfric's *Grammar*," *Peritia* 16 (2002): 26–39; see 29–30 for evidence that Welsh speakers did pronounce these and similar words with short vowels.

12. Possibly this is because Ælfric's preferred *producta syllaba* was also artificial: by this period, both /a/ and /a:/ would have been pronounced as /a/ in stressed syllables by Romance speakers: József Herman, *Vulgar Latin*, trans. Roger Wright (University Park: Pennsylvania State University Press, 2000), 30–31. As Wright pointed out, however, Isidore of Seville (for example) used *producta* to refer to stress rather than quantity, so it seems more likely to me that Ælfric was accustomed to hearing a strong stress on the first syllable of *pater* (and, consequently, that the British may have pronounced the word with a less emphatic initial stress).

13. Anita Guerreau-Jalabert, ed., *Abbon de Fleury: Questions grammaticales* (Paris: Les belles lettres, 1982), 25, 29.

14. Guerreau-Jalabert, 235–41; for discussion of Abbo's strictures on pronunciation, see Wright, *Late Latin and Early Romance*, 136–39.

15. In other words, *isti* were pronouncing <ce> and <ci> as if in the modern English words *case* and *kin*, instead of *chase* and *chin*.

16. See Rebecca Stephenson, *The Politics of Language: Byrhtferth, Ælfric, and the Multilingual Identity of the Benedictine Reform* (Toronto: University of Toronto Press, 2015).

17. For an overview of Aldhelm's life, see Michael Lapidge, "Aldhelm," in *The Wiley Blackwell Encyclopedia of Anglo-Saxon England*, ed. Michael Lapidge et al., 2nd ed. (Oxford: Wiley Blackwell, 2014), 27–29; for a more synthetic and speculative account, see Michael Lapidge, "The Career of Aldhelm," *Anglo-Saxon England* 36 (2007): 15–69.

18. The poem is edited in Ehwald, *Aldhelmi Opera*, 523–28. On the form (and Aldhelm's use of it), see Andy Orchard, *The Poetic Art of Aldhelm* (Cambridge: Cambridge University Press, 1994), 19–72.

19. See Dag Norberg, *An Introduction to the Study of Medieval Latin Versification*, trans. Grant C. Roti and Jacqueline de la Chapelle Skubly; ed. Jan Ziolkowski (Washington, DC: Catholic University of America Press, 2004), with a concise explanation of his notation in the foreword (xxiv). In brief: *8* indicates the number of syllables in a verse and *pp* that stress is fixed on the proparoxytone (i.e., the third syllable from the end), as distinguished from the paroxytone (the penultimate syllable, notated as *p*). In the *Carmen rhythmicum*, two identically structured lines form a couplet: hence, 8pp + 8pp. This notation can be used to describe a wide range of verse structures and stanzaic forms.

20. Ehwald, *Aldhelmi Opera*, 525. Probable alliteration is marked in boldface; possible patterns in boldface italics.

21. For more on Aldhelm's alliterative patterning, see Orchard, *Poetic Art*, 43–54. Orchard notes the alliterative equivalence of *f* and *v* at 49–50. Norberg also comments on the English tendency to equate initial *f* and *v*; see Norberg, *Medieval Latin Versification*, 45.

22. The *Carmen rhythmicum* is two hundred lines long as printed (i.e., one hundred couplets). In addition to lines 34–36 and 39–40 above, *f* and *v* are paired word-initially at lines 23, 70, 96, 106, 112–13, 159, and 171.

23. Robert A. Hall Jr., *Proto-Romance Phonology* (New York: Elsevier, 1976), 59–60. Thus, Latin *vinum* (wine), pronounced with a semivowel in antiquity, was borrowed into Old English as *wīn* (ModE *wine*) but appears in Spanish and Italian as *vino* (with fricative /v/).

24. Wright, *Late Latin and Early Romance*, 100: "no Romance speech has ever merged these two sounds in initial position."

25. A. Campbell, *Old English Grammar* (Oxford: Oxford University Press, 1959), §50(1), 20; Donka Minkova, "Phonemically Contrastive Fricatives in Old English?," *English Language and Linguistics* 15 (2011): 31–59. For evidence that Old English speakers still did not distinguish between *f* and *v* in foreign words in the tenth century, see Janet M. Bately, "The Old English Orosius: The Question of Dictation," *Anglia* 84 (1966): 255–304, 285–87.

26. See Anthony Harvey, "Retrieving the Pronunciation of Early Insular Celtic Scribes: The Case of Dorbbēne," *Celtica* 22 (1991): 48–63, 59–61.

27. An anonymous letter to Aldhelm, thought to have been written by an Irishman, mentions "quod a quodam sancto viro de nostro genere nutritus es" (that you were brought up by a certain holy man of our race; Ehwald, *Aldhelmi Opera*, 494), though this letter's attribution is uncertain. Michael Lapidge has also proposed that Aldhelm studied on Iona ("The Career of Aldhelm"). While the question of Aldhelm's early training is difficult to resolve, his widely circulated letter to Heahfrith, urging him to study in Canterbury rather than Ireland, perhaps ironically demonstrates considerable familiarity with Irish scholars (Ehwald, *Aldhelmi Opera*, 488–94).

28. Ernst Pulgram, *Latin-Romance Phonology: Prosodics and Metrics* (Munich: Wilhelm Fink, 1975), 91.

29. Campbell, *Old English Grammar*, §§72–80, 30–33. We see this in these lines from the Ascension Day poem *Christ II*: **f**erðwerige onfon in **f**yrbaðe, / **w**ælmum biwrecene, **w**raþlic

onlean (in the pool of fire, engulfed by the surge, the despairing ones receive a terrible recompense) (*Christ II* 830–31), which alliterate on *f* and *w* respectively. The prefixes *on-* and *bi-* in *onfon* and *biwrecene* are unstressed and do not alliterate.

30. Pulgram, *Latin-Romance Phonology*, 91; at 104–13 Pulgram argues that many Latin words with stressed prefixes represent the lexicalization of an early emphatic stress.

31. Ehwald, *Aldhelmi Opera*, 526.

32. See Michael W. Herren, ed., *The Hisperica Famina: I. The A-Text* (Toronto: Pontifical Institute of Mediaeval Studies, 1974); and Michael W. Herren, ed., *The Hisperica Famina: II. Related Poems* (Toronto: Pontifical Institute of Mediaeval Studies, 1987).

33. In his influential *De arte metrica*, for instance, Bede describes a rhythmic Ambrosian hymn as "instar iambici metri" (in the likeness of iambic meter); see *Beda Venerabilis Opera Didascalia*, CCSL 123A (Turnhout: Brepols, 1975), §24, 138–39.

34. See Norberg, *Medieval Latin Versification*, esp. 81–129.

35. Most recently edited by Inge Milfull, *The Hymns of the Anglo-Saxon Church* (Cambridge: Cambridge University Press, 1996), no. 61, 253–55. Milfull's base text is the Durham Hymnal (Durham, Cathedral Library, B.III.32, s. xi^{1}); other witnesses in hymnals include London, British Library, Cotton Vespasian D.xii (s. xi^{med}); London, British Library, Cotton Julius A.vi (s. xi); London, British Library, Harley 2961 (s. xi$^{3/4}$), and Cambridge, Corpus Christi College 391 (s. xi$^{3/4}$).

36. The Cuthbert manuscript was written 934 x 942; for a digital facsimile and up-to-date bibliography, see Parker Library on the Web: https://parker.stanford.edu/parker/catalog/qv695jy8078.

37. Milfull, *Hymns*, 253–55.

38. For a concise account of the circulation and liturgical use of hymns, focused especially on early England, see Helmut Gneuss, *Hymnar und Hymnen im englischen Mittelalter* (Tübingen: Max Niemeyer, 1968), 3–6.

39. See Norberg, *Medieval Latin Versification*, 100–105, 116, 133–35.

40. Norberg, 8, provides the particularly striking example of a rhythmic Ambrosian stanza containing a fixed rhythmic pattern, internal rhyme within each verse, and end-rhyme continuing across the stanza.

41. *Carmen rhythmicum*, lines 127–30:

Tum binis stantes classibus
Celebramus concentibus
Matutinam melodiam
Ac synaxis psalmodiam.

[Then, standing in two divisions, we were singing together the matins song and the appointed psalm.] (EHWALD, *ALDHELMI OPERA*, 527)

Line 128 is characteristically ambiguous; *concentibus* might mean "in unison," or it might not.

42. For a digital facsimile, see Parker Library on the Web: https://parker.stanford.edu/parker/catalog/hg904kt9713.

43. David N. Dumville considered the script a precursor to Square minuscule; see his "English Square Minuscule Script: The Background and Earliest Phases," *Anglo-Saxon England* 16 (1987): 147–79, 166–67. Though Dumville did not venture a precise date, his discussion seems to imply he would attribute it to the first decade or so of the tenth century and to an origin in Worcester.

44. In line 6 of the first poem, *falendas* appears for *kalendas*—an unlikely error for a scribe focused on recording the date of his own work but a very plausible one if the exemplar were in some form of Hybrid minuscule. Compare, for instance, the name *Koena* on fol. 40r of the

Durham Liber Vitae (London, British Library, Cotton Domitian A.vii; the name is 10 from the bottom in the left-hand column). Hybrid minuscule *k* has a descender rather than an ascender as in the Caroline minuscule with which the scribe of the CCCC 307 poems appears to be more familiar.

45. M. R. James—to the best of my knowledge these poems' only editor—did not reconstruct the text but made some plausible and ingenious suggestions for emendation; see Montague Rhodes James, *A Descriptive Catalogue of the Manuscripts in the Library of Corpus Christi College Cambridge*, 2 vols. (Cambridge: Cambridge University Press, 1912), 2:105–7.

46. James, 106.

47. This likely also threw off James, who was trained as a Classicist; see S. G. Lubbock, *A Memoir of Montague Rhodes James* (Cambridge: Cambridge University Press, 1939), 15.

48. Text from James, *Descriptive Catalogue*, 2:105–6, checked against the facsimile at Parker Library on the Web.

49. *Includit* is the only word in the poem that begins with a transparent prepositional prefix, so it is difficult to be sure whether this is the poet's usual practice or a sort of license. It is clear, however, that the poet consistently scans prevocalic *i* and *u* as consonants (e.g., *huius* and *metuo* in line 6 both seem to be disyllables).

50. Text from James, *Descriptive Catalogue*, 2:105–6, and the facsimile at Parker Library on the Web. The line-final *puncti versi* are in the manuscript. Italics denote expanded abbreviations; the *d* of *ud* [*recte* ut] in line 8 is legible under an erasure, but has not been corrected (perhaps as a metajoke?).

51. See above, note 44.

52. I use here the scansion system proposed by Nicolay Yakovlev, who posits a basic template of four audible metrical positions filled either by a single or resolved stressed syllable (represented as S or Sr) or by a sequence of unstressed syllables (x). Yakovlev's template generates a range of metrical patterns that effectively matches that of Sievers's widely used classification system. See Nikolay Yakovlev, "The Development of Alliterative Metre from Old to Middle English," (DPhil thesis, Oxford University, 2008), 42–88, esp. 55–56. Eduard Sievers expounded his foundational theory in *Altgermanische Metrik* (Halle: M. Niemeyer, 1893); the standard modern English elaboration is that of A. J. Bliss, *The Metre of Beowulf* (Oxford: Blackwell, 1958). Yakovlev's system allows prefixes to be optionally considered extrametrical, a license that Eadwald appears to have invoked at lines 2a, 7b, and (mirroring 2a, but stretching the definition of *prefix*) 6a.

53. Richard Dance has suggested one further alternative: that *gn* was treated as a single palatalized consonant, which would again allow for resolution and scansion of *dignetur* as Sr x, rendering 8a metrically normal.

54. The essays by Fulk, Elliott, and Frese in Robert Bjork, ed., *The Cynewulf Reader* (New York: Routledge, 2001), provide a helpful entry point into the study of Cynewulf's "signatures" and the authorship questions they raise for the poems in which they are found (*Christ II, Elene, Juliana,* and *Fates of the Apostles*), as well as associated poems like *Guthlac B*; see also Thomas Birkett, *Reading the Runes in Old English and Old Norse Poetry* (Abingdon: Routledge, 2017).

55. For exploration of interlingualism as a phenomenon in earlier medieval English verse, see Alexandra Vance Reider, "The Multilingual English Manuscript Page, *c.* 950–1300" (PhD diss., Yale University, 2019).

56. For many helpful comments and suggestions as this work developed, my grateful thanks to this volume's editors, Steve Justice and Chris Cannon; to the audience and participants of the original "Sound of Writing" conference; and to the audience and organizers of the 2021 ASNC Departmental Colloquium.

CHAPTER SIX

The Writing of Sound

Meredith Martin

> The book has always been mere breaths away from utterance.
>
> CHRISTOPHER CANNON AND MATTHEW RUBERY, INTRODUCTION TO "AURALITY AND LITERACY" (2020)

> A spoken language is . . . a vague and floating entity.
>
> HENRY SWEET, *SPOKEN ENGLISH* (1908)

A Vague and Floating Entity

How do we locate sound in language? How should we physically mark that location on a page? The disciplines of book history, sound studies, and the history of linguistics each have very different answers to this question, but the one thing these disciplines have in common is that when they attempt to answer this question in text, they all rely on the now shared descriptive vocabularies of phonetics (e.g., fricatives, plosives), even when they might disagree about the conventions of marking sound via phonetic symbols or diacritical marks; that is, they use the same language to describe sounds without any real sense that they agree on what those sounds sound like. What might it do to our current approach to poems if we thought about how scholars worried over the ways sound might appear in and through textual form rather than simply relying on this shared descriptive phonetic vocabulary? By shared vocabulary, I mean the descriptive terms we use for sounds as related to their physiological mechanisms as if these terms are transhistorical. The word *fricative*, for example, appears in the *Oxford English Dictionary* from 1863; the Princeton Prosody Archive (prosody.princeton.edu) antedates this to 1855.

The general systematization of pronunciation before this moment is not a given; issues of sound in text were hotly contested in the developing field of phonetics, yet we imagine a transhistorical concept of a "poetic voice" as if it adheres to our now (still shakily) standardized understanding of sounds in English. Often, scholars working in the period between 1750 and 1870 seem to accept sound as fixed, whereas scholars of earlier periods are far less likely to accept as a given the sounds of the poems they discuss. My hunch is that scholarship on earlier periods, before 1750 or so, stabilized versification but not pronunciation, while scholarship on later periods has tended to stabilize both, often using one as evidence for their arguments about the other.[1] Before Saussure, before Derrida's beef with Saussure, before phonotexts or close listening, before the invention of orality and aurality, the concept of sound was unmarked territory.[2] Or rather, it was marked with so many squiggles, dots, waves, invented alphabets, universal alphabets, cosmophonographic symbols, phonetic speech, phonetic diagrams, and complicated diacritics that it is no wonder literary scholars have turned their eyes away from it. How did we arrive at the generally accepted notion that our current concept (a sense of a shared perception) of sound is close enough to the past that we retroproject our contemporary pronunciation—however varied that might be—onto that messy protodisciplinary mash-up of lexicography, philosophy of language, orthography, and prosody that appears in texts that talk about how to mark sound on a page? Or rather, if we don't completely accept that our pronunciation is close enough to the past to generate similar meaning, we at least agree that to do the opposite—to try to accurately imagine what sound *sounded* like in the past—might miss the mark. But despite knowing that the historical sound of spoken language is immeasurably variable, we often teach as if we are able to apprehend historical language just enough to translate it into an imaginary "standard" pronunciation (David Crystal's work on Shakespeare is a useful example).[3] These assumptions about sound have implications for how we teach and write about prosody.[4] Here, I want to document what we might describe as not only a failure of imagination but a failure of research. As I showed in *The Rise and Fall of Meter*, the disciplinary consolidation of "English literature" calcified the teaching of English versification via an acceptance of the accentual-syllabic system; this acceptance was predicated on dismissing advances and discussions that are ongoing in linguistics about how to measure English verse.[5] The moment of disciplinary division between English literary study and linguistics at the beginning of the twentieth century was concurrent with the rise and acceptance of the ideological narrative of English meter as derived from classical scansion. Prosody as a subject persists in both English and linguistics in very different ways. Yet, just as "English" has stabilized a notion of English versification in the classroom (and, in different ways, has disregarded or critiqued various structuralisms and formalisms that rely on and derive from linguistics), it has also stabilized a notion of English pronunciation in the past. Our collective reluctance to historicize the terms we use when we describe sounds in poems results, at times, in a failure of imagination, a lack of historical awareness and nuance, especially when it comes to the concept of sound in writing.[6] I trace this failure via the continued use of terms for pronunciation—for describing sound using terms from phonetics—and show how our imaginary concept of "voice" and "speaker" in English literary study has allowed us to maintain the fiction that our contemporary concepts of speakers and voices have something—have anything—to do with historical sound.

In the historical periods in which I am currently working—roughly from Locke to Saussure—I notice that the discipline of sound studies is late to arrive on the scene; when it does show up, the concepts of a "speaker" and a "voice" often don't have very much to do with sound.[7] Since my approach to teaching prosody is to make sure my students are aware of the varieties and cultural implications of versification and pronunciation (the two parts of prosody), they are often relieved to know that they do not have to change the way they speak when we read poems from the past out loud. But before we read aloud, I am sure to teach them about how unfixed English versification is and that we cannot really know what these poems sounded like. My students find it funny when I imitate Tennyson's own recitation of "The Charge of the Light Brigade," but his aging, yearning, wax-cylinder-undulating tone is impossible for me to erase. The layered mediation of my imitation of a recording of Tennyson's performed voice is an expressive echo I exaggerate on purpose when I teach that poem—a poem already so saturated by its life in circulated print that its various mediations echo in the distance between Tennyson's elegy and the nameless soldiers he elegizes. And I've purposefully layered the prepositions in the prior sentence to illustrate that there is nothing immediate about my reading Tennyson's poem on the page—or hearing him read it—nor should there be for my students. Eric Griffiths's 1989 *The Printed Voice of Victorian Poetry* ventured that we do not read the way that we speak, nor do we read the way that historical speakers spoke. Griffiths, as Yopie Prins has expertly argued, points not to the impossibility of recapturing or historicizing the sound of historical speakers but rather to the view that poetry evokes voice *as an absence*. Prins writes that this evocative absence is "an insight glimpsed in *Seven Types of Ambiguity* by William Empson": that the "absence rather than the presence of voice" in Victorian poetry, despite the proliferation of imaginary voices, makes it distinctive. Griffiths's argument, Prins also writes, is that "poems circulating in nineteenth-century print culture point to an imagined voice that may in fact be unvoiceable." Prins rereads and resituates Empson's "pathos," repeated and amplified by Griffiths. For Empson, as for readers in the present, grace is "given by an enforced subtlety of intonation, from the difficulty of saying it so as to bring out all the implications."[8] Both Empson and Griffiths locate pathos in the choice to perform (to voice) one emphasis (a loss) as opposed to silent (textual) reading that allows for the interplay of various, ambiguous meanings at once.[9] By pointing out this imaginary (mental) voice that contrasts with the speaking voice (and its various emphases), Prins theorizes the distance between the textual mediations of possible voicing and this imaginary voiceless mental voice. To this I would add that, even when scholars are attempting to characterize how sound might have been written via the figuration of voices in metrical or textual form, the imaginary voice that cannot be voiced pulls attention away from the actual page. Prins clarifies: "This is by now a predictable debate in which 'voice' and 'writing' are each in turn idealized: Derrida (preoccupied with inscription) posits the ideality of voice as self-presence while Griffiths (preoccupied with vocalization) posits writing in the abstraction of print."[10] Poems either exceed or do not quite achieve the imagined idealized voices of their imagined idealized original "speakers," but, as Prins shows, reading beyond the concept of a "speaker" allows us to "open up a cultural history of forms."[11] And although Prins's work has helped us relocate our understanding of poetic meter in a broader cultural field, we have yet to do the same for the concept of sound as such, especially as it relates to the concept of meter.

We have a century of critical readings of poems that live in that distance between however we imagine historical speakers spoke and how our apprehension of the poem's soundedness—in the past or present—generates meaning that has little to do with actual sounds. These imagined sounds are *only* textual; they are only possible because of the shared language of phonetics—how we now agree to describe sound (sibilants, plosives, fricatives, liquids). Phonetics gives us a way to attach our perception of sound to meaning, to create (or say we detect) sound symbolism—also called phonetic symbolism—and this has provided *enough* stability to allow us to feel comfortable making claims about the expressive nature of sonic patterns in poems.[12] When we use phonetic terms to describe poems, we are making claims about the apprehension of speech in the past, anachronistically applying them to poems even though the readers, writers, and speakers of these poems (and by *speaker* here I mean oratorical performer) would not have described the sounds of their words in the same way. The historical archive of how sound is described in the eighteenth and nineteenth centuries is rich and understudied, often relating to the natural world, and absolutely aware of and tracking the existence of a soundscape as Murray Schafer defined it in 1969. Texts describe varieties of voices and performances in relation to musical scales, birdsong, wind instruments, mouth shape (often ethnically inflected), climate, emotion, and education.[13] So, in the second part of this essay, my purpose is not to summon an "original speaker" that we cannot hear but to reflect on groups or even generations of speakers whose voices were being trained, who were self-training, or who were learning to pronounce English a certain way for a certain purpose. I am curious about a nonabstract notion of vocalization related to the professions and disciplines (lexicography, rhetoric, elocution) that were concerned with how people pronounced "properly" and for what purposes.

Phonetic descriptions, I think, have in some way allowed us to imagine a standard pronunciation that both universalizes and standardizes an imagined, nonhistorically located speaker. The "mute polyphony" of Eric Griffiths and the impossible subtlety of intonation William Empson yearns for are located in that roving "speaker" of poems who is always somewhere beyond sound. To put it another way, I know that I will influence my students' interpretation of *The Waste Land* if I play them the recording of T. S. Eliot reading it. The transatlantic accent, affected and acquired, transmits so much about Eliot's class position that, hearing it, we cannot but register Eliot's own autobiographical experience in one of the poem's many narrators. Do we protect an idea of Eliot's poem as somehow universal and therefore *not* tied to his personal experience, when we imagine our own voice—or, more likely, some description of the poem's own utterance or the poem's own voiceless voice—in our head reading the poem rather than Eliot's? Does the unvoiced, but really muting *his* voice, aspect of the poem really make it accessible to more readers? Helen Vendler and other writers who rely on the abstract concept of a "lyric" with a "speaker" would say yes.[14] Contrast this concept of a lyric speaker (a whiteness personified? An erasure of difference?) to the layers of mediation we sort through when we read and hear "voices" via recording *and* print technologies. These are the many mediations we might choose to erase when we replace the author's actual recorded voice with our own voice as a stand-in for a transhistorical "lyric voice." How do we square this with the way we may read the textual mediation of an idiom, italic, or capitalization of text: "I said, / What you get married for if you don't want children / HURRY UP PLEASE ITS TIME." We know this is a stage direction, a character in the poem. We know that the capital letters are another character shouting; we know we are in the soundscape of a pub. But do we, as teachers and readers, still fall back into performing an imaginary standard "voicing" of the poem—a white man's speech, a universal and universalizing narrator by the time "the nymphs are departed?" Adding the layer of the recording, if we listen to Eliot's voice reading "the nymphs are departed," it is unmistakably a mid-Atlantic accent, a classed and historically located poet's voice whose education Eliot performs or purposefully deforms in every phoneme. The imagined universal lyric speaker that readers might perform as taking the place of Eliot's mid-Atlantic voicing when we get to "the nymphs are departed" conflates our own historically located readerly performance—out loud or in our heads as we read—with an underimagined notion of sound that I imagine erases Eliot's accent. My hunch is that Eliot's speaker gets to be universal because Eliot's class location is the highest, because sound and voice have been abstracted into "sounding" and "voicing," and because, as Yopie Prins and Virginia Jackson have proven, we insist on the impossibility of voicing at the same time as we argue for the existence of a transhistorical lyric speaker.

I have purposefully chosen examples of performances by Tennyson and Eliot of poems that are explicit about the pitfalls of relying on accurate textual or vocal transmission: " 'Forward, the Light Brigade! Charge for the Guns!' he said" of the first stanza and the repeated "Forward, the Light Brigade" command of the second stanza are the (shouted) mistaken orders that lead the six hundred soldiers into the jaws of Death. The blunder of the poem is that these orders were miscommunicated. *The Waste Land*'s working title was "He Do the Police in Different Voices," and the poem has long been read as a collection of various idiolects and dialects, resulting in countless articles that explore the function of "voice" in the poem.[15] But to read the "voices" in these poems, how often do we put Tennyson's or Eliot's own phonographic performances in conversation with the textual performances? Another reason why these two are helpful and illustrative examples is that students can immediately hear pronunciation differences, and therefore historical distances, in the two performances.[16]

When we rely on the impossibility of voicing a poem—or a word—as the subtext to our insistence that we are connected to an imaginary utterance in the past, we might lose the opportunity to think through these differences and distances. Yet when we do so, we nevertheless rely on what we perceive to be the stability of prosodic effects: "echoing of rhyme, assonance, or alliteration, and rhythmic patterning" in Jonathan Culler's argument. In addition to "voicings," Culler calls these effects the "fundamental dimension of lyric," yet he mutes the fact that all of these effects are textually mediated and each is historically contingent.[17] The ongoing lack of agreement, for instance, on how Gerard Manley Hopkins would have performed his poetry is a case in point.[18] Angela Leighton uses Culler's division between "voice" and "voicings" to sidestep any discussion of performance.[19] The possibility of your voice taking the place of an author's voice, or, rather, having the entire poem *take place nowhere*, is what Jackson powerfully names "the fiction of the lyric speaker" that "locate[s] the poem's conversation in a fictive space in which you and I can share intimacies and priorities without having to share personal information."[20] In this space—the *only* location where sound might be imagined as stable; where rhyme, assonance, alliteration, and rhythmic patterning never change; where you, reader, may disregard the poem's varieties of prosodic or linguistic meaning so as to quickly move past how any prosodic effects may have been perceived in the past—in this place the universal speaker lives. And this is how and why one project of historical prosody and historical poetics is to rethink this concept altogether: this concept of "voice" and "speakers" is what allows scholars who say they are talking about sound in poetry to set aside, Leighton explains, "not only drama and performance poetry, but also much of the heritage of black writing, from Langston Hughes to Patience Agbabi—writing which calls on the voice rather than on what Griffiths and Culler call 'voicing,' and whose logical end is the live audience rather than the solitary reader." But whose logical end does Angela Leighton mean, here? She writes, "My excuse then . . . is that this book focuses on the sound that, in a sense, stays silent on the page while shaping the labor of the ear through which it might, nevertheless, be heard."[21] A poetry held apart from drama, performance, and much of the heritage of black writing is not one that interests me very much. Or, rather, Leighton's method provides a convenient excuse to disregard any poem that troubles the concept of a seamless translation between a past "utterance" that might be considered "universal" (in the Eliot sense) and to make entirely stable any prosodic effects that might back up that translation. I'm concerned with the recourse to prosodic stability as a backdrop to that seamless translation of sounds from the past into our contemporary understanding of phonetics, and I am also curious about why the sound of eighteenth- and nineteenth-century poetry, in particular, seems so silent when the material artifacts of sound are everywhere to be seen.

Why is this the case? The ease of phonetic descriptors and the lie of metrical stability is one reason we have spilled so much critical ink thinking about Eliot's "ghost of meter"—detecting metrical accents or "scanning" for metrical regularity by putting marks on the page to help us apprehend a pattern—and so little time thinking about how Eliot's sounded voice might mean something else. Perhaps another reason is that we really are afraid to get it wrong—that laughter when my students hear my Tennyson impression is born of discomfort. I sound unhinged, unlike how they are used to hearing words sound. Similarly, they are uncomfortable when we sit down to look at a poem written in dialect. Eliot and Pound corresponded in a blatantly raced dialect privately, fully aware of the print mediation of the spoken word in their letters.[22] Idioms, not marks for pronunciation, signal the dialect of a particular social class in *The Waste Land*, yet for white readers, as James Weldon Johnson remarked in 1922, it is altogether too tempting to read the printed marks of racialized dialect as directives to the poem's performance, a symbol of an oral folk form pointing to a preliterate authenticity.[23] Marks indicating social class or racialized speech or regional dialects on the page mean that the present-day reader is confronted directly with the distance between themselves as a performer and the sounds that those marks might mean. But, I tell my students, that distance is part of what marks on pages teach us; marks for dialect are showing us how to read, but they are teaching us how to read for genre rather than sound; that is, the marks for dialect on the page participate in the well-known historical conventions of the genre of dialect poetry, a genre that both references and satirizes the desire for an imaginary original "speaker."

For instance, James Weldon Johnson compares Paul Laurence Dunbar's dialect poetry with Scottish poet Robert Burns's: "Burns took the strong dialect of his people and made it classic; Dunbar took the humble speech of his people and in it wrought music."[24] Though Johnson's reading of Dunbar's dialect poetry contains much of the essentializing folk nostalgia of the early twentieth century, it nevertheless locates dialect in conventions of print rather than in a simplified idea of oral performance. For instance, if we read the first poem in his *Book of American Negro Poetry*, published the same year as *The Waste Land*, as if its dialect marks are a guide to the poem's proper performance, we look past the poem's embeddedness in a long history of dialect writing. Michael Cohen writes that "the prevailing interpretation of dialect as the authenticating oral signature of the printed folk poem transformed poems with no pretense to being oral folklore into a dominant mode of articulation of cultural fantasies about racialized folk."[25] Johnson recognizes that the use of dialect has limited how poems by African Americans have been read by white readers. The move away from dialect poetry, Johnson writes, will "be regretted by the majority of white readers," and he himself feels the loss of "this quaint and musical folk-speech as a medium of expression." Yet the association of dialect with the "speech of the folk" is also, in Johnson's reckoning, "mere mutilation of

English spelling and pronunciation."[26] Dialect poetry of all kinds, and its print mediations, are not evidence of a performance tradition or a simple guide to performance in speech but rather a figure mobilized to fix a particular sonic imaginary to a particular folk imaginary. This is not unique to poetry; it occurs all over fiction as well. Dialect citations should be read as pointers and marks that indicate specific communities, not necessarily guides to actual performance. When we see past the dialect marks to the figure of the folk that these marks both symbolize and send up, we move past one concept of "voice" in performance altogether to see all possible "voicings"—both on and off the page—as multiply mediated readings.[27]

The sounds that Tennyson's and Eliot's recorded voices make—both their pronunciation and their versification—are mediated by print-readable inscriptions, by audio technology, and by prosodic technologies. This is nothing new, but it bears repeating: genres of performance and pronunciation existed long before recording technology, and we can read them through the cultural history of prosody. But we are much more likely to think through the mediations of versification (diacritical marks as media) than we are to think about the mediations of pronunciation (the other side of the prosodic coin). Like my students' embarrassment when I imitate Tennyson, the idea of considering pronunciation and performance as highly mediated lies in tension with a mode of lyric reading that elides a poem's—or a poet's—historical embeddedness. As is clear above, the word *speaker* is now entirely detached from its original meaning as someone who "performs." It is another symptom of our confusion over these terms that the term *speaker* is historically an "orator"—but now the term means its opposite: when we say a poem has a "speaker," we are ventriloquizing as we read and silencing the history of the development of the discipline we might now call "speech and rhetoric." By ignoring whatever does not fit the silences lyric reading requires or by choosing to classify it as "rhetorical" or cued toward live performance, we've arrived at a place where the "the speaker" has become synonymous with the lyric speaker and therefore with lyric reading, the process by which we assume all poems in the past are lyric poems. When we talk about speakers, we are not talking about students trained in the bodily gestures and accents of elocution. The poetic "speakers" in the classroom are not Lord Alfred Tennyson's mediated wax-cylinder waver or T. S. Eliot's mid-Atlantic pronunciation but rather this imaginary speaker-as-person who emanates from that voiceless nowhere-place, that stopped, out-of-history time between the poem's writing and its reception. I think this is what Susan Stewart means when she writes that "the poem itself is an utterance, an expression of a person that we apprehend in turn as the expression of a person."[28] As Jackson has written and discussed widely, by making poems into persons, no matter our intentions, we replace actual sound with abstract sound and erase actual people.[29]

Of course, the "speaker" occupies no space, and the abstract speaker cannot have a body. But when we stop to think about real speakers—and real ways people speak or might speak, the way historical poems intervened in genres of print and genres of pronunciation and performance—we drop out of lyric time and into the messiness of historical poetics. Again, I can see why scholars have avoided that messiness. Even the pronunciation shifts between the early days of the phonograph and the current moment are understudied, and it may be that sociolinguistic and prosodic features are less important to discussions of poetry and sound than the highly mediated ways we may encounter poetry in performance, recorded or live.[30] Yet scholars of the medieval and early modern periods are eager to recreate the sounds of poems prosodically and phonologically alongside considerations of their print mediation.[31] What happened between the early modern period and the advent of phonographic technology is, of course, some version of the stabilization or standardization of pronunciation in English alongside the solidification of one method of teaching meter in English. Several scholars have examined the effects of ongoing efforts to standardize pronunciation in the eighteenth, nineteenth, and even early twentieth centuries with work on Samuel Johnson's dictionary, the elocution movement, grammatical shifts, and the advent of BBC or "Received" English.[32] But these studies of how English became recognizable are to the side of how we think about sound when we read poems—to the side of how we might read poems differently were we able to historicize how we think about and describe sound. My own work, growing from Prins's and Jackson's, shows how the definition of meter in English is and always has been contested.[33] And despite the prevalence of retroprojecting the concept of an imaginary "speaker," the way we think about how poems are spoken seldom considers the difficulty with which scholars attempted to standardize how we write about speech in print. What would a historical poetics of sound in print look like?

Prosody, Grammar, Sound

"It may be observed that accent should be regulated, not by any arbitrary rules of quantity, but by the number and nature of the simple sounds."[34] It would take several books to produce a historical poetics of sound. When scholars understand pronunciation to be historically variable, they tend to think of versification as stabilizing (think of the ottava rima enforcing the odd pronunciation of *Don Juan* rhyming with "true one").[35]

Critics in the decades of formalist reading's reconsideration used variable pronunciations to slide away from the perceived conservatism of close-reading-as-right-reading toward a method of reading closely for metrical disruption, which, at times, meant reading for possible class and social relations implicit in various possible pronunciations and thus to join "neoformalism" to the discipline of cultural studies.[36] Stumbles, stammers, choking, gasping, silence, and a variety of other figures also stood in for the possibility that the poem's prosody was communicating something about the impossibility of its transparent communication; the *affect* of difficult communication takes expressive shape of its own. Not "saying" something directly, the expressive register of prosodic disruption was (and is) often read as the intention of an imagined speaker who is communicating emotionally, through imagined sounds, what they cannot say outright and what only a closely reading scholar can "hear," "see," "read," and "interpret." But even the figure of dysprosodic or inarticulate "speech" presumes the possibility of fluency. Similarly, the impossibility of apprehending historical pronunciation—and the ambiguities that scholars may read them through—presumes that there was a *possible* method of transparently apprehending a poem's intended metrical effects.[37] Thinking about and arguing about these various apprehensions of a poem's effects is pleasurable, and I am not trying to be a prosodic killjoy by once again reminding everyone that in the history of prosody, neither pronunciation nor versification cohered in either a literary or linguistic sense. I do want to make clear, however, that the schemes for fixing sounds in English (in language more broadly, but in English in this specific context) reveals that "sound" as a concept remains unfixed—unstandardized—despite the attempts to fix it in writing, in text. Where and when and how scholars made decisions about versification and pronunciation varied widely. Both subfields of grammar (versification and pronunciation, along with etymology and syntax) were revised hundreds of times over the course of the eighteenth and nineteenth centuries. Grammar books, paratextual grammatical treatises on dictionaries, and pronunciation guides (that sometimes began as attached to grammar books and then circulated and were reprinted on their own) had conflicting pronunciations in English just as they did in Latin; think of the school-specific Eton Grammar and the caricatures of classical scholars searching for the true pronunciation of dead languages. And just as in Classics, so too in English do we generate meaning out of these possibilities—perhaps because an important part of English disciplinary history is classical philology.[38] Just as there were conflicts over questions of accent and quantity in versification, so, too, did scholars argue about the quantity of sounds in English—both how many sounds and how to sound quantity. Historians of language refer to these conflicts to track and think through patterns of language change; shifting accents in pronunciation guides might show the difference between how two generations pronounced particular words. But whether or not historical dictionaries and pronunciation guides should be brought to bear on the study of sound in poetry is a relatively new question. Natalie Houston has been using nineteenth-century versions of John Walker's *Rhyming Dictionary* to apply computational tools to the study of rhyme in Victorian poetry, but other than this computational approach to historical poetics (what she calls "operationalized historical poetics"), scholars of prosody who do not work specifically on rhyme seldom consider the historical contingency of sound in their readings of poetry.[39] Even in the case of using a historical rhyming dictionary like Walker's to think through historical pronunciation, we must consider that various editions of that text and the source text for many of the rhyme words was another poetic handbook first printed in 1702.[40] The culture of reprinting means that the textual evidence of rhyming dictionaries might not be the most efficacious way to measure historical pronunciation. But rhyming dictionaries do show the proximity of poetic discourse, historical pronunciation, and the development of phonetics.

If we put thousands of grammar books, texts about the teaching of poetry, and texts about the teaching of the English language and early phonetics together in a full-text searchable database that combines materials from ECCO and the HathiTrust, as I have been doing for the past ten years with the Princeton Prosody Archive, one result that is immediately visible is how poetic and linguistic terms overlap, shift, and influence one another; the history of versification involves the history of pronunciation and the development of linguistics. The material locations where graphic signs for sound were defined and standardized—or defined and discarded—were also locations where scholars argued about English accents in poems. The standardization of marking accent in speech *and* poetry, the gradual standardization of orthography and the century-long movement to fix graphic signs to (not yet named) phonemes resulting in the International Phonetic Alphabet, and the development of the science of phonetics all contributed to the way we talk about sound in poetry, as well as what texts we might consult to back up our claims. One narrative about versification in English, now understood (or misunderstood or, in any case, widely taught) as accentual-syllabic, depends on a taxonomy derived from Latin poetry, which was, in turn, derived from Greek. Many of the debates about prosody (what I have called elsewhere prosody wars) in the latter half of the nineteenth century, when scholars and teachers looked for an adequate and lofty way to present English meter based on or derived from the Latin, focused on how to measure quantity and accent in English, and one hope for spelling reform was to eradicate confusion over pronunciation in English so as to solve the problem of English meter *and* English pronunciation. If we all know how words should *sound*, then we wouldn't have any problem scanning poems in the same way.

Yet in the eighteenth century, grammar books were concerned with arguing for English grammatical instruction in order to displace Latin as the language of instruction. One of the projects in this effort was to decide how to teach a living language with sounds that were not fixed—could not be easily fixed—by a macron or a breve, which were the signs that helped to guide the Latin pupil as to the proper imagined pronunciation of a dead language. How and what might scholars use to guide future students of the English language—and then English literature—in the proper pronunciation of their language? What marks on the page could signal accent or emphasis, but, more importantly, how could we describe sound in English at all? This mid-to-late eighteenth-century discourse was concerned primarily with *speakers* of English, who were increasingly literate but possessed too much variety in their speech. These texts were friendly to foreign speakers (as in many script traditions) and tested out phonetic signs and symbols on multiple languages and on the poetry of other languages. The gradual standardizing projects of the eighteenth century—Johnson's *Dictionary* (1755) and Thomas Warton's *History of English Poetry* (1774–81), for instance—decreased orthographic variety and, as Paula McDowell has shown, helped to "invent" a concept of the "oral" that was closer to the language of nature.[41] "What is striking about comment on the spoken language," writes Lynda Mugglestone, "and reactions to it, in the late eighteenth and nineteenth centuries, is the rigorous approach adopted toward notions of correctness, manifested in a social as well as a phonemic sense, as orthoepists attempted to codify the spoken language, according to an increasingly class-based system of absolutes."[42] Guidance in English pronunciation was important for several reasons, not least of which was competition with "learned fellow subjects of Scotland and Ireland" who were "making frequent attempts to ascertain, and fix a standard, to the pronunciation of the English tongue."[43] Janet Sorensen writes that the internal politics of grammar and standard pronunciation are crucial to any concept of a nation.[44] And in eighteenth- and nineteenth-century discussions about sound and accent, quantity and syllables, pronunciation and debates over the ways to transcribe the proper marks for phonetic symbols and, eventually, phonemes is bound by the need to invent an English pronunciation—and an English prosody—that will be accepted by the widest possible audience and that will represent the essence of the people speaking those words. John Ash's dictionary is clear on this point:

> The accent and quantity of syllables give that distinction to words, and that pleasing modulation to the voice in pronunciation without which the ear would be perpetually disgusted with the most insufferable monotony. And hence it is, that in all the polished languages, this article has been attended to with great exactness. The Latins and Greeks distinguished all their syllables into long and short, and the latter made use of no less than three distinct marks or characters to point out the different quantity of accent or elevation of the voice in the pronunciation. And I am inclined to think, that if the proper modes of speaking were to be carefully attended to we should find something similar to this in the English language.[45]

Lexicographers wrote about the impact on poetry of their new rules about sound and how to mark it in text. Grammars and pronunciation guides to dictionaries argued over where and how to mark syllabic accents, long and short vowel sounds, multiple accents, and the problem of emphasis or modulation of the voice, what Ash calls "the oratorical accent." I am choosing to focus on discussions of accent that intersect with pronunciation in its print history—that is, the versification that appears in grammar books, pronunciation guides, dictionaries, and histories of language—because there we might locate the particular ways that sound was unfixed even in those texts that aimed to fix it via semantic accent, pronunciation, or emphasis. For instance, Ash worries that "this emphasis or modulation of the voice . . . frequently occurs, and sometimes with great advantage, in numerous compositions, where an accented syllable would destroy all the harmony of the verse. The place where the emphasis should be laid is sometimes exceedingly obvious, but to point out the best method of laying on this emphasis, is a task to which I profess myself to be exceedingly inadequate."[46]

Thomas Sheridan, William Perry, and John Walker, though hardly considered influential in the history of sound in poetry, nevertheless worked on a series of revised dictionaries to establish the diacritical system of marking accents that is still followed by and large in guides to versification (although not in guides to pronunciation), despite their disagreement about how many sounds English had or how to mark them. In 1775, Sheridan wrote that "there are in our tongue 28 simple sounds, whereof 19 are consonants, and 9 vowels."[47] He published several versions of a dictionary, each with subtitles that emphasized either pronunciation or "a complete guide to sound and meaning." His *General Pronouncing Dictionary* went through fifteen editions between 1798 and 1830; the subtitle of the *Complete Dictionary of the English Language* reads: "both with regard to sound and meaning. One main object of which is, to establish a plain and permanent standard of pronunciation. To which is prefixed a prosodial grammar."[48] The grammars, accents, and sounds of English had a direct effect not only on English poetry but on the concept of Englishness writ large.

Revised from the rhetorical grammar of his general dictionary, Sheridan's prosodical grammar contained the appendix "Rules to Be Observed by the Natives of Ireland, in Order to Attain a Just Pronunciation of English" and "Observations with Regard to the Pronunciation of the Natives of Scotland and Wales," as well as "Directions to Foreigners." Sheridan himself was a native of Ireland and a stage actor, who is primarily referred to as an elocutionist when he is mentioned at all in literary history. In 1788, William Perry's revised *Royal Standard Dictionary* asserted, "We have 14 distinct articulate sounds in our vowels, besides the compound sounds of the diphthongs."[49] In an earlier version of the same dictionary, Perry included the diphthongs in his original count, bringing the vowel sounds to twenty-eight—just over three times the number of vowel sounds counted by Sheridan. The complete title to William Perry's *Royal Standard English Dictionary in which the words are not only rationally divided into syllables, accurately accented, their part of speech properly distinguished, and their various significations arranged in one line; but likewise by a key to this work, Comprising the various Sounds of the Vowels and Consonants, denoted by typographical characters, and illustrated by Examples which render it intelligible to the weakest capacity etc.* is still too long to reproduce. This text influenced Thomas Sheridan's revisions to his *Lectures on the Art of Reading*, as well as the later editions of Sheridan's dictionary, and in the lexicographers' prefaces and engagements with one another in a series of grammars (Perry's is "comprehensive"), you can read Perry taking the Irish scholar to task for missing particular vowel sounds.[50] Though not enough is known about Perry to determine whether he was English or Scottish, he identified as a Scottish scholar later in his life. His complicated representational system adopted grave and acute accent marks to indicate accentuation and italics to denote mute vowels; he eventually had to include a key to his phonetic symbols as they became more complicated. But he is also thought of, alongside Sheridan and Walker, as an early adopter of a more precise approach to the sounds of English. Perry writes, in 1775:

> It is now requisite that I should take notice of a singularity in the following work which regards the right use of the *acute* and *grave* accents. The celebrated author

above mentioned [Sheridan] is, among others, a zealous advocate for unity of accent; and indeed, most of our lexicographers have made use of the *acute* accent only, which they have placed indiscriminately over *long* and *short* syllables; nay they go so far as to tell us, that the accent always makes the syllable long; than which nothing can be more absurd, as it tends to a total annihilation of the harmony of the verse, which conflicts in the pleasing variety of long and short, accented and unaccented syllables. Contrary to such an impropriety, I have ventured to make a due distinction, by the proper use of the *grave* or *acute* accents; the former being affixed to *flat* and *slowly* accented syllables, and the latter to *sharp* and *quickly* accented.[51]

Though Perry was not the inventor of this distinction, the influence of his system helped to standardize these marks in print; moreover, he agreed that accent and quantity were improperly marked in English verse: "That which we call *accent* does by no means correspond with what the ancients called *quantity*, though it is arbitrarily implied to signify the same thing. . . . The ancient laws of prosody are by no means conformable to the genius of our language; they are better adapted to the pronunciation of a *North Briton* than to an *Englishman*" (xlvii). He argues, "By this indiscriminate use of *accent* and long *quantity*, allowing *strength* to supply the place of *length*, the harmony of verse is marred, which, however, is by no means inconsistent with the rules of oratory. If our lexicographers and poets were universally to adopt a plurality of accent, and make the proper distinction between long and short syllables as the Greeks did, by the right application of the *grave* or *acute* accent, it would tend to free our verse from this glaring absurdity" (xlvii). Yet the history of prosody, as we tend to teach it, does not include this crucial history of the indeterminacy of sound in writing about the English language. Nor do we think through the ways that "accent" (both as mark and later as "beat") was accidentally codified by those who did not necessarily identify as English, despite their reservations about it, and that the imagined "fixity" of a concept like accent was concurrently promoted as the most "English" (as in, the most "Anglo-Saxon") and the least "Classical" of poetic effects.

As should now be quite clear, these deliberations about how accent should be indicated on the page as a guide for pronunciation in turn influenced how writers on both language and poetry began to blur the distinctions between a speaker's "natural" or spoken accent (that which had been acquired by careful practice with these pronunciation guides) and a performed or elocutionary emphasis—an oratorical accent—neither of which was exactly the same thing as what these authors understood to be metrical stress.[52] According to Esther Sheldon, by the end of the eighteenth century, the diacritical system "approximately as we know it in our modern dictionaries had been worked out."[53] These late eighteenth-century examples provide just one location where the attempt to fix certain kinds of pronunciation with graphical marks presses against the hope that poetry's measure will become similarly fixed. In a canny attempt to argue against his own books' redundancy, Walker's ubiquitous pronouncing dictionary, first published in 1791, asks: "What will it avail us, it may be said, to know the pronunciation of the present day, if, in a few years, it will be altered? And how are we to know even what the present pronunciation is, when the same words are often differently pronounced by different speakers, and those, perhaps, of equal numbers, and reputation? To this it may be answered, that the fluctuation of our language, with respect to its pronunciation, seems, to have been greatly exaggerated."[54]

Walker went on to have a successful career as both an orthoepist and promoter of his pronouncing dictionary, which absorbed many of the marks that Sheridan and Perry labored to establish. But the contention that "the fluctuation of our language . . . has been greatly exaggerated" would be hard to maintain, then or now. Over the course of the nineteenth century, the grounds of linguistics and phonetics shifted, as did the grounds of literary study. But some of our readings seem to be back with Walker rather than with Henry Sweet, thought of as the father of modern phonetics, who wrote in 1908: "A standard spoken language is, strictly speaking, an abstraction. No two speakers of Standard English pronounce exactly alike."[55]

But what do these marks matter? Scholars don't need to know the International Phonetic Alphabet to adopt phonetic descriptors for sonic effects in poems, but our failure of imagination when it comes to historical sound hides from view these subtle, yet extremely influential, discussions and debates about how to render sound in text. By expanding and historicizing these discussions of the voice, of sound, of accents, and of marks when we talk about poetic "speakers," we can finally begin to imagine persons and subjects in historical soundscapes and mediated print environments, or consider the debate over whether multisyllabic words could have more than one accent, or think about how a poem's intersection with historical versification and historical pronunciation might reveal a more complicated view of the political and social valences of poetry. As a scholar of prosody, I find it impossible to consider poetic form outside the ways that it was taught and circulated in the eighteenth and nineteenth centuries. We abstract the concept of "speakers" from the concept of "speech" when we talk about sound. We seem to also abstract the concepts of "stress" and "accent" when we talk about poems. When Allen Grossman writes that "stress is the inscription of the subjective or meaning-intending volition of the speaker" in his essay *Summa Lyrica*, he is referring to intonation and emphasis, what he calls "natural" stress, that which a speaker or an orator might decide to emphasize in addition to the prosodic stress, or that related to a metrical pattern, in the poem. Yet he, like most theorists, stabilizes "natural" stress in English speech as fixed, shared, pronunciation, just as he contrasts the variability of where we might locate prosodic stress in a line as with what he believes is the more objective and fixed count of syllables.[56] But the historical record shows clearly that this is not the case. There is no such thing as natural stress in English; the stress you learn is the stress that becomes natural to you. Stress in English cannot be universalized because there is no one way to sound English out loud; there is no one way to pronounce the sound of an English word. The "standard" sound of stress in the eighteenth century might be bound to accented syllables, to concepts of emphasis in elocution, to the rising interest in Anglo-Saxon metrical norms that accompanied the development of comparative linguistics. The historical marks for sound on the page give us a glimpse at the richness of engagement with the sound of writing over more than a century, and these failed attempts to fix sound to text should not be read as a reprimand to scholars, instructing them to be more accurate in their renditions; rather, it is simply to acknowledge that their retroprojections of sound are located in the present and not the past. To talk about sound in the past is to talk about the text of sound, and the text of sound in the past is long past due for translation.

NOTES

1. It would be a fascinating case study to put the concept of sound in George Gascoigne's *Certayne Notes of Instruction* (1575) beside that of John Hart's *Orthographie* (1569), for instance (though the latter wasn't republished until 1850, in a moment of frenetic phonetic activity in England).

2. Derrida's beef was not exactly with Saussure but with a concept of Saussure's thoughts found in the 1916 *Cours de linguistique générale*, which was compiled by Charles Bally and Albert Sechehaye from Saussure's lecture notes from the University of Geneva between 1906 and 1911. This disagreement is elaborated in Derrida's *Of Grammatology* (Baltimore: Johns Hopkins University Press, 1976). See Garrett Stewart, *Reading Voices: Literature and Phonotext* (Berkeley: University of California Press, 1990).

3. See David Crystal's website: http://originalpronunciation.com/GBR/Home; T. L. Burton and K. K. Ruthven, "Dialect Poetry, William Barnes and the Literary Canon," *ELH* 76 (2009): 309–41; T. L. Burton, *William Barnes's Dialect Poems: A Pronunciation Guide* (Adelaide: Chaucer Studio Press, 2010); and T. L. Burton *The Sound of William Barnes's Dialect Poems 1: Poems of Rurual Life in the Dorset Dialect, First Collection (1844)* (Adelaide: University of Adelaide Press,

2013). By contrast, in Susan Stewart's "Letter on Sound," the opening essay in Charles Bernstein's *Close Listening* (New York: Oxford University Press, 1998), Stewart writes that this sort of work is a "an absurd exercise in ventriloquism" (17n2). In its chapter form, expanded in Stewart's *Poetry and the Fate of the Senses* (Chicago: University of Chicago Press, 2001), the evocative term *ventriloquism* no longer appears.

4. I find the assumptions of American vs. British pronunciation fascinating, yet most teaching texts on prosody have very little to say about these variations. If there is a diacritical mark, it is interpreted as a sign for emphasis, not pronunciation. This shift (from pronunciation to emphasis) has a long history in English. One easy way to address the elision of this history, however, is to point out to students that idiomatic writing, dialect writing, and disruptions of a concept of "standard" English, in pre-1880s writing largely by and for white people, paralleled the developments of those "standards." For instance, parallel to the *New English Dictionary* project was Joseph Wright's *English Dialect Dictionary* (1898) and Samuel Johnson's suppression of Scots idioms and dialects in his *Dictionary of the English Language* (1755), which inspired Webster to define American English. Here, then, are examples of how the standardization of sound in text either erased communities of speakers or inspired their preservation. Playing one scene from *Pygmalion* with Henry Higgins teaching Eliza is a simple way to characterize this method or process of standardization becoming abstraction for students. Who is left out of the category of "the speaker" when standardized English is the only way we read for sound in poems?

5. See Meredith Martin, *The Rise and Fall of Meter: Poetry and English National Culture, 1860–1930* (Princeton, NJ: Princeton University Press, 2012).

6. I am less concerned with the tangible effects of reading poems from the past in performance today; these are "readings" or "adaptations" just as modern ideas of musical interpretation run up against original instrumentation. In writing about poetry, however, we tend not to think about how unstable the concepts of prosody and pronunciation were in the past. We therefore artificially close the historical distance between our contemporary linguistic or prosodic descriptive terms and past concepts of sound that provide useful, and sometimes crucial, ideological contexts.

7. I refer here specifically to sound studies in relation to poetic language and pronunciation, or sound that might be produced by a (real or imagined) voice or a speaker. John M. Picker's foundational book *Victorian Soundscapes* (Oxford: Oxford University Press, 2003) and works that follow offer a good introduction. In addition to Yopie Prins, I am drawing on helpful work from Max Cavitch, "Steven Crane's Refrain," *ESQ: A Journal of the American Renaissance* 54 (2008): 33–53; Nadia Nurhussein, *Rhetorics of Literacy: The Cultivation of American Dialect Poetry* (Columbus: Ohio State University Press, 2013); and Lisa Gitelman, *Scripts, Grooves, and Writing Machines: Representing Technology in the Edison Era* (Stanford, CA: Stanford University Press, 1999). Gitelman discusses "the potential failure of textual representation to recuperate aural experience" (52). How these concepts of sound and meter bear on notions of metrical form and prosody in the twentieth century is discussed by Ben Glaser in his *Modernism's Metronome* (Baltimore: Johns Hopkins University Press, 2020).

8. Eric Griffiths, *The Printed Voice of Victorian Poetry* (New York: Oxford University Press, 1989), 60; William Empson, *Seven Types of Ambiguity* (London: Hogarth, 1984), 27; Yopie Prins, "Voice Inverse," *Victorian Poetry* 42 (2004): 43–60, 45.

9. Neither Griffiths nor Empson takes into account actual reading practices in their study; rather, each focuses on a scene of reading taking place between one poem on a page (not voiced in real time by its author) and one reader (silently reading and holding multiple ambiguous "readings" of that poem in their head vs. reading the poem aloud). For an early overview of nineteenth-century reading, see Michael Cohen's useful review, "Reading the Nineteenth

Century," *American Literary History* 26, no. 2 (2014): 406–17; see also Matthew Bradley and Juliet John, eds., *Reading and the Victorians* (London: Routledge, 2015).

10. Prins, "Voice Inverse," 46.

11. Prins, 53.

12. Reuven Tsur has called the expressive effects of vowel sounds "acoustic energy," a phrase mobilized by Susan Stewart in her *Poetry and the Fate of the Senses*. See Reuven Tsur and Chen Gani, "Phonetic Symbolism: Double-Edgedness and Aspect-Switching," UConn Literary Universals Project (2019), https://literary-universals.uconn.edu/2019/07/20/phonetic-symbolism-double-edgedness-and-aspect-switching/#; and Reuven Tsur, *What Makes Sound Patterns Expressive* (Durham, NC: Duke University Press, 1992). See also Niklas Erben Johansson, Andrey Anikin, Gerd Carling, and Arthur Holmer, "The Typology of Sound Symbolism: Defining Macro-Concepts via Their Semantic and Phonetic Features," *Linguistic Typology* 24 (2020): 253–310.

13. William Gardner, *The Music of Nature; or, An Attempt to Prove That What Is Passionate and Pleasing in the Art of Singing, Speaking, and Performing upon Musical Instruments, Is Derived from the Sounds of the Animated World* (London: Longman, Rees, Orme, Brown, Green, and Longman, 1832) is by far my favorite example of this discourse.

14. Vendler argues that "a lyric is *a role offered to a reader*; the reader is to be the voice reading the poem." Helen Vendler, "*Tintern Abbey*: Two Assaults," in *Wordsworth in Context*, ed. Pauline Fletcher and John Murphy (Cranbury, NJ: Associated University Presses, 1992), 173–90, 184. This view was brought to my attention by way of Virginia Jackson and Yopie Prins, eds., *The Lyric Theory Reader: A Critical Anthology* (Baltimore: Johns Hopkins University Press, 2014). In the introduction to the sonnets of Shakespeare, Vendler further insists that "the act of the lyric is to offer its reader a script to say"; see Helen Vendler, *The Art of Shakespeare's Sonnets* (Cambridge, MA: Harvard University Press, 1997), 17. I am grateful to an anonymous reader for this citation. See also Angela Leighton, *Hearing Things: The Work of Sound in Literature* (Cambridge, MA: Harvard University Press, 2018).

15. There is even a website based on a class experiment that explores the poem's implied polyvocality: *He Do the Police in Different Voices*; see esp. "What the Class Said: Introduction and Background," http://hedothepolice.org/class.

16. Langston Hughes's "The Negro Speaks of Rivers" assumes, in its very title, that someone might use his recorded voice as the "text" instead of the poem's textual form and, in so doing, forces readers to rethink a category of universal "speaker" that might be performing or even reinforcing a politics of respectability. There are deeper political and racial histories to explore in twentieth-century vocal performances, which might lead fruitfully back to a reconsideration of the assumptions we bring to our readings of poems that do not present this complicated, multimediated layering of phonographic form but are no less mediated by complicated histories of the media of prosody.

17. Jonathan Culler, *Theory of the Lyric* (Cambridge, MA: Harvard University Press, 2015), 35.

18. See Meredith Martin, "Prosody and Meter: Early Modern to 19th Century," in *Oxford Bibliographies in British and Irish Literature*, ed. Andrew Hadfield (Oxford: Oxford University Press, 2009–). See also Martin, *Rise and Fall of Meter*.

19. Leighton, *Hearing Things*, 7.

20. Virginia Jackson, "Historical Poetics and the Dream of Interpretation: A Response to Paul Fry," *MLQ* 81 (Sept. 2020): 289–318, 293.

21. Leighton, *Hearing Things*, 18.

22. On T. S. Eliot's use of racialized dialect, see Michael North, "The Dialect in/of Modernism: Pound and Eliot's Racialized Masquerade," *American Literary History* 4 (1992): 56–76.

23. James Weldon Johnson, *The Book of American Negro Poetry* (New York: Harcourt, Brace, 1922).

24. Johnson, 70.

25. Michael Cohen, "Paul Laurence Dunbar and the Genres of Dialect," *African American Review* 41 (2007): 247–57, 250.

26. Johnson, *Book of American Negro Poetry*, 1922 ed., xxxix–xli, xl.

27. See Prins, "Voice Inverse"; and Yopie Prins "Historical Poetics, Dysprosody, and *The Science of English Verse*," *PMLA* 123 (2008): 229–34.

28. Stewart, *Poetry and the Fate of the Senses*, 68.

29. See Virginia Jackson, *Before Modernism: Inventing American Lyric* (Princeton, NJ: Princeton University Press, 2023); Virginia Jackson, "Apostrophe, Animation, and Racism," *Critical Inquiry* 48 (2022): 652–75; and Jackson, "Historical Poetics and the Dream."

30. See Marit J. MacArthur, "Monotony, the Churches of Poetry Reading, and Sound Studies," *PMLA* 131 (2016): 38–63; and Tanya Clement, "Anne Sexton Listening to Anne Sexton," *PMLA* 135 (2020): 387–92.

31. The *PMLA* "theories and methodology" cluster on "Aurality and Literacy" (135 [2020]: 350–418), edited by Christopher Cannon and Matthew Rubery, includes Paula McDowell, an amazing scholar of the invention of oral cultures in the eighteenth and nineteenth centuries, but her essay for that volume focuses on the influence of the elocutionary movement on theories of media history (see Paula McDowell, "Elsie McLuhan's Vocal Science," *PMLA* 135 [2020]: 378–86). Like McDowell, I urge a more careful consideration of the overlapping ways sound was scripted and thought to be meaning-making in the eighteenth and nineteenth centuries. Johanna Drucker's work—and work by contemporary book historians and media theorists—is invested in the graphical representation of sound in poetry but not in the discourse of sound in versification and pronunciation. See, for example, her *Visualization and Interpretation: Humanistic Approaches to Display* (Cambridge, MA: MIT Press, 2020); and *Graphesis: Visual Forms of Knowledge Production* (Cambridge, MA: Harvard University Press, 2014).

32. Manfred Görlach, *Studies in the History of the English Language* (Heidelberg: Carl Winter, 1990); Paula McDowell, *The Invention of the Oral* (Chicago: University of Chicago Press, 2017); Jeff Strabone, "Samuel Johnson: Standardizer of English, Preserver of Gaelic," *ELH* 77 (2010): 237–65; James Mulholland, *Sounding Imperial: Poetic Voice and the Politics of Empire, 1730–1820* (Baltimore: Johns Hopkins University Press, 2013).

33. See Martin, "Prosody and Meter"; see also Martin, *The Rise and Fall of Meter*; Yopie Prins, "Victorian Meters," in *The Cambridge Companion to Victorian Poetry* (Cambridge: Cambridge University Press, 2000), 89–113; and Prins, "Voice Inverse."

34. William Enfield's *The Speaker* (1774), xv–xvi: Rule V: Pronounce every word consisting of more than one syllable with its proper accent.

35. See William Logan, "Keats and the Pronunciation of 'Cortez,'" *New Criterion* 39 (2020): 20–25, for an example of stable versification as an excuse for (in this case poor) implied pronunciation.

36. I use Susan Wolfson's distinction between "formalist" reading (or "a concern for how poetic form is articulated and valued") and formalism here from her *Formal Charges* (Stanford, CA: Stanford University Press, 1999), 235n1. Herbert Tucker deploys this technique beautifully at the end of "The Fix of Form: An Open Letter," *Victorian Literature and Culture* 27 (1999): 531–35. Lynda Mugglestone's work on John Keats is also in this vein. See her "The Fallacy of the Cockney Rhyme: From Keats and Earlier to Auden," *Review of English Studies* 42 (1991): 57–66.

37. Prosodic readings of this kind are so common it is difficult to choose only a few

examples. Two will have to suffice: "Here the jolting punctuation and radically elliptical compression create a jarring separation between the semantic meaning of the words—her will is consonant with God's—and the disrupted rhythm, which requires multiple breaths within the line. It is as though the speaker is gasping through her lines." Marion Wells, "The Tears of Rachel: Lament and Affective Improvisation in Mary Carey's *Spiritual Dialogue, Meditations and Poems*," *ELH* 86 (2019): 669–97. "The prevalence of the guttural 'g' in this first line instantiate[s] repeated acts of pronunciation that draw attention to the role of the throat, which constricts rather than opens the pharyngeal airways. This constriction further implies a gasping for breath, suggestively staging suffocation and asphyxiation often characterizing the atrocities of war." Suzanne Zelazo, "Sounding Eyes: Mina Loy's Acoustic Subjectivity in 'The Song of the Nightingale Is like the Scent of Syringa,' " *English Studies in Canada* 33 (2007): 78–79.

38. The difficulty of reconstructing actual sound in the classical languages (despite the variety of texts asserting that Latin or Greek sounded a certain way) and the reliance on rules of versification to attempt such a reconstruction may be one reason that twentieth-century readings of nineteenth-century English versification keep proliferating imagined sounds of English. Like the cypher of Sappho, classical versification has stood in for our inability to engage with historical sound to begin with. And, again, that is not to say that engagement with classical versification—*how it might sound in English*—has not been fruitful and provided some friction against which other scholars who do think about historical sound might stake claims, but it is to say that the sound of classical versification—its problems and its indeterminacy, the fact that one would know an Eton man for his Latin pronunciation in the nineteenth century—have overshadowed the same problems and indeterminacy in English versification and how English poetry might sound.

39. Many of Walker's rhymes were lifted directly from Edward Bysshe's *The Art of English Poetry* so are themselves an inadequate measure. See Natalie Houston, "Distant Reading Nineteenth-Century British Poetry with Rhyme Networks," *Understanding Rhyme through Network Analysis* (abstracts of papers given at the 2020 Digital Humanities Conference: https://dh2020.adho.org/wp-content/uploads/2020/07/134_UnderstandingRhymeThroughNetwork Analysis.html).

40. Edward Bysshe, *The Art of English Poetry* (1702). See also A. Dwight Culler, "Edward Bysshe and the Poets Handbook," *PMLA* 63 (1948): 858–85; and Stephen Jarrod Bernard, "Edward Bysshe and 'The Art of English Poetry': Reading Writing in the Eighteenth Century," *Eighteenth-Century Studies* 46 (2012): 113–29.

41. McDowell, *Invention of the Oral*. See also the 1998 special issue of *The Yearbook of English Studies* 28: "Eighteenth-Century Lexis and Lexicography," ed. Andrew Gurr, especially the essays by Anne McDermott, "Johnson's 'Dictionary' and the Canon: Authors and Authority" (44–65); and Nicholas Hudson, "Johnson's 'Dictionary' and the Politics of 'Standard English,' " (77–93). See also Strabone, "Samuel Johnson"; Jacqueline George, "Public Reading and Lyric Pleasure: Eighteenth Century Elocutionary Debates and Poetic Practices," *ELH* 76 (2009): 371–97; David Fairer, "The Origins of Warton's History of English Poetry," *Review of English Studies*, n.s., 32 (1981): 37–63; and Manfred Görlach, *Eighteenth-Century English* (Heidelberg: Carl Winter, 2001).

42. Lynda Mugglestone, "Prescription, Pronunciation, and Issues of Class in the Late Eighteenth and Nineteenth Centuries," *Sentences for Alan Ward: Essays Presented to Alan Ward on the Occasion of His Retirement from Wadham College*, ed. Dan M. Reeks (Oxford: Bosphoros, 1988), 175–82.

43. William Kenrick, *A Rhetorical Grammar of the English Language* (London: R. Cadell, 1773).

44. Janet Sorensen's *The Grammar of Empire in Eighteenth-Century British Writing* (Cambridge: Cambridge University Press, 2000); Andrew Elfenbein's *Romanticism and the Rise of English* (Stanford, CA: Stanford University Press, 2009); and Haruko Momma's *From Philology to English Studies: Language and Culture in the Nineteenth Century* (Cambridge: Cambridge University Press, 2015) together chart a path through an undertheorized discourse about language and nation that might help us think differently about what we mean when we talk about sound in English poetry. Sorensen lays out the important ways that Samuel Johnson, Adam Smith, and Hugh Blair navigate the integration of the inland empire as a foundational part of English polite speech; Elfenbein tracks historical grammatical change and its impact on Romantic era poetry; and Momma provides a comprehensive and compelling account of the continuities between English studies and philology, showing how our study of literature is scaffolded on the work of scholars whose primary aim was to find and fix both the origins and futures of language.

45. John Ash, "Dissertation VI: On Accent, Emphasis, and Quantity," in *The New and Complete Dictionary of the English Language: To Which Is Prefixed a Comprehensive Grammar*, 2 vols. (London: Printed for Edward and Charles Dilly and R. Baldwin, 1775), 1:23–25.

46. Ash, 1:25.

47. Thomas Sheridan, *Lectures on the Art of Reading* (London: J. Dodsley, Pall-Mall, J. Wilkie, St. Paul's Church-Yard; E. and C. Dilly, in the Poultry; and T. Davies, Russel-Street, Covent Garden, 1775), 13.

48. Thomas Sheridan, *A General Pronouncing and Explanatory Dictionary of the English Language* (London: Vernor and Hood, 1798); Thomas Sheridan, *A Complete Dictionary of the English Language* (London: Charles Dilly, in the Poultry, 1789).

49. William Perry, *The Royal Standard English Dictionary* (Worcester, MA: Isaiah Thomas, 1788), 10.

50. For more on this conflict, see Massimo Sturiale, "William Perry's *The Royal Standard English Dictionary*," *Historiographica Linguistica* 33 (2006): 139–68.

51. William Perry, *The Royal Standard Dictionary* (London: David Willison, 1775), 8–9.

52. See Richard Mulcaster's, *Elementarie*, ed. with an introduction by E. T. Campagna (1582; Oxford: Clarendon Press, 1925), 121:

> The particular *rule* examineth the force of all such characts, as we vse in writing, whereof there be two kindes: the one signifying and sounding: the other signifying, but not sounding. Those characts which signify but sound not, ar certain notes, which we vse in the writing of our English túg for the qualifying of words, & sentences in their pronouncing, by that which is sene in the form of our writing, which can be núber thirtene, in name & form these: *Cõma* , *Colon* : *Period* . *Parenthesis* (.) *interrogation* ? the long time — the short time ˘ the sharp accent ´ the flat accét ` the ſtreight accét | the ſeuerer “ the vniter the breaker = I vse the foré and originall names in most of these, bycause both the notes themselues be of a foren brede, and theie be commonlie best known by their own cuntrie names : I might darken more if I should deuise new names, then by enfranchising of the foren, a thing comon to all speches, which vse the translate terms of anie Art.

53. Esther K. Sheldon, "Pronouncing Systems in Eighteenth-Century Dictionaries," *Language* 22 (1946): 27–47, 27.

54. John Walker, preface to *A Critical Pronouncing Dictionary and Expositor of the English Language* (London: G. G. J. and Robinson, Paternoster Row and T. Cadell, in the Strand, 1791), iii–viii, vi.

55. Henry Sweet, *The Sounds of English* (Oxford: Clarendon Press, 1908), 8.

56. See Allen Grossman, *Summa Lyrica: A Primer of the Commonplaces in Speculative Poetics*, in *The Sighted Singer: Two Works on Poetry for Readers and Writers*, with Mark Halliday (Baltimore: Johns Hopkins University Press, 1992), 373–74:

> Stress both in the natural language and in the context of the poem points diacritically to the meaning-bearing element in the word. Where there is dispute about stress the reader need only accept as an obligation the semantic consequences of any given stressing. . . . Stressing is the inscription of the subjective or meaning-intending volition of the speaker (this is for the reader). We may dispute about stress. Syllable count, by contrast, is by its nature at the other extreme of intersubjectivity. It has the character of the "objective" and we do not dispute about it, only correct one another with the understanding that the solution to the counting problem will be univocal. Stress is the point of presence of the hermeneutic issue in the substance of the hermeneutic object itself.

CHAPTER SEVEN

Music Writing and Music History in a Thirteenth-Century Song

Sean Curran

In this essay, I am concerned with the history *of* and the history *in* the genre of the motet in the mid-thirteenth century, and I pursue that history through an account—by turns literary critical, music analytical, and paleographical—of a single piece that exemplifies, traces, and characterizes it.[1]

To a new listener, motets of the "polytextual" sort that are my particular concern usually make an impression of complexity: three or even four voices simultaneously putting forth different texts, often in different languages (Latin and French), and set to different melodies. The sonic unruliness that results has provoked varied responses. Haunting them all has been the question of how so abstruse a sound could make sense to historical listeners both medieval and modern.[2] One would wish for clear social-historical data in considering that question. Who sang these pieces? How? Under what circumstances? For whom? But the motet's was a repertory that circulated almost entirely anonymously and without composer attributions, and the social practices that carried it did not generate most forms of ancillary documentation (records of payment to musicians, for example), which music historians handling later periods conventionally adduce when answering such social-historical questions.

Lacking much documentation of the motet's social and institutional milieu, scholarship has tried to infer one from its constitutive parts and has found itself looking in two quite different directions. In one direction, the motet with French text may be viewed against the backdrop of monophonic songs with texts in vernacular Old French (the so-called *trouvère* repertory). In a different direction are the ivory towers of the Cathedral of Notre Dame (to whose repertory of liturgical polyphony the earliest surviving, Latin-texted motets are closely related: see below) and the University of Paris that was growing up around it. It is this latter pole to which the needle of the historiographical compass has, by default and almost inevitably, pointed (or, when it has twitched, to which it has snapped back), especially in accounting for polytextual motets. To whom else could such a sophisticatedly complex music have made sense? This side of the field has taken the genre's sonic and discursive complexity to confirm that the motet's home was the Cathedral and University of Paris; that the makers, performers, and audiences were the learned; and, above all, that the condition of the polytextual motet's possibility was *writing*.

After this setup, one might suppose the aim of this essay is to set out a middle ground on which the historiographical sides may meet. That is not so—or, not quite.[3] This is because, as we will see shortly, the modern disciplinary predilection for the motet's writtenness was shared, or rather was stridently urged, by just the thirteenth-century Parisian academics in question. Moreover, we will see that these presuppositions could be voiced compositionally from within a motet *and* be subjected by its articulate formal design to skeptical investigation. Thus, my rather different aim here is to show that our unevenly divided historiography originated *and was self-consciously historiographical in* the thirteenth century, when (at one or another level of cultural consciousness and by social processes only blurrily perceptible) decisions were being made about how and precisely which skills of writing and of reading would henceforth structure the field of musical production.[4] To offer a manner of reading a motet capable of supporting such a claim is one of my primary goals.

I take as a case study the motet *Par une matinee* (807) / *Mellis stilla* (808) / ALLELUYA (unidentified), and my argument proceeds by the following steps.[5] First, I sketch the history and characteristics of the thirteenth-century motet to illustrate why the form has so often been taken as definitionally learned (and also why the historiographical compass needle has twitched). That will lead us briefly to reexamine a much-mined passage on the social reach of the genre from a contemporary commentator, Johannes de Grocheio, who asserted that it *should* be definitionally learned. From the manner in which he makes the assertion will be pressed new evidence that he knew it was not. Then, we take up the motet itself, treating its voices in turn, starting from its triplum (that is, one could translate creatively, the "third voice up" in each system of the edition of the piece presented in appendix 1), and only then moving to consider at length the tenor-motetus pair (the "bottom" and "middle" voices of my score), which affords the motet its most salient structural scaffolding. We will see that the Old French triplum *Par une matinee* swaggers with the writerly clerical confidence found in Grocheio: a calculated effect reducible neither to the triplum's text nor to its music alone but that is produced uniquely by their brilliant conjunction. That analysis will show that the triplum was composed with a sophisticated knowledge of the formal devices that lent shape to contemporaneous Old French monophonic songs, here bent to a statement (in its own way as articulate and as questionable as was Grocheio's) about the distinguishing *writtenness* of the motet genre, about its merit to be documented, and about its historical worthiness.[6] What permits us not only to raise but to provide new answers to such questions are some suspicious features of the tenor (which, for this period, "should" be a quotation from a plainchant: the genre-sketch in the next section will explain why) and of its unusual and striking fit to the motetus *Mellis stilla*. But more striking still is the variety of manuscripts (and of *kinds* of books) that report *Mellis stilla* under several different but recognizably familiar forms and in manners of writing quite foreign to the domain staked out so proudly by *Par une matinee*. Having followed *Mellis stilla* across the length and breadth of the medieval Latin West, we will—at last—be in a position to listen again to all of our motet's voices, together, and to hear with altered understanding an old form of art whose proud novelty was to stake a claim to have been made worthy of history.

Histories of the Motet

The thirteenth-century motet is a genre that may benefit from introduction.[7] The motet was probably born when musicians at the Cathedral of Notre Dame experimented with supplying words to the melismatic "discant clausulae" that studded their polyphonic settings of chants for the Mass and Office on major liturgical feasts.[8] This sort of discant was characterized by the use of measured, proportional rhythm. The original pitches of the chant would be disposed into short phrases of a repeating rhythmic pattern to create a "tenor" (named from Latin *tenēre*, "to hold," with good sense: this foundational part literally holds the music together). Above the tenor would be crafted one, two, or three further new voices, also measured into "long" and "short" notes (*longae* and *breves*) related in proportion to one another in patterns characteristic of one of six flexible rhythmic systems—the "rhythmic modes." Against the regularly periodic phrases of a tenor's "rhythmic ostinato,"[9] upper voices (*duplum, triplum, quadruplum*) could phrase in myriad and varied ways, from the highly regular to the artfully unpredictable. By consequence, when poetry was added to the music (similar to the intensively rhyming, accentual sort of Latin *ritmus* so popular in Paris of the twelfth century and showcased in the genre of the sequence, especially as associated with the Abbey of St. Victor), its versification could display a similar abundance and variety of formal designs.[10] By mid-century, motets were being composed from scratch in one, two, or three voices in any combination of French, Latin, or both, all sung simultaneously above a chant-derived tenor. Often, however, one or more of the upper voices of these motets we call "polytextual" will share its music with another motet-voice, reported elsewhere and perhaps in another language, forming complex webs of citation and recomposition whose charting has been the stuff of industrious scholarship for several generations.[11] A final detail is that French-texted motets often contain snippets of citations, too (or stichs of poetry or melody crafted to sound as if they *might* be citations); among the words medieval people used to describe this phenomenon (which we call a "refrain") was the term *motet*, and this may be the source of the Latin term *motetus*.[12]

It has in recent years become a happy convention of music-historical scholarship to characterize the motet by—and to champion—its manifold and creatively rich hybridities.[13] As the foregoing stylistic narrative will already have communicated, motets of our period bear resemblances to and quotations from several different repertories of song, both liturgical and worldly, and this range of deictic reference compounds the fundamental problem, already mentioned, that we have almost no empirical evidence about the performance practices associated with this music.

This deictic plurality has caused the occasional historiographical vacillations away from the Parisian and scholastic paradigm. Certainly, it has long been observed that some motets were collected into books of a sort we have come to call *chansonniers*; and relating motets with Old French texts to Old French monophonic songs, scholarship has from time to time supposed that *vernacular* polyphonic practices might have surrounded, or complemented, or even influenced in some way the polytextual motet of the mid-thirteenth century.[14] Nevertheless, these have remained largely beyond scholarly discussion under the assumption that they were unwritten and are therefore lost to us.[15] Polyphonic sources whose contents are not polytextual, or whose writing is not easily placed on a developmental line from modal to Franconian notations, have often been designated "peripheral," "simple," or even "primitive,"[16] this notwithstanding predictable and sustained critiques of "center" versus "periphery" models and of evolutionary ones that prioritize the development of notations at the expense of the social practices sustaining their creation.[17] In our most recent histories, the motet's learnedness still seems to place it squarely in Paris, around Notre Dame and the University. In general, the polytextual motet has seemed too complicated to have been conceived other than in writing and too abstruse in its sound to have been meaningful to anyone except university men.[18]

A medieval advocate for this view has been found in the *Ars musice* of Johannes de Grocheio, our lone thirteenth-century commentator on matters music-sociological.[19] Of the motet, he writes, "This song, moreover, ought not to be yielded up before common people [*coram vulgalibus*]—because they do not pay attention to its subtlety, and neither are they delighted in hearing it—but before those with letters [*coram litteratis*] and those who are seeking out the subtleties of the arts."[20] I am not the first to find these words suspicious, but I may be the first to find them genuinely audacious.[21] It is not the prescription in itself that is remarkable; Grocheio makes plenty of those. It is rather that this is the only *negative* such prescription in the whole treatise—the only time, that is, that Grocheio opines on how or by whom a musical genre should *not* be made rather than by whom it should.[22] But what marks his words as polemical, I think, is how they rupture the form he declaredly aspires to create in the treatise.[23] This form, which has been long in the making by the time the motet is discussed, takes Paris as adequate synecdoche for the world at large: to account for the music of Paris will be to account for what is important everywhere, he asserts, because "in our times, the principles of whatever liberal art you like are diligently investigated in Paris, and their practices and those of pretty much all of the mechanical arts are found there too."[24] Grocheio proceeds to divide his synecdochic musical Paris into three "membra generalia" or "general branches" (60, par. 6.2). But each of the three branches is defined untidily by a bundle of concepts, which results in overloaded and unparallel constructions: "We say that one branch concerns monophonic [*simplici*] or civil music, which we call *vulgalis*. On the other hand, another concerns polyphonic [*composita*] music or regulated [i.e., by modal rhythm] or canonic, which they call rhythmically-measured music [*musica mensurata*]. But the third kind is what is effected from these two and to which these two are, as it were, ordered for the better. This is called ecclesiastical, and it is assigned for the praise of the Creator."[25]

So when Grocheio gets around to his discussion of the motet—part of his second, "canonic" *membrum* of music—the *vulgalibus* (whoever they are) should have no business in this part of the treatise, and they arrive here only to be scorned. Whatever they were doing with the motet, it would seem, they did it loud enough to bring the walls of Grocheio's musical Paris tumbling down. From this it should be clear that this prevalent view of the social history of the early motet is not some merely modern belief; it has medieval origins, and its expression in Grocheio's treatise gives us reason to wonder what we're missing.

Not so evident, and therefore the major purpose of this essay to disclose, is that—as I will argue—opinions about the social life of music could also be articulated compositionally; that is, they could be rendered available for recognition to us as to interested medieval parties of Grocheio's sort as the cumulative product of the various structured lines of verbal and musical thought a motet puts forth in time for minds to follow.[26] They may especially be perceived through pieces that direct conscious attention to effects of musical style that their poetic texts construe as distinctively writerly.

To make that case, I offer an extended analysis of *Par une matinee / Mellis stilla / Alleluya*. In its musical style as much as in its text, the motet's triplum is as confident an advocate as Grocheio for the unique power of music writing to manipulate style and to divide categories of people by kinds of literate musical skill they ought to have. But ironically, this bilingual version of the piece seems only to have had very limited circulation and is now found in only two sources: the "La Clayette" manuscript (Paris, BnF n.a.fr. 13521) and the Montpellier Codex (Montpellier, Bibliothèque universitaire Historique de Médecine, H 196). Meanwhile, elements of the same piece—especially the motetus *Mellis stilla*—are found in various and telling configurations across sixteen known manuscripts; smaller units of its text appear in still further songs.[27] I give a detailed reading of La Clayette's version of the piece in tandem with a paleographical examination of some of the other manuscript witnesses to suggest that this motet's different voices tell competing stories about the motet as a written genre. *Par une matinee* was composed with an agenda, one that *Mellis stilla* can be used to question.

It is by now uncontroversial when dealing with works of the fourteenth century, whose *ars nova* notations were more powerful still than those of the thirteenth, to find in songs explicit compositional play with the idea of the power that resides in their notation.[28] Guillaume de Machaut—secretary, composer, and consummate historical obfuscator—was well aware of the power of music books to shape his legacy and of their capacity to be tools with which to tell stories about the historical import of his prowess as a composer.[29] The piece I examine here shows Machaut was late to the game in recognizing that music writing could manipulate the historical record. Pieces like *Mellis stilla* offer the opportunity to listen for the perceived musical conditions that made declarations of music-technological prowess possible. In adumbrating those conditions, we find that compositions such as *Par une matinee* were manipulations bound up with the creation of a written historical record for polyphony and that they promoted the idea of written music's difference from "oral" cultures. Over time, their manipulations have come to seem transparently factual as witnesses to the social practice of polyphony *tout court*. They are not.

Polyphony, Out of Earshot

Consider the Old French poem *Par une matinee*, the triplum of our polytextual motet.[30] (Appendix 1 presents [a] the texts and translations of the motet's parts, [b] an edition of the piece, and [c] an analytical transcription of the triplum.) If we follow it closely, it will lead us to one song concealed within another.

Like most vernacular motet texts, this one bears many generic hallmarks of the Old French lyric world by which it was originally surrounded.[31] An unnamed narrator—after the manner of a pastourelle, let's call him a "chevalier"—recounts a journey he made into a grove pleasantly bustling with birdsong.[32] There, he overhears "little Marot"; in her sobs and sighs he takes an equal (though more sinister) aural delight. Hers is not a happy song: the Old French verb *dementer*, here in present active participle ("dementant," v. 19), means something stronger than "grieving" or "lamenting"; it is not without the connotations of modern English "demented."[33] Perhaps having heard her cries, however, Marot's lover, Robin, arrives, singing ("chantent," v. 21), and it's not too long before she and Robin exit the scene, happily occupied in what the narrator describes as "games" ("ieus," v. 26).

Before we think about the musical setting of this motet—its most overtly musical sounds—it is worth listening more closely to the soundscape the lyric describes. It would seem on a first reading to record three sorts of sound: Marot's lament (v. 4), which later (vv. 15–18) morphs into a more formal utterance; the birdsong (vv. 7–8); then Robin's singing (v. 21). It is no surprise that we get birdsong, a standard attribute of the nature opening in all sorts of contemporaneous lyrics.[34] But the jarring pleonasm with which it is reported by verses 7–8—"un *chant* mout jolif / doiseillonnez *chantanz*" (a song of singing birds)—makes Marot's human vocalization seem only ambiguously musical by comparison, given that it is introduced by a form of the less obviously melodic verb *dire*, "disant" (v. 14)—significantly, another present participle.[35] So when Robin arrives in the act of singing (yet again with a present participle, "chantent," v. 21), sonic clarity returns—which is all the more curious, for the "muffled" middle section of this ABA′-form of imagined vocal timbres contained the narration of an actual performance. We will ponder what lies behind that sounded haze shortly, but this is not the song for which we are searching.

Rather, we should listen closely to the moment Marot runs to greet Robin, at verses 22–23, when, as the chevalier reports, "encontre li sen uet marot / mout grant ioie fesant." To this point, all of Marot's actions have been (at least implicitly) sonic—she sighs, she mourns, and she makes a performance articulate enough for words to be discerned from it—and they have all been introduced with participles. We might go so far as to say that for Marot, the relation of emotion to sonic expression has been an unpremeditated one and that when she acts an emotion in a present participle, it is identifiable to the chevalier only insofar as it makes a trace he can *hear*. So notice that in verse 23, Marot is again *making* her *joie*. Like her other participles, *fesant* can be understood as a verb of performance: it makes sense to "faire une chanson" after all. So I submit that it is the sonic trace of Marot's joy that she is *making* "encontre" the singing Robin and that encased within this emotive metonym is a faintly audible music to which the word *encontre* gestures knowingly. Whether used as a preposition or an adjective, *encontre* connotes opposition, of one thing being against another; most simply, it suggests the two characters stand face-to-face or side by side.[36] But sharing its root with Latin *contrapunctus* (counterpoint), it brings music with it, too, in this period when theoretical prescriptions for singing harmonies were coming to be expressed with the idiom "punctus *contra* punctum."[37] So, Robin's declared song is only half of what the chevalier heard, albeit that it is all he reports directly. It is what the lovers are singing *together* that is our concealed song. As they go on their way (to who knows where), *polyphony* wanders off beyond audible horizons.

Reading Marot's Song

How does the music of the triplum *Par une matinee* respond to the shifts of voice described in its text and their implied registers of performance? The most revealing answers to that question come when we view the triplum from a new perspective, looking closely as we do so at its medieval notation.

To help with that, appendix 1(c) gives an analytical transcription of the triplum in which lines are divided wherever there is a notated rest, thus to make its phrase structure plain to the eye.[38] As with the transcription into modern notation in appendix 1(b), dotted bar lines are added to group the notes into measures of a duration called by most theorists in the second half of the thirteenth century the "perfect long" or the "perfection."

In appendix 1(c), I also preserve the note shapes used in the La Clayette manuscript.[39] Of these, there are three basic forms for representing one note sung to one syllable, each corresponding to one of the three rhythmic entities found in *musica mensurata* (i.e., "mensural" or "proportionally measured" polyphony of the thirteenth century): (1) the *longa* (henceforth the "long," or simply "L"); (2) the *brevis* (now conventionally anglicized as the "breve," here abbreviated "B"); and (3) the *semibrevis* (the "semibreve," or "S"). Graphically, the long is formed with a square notehead plus a descending tail on the right (and is identical in form to the *virga* of contemporary chant manuscripts, from whose notational script it was borrowed and applied to this very different kind of rhythmic situation).[40] The breve was represented by a square notehead with no tail (thus corresponding to the *punctus* of chant books); the semibreve was represented with a rhomb (usually found in chant books as a component of a descending multinote figure called a *climacus*).[41]

Graphical forms used in this manner of notating were more thoroughly dependent than are modern notational forms on the local context of their use for correct rhythmic realization, and evaluation depends particularly on the signs' position relative to one another in a given series of pitches. Thus, by the time the triplum *Par une matinee* was composed (which I take to have been the third quarter of the thirteenth century), two species of long shared the same *virga* sign (the *longa perfecta*, containing three *tempora* or units of time; and the *longa imperfecta*, containing two *tempora*), and two species of breve (the *brevis recta*, the "correct breve," which lasted for one *tempus*; and the *brevis altera*, the "other kind of breve," which lasted for two *tempora*). This much is enough to illustrate that there is in this notation a still wider gap between sight and sound—between the graphical form of a note and the empirical duration it is intended to represent—than modern music-readers are habituated to navigate in performance from notations that developed later.[42]

Now, the decision to realize a long as *perfecta* or *imperfecta* and a breve as *recta* or *altera* was well governed by principles of widespread acceptance and put forth in a developing canon of music-theoretical treatises about *musica mensurata* ("[rhythmically] measured music").[43] But the third note-shape, the rhomboid *semibrevis*, enjoyed no such authoritative governance in the mid-thirteenth century (either as a sound or as a notational sight). The sign enjoyed, instead, a flexibility of application to any rhythmic values shorter than the breve—but with the result of concomitant uncertainties, in particular cases, about precisely what sounded rhythms the written signs were intended to communicate.[44] That is to say, despite nascent attempts to submit it to theoretical governance, the semibreve remained for the most part *ultra mensuram*, "beyond measurement" in practice ("beyond," that is, because its quick sounds were too short to register on the scale of measurement set by the arbiter of the *tempus*).[45]

Through what follows, I will suggest that these uncertainties could be the basis of creative musicopoetic play on the part of composers. To preserve the medieval notation in appendix 1(c)'s transcription, then, is to empower criticism with readier access to that play. Meanwhile, to view the triplum in terms of its phrase lengths is to see that its narrator is not only well versed in the topical world of Old French monophonic songs; he is also familiar with, and turns to representational purpose, the devices that give them form.

In midcentury motet style, and especially in bilingual motets, we might expect the upper voices to fall into an array of varying phrase lengths against the tenor *ordines*.[46] That is true of *Par une matinee*, whose phrases range in duration from two perfect longs (henceforth 2L) to 6L. But closer inspection finds this stylistic resource to be subject to careful control from the outset and responsive to the verse structure in a way that orders a style that in other motets might merely be artfully unruly into a form suggestive of monophonic song.

Musical notation of this period is fundamentally syllabic in conception, one syllable of text corresponding to one grapheme in the music (and short melodic flourishes on the same syllable grouped into one multipitch figure, called a "ligature" when the constituent pitches are graphically joined, or a *coniunctura* when they show internal separation). Scanning verses 1 to 7 with a notator's eye thus yields a syllable-structure of 7676 555, segmenting as a quatrain with cross-rhyme plus a tercet of b-rhymed lines (abab bbb).[47]

As set in melody, the triplum begins with two phrases each of 4L, each carrying two verses of poetry (a verse of seven syllables followed by one of six in each case). Their phraseological parallelism redoubles the verse rhyme, for the ab pair in phrase I is answered by the ab′ pair of phrase II. Moreover, the parallel is articulated tonally, with phrase I's open termination on *b* answered by phrase II's closed arrival at *c*.[48] If the musical phraseology projects the first four verses as a quatrain, phrase III can then be understood as an answering tercet. Setting three five-syllable verses (5–7) each over a span of 2L, the phrase is shaped to articulate the verses' rhyme syllables with an internal pattern inaugurated by the pair of 1L melismata at mm. 10 and 12 (to end verses 5 and 6) and completed by the emphatic, one-note articulation (for the rhyme syllable of verse 7) on the downbeat of m. 14. Moreover, that arrival also signals that a higher-level milestone has been reached, for it returns the triplum to the same pitch (*a*) from which it departed on its journey in phrase I.

The sum of all this is remarkable: the versification shows that the poet-composer frames what would otherwise be merely the beginning of a motet triplum as the beginning of a *song*. And because the purpose of that song is to tell the encounter the chevalier claims to have had with Marot, he thereby figures the chevalier as *author* of the song he sings.[49] The details are intricate but clear in their bearing. We have a miniaturization of a seven-line strophe divided as a quatrain and a tercet articulated in the music by an XXY form—that is, by the cornerstone music-formal unit of thirteenth-century Old French vernacular monophony, and later of the fourteenth-century *formes fixes*.[50] Thus the motet's poet-composer complements the text's pastourelle topic with a gesture toward a monophonic song's strophic structure.

What comes next confirms the suggestion that there is a strophism-in-miniature afoot: fundamentals of both the versification structure of verses 1–7 and the musical XXY form of phrases I–III proceed to repeat (with interpretable variation) in verses 8–14 and phrases IV–VIII. Thus, again, the poetry segments into a quatrain plus tercet with the respective syllable counts 6776 (the count of the first two verses thus reversed) and 565 (where the six-syllable verse is segmented by the musical phrasing as 1+5); their emerging rhyme scheme (again disregarding the terminal consonants of uncertain phonemic value) again reinforces that segmentation and could be represented as cdc[d/b] bbc. (The ambiguity I label "[d/b]" will be addressed presently.) Like phrases I and II, phrases IV and V also each last 4L, each set a poetic couplet (verses 8–9 and 10–11, respectively); once again, there follows a tercet (vv. 12–14) of which each verse is carried through 2L (phrases VI–VIII, mm. 23–24, 26–27, and 28–29 respectively; I will deal with the extraneous m. 25 in a moment, too), the rhyme syllables placed on the downbeat of the second long in each case, and each also serving as the only phonetic event in a whole 1L measure.

This all constitutes an interpretable *gesture*: a *representation* of monophonic form rather than a direct reproduction. The fact is suggested by the ways in which the device of strophic repetition is implied but adapted, and to contrastively interpretable results. Thus, the quatrain of verses 8–11 also points toward cross-rhyme, to that extent constituting a repeat of the form of verses 1–4. But verses 9 and 11 (which should correspond with one another under this interpretation) are aparallel, because verse 9 has the diphthong "moi," where verse 11 has disyllabic "o-ï."

While they do not rhyme to the ear, their identical manuscript orthography means they *do* rhyme to the *eye*.[51] (This is why I labeled the rhyme of verse 11 as "[d/b]"; to the ear, verse 11 reverts to the b-rhyme introduced in verse 2.) Our narrator is not only a versifier, then; he is a literate one who imagines how his song will be beheld on the page once he is done.

Other departures from the established formal shaping, however, connote rather less narratorial cerebration. Considering pitch structure, we find that the *ouvert-clos* (*b-c*) relationship of phrases I and II is switched to yield "*clos-ouvert*" in phrases IV and V (*closed c* at m. 18, answered by *open b* at m. 22); this stall in melodic logic is doubled by the repetition at the start of phrase V (that is, in the middle of the new quatrain) of the intonation figure (*a-a-G-a-c*) with which the triplum set off in m. 1. Thus, components of the first "strophe's" form recur scrambled as this second one comes about; and the imperfect repetition suggests a narrative divide between the figural singer (whose voice is losing its composure) and his figured song (to whose correct formal rendition he nevertheless aspires).

Thus, as he prepares himself to report Marot's emotive arousal, the chevalier suffers a loss of vocal control that betrays his own. The comedic high point is literally that: the effusive top *g* in m. 25 is the highest note we hear in the piece. To boot, it sets the *first* syllable of a new verse (indeed, the conjunction *et*) as the most exposed of musical phrase *endings*; it teeters on a verge where articulate expression passes into a vocable or an index of emotional extremity, as if the *et* were a fragmentary first syllable "hé" awaiting a "-las" not granted (the verse and voice breaking off into the momentary silence of m. 25^3).[52] Following the effusion, the cohesion of his strophe is imperiled: each is now set to a separate phrase (nos. VI–VIII), the rests breaking the line so as to suggest our narrator needs to catch his breath.

Finally, we hear what Marot has to say. Against the narrator's clever composing, her performance comes up short. If she achieves a strophe at all, it comprises only a modest four verses (nos. 15–18, phrases IX–XI), rather than the narrator's grander seven, and no rhyme-scheme to speak of (that problem, again, of the phonemic status of the terminal consonants). It also seems to break off before reaching a proper close: her final words, "por quoi demorez uoz tant?," would constitute an "imperfect" phrase ending according to thirteenth-century theorists, finishing as they do on the final breve of a perfection (at m. 36^3) rather than on the first breve of a new one.[53] And as her diction dissolves into rapid-fire syllables, it is as if her voice becomes sheer, unprocessed vocal sound. Precisely at stake, it seems, is just what kind of human sounding practice our narrator is representing: whether it is singing or just emotive noise and how the two should be distinguished. This sustains an ambiguity the narrator evidently courts when he introduces her song with the participle *disant*. Again: from *dire*, this verb's semantic range can encompass both song and speech, but it is not specifically either.[54] The point is only redoubled by a nasty bit of mimicry on the narrator's part: perhaps cutting short the reportage, he finishes phrase XI, which Marot had begun, by echoing the texture and contour of her final utterance from m. 36 in descending melodic sequence at m. 37 to the words "issi se uait dementant." The deictic *issi* (like this) is provocatively positioned right on the semibreves whose interpretation is at stake. *Like what?*, we might ask. What kind of noise *is* Marot making?

The triplum asserts two antithetical answers with equal force. When we first hear words from her (see m. 30), they come out in a triplet rhythm we have heard once before: back in phrase IV (see m. 15), where it figured the "song of the singing birds." The purpose of the pleonasm is now clear: it tells us that Marot is indeed singing—at least, insofar as birds sing (an open question: see below). Perhaps it was her song the narrator had heard echoing through the woods all along.

The contrastive assertion is made through the graphical forms of the notation in which Marot's sound is recorded. According to notation theorists of the mid-thirteenth century, a single breve could not be broken into any more than three semibreves, and no sign was yet in use that could capture smaller values.[55] Moreover, as Elizabeth Eva Leach has shown, subbreve note values used by singers were often metaphorized as avian in the theoretical tradition because, like birdsong, they were an unwritable and therefore irrational utterance.[56] So as Marot's song takes flight, her syllables get so fast as almost to become nonsense: four semibreves must be pressed into the space where both music theory and contemporaneous musical scripts can unambiguously handle only three. Heard that way, Marot's sound is an irrational chirping, *no more* articulate than the birdsong by which she is surrounded.

The brilliance of this is that the narrator has created an array of written signs that can stand figuratively for the unwritable. In the fiction he narrates, countless smaller notes, countless lost sounds, might once have lain beyond the representational barrier he puts up.[57]

Still more brilliant is the representation's double edge. Marot might perfectly well be singing or wailing: because both options are deliberately kept in play, the narrator admits that the two categories *are* in principle distinguishable. But his *polemical* position is that the distinction basically doesn't matter, because if this is anything less than literate music, who cares? Emerging from all of this is a startlingly modern construction of a category of "oral music," as that amorphous zone inversely constituted by the written. Pastourelles such as this always work on an autobiographical and historical logic: that they render in sung form an encounter that took place, once upon a time. Here the narrator admits to the realm of the hearable, the repeatable, and so, I contend, to the musically historical, only that which is made in a writerly way. He had always been listening to her song as much with his *eyes* as with his ears. When first he met her, the narrator had *read* Marot's song; yet in doing so, he invented its illegibility.

This brings us to the first of several conclusions about our own historiographies of the early motet, which this analysis permits us to see in a long view *from ahead* rather than in the retrospective vista I set out earlier. One reason our historiographies about the motet's distinguished relation to writing are hard to think around is that motets themselves were among the vehicles by which thought on the distinction of music writing was relayed. Polytextual motets of the mid-thirteenth century could manifest the same self-consciousness about the technological and social significance of written composition as does Grocheio. That is to say, already in the thirteenth century, the motet had a *historiographical* voice.

The Many Faces of *Mellis stilla*

That voice might also be unreliable—and certainly *is*, in what it says through *Par une matinee*. Before we go on to think about the apparently *polyphonic* song to which the narrator gestures, let us stop to consider the motetus, which will clarify why *Par une matinee* should be understood to dissemble.

Mellis stilla is one of the most widely attested pieces in the motet repertoire, appearing under a variety of guises related to the motet version in sixteen extant manuscripts of origins as distant as England and Spain, Italy and the Rhineland (and this is not to mention still further pieces sharing the words *Mellis stilla* whose relation to the motet is less clear). Appendix 2 lists its sources. Certainly the breadth of its transmission contrasts with the limited circulation enjoyed by *Par une matinee*, which is reported only by the Montpellier Codex (of which the relevant portion is of demonstrated Parisian production) and the La Clayette manuscript. So among other questions, we are entitled to ask what aesthetic properties allowed *Mellis stilla* to get legs and to wander so far.

One such property is the lucid salience of its text's sonic design and the several ways its rhythmic structure and other phonic properties make seriality and repetition basic components of the poem's style. *Mellis stilla* (drop of honey) comprises eight verses of accentual, rhyming poetry of a kind known in the thirteenth century as *ritmus*. All verses share a terminal sound in *-a*, one that chimes out the more clearly for the choice to set each of the eight as a separate melodic phrase, aligned precisely with one each of the eight statements of the tenor *talea*. Within each line, the thirteen syllables of each verse are articulated into three "limbs" of 4 + 4 + 5 syllables by rhyming the fourth and eighth syllables (which always coincide with a word boundary) with one another.[58] With audible regularity, limbs correspond with discrete phraselets, frequently in parataxis and often voicing Marian epithets. Of these, some are commonplace (e.g., *maris stella*, "star of the sea," or *Iesse virgula*, "rod of Jesse"), but others are less familiar (e.g., *mamilla stillans mella*, a "nipple" or "budding breast dripping with honey"; so Mary is both provider of sweetness and the sweetness provided). At a still closer analytical range, repetition inheres in the poem's remarkable economy of phonemic means (a property announced by the dense recurrence of *m*'s and *l*'s in the opening two verses).[59] So densely and yet so freely does the humble fund of language sounds form micropatterns that the text sounds like a set of mere phonemes in easy rotation whose permutations felicitously generate ever more attributes of Mary's glory. The aesthetic yield of the poem is one of an abundance that suggests limitlessness—that this patchwork of epithets might extend indefinitely or be configured in another way.

Though she is not named, there cannot be any doubt about the poem's addressee; she is already known, familiar. The possible identity of the speaker is productively underdetermined, remaining so even once grammatical markers of person finally appear after the poem's last-minute transition from praise and invocation into prayer triggered by the words "detur ut purgetur" in verse 7. The text asks for a purging to occur but does not specify whether the singer him- or herself will be among the "purgati" (v. 8). Just as it permits performance by one or by many, then, the text invites endless repetition in the hope that the singer might attain what the answer to their prayer does not directly guarantee. As such, the text might be sung as well by many people as by one alone. We might say, by way of synthesis, that *Mellis stilla*'s personal tone offers a private devotional experience in praise of the Virgin, an experience that need be no less intimate if shared simultaneously (or, for that matter, in series) by several speakers.

The poem's balance of freedom of effect and organization of structure is shared by its melody. Let us return to appendix 1(b) and consider the motetus. Throughout, the trochaic accentual feet of *Mellis stilla*'s verses are set in the long-breve pattern of rhythmic mode 1, thus aligning the long of the modal foot with the stressed syllable of the meter; poetry and music reinforce one another's structural salience at the level of the syllable, as well as at the higher-level pairing of verse with phrase. A default *fractio* pattern divides the long into two pitches,[60] producing a melody almost entirely conjunct in motion, seldom passing through more than a fourth (more often only a third) in one direction before turning in the other. The pitches on which the melody comes to rest at the end of each phrase trace out a pattern of their own: *c-d-e-d* | *c-d-e-d* (where "|" represents the phrases' grouping against the two tenor *cursūs*). Yet while the motetus comes to rest on *d* (and, in polyphonic performance, forms an octave with the tenor, which is on *D*), having the last tonal word does not confer on *d* the sense of a "final" in any of our more system-regulating definitions of the term; rather, it is *c* that seems the center of pitch-reference.[61] This is made clear by the counterpoint of the opening verse. The three limbs in each verse match here and throughout with the disposition of the tenor *ordines* within each *talea*. In the first verse (mm. 1–7), the three tenor *ordines* create a miniature motion toward (mm. 1–2), away from (mm. 3–4), and then back to *C* (mm. 5–7), conferring on *D* the function of a penultimate sonority through which to approach the tenor melody's actual musical "home." Thus, there is a structural incompleteness in the pitch pattern traced by the phrase endings (for the *D*/*d* dyad on which the tenor-motetus pair concludes the first *cursus* at m. 28 and the second at m. 57 has acquired a precadential, "unfinished" character). Moreover, there comes a momentary hint of strophic return in the melodic repetition heard in the motetus at the opening of verse 5 (as mm. 29–31 echo mm. 1–3, a recurrence aligned with the beginning of the new tenor *cursus*); it is reinforced by a dovetail join that extends the sense of tonal openness into the new verse (which starts with the *d* on which the previous had ended), and then resolves it to *c* at m. 30. Thus, the join of verses 4 and 5 displays a mechanism by which the piece might be extended when that new *cursus* comes full circle, as if the song had halted for only a moment and might begin its mellifluous journey again.

As should be clear by now, I find a reciprocity (as distinct from a direct causality) between the piece's sense of artful freedom and its wide dissemination.[62] It is a reciprocity that requires qualification. The foregoing account of the piece bears many hallmarks that musical medievalists have used to account for the composition and transmission of music in "oral" cultures. Both text and music contain repetitive figures in an audibly patchworked configuration, whose succession is fitted within a simple overarching (so, an argument might go, perhaps preextemporizational) plan. Scholars of chant, in particular, but also of early polyphony, find such characteristics the necessary consequence of the unwritten creation of pieces of music, which would be not so much "transmitted" as "recreated" or "reextemporized" at each new iteration.[63] Much of this work has very successfully revealed the conditions that impinged on music making in the centuries before written composition was demonstrably ubiquitous. In the case of this piece, however, there is good reason to question whether the esthetic judgment that the piece sounds free necessitates the poietic conclusion that it sounds that way as a consequence of how it was made; and it is one purpose of my discussion of *Mellis stilla* to test the logical assumptions that attend hypotheses of oral or written composition, especially for the genre of the motet.[64]

Mellis stilla has been problematic for some of the usual procedures of motet scholarship and perhaps not problematic enough for some others. In almost all its sources, it *is* presented as a motet, perhaps, indeed, a forward-looking one.[65] Meanwhile, as a motet from midcentury, almost by definition it should be founded on a borrowed snippet of plainchant in the tenor voice, but (as I have mentioned) scholars have not located a liturgical source for the precise series of pitches that build our motet's tenor. Part of the problem—and perhaps of the solution—is that medieval scribes do not seem to have known the origins of the tenor melody any better than we do (at least when we consider their testimony in sum). It is variously given the incipit "Alleluia" or "Domino"—both suspiciously encompassing and underspecific incipits—or just left undesignated.[66] Taking her cue from the "Domino" incipits, Marie Louise Göllner once proposed that the tenor is a paraphrase of the "domino" melisma from the Easter Day Gradual "Haec dies," but I struggle to accept that suggestion, for reasons too detailed to enumerate here.[67]

In any case, I think there is a much simpler solution, which is to suppose that the motet tenor did not originate as a chant at all. Rather, I propose, it was composed with or for the first four verses of the *Mellis stilla* melody—to whose poetic form the tenor's rhythmic structure is so unusually transparent, and against which it so consistently forms the "directed progressions" (that is, the intervallic progression of a major sixth resolving to an octave) that would become the grammatical cornerstone of fourteenth-century counterpoint.[68] The tenor melody would then have been repeated to serve as the foundation for composing *Mellis stilla*'s second half.[69] There are any number of ways in which this could have been done, in writing or without it.[70] Loosening *Mellis stilla* from the assumption that its tenor is a chant also loosens the conceptual tethers that would make us think of it as a liturgical piece and the compositional work of a literate and professional singer-liturgist. Who knows where it might have been composed, or how?

Based on the piece's manuscript transmission, that could have happened pretty much anywhere; there's no reason to suppose it was Paris.[71] Beyond La Clayette and the Montpellier Codex, *Mellis stilla* found a home in a rich variety of books of broad geographical origin (listed with some annotations and references to further scholarly commentary in appendix 3). They include a collection of French texts whose cornerstone is the *Miracles de Nostre Dame* by Gautier de Coinci (Paris, Bibliothèque de l'Arsenal, MS 3517–18); a portable psalter from England, whose prayers are grammatically inflected for use by women and cannot be shown to have been in monastic, as opposed to lay, ownership (Oxford, Bodleian, MS Rawlinson G 18); and a Pisan *laudario* (Ars8521), from which it would have been sung by the pious members of a *laudese* confraternity. This last, physically enormous book is fascinating. It is heavily worn from use; yet most pages (including 180r, where we find *Mellis stilla*) were not even ruled to receive staves, and those that were did not receive their notation. So without notation to guide us, who are we to say that the confraternity members who sang from it together without the notation to guide *them* sang only *Mellis stilla*'s melody and not also its tenor accompaniment?[72] Our only grounds to do so would be that they were not in holy orders—which would be to assert precisely the conjunction of music-writing and clerisy on which Grocheio would have us set the genre of the motet as a seal.

Most of these manuscripts are available in online facsimiles (and are so indicated with links in appendix 3). I invite the reader to flip through them; this much will be enough to communicate that they vary widely in their notational orthography.[73] Some of *Mellis stilla*'s scribes seem to have known very little about rhythmic notation; indeed, some had almost no calligraphic expertise at all—the scribe of Boulogne-sur-Mer, Bibliothèque municipale, MS 119, fol. 1v, for instance, who copied *Mellis stilla* in the monophonic (so-called "Messine") neumes of his region and who, frankly, made a mess of his copy, especially in terms of its ruling and page preparation. But here, as across the sources, it is the *notation itself* rather than the substance of the melody notated that displays the greater variation. The same is true of the notation treatises from the period that use the incipit of *Mellis stilla* as an example (of which digitized copies of the critical editions are also available online, as indicated in appendix 2; thus, the examples are not reproduced here).[74] Each theorist uses the melody fragment to illustrate the rhythmic value of a notational form, but the forms so illustrated vary across the set.[75] For their notational differences, however, the manner of reading that the examples assume is the same: each author uses a familiar incipit to bring to mind a song he expects most readers will know—indeed, he chooses it *because* it is so widely known—so that readers may judge how successfully that notation encapsulates the melody ringing in their ears. That is to say, the condition of *Mellis stilla*'s written exemplarity is that it was known from beyond that immediate instance of writing, from who knows what other contexts that lay beyond the book.

In sum, the testimonies of *Mellis stilla* suggest the melody passed through many circumstances of performance and through textualities other than that by which *Par une matinee*'s narrator would render Marot silent. *Par une matinee* is, among other things, a song about written musical records: about who gets to make them and what music is record-worthy. But *Mellis stilla*, the song against which the narrator's own is unfurled, neatly reverses pretty much every principle for which he seems to stand.

In our bilingual motet, a song from beyond an elite tradition is hidden in plain sight. That it wandered over boundaries demarcated by kinds of writing suggests they were more porous than either the triplum's narrator, or Grocheio, or many motet scholars would have us believe. I reach no firm answer to the question, "What musical practices lay behind Grocheio's directive *non debet*?" At least not for now. Perhaps Grocheio knew several: like the precise sound of Marot's voice beyond underdetermined semibreves, we cannot know what might have been heard beyond the veil through which Grocheio incites us to listen in the very act of telling us not to try. But *Mellis stilla* points to directions we might pursue should we seek firmer answers. It suggests we may yet learn something of the polyphonic practices by which the motet was surrounded, because they have left traces *in* the motet repertoire to a greater degree than Grocheio would lead us to suspect. There may be unexpected voices recorded in the archive, waiting to be heard.[76]

Listening Again

Perhaps the composer of our bilingual motet (if not his chevalier) knew as much. But let's acquit ourselves of the chevalier first.

We had left him some pages ago (and at the end of his eleventh phrase) at the top of his own voice, in a remediating ventriloquy of Marot's: a gesture that purports to reveal the sonic kernel of the encounter that inspired his own song. In the remainder of the triplum, he wraps up the encounter with Marot, announces the arrival of Robin, and takes his own leave. In so doing, he regains his vocal composure and then rejoins the strophic structure from which he had departed in his reportage and his excitement.

In detail. After the fireworks of phrase XI and its tonally open ending on *d* (m. 38), the opening of phrase XII (m. 39) returns the chevalier's diction to the rhythmic default established at the very opening; this is how he recovers his vocal composure. Then the 3L phrase XII comes to rest on the closed sonority of *c*, from which Marot's reported song had departed at the start of phrase IX (m. 30); thus, the chevalier closes off musically what is also a close of syntax in the poetry and the close of the local narrative episode. Indeed, perhaps he stakes another claim to composerhood by interpolating Marot's reported utterance as a stub onto which to graft a more songlike ending than that at which she herself had arrived at the close of m. 36.[77]

He himself is not done, however, and finishes phrase XIII on an *open d* (and because that phrase, like XII, is also of 3L, the closed-to-open contrast of mm. 41 and 44 is made the more salient). We can hear the end of phrase XIII as a point of tonal suspense; and of several possibilities latent in that moment, one is that (because the melodic logic has not yet reached a conclusion) there is more yet to be said about the arrival of Robin that the chevalier has just announced. The suspense is partly satisfied by the return it cues to the 4L phraseology for the couplet of verses 22 and 23 in phrase XIV: a recapitulation of the phraseological hallmark (the musical X-section) of the strophic structure with which his song began and that he now rejoins, and of which the effect of an answer to the tonal question just posed is driven home by an emphatic five iterations of the referential pitch *c* in phrase XIV's first two longs (mm. 45–46). This third and final strophe is both abbreviated and expanded, but the underlying shape that builds the gesture is clear. It is abbreviated because it begins with only one couplet-setting phrase of 4L, not two, before we hear the three expected 2L limbs of the strophe's tercet (in phrases XV, XVI, and mm. 53–54 of phrase XVII). It is expanded, however, because, in a final display of composerly prowess, the neumatic flourish on *-nant* (m. 54) that marks the end of the usual 2L limb is recast as an approach to the apex of a melodic arc by an unexpected phrase extension, through which the melody descends to, decorates with auxiliaries, and finally cadences on *a*. Niftily, the chevalier has arrived back at the pitch from which his whole song began. Still more impressive is the result of the unexpected extra verse of poetry the phrase-extension carries, which yields "lor ieus demenant / vont || et ie men part atant." This redistributes the parts of two verses rhyming in *-ant* as an alexandrine of two hexasyllabic hemistichs separated by a caesura. The pronounced shift of poetic design at the final moment palpably courts the conceit of the *envoi*: usually a separate verse-couplet or other song-segment capping (and perhaps recapitulating part of) the form of the stanzas it follows, and which synecdochically imagines the safe passage of the whole song to its recipient.[78] Thus, the chevalier's declaration of departure is redoubled by its formal setting in song and not (or, not only) because this is where the piece reaches an end. Rather, it is because in this most virtuosically versified, grammatically self-contained gesture of the piece—which is the only time the narrator names himself as a *je*—it is as if a genie were being syphoned into the *envoi*'s musicopoetic bottle.[79] And *as* an *envoie*, it harbors the possibility that its synecdoche may be unpacked and the genie escape. The chevalier waits to be sung into existence once again, tall historical stories and all.

But, at last, let us listen again to measures 45 and 46, where the triplum's narrator reaches the word *encontre* and its veiled gesture toward polyphonic song, and where that plethora of *c*'s (articulated five times in two measures) announces the return of the strophic form with a return to a tonal home. If we think across the whole texture of the motet at this moment, something else, quite marvelous, comes within earshot. Notice that the whole texture pares down here, such that the triplum and motetus are like variants of one another: of nine pitch-articulations in the triplum, seven are on the same note simultaneously being sounded by the motetus. As if three voices were singing only two parts, the triplum becomes nearly indistinguishable from *Mellis stilla*'s dyadic frame. I like to hear this sudden transparency to the prayer against which the triplum was composed as a suggestion that it is *Mellis stilla* that Robin and Marion are singing as they go off into the sunset, *encontre* one another. Certainly the texture of the piece conspires to pose a question: "If you can learn to sing in two parts, how much more difficult is it to sing in three, really?"[80] (That is not a question Grocheio would have liked us to ask. Mostly we haven't.) So perhaps the triplum's *composer*, hearing the whole piece, takes stock of something the triplum's *narrator* would find unthinkable: that polyphony both within and beyond the genre of the motet might not be so different from polyphony more proud of its writtenness.

In any case, we learn that the games the lovers went off to play were innocent after all. Here, in corroboration of its other written traces, *Mellis stilla* intimates that vernacular music could be sung in the Latin tongue.[81]

APPENDIX 1

A bilingual motet of the mid-thirteenth century, in three parts, Triplum: *Par une matinee*/Motetus: *Mellis stilla*/Tenor: ALLELUYA. Texts, translation, and musical transcription. Transcribed from MS Paris, BnF, nouv. acq. fr. 13521 (the "La Clayette" manuscript), fols. 374v–75r. Also found in MS Montpellier, Bibl. universitaire Historique de Médecine, MS H 196 (the "Montpellier Codex"), fols. 72v–75r. I preserve La Clayette's readings and orthography except in cases of unquestionable error, in which case the Montpellier reading is supplied in square brackets.

(a) Texts

Triplum

PAr vne matinee	Upon a morning
el mois iolif dauril	in the jolly month of April,
mariete ai troue[e]	I found little Marot
regretant son ami	crying for her lover,
en un pre flori	in a flowery meadow,
souz un glai foilli	on a leafy sedge.
un chant mout iolif	I heard a very jolly song
doiseillonnez chantanz	from the singing birds
en un bochet entour moi	in the woods around me,
si cum aloie esbatant	as I went along having a good time
et pensant ai oi	and daydreaming.
sen fui esioi	I took great joy in it
et sen fui resbaudiz	and was cheered.
soi marot disant	Then I heard Marot saying,
biaus douz amis robin	"Handsome, sweet friend Robin,
que iaim mout *et* desir	whom I love and desire very much,
amourous *et* iolis	who are loving and good-natured,
por quoi demorez uos tant	why do you tarry so long?"
issi se uait dementant	In this way she went on mourning,
la bele la blonde en soupirant	the beautiful, blonde, sighing.
dilec a pou uenoit robin chantent	Then, after a while, Robin came along, singing;
encontre li sen uet marot	Marot runs up to meet him,
mout grant ioie fesant	making great merry.
trestout maintenant	Straight away
icil dui amant	these two lovers
lor ieus demenant uont	go off, making their games,
et ie men part ata*n*t.	and at this point I take my leave.

Motetus

MEllis stilla maris stella [r]osa pr[i]mula	Drop of honey, star of the sea, primrose,
tu mamilla stillans mella iesse uirgula	you, little breast dripping with honey, rod of Jesse,
expers paris uirgo paris patrem filia	without peer, virgin daughter who gives birth to the Father;
ordo stupet cuius su[p]plet uicem gracia	order is astounded [by the virgin birth], for which grace makes good the repayment.
mediatrix uite datrix mundi domina	Mediator, giver of life, mistress of the world,
uia uite mortis trite tu uictoria	way of life, you the victory of death downtrodden,
per te detur ut purgetur fecis scoria	through you, may it be granted that this slaggish sediment be cleansed,
qua purgati tua grati sint memoria.	by which those thus purged might be grateful in your remembrance.

Tenor

ALLELUYA	Alleluia
(or DOMINO in some manuscripts)	(To the Lord)

(b) Score

*As **birdsong** is reported, first breve fractures into three semibreves*

Marot's song (as ventriloquised by the chevalier)
Three statements of the three-semibreve "birdsong" figure
29
sant 15 biaus douz a-mis ro - bin 16 que iaim mout et de - sir 17 a-mou-rous et io - lis 18 por
5 me - di - a - trix ui - te da - trix mun - di do - mi - na
Cursus II
Marot's reported voice fractures into rapid-fire semibreves...
...which the chevalier repeats in mockery
6
quoi de-morez uos tant 19 is-si se uait de - men - tant 20 la be - le la blondeen sou - pi - rant 21 di - lec a pou
6 ui - a ui - te mor - tis tri - te tu uic - to - ri - a
Dense unisons between triplum and motetus
3
ue-noit ro-bin chan - tent 22 en-con-tre li sen uet ma-rot 23 mout grant io - ie fe - sant 24 tres-tout-main - te -
7 per te de - tur ut pur - ge - tur fe - cis sco - ri - a
0
nant 25 i - cil dui a - mant 26 lor ieus de - me - nant uont 27 et ie men part a - tant.
8 qua pur - ga - ti tu - a gra - ti sint me - mo - ri - a.

(c) Analytical Transcription of the Triplum Par une matinee

PHRASE LENGTH

1 Long	2L	3L	4L	5L	6L

PHRASE

Chevalier's "strophe" 1

Quatrain

I
(1) PAr v- ne ma - (2) ti-nee el mois io - lif da - uril

5
II
(3) ma-ri-ete ai tro-ue-[e] (4) re - gretant son a - mi

Tercet

9
III
(5) en un pre flo - ri (6) souz un glai foil - li (7) un chant mout io - lif

Chevalier's "strophe" 2

Quatrain

15
IV
(8) doiseillonnez chan - (9) tanz en un bo - chet en - tour moi

19
V
(10) si cum a - loie es-ba-tant (11) *et* pensant ai o - i

Tercet

23
VI
(12) sen fui es - io - i (13) *et*

! *The chevalier's vocal exclamation disrupts the repeating "stophic" logic*

26
VII
sen fui es - bau - diz

28
VIII
(14) soi ma-rot di - sant

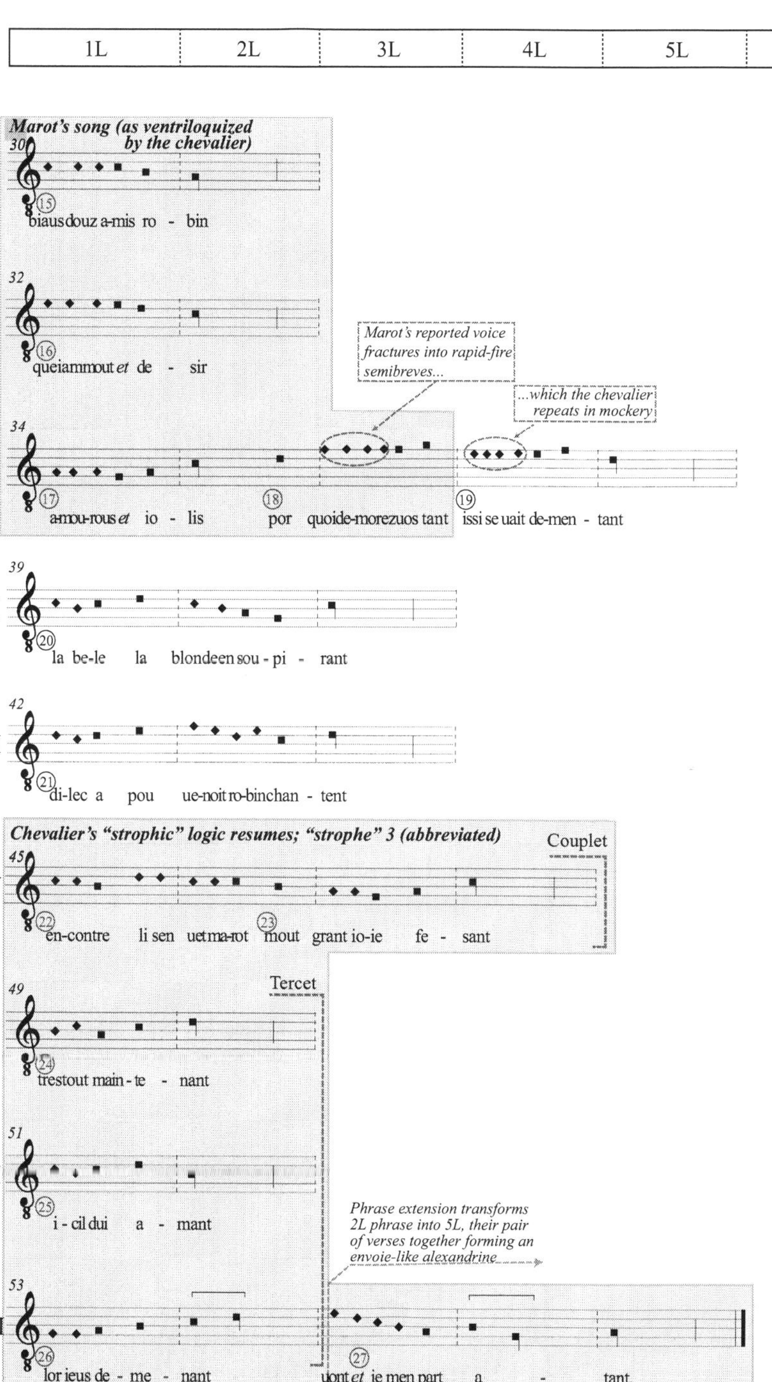

1L
2L
3L
4L
5L
6L
Marot's song (as ventriloquized by the chevalier)
IX
X
XI
XII
XIII
biausdouz a-mis ro - bin
queiammout et de - sir
a-mou-rous et io - lis
por quoide-morezuos tant
issi se uait de-men - tant
la be-le la blondeen sou - pi - rant
di-lec a pou ue-noit ro-binchan - tent
Marot's reported voice fractures into rapid-fire semibreves...
...which the chevalier repeats in mockery
Chevalier's "strophic" logic resumes; "strophe" 3 (abbreviated)
Couplet
XIV
XV
XVI
XVII
en-contre li sen uet ma-rot mout grant io-ie fe - sant
Tercet
trestout main - te - nant
i - cil dui a - mant
lor ieus de - me - nant
uont et ie men part a - tant.
Phrase extension transforms 2L phrase into 5L, their pair of verses together forming an envoie-like alexandrine

APPENDIX 2

Network of Manuscript Witnesses and Related Songs for *Par une matinee* / *Mellis stilla* / ALLELUYA

This section presents a complete list of manuscript witnesses for my case-study motet and for all further pieces related to it by shared music or text. Presented first are those versions of the piece that "reuse" one or more of its constituent voices in full. There follows a list of pieces related by partial use of one or another of the voice parts: these comprise another motet, a set of pieces related by a supposed use of an Old French refrain, and Latin songs (often sequences) whose texts show awareness of the *Mellis stilla* topos. Finally, there follows a list of references to *Par une matinee* or *Mellis stilla* in Latin texts of music theory.

Entries are arranged in descending order of the number of voice parts transmitted; position in the list should not be understood to indicate chronological priority either of pieces or of their manuscripts. Appendix 3 gives a key to the manuscript sigla used here and a brief characterization of each manuscript's contents with a broad indication of its date.

Information on motets is taken from Hendrik van der Werf, *Integrated Directory of Organa, Clausulae, and Motets of the Thirteenth Century* (Rochester, NY: H. van der Werf, 1989).

Refrain identifications are those offered in the database *Refrain: Music, Poetry, Citation; The Medieval Refrain*, by Anne Ibos-Augé and Mark Everist, www.refrain.ac.uk; a cornerstone of the database is the still-foundational bibliographical work of Nico H. J. van den Boogaard, *Rondeaux et refrains du XIIe siècle au début du XIVe*, Bibliothèque française et romane, série D: Initiation, textes et documents, 3 (Paris: Klincksieck, 1969), whence the "vdB" tag under which refrains are indexed in the database.

Sequences are identified by their number in the database *Clavis sequentiarum*, by Calvin Bower, recently incorporated into the *Cantus Database*, http://cantus.uwaterloo.ca. Where a sequence's text was printed in *Analecta Hymnica*, its number is usually a compound of five digits of which the first two indicate the *AH* volume number, the last three a text's position in that volume. Great service to the disciplines has been rendered by David Hiley et al. in forming from the relevant *AH* volumes a searchable database of sequence texts; see their full collection of *AH* references at www.uni-regensburg.de/Fakultaeten/phil_Fak_I/Musikwissenschaft/cantus.

Theoretical citations were identified in Gordon A. Anderson, ed., *Motets of the Manuscript La Clayette: Paris, Bibliothèque nationale, nouv. acq. fr. 13521*, with French texts ed. and trans. Elizabeth A. Close ([Rome]: American Institute of Musicology, 1975), xxxviii. I retain Anderson's sigla for the treatises, supplying updated references to the critical editions of record.

Three-Voice Versions

(i) Triplum: *Par une matinee* (807)
Motetus: *Mellis stilla* (808)
Tenor: DOMINO II (unidentified)

Witnesses:
Mo, fol. 72v–75r (Tenor incipit: "Domine.")
Cl, fol. 374v–75r (Tenor incipit: "Alleluya.")

(ii) Triplum: *O Maria mater pia spes fidelium* (809) [= music of (807) and (810)]
Motetus: *Mellis stilla* (808)
Tenor: DOMINO II (unidentified)

Witness:

PsAr, fol. 40v–41v (incomplete copy; Tenor incipit "Domino")

(iii) Triplum: *Virginis preconia cum melodia* (810) [= music of (807) and (809)]
Motetus: *Mellis stilla* (808)
Tenor: DOMINO II (unidentified)

Witnesses:

Ba, fol. 36r–36v (Tenor incipit: "Domino")

(iv) Triplum: *Mal d'amors prenes m'amie* (811)
Motetus: *Dame je me clamerai a amor* (812)
Tenor: DOMINO II (unidentified)

Witness:

Mo, fol. 209v–11r (Tenor incipit: "Domino.")
[Tenor is identical to that of (i) through (iii) in both pitch content and talea structure but sets only one cursus.]

(v) Triplum: *Par une matinee el moys ioli d'avril jouer alai* (896)
Motetus: *O clemencie fons* (897)
Tenor: D'UN JOLI DART (R1256)

Witness:

Mo, fol. 353v–54v
[For its first seven words, the melody and text of the triplum (896) are identical to (807); the rest of the part appears to be newly composed.]

(vi) Triplum: [*Mellis stilla*]
Motetus: *Mellis stilla* (808)
Tenor: DOMINO II (unidentified)

Witness:

Hu, 166r–66v (Tenor incipit: "tenura sso de este canto que vedes aqui", almost illegible because of damage to the leaf)
[A conductus motet: to the core of *Mellis stilla* (808) / DOMINO II is added a new triplum syllabified with the *Mellis stilla* text; its pitches are not related to the melody shared by the (807)-(809)-(810) group.]

Two-voice versions:

Two-voice Latin motet:

(vii) Motetus: *Mellis stilla* (808)
Tenor: DOMINO II (unidentified)

Witnesses:

Ars3517, fol. 3r (Tenor incipit: undesignated)
Ars135, fol. 290v (Tenor incipit: "[D]omino.")
Ca, fol. 129v (Tenor incipit: undesignated)
Lyell72, fol. 173r (Tenor incipit: undesignated)
MüC, fol. 73r–v (Tenor incipit: undesignated)

Conductus version:

(viii) Upper voice: [*Mellis stilla*] (808)

Lower voice: *Mellis stilla* (= based on DOMINO II)

Witness:

OxRawlG, fol. 106v (Tenor is texted)

[The upper voice is a nonmensural copy of the usual *Mellis stilla* melody; the lower voice is based on the motet's melismatic tenor, syllabified here for the *Mellis stilla* text and harmonically reworked; the voices are laid out in score.]

Monophonic versions:

(ix) Voice 1: *Mellis stilla*

Witness:

Todi, fol. 33r

[The song is an addition on the bottom margin, in a different hand from that of the writing block's copyist. Curiously, the melody reported is not that of the motetus (808) but essentially a syllabification of the tenor melody DOMINO II (one independent of the OxRawlG rendition, though derived from similar contrapuntal procedures).]

(x) Voice 1: *Mellis stilla* (808)

Witness:

Boul, fol. 1v (the inner face of what is now a flyleaf but was originally the front pastedown)

Text-only version:

(xi) Voice 1: *Mellis stilla*

Witness:

Ars8521, fol. 180r

Version indeterminate:

(xii) Tenor: DOMINO II (Tenor incipit: "Tenor de Mellis stilla.")

Witness:

CCCC8, binding strip between fols. 256v–57r

(xiii) Voice 1: *Mellis stilla maris*

Witness:

Be, fol. 116v (Tenor incipit: undesignated)

[*Mellis stilla* is the second item in a list of incipits conventionally understood to represent the index of a lost music manuscript.]

Further connected pieces

(xiv) Sequence:

Incipit: *Mellis stilla maris stella* | *Cuius dulcor vincit mella* | *Cuius splendor sidera*

Reference: AH09087

Witnesses:

Add710, fol. 121v–22v

Lat1107, fol. 369v–70v

[Three verses of the *Mellis stilla* text are quoted in verses 1a, 2a, and 2b of the sequence, without melodic quotation (the melody is that of *Hodierne lux diei*, AH54219).]

(xv) Sequence:
Incipit: *Mellis stilla* | *De spinis exiit* | *Maris stella*
Reference: AH10077

Witness:
Dublin, Trinity College, MS 82 (the "Kilcormac Missal," with fragment of a Sarum Antiphoner).

(xvi) Sequence [?]:
Incipit: *Ave salus gentium* | *Mater regis gloriae* | . . . *Mellis stilla* | *maris stella* | *Rosa primula* [etc.]
Reference: AH34120 [not in *Clavis sequentiarum*]
[As presented in *AH*, the sequence includes the text of *Mellis stilla* (as verses 4a–7b; this portion is identical to the motet text in all but a minor change in the final b-versicle), fronted by an opening verse and then two paired versicles (1–3b), which are also in praise of Mary. Unnotated.]

Witness:
Utrecht, Universiteitsbibliotheek, MS 369, fol. 121v
[A Cistercian book of prayers, dated 1477.
Online: https://utrechtuniversity.on.worldcat.org/oclc/965420426]

(xvii) Sequence:
Incipit: *Matri consolationis* | *Filii salvationis*
Reference: AH54238
[The phrase "mellis stilla maris stella" occurs in stanza 7 of a substantial song of twelve stanzas (in six metrical pairs).]

Witnesses:
Graz, Universitätsbibliothek, MS 756 (dated 1345), fol. 190v–91v
[Notated in unheighted neumes; precise melody unrecoverable, though neumes over the phrase "mellis stilla maris stella" do not correspond to the texture and contour of the motet-incipit.]
Salzburg, Erzabtei St. Peter, Benediktinerstift, Bibliothek, MS a.III.20 (s.xvi)

Refrains

Par une matinee (807) is identified by Anne Ibos-Augé and Mark Everist in the database *Refrain* as a source for the refrain that, following van den Boogaard, they index s.v. "vdB 220: Biaus doz amis, por quoi demorés tant!," http://refrain.ac.uk/view/abstract_item/220.html. The vdB 220 tag appears in one other work, motet-voice (28), *Pour moi deduire et pour moi deporter*, as follows:

Motet
Quadruplum: *A diu commant cele* (27)
Triplum: *Por moi deduire et por moi deporter* (28)
Motetus: *En non diu queque nus die* (29)
Tenor: OMNES (M1)

Witnesses:

Mo, 36v–39r

[The melodies are quite dissimilar; any citational force is generated by the text alone.]

Theoretical citations

1. Anon II:
Edition: Anonymous II, *Tractatus de Discantu [Concerning Discant]*, ed. and trans. by Albert Seay, Texts/Translations, no. 1 (Colorado Springs: Colorado College Music Press, 1978). *Mellis stilla* citation at 14 (trans. 15).
Online at *Thesaurus Musicarum Latinarum*: https://chmtl.indiana.edu/tml/13th/ANOTDD.

2. Anon MüC:
Edition: Anonymous, *Practica musicae artis mensurabilis*, ed. Marie Louise Göllner in Göllner, *The Manuscript Cod. lat. 5539 of the Bavarian State Library, with an Edition of the Original Treatises and of the Two-voice Organal Settings* ([Neuhausen-Stuttgart]: American Institute of Musicology / Hänssler-Verlag, 1993), 101–8 (with discussion at 98–100). *Mellis stilla* citation at 107.
Online at *Thesaurus Musicarum Latinarum*: https://chmtl.indiana.edu/tml/13th/ANOPRA.

3. Anon Pavia:
There is no critical edition of this treatise, and I have been unable to consult the manuscript (although I include its details for reference).
Manuscript: Pavia, Biblioteca Universitaria, MS Aldini 361. *Mellis stilla* citation at fol. 65v.

4. *Doc VI*:
Edition: Anonymous, *Ars musicae mensurabilis secundum Franconem*, ed. Gilbert Reaney and André Gilles, Corpus Scriptorum de Musica 15 (N.p.: American Institute of Musicology, 1971). *Mellis stilla* citation at 44.
Online at *Thesaurus Musicarum Latinarum*: https://chmtl.indiana.edu/tml/13th/ANOFIG.

5. Petrus:
Edition: Petrus Picardus, *Ars motettorum compilata breviter*, ed. Alberto Gallo, Corpus Scriptorum de Musica 15 (N.p.: American Institute of Musicology, 1971). *Mellis stilla* citation at 17.
Online at *Thesaurus Musicarum Latinarum*: https://chmtl.indiana.edu/tml/13th/ANOFIG

APPENDIX 3

Manuscript Sigla Used in This Study

Sigla are largely those deployed in Hendrik van der Werf, *Integrated Directory of Organa, Clausulae, and Motets of the Thirteenth Century* (Rochester, NY: H. van der Werf, 1989). A URL has been provided for any manuscript known to be digitized at the time of writing. Manuscript descriptions may be found in Gilbert Reaney, *Manuscripts of Polyphonic Music, 11th–Early 14th Century,*

Répertoire International des Sources Musicales, ser. B, vol. 4, pt. 1 (Munich: G. Henle, 1966) (henceforth RISM B/IV/1). Further information on most items in this list can be found in the Digital Image Archive of Medieval Music (DIAMM), where further bibliographical references are also available. Sources of *Mellis stilla* have their sigla presented in bold type.

Siglum	Manuscript and comments
Add710	Cambridge, University Library, MS Add. 710 (the "Dublin Troper").
Ars135 (also ArsA)	Paris, Bibliothèque de l'Arsenal, MS 135. The manuscript is a Sarum Gradual of the thirteenth century, of English provenance, to which polyphonic items were added later, possibly in the early fourteenth century (see RISM B/IV/1, 369–71). Online: https://gallica.bnf.fr/ark:/12148/btv1b550057271/f592.item.r=arsenal%20 135.
Ars3517 (also ArsB)	Paris, Bibliothèque de l'Arsenal, MSS 3517–18. (Manuscript also known as Gautier D-1.) Online: https://gallica.bnf.fr/ark:/12148/btv1b55006913x/f11.item. Literary codex containing the *Miracles de Nostre Dame*, by Gautier de Coinci. Originally a single manuscript, it is now bound in two volumes; the music occupies preliminary leaves (but not flyleaves) in MS 3517 (fols. 1r–4v). RISM B/IV/1, p. 371, dates the codex to the second half of the thirteenth century and suggests the textual script locates the book in eastern France. It may yet be determined at what stage of binding the polyphonic items were included with the literary collection.
Ars8521 (also ArsC)	Paris, Bibliothèque de l'Arsenal, MS 8521. Online: https://gallica.bnf.fr/ark:/12148/btv1b52502464t/f377.item. The manuscript is a *laudario* used by a confraternity in Pisa. Blake Wilson dates it simply as "fourteenth century" (Blake Wilson, *Music and Merchants: The "Laudesi" Companies of Republican Florence* [Oxford: Clarendon Press, 1992], 154). *Mellis stilla* was copied as one of a collection of Latin texts at the back of the book for which space was never left for the addition of music. By contrast, the rest of the manuscript was almost entirely ruled with staves, but notation was never written on them.
Ba	Bamberg, Staatsbibliothek, MS Lit. 115 (*olim* Ed. IV. 6). A Parisian (?) anthology of motets, of which this section was probably copied in the third quarter of the thirteenth century (see *Grove Music Online,* s.v. "Sources."). Online: https://nbn-resolving.org/urn:nbn:de:bvb:22-dtl-0000002752.
Be	Besançon, Bibliothèque municipale, MS I, 716. *Mellis stilla* is the second item in this list of pieces understood to report the contents of a lost motet manuscript. The most recent description and study remains Friedrich Ludwig, *Repertorium organorum recentioris et motetorum vetustissimi stili*, vol. 1, pt. 2, ed. Luther Dittmer (New York: Institute of Mediaeval Music; and Hildesheim: Georg Olms, 1964), 505–13. Online: https://data.biblissima.fr/entity/Q131412.
Boul	Boulogne-sur-Mer, Bibliothèque municipale, MS 119 (*olim* 148). Online: https://bvmm.irht.cnrs.fr/iiif/20304/canvas/canvas-1891780/view.
Ca	Cambrai, Médiathèque municipale, MS A 410 (*olim* 346). The manuscript is a miscellany containing a collection of letters and Latin poems on the Schism of the Bishopric of Liège, among other literary works of Flemish origin. The main body of the manuscript was copied in the twelfth

century, while its ten motets were added by a thirteenth-century hand. (See RISM B/IV/1, 261–63.)
Online: https://www.diamm.ac.uk/sources/270/#/.

CCCC8 Cambridge, Corpus Christi College, MS 8.
Jacques Handschin ("The Summer Canon and Its Background: II," *Musica Disciplina* 5 [1951]: 84) mentions being able to see a binding strip between fols. 256v and 257r with the words "Tenor de mellis stilla." (Thanks to Theodoretus Breen for bringing this to my attention.) Incipit is no longer visible (though edges of some notes can be seen); the constitution of the music manuscript from which this binding material was taken is unknown (c. 1300?). See, most recently, Amy Williamson, "English Polyphonic Music around 1300: Genre and Repertory in Cambridge, Corpus Christi MS 8," *Musica Disciplina* 58 (2013): 373–91.
Online: https://parker.stanford.edu/parker/catalog/cv176gb0028.

Cl Paris, Bibliothèque nationale de France, MS nouvelles acquisitions françaises 13521 (the "La Clayette" manuscript).
An Old French literary anthology, produced in fascicular units between the 1260s and ca. 1300. The motet collection was present in the earliest of three identifiable bindings.
Online: https://gallica.bnf.fr/ark:/12148/btv1b530121530/f765.item.

F Florence, Biblioteca Medicea Laurenziana, MS Plut. 29.1.
Online: http://teca.bmlonline.it/ImageViewer/servlet/ImageViewer?idr=TECA0000342136&keyworks=Plut.29.01.

Hu Burgos, Monasterio de Las Huelgas, MS XI.
A manuscript made ca. 1300 for the Cistercian convent of Las Huelgas, where it remains. The book contains a broad variety of monophonic and polyphonic materials for the liturgy and devotional life of the institution. For a detailed account of the book's production history, see Nicolas Bell, "The Codex," in *The Las Huelgas Music Codex: A Companion Study to the Facsimile* (Madrid: Testimonio Compañia Editorial, 2003), 19–39.
[Not presently available online.]

Lat1107 Paris, Bibliothèque nationale de France, MS Latin 1107.
Missal of the Royal Abbey of Saint-Denis, s.xiii^{2}.
Online: https://gallica.bnf.fr/ark:/12148/btv1b10033022b/f384.item.r=latin%20 1107.

Lyell72 Oxford, Bodleian Library, MS Lyell 72.
The manuscript is a processional. Gilbert Reaney (RISM B/IV/1, 564–66) considers it an Italian manuscript of the thirteenth century; Jane Disley believes the book to have been made for a "Dominican house in the Patriarchate of Aquileia, in the Dominican province of lower Lombardy" and "probably [in] the first quarter" of the fourteenth century. Jane Disley, "The Dominican Processional Oxford, Bodleian Library, MS. Lyell 72 (GB-OL72)," in *Le polifonie primitive in Friuli e in Europa*, ed. Cesare Corsi and Pierluigi Petrobelli (Rome: Torre d'Orfeo, 1980), 217–27, 222. *Mellis stilla* is one of several polyphonic compositions incorporated within a collection of sequences, and its *mise en page* is continuous with those items.
[Not presently available online.]

Mo Montpellier, Bibliothèque universitaire Historique de Médecine, MS H 196 (the "Montpellier Codex").

A Parisian anthology of motets, probably of layered compilation; the fascicle containing our motet (the third of eight) probably copied in the 1270s.
Online: https://ged.biu-montpellier.fr/florabium/jsp/nodoc.jsp?NODOC=2015_DOC_MONT_MBUM_26.

MüC Munich, Bayerische Staatsbibliothek, MS Lat. 5539.
The manuscript is a compendium of miscellaneous paraliturgical songs, both monophonic and polyphonic, and contains a music-theory treatise. Marie Louise Göllner states that "the manuscript was begun in Regensburg shortly before 1300 as part of the musical reform instigated by Bishop Heinrich II at the Cathedral [there]." See Marie Louise Göllner, *The Manuscript Cod. lat. 5539 of the Bavarian State Library; with an Edition of the Original Treatises and of the Two-Voice Organal Settings* (Neuhausen-Stuttgart: Hänssler-Verlag / American Institute of Musicology, 1993), 14. *Mellis stilla* is embedded within a continuously copied group of items introduced with the rubric "incipiunt tropi": it seems to have been understood by its copyist as a kind of polyphonic trope.
Online: urn:nbn:de:bvb:12-bsb00079147-6.

N Paris, Bibliothèque nationale de France, MS français 12615 (the "Chansonnier de Noailles").

OxRawlG Oxford, Bodleian Library, MS Rawlinson G 18.
The manuscript is a psalter tailored for private devotion. Obits in the calendar indicate a connection to Burnham Priory in Buckinghamshire, England, though there is no reason to presume the manuscript itself was housed there rather than owned by a lay patron of the house. The psalter is of the early thirteenth century, and *Mellis stilla* was added at the end of the book in the later thirteenth century, along with a Passion poem in Anglo-Norman and a notated Middle English lyric, *Worldes blis*. *Mellis stilla* is arranged as a two-part song, as the first item of an ad hoc formulary whose expressed devotional purpose is to reestablish "concordia" between the hearts of the two singers. I am preparing a study of this manuscript. (See RISM B/IV/1, 574–75.)
Online: https://www.diamm.ac.uk/sources/940/#/.

PsAr Paris, Bibliothèque nationale de France, MS Latin 11266.
A Parisian music-theory manuscript containing the treatise of Lambertus, to which seven motets in three parts were added later. Mark Everist considers it a manuscript of the early 1280s. See Mark Everist, "Music and Theory in Late Thirteenth-Century Paris: The Manuscript Paris, Bibliothèque nationale fonds lat. 11266," *Royal Musical Association Research Chronicle* 17 (1981): 52–64.
Online: https://gallica.bnf.fr/ark:/12148/btv1b8432482r/f86.item.

R Paris, Bibliothèque nationale de France, MS français 844 (the "Chansonnier du Roi").

Todi Todi, Biblioteca communale, MS 73.
The copy is apparently heavily erroneous, and verse 6 is missing entirely from the melody. I have consulted it from the black-and-white reproduction in Agostino Ziino "Some Observations," 496.
[Not presently available online.]

NOTES

1. An earlier version of this material appeared as "The Place of Writing in the Production of Polyphony," chapter 4 of my "Vernacular Book Production, Vernacular Polyphony, and the Motets of the 'La Clayette' Manuscript (Paris, Bibliothèque nationale de France, nouvelles acquisitions françaises 13521)" (PhD diss., University of California, Berkeley, 2013). Some of my views have changed in the interim, and so have some features of the terrain; where there is overlap, the present version supersedes what was written there. Deep thanks to all who have read and supported this work, particularly Nicolas Bell, Margaret Bent, Richard Crocker, Emma Dillon, Susan Rankin, Mary Ann Smart, Richard Taruskin, and, especially, Steven Justice.

For brilliant, contrastive historical accounts of the motet in the thirteenth century, see Richard L. Crocker, "French Polyphony of the Thirteenth Century," in *The Early Middle Ages to 1300*, ed. Richard L. Crocker and David Hiley, vol. 2 of *The New Oxford History of Music*, 2nd ed. (Oxford: Oxford University Press, 1990), 636–78; and Richard Taruskin, "Music for an Intellectual and Political Elite: The Thirteenth-Century Motet," in *The Oxford History of Western Music* (Oxford: Oxford University Press, 2005), 1:207–45. The gold standard music analytical study of the genre remains Mark Everist, *French Motets in the Thirteenth Century: Music, Poetry, and Genre* (Cambridge: Cambridge University Press, 1994); and of the genre's poetry, Sylvia Huot, *Allegorical Play in the Old French Motet: The Sacred and the Profane in Thirteenth-Century Polyphony* (Stanford, CA: Stanford University Press, 1997). A longer historical view is covered in Jared C. Hartt, ed., *A Critical Companion to Medieval Motets* (Woodbridge, UK: Boydell, 2018).

2. Such work was catalyzed in reaction to a polemic launched by Christopher Page, advocating against the examination of intertextual references in polytextual motets on the grounds that the sonic difficulty of the genre makes them inaudible. See Christopher Page, *Discarding Images: Reflections on Music and Culture in Medieval France* (Oxford: Clarendon Press, 1993), 65–111; and Christopher Page, "Around the Performance of a 13th-Century Motet," *Early Music* 28 (2000): 343–57. Influential responses include Dolores Pesce, ed., *Hearing the Motet: Essays on the Motet of the Middle Ages and Renaissance* (New York: Oxford University Press, 1997), esp. the essay of Margaret Bent, "Polyphony of Texts and Music in the Fourteenth Century: *Tribum que non abhorruit / Quoniam secta latronum / Merito hec patimur* and Its 'Quotations,'" 82–103; Suzannah Clark, "'S'en dirai chançonete': Hearing Text and Music in a Medieval Motet," *Plainsong and Medieval Music* 16 (2007): 31–59; and Emma Dillon, *The Sense of Sound: Musical Meaning in France, 1260–1330* (Oxford: Oxford University Press, 2012). For my position on those debates, see Sean Curran, "Hockets Broken and Integrated in Early Mensural Theory and an Early Motet," *Early Music History* 36 (2017): 31–104.

3. I have made points of that sort elsewhere, presenting evidence that one of the most important collections of midcentury polytextual motets (the "La Clayette" manuscript) usually thought to have been of Parisian origin shows ample signs, instead, of production in an environment where access to written musical exemplars was not as reliable as we might expect the Parisian book market to have enjoyed. See Sean Curran, "Composing a Codex: The Motets in the 'La Clayette' Manuscript," in *Medieval Music in Practice: Studies in Honor of Richard Crocker*, ed. Judith A. Peraino (Middleton, WI: American Institute of Musicology, 2013), 219–53. Moreover, wherever La Clayette was compiled, the manner of its motets' layout permitted, indeed anticipated, a performance practice akin to literary praelection in which a single *reader* would teach motets to the other singers a piece required, building up the parts of the polyphonic edifice incrementally and through live instruction; the only skill required to sing this complicated music would, under such a model, turn out to be the willingness to be taught. See Sean

Curran, "Reading and Rhythm in the 'La Clayette' Manuscript (Paris, Bibliothèque nationale de France, nouv. acq. fr. 13521)," *Plainsong and Medieval Music* 23 (2014): 125–51.

4. A way of conceiving matters that is indebted to Pierre Bourdieu, *The Field of Cultural Production* (New York: Columbia University Press, 1993). Edward H. Roesner seems to have meant something like this when he writes that "the music of Paris was the first body of polyphony to be conceived and disseminated primarily in writing rather than orally—indeed, it is in this repertory that we can discern the beginnings of musical 'composition' in the modern sense." See Edward H. Roesner, ed., *Le Magnus Liber Organi de Notre-Dame de Paris*, vol. 1, *Les Quadrupla et Tripla de Paris*, with plainchants ed. Michel Huglo (Monaco: Éditions de L'Oiseau-Lyre, 1993), lvii.

5. Numbers after a motet title report the motet's position in the index by Hendrik van der Werf, *Integrated Directory of Organa, Clausulae, and Motets of the Thirteenth Century* (Rochester, NY: H. van der Werf, 1989); throughout the present essay, I standardize motet references to the numbers given in this resource.

6. I am influenced here by Maura Nolan, who has drawn attention to the "*writtenness* of the past, to its production of textual forms of representation," and who observes that "medieval people . . . *did* create artifacts they hoped would speak to the future." See Maura Nolan, "Historicism after Historicism," in *The Post-Historical Middle Ages*, ed. Elizabeth Scala and Sylvia Federico (New York: Palgrave Macmillan, 2009), 63–86, 69 (emphasis in original).

7. My section title nods to Bettina Varwig, *Histories of Heinrich Schütz* (Cambridge: Cambridge University Press, 2011).

8. This origin story has come under fire recently because philological work has suggested that some passages of melismatic discant, some clausulae, and some of the Latin motets as reported in the anthology manuscript known as "F" may at some prior stage of recension have had French texts that were stripped from them for inclusion in this, the most liturgically orderly of the sources of the Notre Dame repertoire. See, e.g., Catherine A. Bradley, "Contrafacta and Transcribed Motets: Vernacular Influences on Latin Motets and Clausulae in the Florence Manuscript," *Early Music History* 32 (2013): 1–70. But there is a risk in such revisionisms of conflating the history of genres with the transmission history of particular samples of the genre. Richard Taruskin made that point about the relation of motets to clausulae in MS F in *The Oxford History of Western Music* (Oxford: Oxford University Press, 2005), 1:210. On the musical and liturgical history of Notre Dame, see Craig Wright, *Music and Ceremony at Notre Dame of Paris, 500–1500* (Cambridge: Cambridge University Press, 1989).

9. Thomas B. Payne's apt characterization; see Philip the Chancellor, *Motets and Prosulas*, ed. Thomas B. Payne (Middleton, WI: A-R Editions, 2011), xiii.

10. On *ritmus* in this period, see Margot Fassler, "Accent, Meter, and Rhythm in Medieval Treatises 'De Rithmis,'" *Journal of Musicology* 5 (1987): 164–90; and Christopher Page, *Latin Poetry and Conductus Rhythm in Medieval France* (London: Royal Musical Association, 1997).

11. The foundational bibliographical work (not all of it published in his lifetime) remains that of Friedrich Ludwig, *Repertorium organorum et motetorum vetustissimi stili*, pt. 1, *Handschriften in Quadrat-Notation* (Halle: M. Niemeyer, 1910), repr., ed. Luther Dittmer (New York: Institute of Medieval Music; and Hildesheim: Georg Olms, 1964); pt. 2, *Handschriften in Mensuralnotation*, ed. Friedrich Gennrich (Langen bei Frankfurt, 1961). This was built on by Ludwig's student Friedrich Gennrich, *Bibliographie der ältesten französischen und lateinischen Motetten* (Darmstadt: n.p., 1957). Subsequent discoveries were incorporated into Van der Werf, *Integrated Directory*.

12. These issues of terminology have been hotly debated. For a conspectus of scholarly positions taken on the word *motet* to his time of writing, see Michael Beiche, s.v. "Motet/

motetus / mottetto / Motette" (2004), in *Handwörterbuch der musikalischen Terminologie*, ed. H. H. Eggebrecht and Albrecht Riethmüller (Stuttgart: Franz Steiner, 1972–2006); online at http://daten.digitale-sammlungen.de/bsb00070512/image_223. For a synoptic presentation of the relevant lexicographical data in Latin, see *Lexicon Musicum Latinum Medii Aevi*, s.v. "motetus -i," digital edition in the Wörterbuchnetz of the Trier Center for Digital Humanities, version 01/21, www.woerterbuchnetz.de/LmL/motetus. The terminological sketch I offer here distills the findings of Klaus Hoffmann, "Zur Entstehungs- und Frühgeschichte des Terminus Motette," *Acta Musicologica* 42, no. 3–4 (1970): 138–50; and in light of their development by Judith A. Peraino, *Giving Voice to Love: Song and Self-Expression from the Troubadours to Guillaume de Machaut* (Oxford: Oxford University Press, 2012), 192–95; and Elizabeth Eva Leach, "The Genre(s) of Medieval Motets," in *A Critical Companion to Medieval Motets*, ed. Jared C. Hartt (Woodbridge, UK: Boydell, 2018), 15–41, esp. 16–22. For comprehensive recent accounts of the vast scholarship on refrains, see Clark, " 'S'en dirai chançonete,' " esp. 44–54; and Jennifer Saltzstein, *The Refrain and the Rise of the Vernacular in Medieval French Music and Poetry* (Woodbridge, UK: D. S. Brewer, 2013), 1–34.

13. The critical discussion of hybridity is a development I associate particularly with work by Ardis Butterfield, Judith A. Peraino, and Anna Zayaruznaya. See Ardis Butterfield, "*Enté*: A Survey and Reassessment of the Term in Thirteenth- and Fourteenth-Century Music and Poetry," *Early Music History* 22 (2003): 67–101; Judith A. Peraino, "The Hybrid Voice of Monophonic Motets," in *Giving Voice to Love: Song and Self-Expression from the Troubadours to Guillaume de Machaut* (Oxford: Oxford University Press, 2012), 186–234; and (on motets of the fourteenth century) Anna Zayaruznaya, *The Monstrous New Art: Divided Forms in the Late Medieval Motet* (Cambridge: Cambridge University Press, 2015). On the musicological valorizations of unity and organicism against which previous generations of scholarship variously found the motet to fall foul and therefore to be in need of defense, see Zayaruznaya, 1–20.

14. Thus, Ludwig discussed the motet collections of the chansonniers R and N in *Repertorium*, 1:285–305. That motets were collected into these (and other similar) books is certainly evidence that motets made some sense to scribes primarily interested in Old French monophony and probably working in Artois. (For concise descriptions and references to the relevant scholarly literature, see *Grove Music Online*, s.v. "Sources, MS," §III, "Secular Monophony," pt. 4, "French," by Elizabeth Aubrey, www.oxfordmusiconline.com.) Exactly what understanding those scribes took from motets, however, remains open to interpretation given that the tenors are notoriously poorly copied (riddled with errors and often missing); on which, see Mary E. Wolinski, "Tenors Lost and Found: The Reconstruction of Motets in Two Medieval Chansonniers," in *Critica Musica: Essays in Honor of Paul Brainard*, ed. John Knowles (Amsterdam: Gordon and Breach, 1996), 461–82. The motets of MS N are now reconstructed in the careful edition, Gaël Saint-Cricq, ed., with Eglal Doss-Quinby and Samuel N. Rosenberg, *Motets from the Chansonnier de Noailles* (Middleton, WI: A-R Editions, 2017).

15. On the vernacular character of Old French motet texts, for instance, see the historiographical tradition that emphasizes the vernacularity of the French motet, and which runs from Edmond de Coussemaker, *L'Art harmonique au XIIe et XIIIe siècle* (Paris: A. Durand, 1865), to the brilliant observations of Christopher Page, esp. *The Owl and the Nightingale: Musical Life and Ideas in France, 1100–1300* (London: Dent, 1989), esp. 116–25 and 148–54; and Page, *Discarding Images*, 43–111; and those studies that have followed in its wake. That tradition is helpfully summarized (apparently with endorsement) by Karl Kügle, s.v. "Motette," §B, "Historische Entwicklung," pt. 1, "Entstehung" (1997), in *MGG Online*, ed. Laurenz Lütteken, www.mgg-online.com/mgg/stable/58097. Rather more alert to the sophistication of Old French motet poetry—that is, in a way that invites the distinction between literary and musical conceptions of vernacularity I pursue here—is Huot, *Allegorical Play*.

Among other genres of the written tradition, the conductus—often but not uniquely a polyphonic genre—had until recently also fallen foul of a bias in favor of the longer-lived, often showier polytextual motet; but the imbalance is being righted. See Mark Everist, *Discovering Medieval Song: Latin Poetry and Music in the Conductus* (Cambridge: Cambridge University Press, 2018).

16. See, e.g., the variety of interpretations evident in the contributions to Cesare Corsi and Pierluigi Petrobelli, eds., *Le polifonie primitive in Friuli e in Europa* (Rome: Torre d'Orfeo, 1980); and Giulio Cattin and F. Alberto Gallo, eds., *Un millennio di polifonia tra oralità e scrittura* (Bologna: Società editrice Il Mulino, 2002).

17. An early critique, directly related to the motet, was implicit in Ernest H. Sanders, "Peripheral Polyphony of the Thirteenth Century," *Journal of the American Musicological Society* 17 (1964): 261–87. See also Reinhard Strohm, "Center and Periphery; Mainstream and Provincial Music," in *A Companion to Medieval and Renaissance Music*, ed. David Fallows and Tess Knighton (London: Dent, 1992), 55–59.

18. For examples see the comments in Edward H. Roesner, introduction to *Ars antiqua: Organum, Conductus, Motet* (Farnham: Ashgate, 2009), xi–xix; and Taruskin, "Music for an Intellectual and Political Elite."

19. The edition of reference is now Johannes de Grocheio, *Ars musice*, ed. and trans. Constant J. Mews, John N. Crossley, Catherine Jeffreys, Leigh McKinnon, and Carol J. Williams (Kalamazoo, MI: Medieval Institute Publications, 2011). I cite from it using the numbers with which the editors helpfully front each paragraph; and I give a page number for both the Latin and (for completion) their facing-page translation—which is very good, though I have usually tweaked it, nonetheless (I signal when I have done so). All references are henceforth reported in parentheses (whether in the main text or a note). Were the disciplines to expand their conception of "music-theory texts" into "texts transmitting musical knowledge," one wonders whether Grocheio might be found not to be our "lone" sociological commentator after all.

20. Grocheio, *Ars musice*, 85, par. 19.1 (translation adapted). Latin: "Cantus autem iste non debet coram vulgalibus propinari. eo quod eius subtilitatem non advertunt nec in eius auditu delectantur. Sed coram litteratis et illis, qui subtilitates artium sunt quaerentes" (84).

21. In her pathbreaking study of Old French motet poetry, Sylvia Huot wisely observed of Grocheio's comments that "this does not necessarily mean, of course, that motets never were performed for and by the vu[l]galibus, a term by which Grocheio designates the uneducated and presumably undiscerning laity. Indeed, if Grocheio troubled to make the point, it may be because motets were being performed in contexts he disapproved of." Huot, *Allegorical Play*, 9. Christopher Page countered claims of the motet's elitism rather differently, arguing that Grocheio's clerics would have included everyone in orders from great dignitaries to novices. See Page, *Discarding Images*, esp. 83. For a critique of that view, pointing out that it leaves the motet fundamentally clerical and writerly in its ethos, see Curran, "Reading and Rhythm," esp. 145–46. Taruskin, in "Music for an Intellectual and Political Elite," astutely cautions that the "ostensibly descriptive content [of Grocheio's treatise] should be scrutinized with an eye out for covert prescription" (207); yet he finds this passage on the motet to be "the one part of Grocheio's treatise that does have a realistic ring, and which can be taken as truly descriptive" (208), and he characterizes the motet as "the music of Grocheio's own class" (208). I record herewith my heartfelt thanks to Professor Taruskin for his good cheer in supporting my revisionist instincts about the motet. The specialist positions are helpfully examined in Jennifer Saltzstein, "Clerics, Courtiers, and the Vernacular Two-Voice Motet: The Case of *Fines amouretes / Fiat* and the *Roman de la poire*," in *A Critical Companion to Medieval Motets*, ed. Jared C. Hartt (Woodbridge, UK: Boydell, 2018), 193–203.

22. This is particularly surprising because similar remarks are *not* present in the third and

final section of his treatise, which concerns ecclesiastical music—where the correct reproduction of ritual song in the course of a liturgical event might to some commentators have been a matter of theological or doctrinal consequence.

23. Aspects of the treatise's form (but not the rupture I identify here) are examined in Judith A. Peraino, "Re-placing Medieval Music," *Journal of the American Musicological Society* 54, no. 2 (2001): 209–64, esp. 219–25; and John Haines and Patricia DeWitt, "Johannes de Grocheio and Aristotelian Natural Philosophy," *Early Music History* 27 (2008): 47–98, esp. 81–82.

24. Grocheio, *Ars musice*, 61, par. 6.1 (translation adapted). The Latin (of which the corresponding passage to my translation is the final sentence) reads as follows: "Nobis vero non est facile musicam dividere recte, eo quod in recta divisione membra dividentia debent totam naturam totius divisi evacuare. Partes autem musice plures sunt et diverse secundum diversos usus. Si tamen eam diviserimus secundum quod homines parisius ea utuntur, et prout ad usum vel convictum civium est necessaria, et eius membra ut oportet pertractemus, videbitur sufficienter nostra intentio terminari. Eo quod diebus nostris principia cuiuslibet artis liberalis diligenter parisius inquiruntur, et usus earum et fere omnium mechanicarum inveniuntur" (60).

25. Grocheio, *Ars musice*, 61, par. 6.2 (translation adapted). The Latin: "Unum autem membrum dicimus de simplici musica vel civili, quam vulgalem musicam appellamus. Aliud autem de musica composita vel regulari vel canonica, quam appellant musicam mensuratam. Sed tertium genus est quod ex istis duobus efficitur et ad quod ista duo tamquam ad melius ordinantur: Quod ecclesiasticum dicitur: Et ad laudandum creatorem deputatum est" (60).

26. For more on motets as vehicles that aspire to carry shapes of thought across time, see Sean Curran, "Feeling the Polemic of an Early Motet," in *Polemic: Language as Violence in Medieval and Early Modern Discourse*, ed. Almut Suerbaum, George Southcombe, and Benjamin Thompson (Aldershot: Ashgate, 2015), 65–94; Sean Curran, "Writing, Performance, and Devotion in the Thirteenth-Century Motet: The 'La Clayette' Manuscript," in *Manuscripts and Medieval Song: Inscription, Performance, Context*, ed. Helen Deeming and Elizabeth Eva Leach (Cambridge: Cambridge University Press, 2015), 193–220, esp. 208–20; and Curran, "Hockets Broken and Integrated," esp. 64–104. With typical vision, Emma Dillon points the way to such work in her thoughtful study of prayer texts in motets. See Dillon, *The Sense of Sound*, 184–328.

27. Appendix 2 lists all of these versions and their witnesses, including all sources of *Mellis stilla* I have identified, to indicate the breadth of the music's geographical reach, while appendix 3 reports the full shelfmarks for sigla.

28. Among several publications, see Elizabeth Eva Leach, "Nature's Forge and Mechanical Production: Writing, Reading and Performing Song," in *Rhetoric beyond Words: Delight and Persuasion in the Arts of the Middle Ages*, ed. Mary Carruthers (Cambridge: Cambridge University Press, 2010), 72–95; and Anne Stone, "Self-Reflexive Songs and Their Readers in the Late Fourteenth Century," *Early Music* 31 (2003): 180–94.

29. See Elizabeth Eva Leach, "Death of a Lover and the Birth of the Polyphonic Ballade: Machaut's Notated Ballades 1–5," *Journal of Musicology* 19 (2002): 461–502. My characterization of Machaut adapts the title of Leach's book, *Guillaume de Machaut: Secretary, Poet, Musician* (Ithaca, NY: Cornell University Press, 2011).

30. Transcribed taking La Clayette (fols. 374v–75r) as the base manuscript. The piece has been edited several times before: from La Clayette, e.g., in Gordon A. Anderson, ed., *The Motets of the Manuscript La Clayette: Paris, Bibliothèque nationale, nouv. acq. f. fr. 13521*, with texts ed. and trans. Elizabeth A. Close, Corpus mensurabilis musicae 68 ([Rome]: American Institute of Musicology, 1975), 20–21 (for the score) and xxxviii–xxxix (for commentary); and from Mo, e.g., by Yvonne Rokseth, *Polyphonies du XIIIe siècle: Le manuscrit H 196 de la Faculté de Médecine de*

Montpellier, 4 vols. (Paris: Oiseau-Lyre, 1935–39), 2:98–100; and Hans Tischler, ed., *The Montpellier Codex*, Recent Researches in the Music of the Middle Ages and Early Renaissance 2–3, 4–5, 6–7, 8 (Madison, WI: A-R Editions, 1978–85), no. 40, 2:13–15. Although I have consulted all these editions, I have transcribed the piece afresh. All translations are my own unless otherwise indicated.

31. On the relations between motet poetry and Old French monophonic lyric, see (among others) Beverly Jean Evans, "The Unity of Text and Music in the Late Thirteenth-Century French Motet: A Study of Selected Works from the Montpellier Manuscript, Fascicle VII" (PhD diss., University of Pennsylvania, 1983); Christopher Page, *Discarding Images*, esp. "The Rise of the Vernacular Motet" (43–64) and "Johannes de Grocheio, the *Litterati*, and Verbal *Subtilitas* in the Ars Antiqua Motet" (65–111); Sylvia Huot, *Allegorical Play*; and Ardis Butterfield, *Poetry and Music in Medieval France, from Jean Renart to Guillaume de Machaut* (Cambridge: Cambridge University Press, 2002).

32. On the pastourelle references in motet texts, see Evans, "The Register of the 'Je narratif': Manifestations of the *Bonne vie* and the *Pastourelle*," in "Unity of Text and Music," 91–179. For a large selection of pastourelle texts, see William Paden, ed., *The Medieval Pastourelle*, 2 vols. (New York: Garland, 1987). We should acknowledge the disturbing implications of sexual violence, both in the pastourelle genre and this example of its invocation in a motet. For compassionate models of how to do so, see Katherine Gravdal, *Ravishing Maidens: Writing Rape in Medieval French Literature* (Philadelphia: University of Pennsylvania Press, 1991); and Jennifer Saltzstein, "Rape and Repentance in Two Medieval Motets," *Journal of the American Musicological Society* 70, no. 3 (2017): 583–616.

33 Two excellent recent lexicographical accounts appear in the *Anglo-Norman Dictionary (AND² Online Edition)*, s.v. "dementer" (https://anglo-norman.net/entry/dementer) and s.v. "desmentir²" (https://anglo-norman.net/entry/desmentir_2).

34. On the nature opening in Old French lyric repertories, see Jennifer Saltzstein, "Songs of Nature in Medieval Northern France: Landscape, Identity, and Environment," *Journal of the American Musicological Society* 72, no. 1 (2019): 115–80.

35. The verbs *chanter* and *dire* had overlapping semantic fields in the thirteenth century, and the latter could embrace the envoiced register we typically reserve for "song." An excellent example is contained in the quotation Suzannah Clark uses to head her influential article on refrain citation and motet analysis (to which I here acknowledge many debts of method): Clark, " 'S'en dirai chançonete.' " The broader semantic range of the Old French verb *dire* is partly an inheritance from its Latin origins in the verb *dico, dicere*, which could also be used to emphasize the performed, vocal aspect of a public utterance. See C. T. Lewis and C. Short, *A Latin Dictionary*, s.v. "dico, dicere." In any case, "disant" in verse 14 is contrastively at odds with the emphasis given to the avian singing in verses 7–8

36. See the range of uses conveniently presented in the *Anglo-Norman Dictionary (AND² Online Edition)*, s.v. "encontre¹" (https://anglo-norman.net/entry/encontre_1).

37. For a historical overview of the term's emergence, see Sarah Fuller, "Organum—*Discantus*—*Contrapunctus* in the Middle Ages," in *The Cambridge History of Western Music Theory*, ed. Thomas Christensen (Cambridge: Cambridge University Press, 2002), 477–502.

Although, as Fuller reminds us, theorists usually discussed the two-part framework of thirteenth-century polyphony with the Latin term *discantus*, I would argue this does not preclude a polyphonic reading of Robin and Marot's implied song at the end of this triplum. The noun *contrapunctus* was indeed known in the thirteenth century, as attested in *Lexicon Musicum Latinum*, s.v. "contrapunctus -i" (www.woerterbuchnetz.de/LmL/contrapunctus). Moreover, the Latin *contra* is used consistently in treatises that give instructions on how to sing sanctioned dyadic progressions in two voices. Thus, the anonymous thirteenth-century author of a *Tractatus de musica plana et organica* states that "si cantus ascendat duas voces, et organum incipiat in dyapente, descendet quatuor voces et erit cum cantu, verbi gratia: contra ut re, sol re; contra re mi, la mi; contra mi fa, mi fa; contra fa sol, fa ut, sol fa, sol re." Here, "contra" is unambiguously a preposition describing an operation of polyphony-making. See *Scriptorum de musica medii aevi*, ed. Edmond de Coussemaker (Paris: Durand, 1864–76; repr. Hildesheim: Olms, 1963), 2:494; via *Thesaurus Musicarum Latinarum* (https://chmtl.indiana.edu/tml/13th/ANOMUPO). Moreover, the teaching of music "punctus contra punctum" becomes widespread soon after 1300, precisely as polyphonic vernacular songs in a note-against-note style first find their way into written records. There is every reason to understand them as the first written traces of oral practices in circulation for some decades.

Mark Everist has addressed some of these complicated issues, including the relationship of motet style to song composition at the end of the thirteenth century; paths indicated by Everist have recently been explored by Gaël Saint-Cricq and Matthew P. Thomson. See (among several others) Mark Everist, "Motets, French Tenors, and the Polyphonic Chanson ca. 1300," *Journal of Musicology* 24 (2007): 365–406; and Mark Everist, "'Souspirant en terre estrainge': The Polyphonic Rondeau from Adam de la Halle to Guillaume de Machaut," *Early Music History* 26 (2007): 1–42; Gaël Saint-Cricq, "A New Link between the Motet and Trouvère Chanson: The *Pedes-cum-cauda* Motet," *Early Music History* 32 (2013): 179–223; Gaël Saint-Cricq, "Motets in Chansonniers and the Other Culture of the French Thirteenth-Century Motet," in *A Critical Companion to Medieval Motets*, ed. Jared C. Hartt (Woodbridge, UK: Boydell, 2018), 225–42; Matthew P. Thomson, "Building a Motet around Quoted Material: Textual and Musical Structure in Motets Based on Monophonic Songs," in *A Critical Companion to Medieval Motets*, ed. Jared C. Hartt (Woodbridge, UK: Boydell, 2018), 243–60.

38. It might be helpful to clarify (because the word can have other implications in different repertorial or music-theoretical situations) that for the present purposes, I define a *phrase* as a string of consecutively produced pitches, where each string so defined is demarcated by a silence (a "rest") before and after it. The phrase structure of upper voices in relation to their tenor has long been a topic of analytical interest to scholars of the motet; relevant studies are too numerous to report here, but my analysis is particularly indebted to Suzannah Clark's demonstration that the pattern of a voice part's phrase lengths over the course of a thirteenth-century motet may gesture in interpretatively significant ways toward the forms of vernacular monophonic song: see Clark, "'S'en dirai chançonete.'" I have also found influential the techniques developed by Anna Zayaruznaya for visualizing and interpreting musicopoetically the upper-voice forms of fourteenth-century motets: see Zayaruznaya, *The Monstrous New Art*; and Anna Zayaruznaya, *Upper-Voice Structures and Compositional Process in the Ars nova Motet* (London: Routledge, 2018). For an extended analysis of the representational value of upper-voice forms in another motet with opinions about singers and singing, see Curran, "Hockets Broken and Integrated," esp. 75–85. Of course, the transcriptions represent analyses in themselves, for they each prioritize one aspect of the piece's style (the isorhythmic structure of the tenor, in appendix 1(b); and phrase length, in appendix 1(c) at the expense of the clarity (or even presence) of others. On the inherently analytical (and potentially distorting) nature of transcriptions and editions, see Margaret Bent, "Editing Early Music: The Dilemma of Translation," in *Counterpoint, Composition, and Musica Ficta* (London: Routledge, 2002), 219–40.

39. Readers interested to make a start with medieval musical notation may turn to the wonderful resource recently created by Margot Fassler, "A Medieval Music Primer," the appendix to her *Music in the Medieval West* (New York: Norton, 2014), A1–32. For a historical narrative of medieval music-writing, see Thomas Forrest Kelly, *Capturing Music: The Story of Notation* (New York: Norton, 2015). For a judicious guide to the notations used for motets over the genre's medieval life (and the extensive scholarship they have stimulated), see Karen Desmond, "Nota-

tion," in *A Critical Companion to Medieval Motets*, ed. Jared C. Hartt (Woodbridge, UK: Boydell, 2018), 103–30. For an in-depth treatment of the habits of La Clayette's notator, see Curran, "Reading and Rhythm."

40. This repurposing of the *virga* and *punctus* of chant notation as the *longa* and *brevis* of *musica mensurata* has often been attributed to the theorist Franco of Cologne (whence the common epithet "Franconian notation"). On Franco, see *Grove Music Online*, s.v. "Franco of Cologne," by Andrew Hughes (www.oxfordmusiconline.com) and the studies cited there. But there is no particular reason to suppose that scribes learned their craft from theorists rather than that theorists synthesized into intellectual systems notational strategies that began in scribal practice; doubtless theory and practice existed in productive interplay. See the important critique offered in Nicolas Bell, *The Las Huelgas Music Codex: A Companion Study to the Facsimile* (Madrid: Testimonio Compañía Editorial, 2003), esp. 82–88.

41. Another feature of this "early mensural notation" is that several consecutive, different pitches sung to the same syllable could be represented with a single graphical form that, for music of this period, we call a "ligature." In the transcription presented in appendix 1(c), however, I resolve ligatures into their constituent individual notes and their appropriate shapes; a series of notes that had been ligated in the manuscript is indicated with a square bracket above the score.

42. Margaret Bent has aptly characterized this property (as it appears in fourteenth- and fifteenth-century music-writing) by calling the notations "under-prescriptive by our standards." See Margaret Bent, "The Grammar of Early Music: Preconditions for Analysis," in *Tonal Structures in Early Music*, ed. Cristle Collins Judd (New York: Garland, 1998), 15–59, 25.

43. For a thorough study of that canon, see Sandra Pinegar, "Textual and Conceptual Relationships among Theoretical Writings on Measurable Music of the Thirteenth and Early Fourteenth Centuries" (PhD diss., Columbia University, 1991).

44. For the lexical evidence, see *Lexicon Musicum Latinum Medii Aevi*, s.v. "semibrevis -is f. et semibrevis -e" (www.woerterbuchnetz.de/LmL/semibrevis); for theoretical analysis with which mine here concurs, see Pinegar, "Textual and Conceptual Relationships," 313–14.

45. Semibreves are characterized as "ultra mensuram" in perhaps the earliest of the treatises on *musica mensurata*, the so-called *Discantus positio vulgaris* reported in the later work by Hieronymus of Moravia, *Tractatus de musica*, ed. S. M. Cserba (Regensburg: Pustet, 1935), 189–94, 189: "Mensurabile est, quod mensura unius temporis vel plurium mensuratur. Ultra mensuram sunt, quae minus quam uno tempore . . . mensurantur, ut semibreves." What came to concern theorists of the latter part of the century was the question of whether and how the division of a *tempus* into three semibreves could be reconciled with division into two. The first theorist to prescribe behaviors for the semibreve was Lambertus, who specified that three semibreves placed for a breve of one *tempus* should be of equal duration (i.e., as in a modern "triplet"), while two semibreves placed for one *tempus* should be performed unequally in the proportion 1:2; but even here there is ambiguity, because Lambertus seems unconcerned whether the shorter or the longer semibreve should be placed first. See *The "Ars Musica" Attributed to Magister Lambertus/Aristoteles*, ed. Christian Meyer, trans. Karen Desmond, with an introduction and critical notes by Meyer, trans. Barbara Haggh-Huglo (Farnham: Ashgate, 2015), 76: "Solo recta brevis moderatur tempore quevis—seipsamque in duas diminuit partes non equales vel in tres tantummodo equales et indivisibiles. Quarum prima pars duarum semibrevis minor appellatur, secunda vero maior, *et econverso*" (emphasis added). Among motets of the La Clayette manuscript and the Old Corpus of the Montpellier Codex (i.e., fascicles 2–6 of this composite, eight-fascicle manuscript), division of the *brevis recta* into more than three texted semibreves occurs only in this piece; see Desmond, "Notation," esp. 152–53. In a new study that arrived as the present volume was going to press (precluding engagement here), Catherine A. Bradley has

also considered the four-semibreve groups in *Par une matinee*. See Catherine A. Bradley, *Authorship and Identity in Late Thirteenth-Century Motets* (London: Routledge, 2022), 81.

46. The best narrative of the stylistic development of the thirteenth-century motet remains Crocker, "French Polyphony."

47. This way of scanning departs from the modern convention in romance prosody of omitting a final unstressed syllable from a line's count. The departure needs no defense; if such syllables counted for thirteenth-century notators, they must count for us, too. Labeling rhymes (or, indeed, characterizing some verse-end sounds *as* rhymes rather than assonances) is trickier here, because the rhyme-vowel, especially the vowel represented by orthographic <i> (the b-rhyme of the opening quatrain), is ended with a variety of consonant codas of uncertain phonemic value (at least in the La Clayette copy; the scribe of Mo—whose witness can on other grounds be declared poorer—reports zero-endings for most <i> rhymes). If we assume that phonemic distinctions are registered by the terminal consonants, a rhyme-notation that would capture the play of vocalic sameness and consonantal difference for verses 1 to 7 would be abab′b′b′b″. The clumsiness of the labels notwithstanding, they highlight how a consonantal sound change is used in line 4 and then 7 to articulate the rounding off of the quatrain and the tercet.

48. This analysis designates pitches in accordance with their construal in the medieval gamut, *A–G* in the lower octave and *a–g* in the upper (with *c* corresponding to the note called "middle *c*" in familiar modern usage); note names are put in italics to distinguish them from rhyme designations. Though the terminology of *ouvert/clos* pitch structure is primarily associated with the design of fourteenth-century *formes fixes* chansons, there is precedent for adapting them for use in the analysis of thirteenth-century music. The terms are applied to paired melodic phrases of thirteenth-century discant in Fritz Reckow, "Das Organum," in *Gattungen der Musik in Einzeldarstellungen: Gedenkschrift Leo Schrade*, ed. Wulf Arlt, Ernst Lichtenhahn, and Hans Oesch (Bern: Francke, 1973), 434–96, 477; and Reckow's use of the terminology is endorsed and expanded to motets in Alejandro Enrique Planchart, "The Flower's Children," *Journal of Musicological Research* 22 (2003): 303–48, 309. Important for the following argument, contemporaneous monophonic songs are usually found to have been composed with planned pitch structures organized (at least in part) by the initial and final notes of each verse within the strophe. Studies that influence my analysis here include Elizabeth Aubrey, "Form," in *The Music of the Troubadours* (Bloomington: Indiana University Press, 1996), 132–97; Elizabeth Eva Leach, "Do Trouvère Melodies Mean Anything?," *Music Analysis* 38 nos. 1–2 (2019): 3–46; Fiona McAlpine, "Authenticity and *Auteur*: The Songs of Hugues de Berzé," *Plainsong and Medieval Music* 4 (1995): 13–32; and Mary O'Neill, "The Melodic Art of the Trouvères: Orality and the Question of Melodic Variants," in *Courtly Love Songs of Medieval France: Transmission and Style in the Trouvère Repertoire* (Oxford: Oxford University Press, 2006), 53–92.

49. My interpretive method here is indebted to Carolyn Abbate, *Unsung Voices: Opera and Musical Narrative in the Nineteenth Century* (Princeton, NJ: Princeton University Press, 1991), particularly "Wotan's Monologue and the Morality of Musical Narration," 156–205; and esp. to Clark, "'S'en dirai chançonete,'" 36–40.

50. For a history of this development (labeling the form AAB, which is more usual, even though XXY is a clearer nomenclature in the present context), see Taruskin, *Oxford History of Western Music*, 1:121–26; and on AAB upper-voice structures in thirteenth-century motets, see Saint-Cricq, "A New Link."

51. To view their manuscript orthography, see Cl, fol. 375r, column a, lines 2 and 3, online at https://gallica.bnf.fr/ark:/12148/btv1b530121530/f755.item.

52. On emotive vocables in the thirteenth-century motet, see Emma Dillon, "Madness and the Eloquence of Nonsense," in *The Sense of Sound: Musical Meaning in France, 1260–1330*

(Oxford: Oxford University Press, 2012), 129–73. See also Emma Dillon, "Representing Obscene Sound," in *Medieval Obscenities*, ed. Nicola McDonald (Woodbridge, UK: Boydell and Brewer; York Medieval Press, 2006), 55–84.

53. For more on imperfect modes, see Mary E. Wolinski, "Hocketing and the Imperfect Modes in Relation to Poetic Expression in the Thirteenth Century," *Musica Disciplina* 58 (2013): 393–411. One may ask whether Marot's reported song here counts as a "refrain." Nico H. J. van den Boogaard (whose bibliographical survey remains foundational to present scholarship) considered Marot's reported song to be one; our triplum is a concordance to refrain no. 220 of his catalogue, to which he gives the textual form "Biaus doz amis, / por quoi demorés tant?" See Boogaard, *Rondeaux et refrains du XIIe siècle au début du XIVe* (Paris: Klincksieck, 1969), 220. This is taken over into the Southampton *Refrain* Database, s.v. "vdB 220," by Anne Ibos-Augé and Mark Everist, in *Music, Poetry, Citation: The Medieval Refrain* (http://refrain.ac.uk/view/abstract_item/220.html). The only other listed concordance of the refrain is motet no. 28, which appears in the Montpellier Codex as the triplum of a four-part French motet, *A dieu conmant* (27) / *Pour moi deduire et pour moi deporter* (28) / *En nom dieu que que nus die* (29) / Omnes (M1), *Mo* fascicle 2, no. 24, fol. 36 verso; and also as the triplum to a three-part bilingual motet found only in La Clayette, *Pour renvoisier et por moi deporter* (28) / *Mulier omnis peccati facta est initium* (30) / Omnes (M1), La Clayette no. 26, fol. 379 verso. (Of these two pieces, the Latin and French motetus parts share the same melody.) Van den Boogaard takes the "refrain" of the four-part motet in *Mo* as his indexed form. As can be seen immediately, it contains far fewer verses than the version reported as Marot's song in our motet; nor does it have the same melody. Boogaard's assertion of a direct refrain citation must therefore be rejected.

54. See note 35, above.

55. For a conspectus of theoretical views, see Wolf Frobenius, "Semibrevis" (1971), in *Handwörterbuch der musikalischen Terminologie*, ed. Heinz Heinrich Eggebrecht (Wiesbaden: F. Steiner, 1971–2005), www.musiconn.de/id/hmt/hmt2bsb00070513f511t520/ft/bsb00070513f511t520?page=511&c=solrSearchHmT.

56. Elizabeth Eva Leach, "'The Little Pipe Sings Sweetly as the Fowler Deceives the Bird': Sirens in the Middle Ages," *Music & Letters* 87 (2006): 187–211; Elizabeth Eva Leach, "Gendering the Semitone, Sexing the Leading Tone: Fourteenth-Century Music Theory and the Directed Progression," *Music Theory Spectrum* 28 (2006): 1–21; and Elizabeth Eva Leach, *Sung Birds: Music, Nature, and Poetry in the Later Middle Ages* (Ithaca, NY: Cornell University Press, 2007).

57. I owe a debt to Carolyn Abbate's analysis of how music present may represent music not directly heard. See Carolyn Abbate, *In Search of Opera* (Princeton, NJ: Princeton University Press, 2001).

58. To use the word *member* to describe a unit with partitive relationship to some higher entity of verse would seem to have the historical sanction of Johannes de Garlandia (the grammarian; he may or may not be Garlandia the music theorist). See Johannes de Garlandia, *Parisiana Poetria*, ed. and trans. Traugott Lawler (Cambridge, MA: Harvard University Press, 2020), chap. 7 §28, 282.

59. Dolores Pesce has compellingly addressed this kind of phonemic play in motet texts in "The Significance of Text in Thirteenth-Century Latin Motets," *Acta Musicologica* 58, no. 1 (1986): 91–117, esp. 93–94. For a study of the corpus of explicitly devotional motet texts in French, see Mark Everist, "Devotional Forms," in *French Motets in the Thirteenth Century: Music, Poetry, and Genre* (Cambridge: Cambridge University Press, 1994), 126–47. See also David J. Rothenberg, "The Marian Symbolism of Spring, ca. 1200–ca. 1500: Two Case Studies," *Journal of the American Musicological Society* 59 (2006): 319–98, esp. 329–54. This material is developed further in David J. Rothenberg, *The Flower of Paradise: Marian Devotion and Secular Song in Medieval and Renaissance Music* (Oxford: Oxford University Press, 2011), esp. "The Assumption

Story in Two Thirteenth-Century Motet Families" (24–57) and "Springtime and Renewal over the *In seculum* Tenor" (58–91).

60. *Fractio modi* is a concept derived from contemporaneous theorists; it describes the breaking of a larger rhythmic value into several smaller ones whose sum is equivalent to it. See Norman Smith, "The Notation of *Fractio Modi*," in *Studies in Medieval Music: Festschrift for Ernest H. Sanders*, ed. Peter M. Lefferts and Brian Seirup, *Current Musicology* 45–47 (1990): 283–304.

61. Still the most important overview of the many meanings—medieval and modern—of the concept of mode is Harold Powers, s.v. "Mode," in *The New Grove Dictionary of Music and Musicians*, ed. Stanley Sadie (London: Macmillan, 1980), 12:376–450. An updated version appears in *Grove Music Online*, s.v. "Mode," by Powers et al., www.oxfordmusiconline.com. My observations in this analysis of *Mellis stilla* and its tenor take inspiration from Richard L. Crocker's observation that "in any given motet . . . the final may be different from the central note or lie outside the locus" (that is, the locus of tenor motion over the course of the piece, before its final note). Crocker, "French Polyphony," 667.

62. Friedrich Ludwig interpreted the connection of style and circulation similarly (though he came down perhaps a bit more heavily on the side of causality): "Dazu kam, dass auch der 2 st. Unterbau zu den beliebtesten und verbreitetsten Marien-Motetten gehörte, was er wohl seiner fliessenden Melodik, die wie in 4,54 und 4,58 im 2. Teil über dem gleichen Tenor viele melodische Wendungen des 1. Teils wiederholt, seinem durchsichtigen Aufbau (Mot. und T. pausieren stets gemeinsam) und seiner aparten 7 taktigen Periodenbildung verdankt." Ludwig, *Repertorium*, 2:406.

63. Such studies would be too numerous to list here, but the work of Leo Treitler has been particularly influential in such branches of scholarship. Especially pertinent to the current discussion is Leo Treitler, "The Vatican Organum Treatise and the Organum of Notre Dame of Paris: Perspectives on the Development of a Literate Music Culture in Europe," in *With Voice and Pen: Coming to Know Medieval Song and How It Was Made* (Oxford: Oxford University Press, 2003), 68–83, and the other essays collected in that volume. Two further careful studies must be acknowledged. Anna-Maria Busse Berger's thoughtful examination of the role played by mnemotechnics in the creation of Notre Dame polyphony also might have much to reveal about a piece like this. She suggests that modal rhythm, by analogy with regularly accentual versification (which our motet also displays), was a tool of mnemotechnic manipulation, allowing for the extemporized alignment and creation of discant clausulae and perhaps even the elaborate four-part organa attributed to Perotin. Anna-Maria Busse Berger, *Medieval Music and the Art of Memory* (Berkeley: University of California Press, 2005), esp. "The Memorization of Organum, Discant, and Counterpoint Treatises" (111–58) and "Compositional Process and the Transmission of Notre Dame Polyphony" (161–97). Susan Rankin's work on the relations of orality and writing in early polyphony must be a touchstone for all subsequent accounts. For her thought on Parisian polyphony, see esp. Susan Rankin, "Thirteenth-Century Notations and Arts of Performance," in *Vom Preis des Fortschritts: Gewinn und Verlust in der Musikgeschichte*, ed. Andreas Haug and Andreas Dorschel (Vienna: Universal Edition, 2008), 110–40.

64. I follow Richard Taruskin's distinction between poiesis and esthesis. See his "The Poietic Fallacy," in *The Danger of Music and Other Anti-utopian Essays* (Berkeley: University of California Press, 2008), 301–29. For a critique of the role "oral vs. written" dichotomies have played in the historiography of Gregorian chant, see Richard L. Crocker, "Gregorian Studies in the Twenty-First Century," *Plainsong and Medieval Music* 4 (1995): 33–86, esp. 49–63.

65. Agostino Ziino finds its tenor's rhythmic pattern to presage fourteenth-century isorhythmic structuring. See Agostino Ziino, "Some Observations on the Motet *Mellis stilla—Domino*," *Revista de Musicología* 13, no. 2 (1990): 487–99, 490. The term *isorhythm* may not be

as appropriate to the fourteenth-century motet as it seemed at Ziino's time of writing, however. See Margaret Bent, "What Is Isorhythm?," in *Quomodo cantabimus canticum? Studies in Honor of Edward H. Roesner*, ed. David Butler Cannata et al. (Middleton, WI: American Institute of Musicology, 2008), 121–43.

66. By the thirteenth century, Alleluia melodies had long been reused from one liturgical situation to another and were often supplied in the process with new texts. For an overview with references to the further bibliography, see James W. McKinnon and Christian Thodberg, s.v. "Alleluia," in *Grove Music Online*, www.oxfordmusiconline.com. Meanwhile, the versicle *Benedicamus domino* was (as Anne Walters Robertson has pointed out) stipulated for all sorts of liturgical situations; good snippets of melody for singing it with were regularly borrowed *ad libitum* from all sorts of chants (including Alleluias). See Robertson, "*Benedicamus domino*: The Unwritten Tradition," *Journal of the American Musicological Society* 41, no. 1 (1988): 1–62. That melodies commonly shuffle between contexts in these genres makes the incipits *Domino* and *Alleluia*, in my view, entirely plausible guesses for a scribe tasked with copying an unfamiliar motet-tenor. Perhaps one of them was correct, and a source melody for *Mellis stilla*'s tenor will present itself in due course with still more thorough bibliographical work on the relevant repertories.

67. See Marie Louise Göllner, *The Manuscript Cod. lat. 5539 of the Bavarian State Library; with an Edition of the Original Treatises and of the Two-Voice Organal Settings* (Neuhausen-Stuttgart: Hänssler-Verlag / American Institute of Musicology, 1993), 145. The chant as sung at Notre Dame (and taken here as my text for analysis) can be consulted in the early thirteenth-century missal Paris, Bibliothèque nationale de France, Latin 1112, fol. 105v, column b, lines 7–13 (where the "domino" melisma falls at line 10). See online at https://gallica.bnf.fr/ark:/12148/btv1b6000450z/f220.item.r=latin%201112. My techniques for analyzing melody here blend strategies developed by Richard L. Crocker and Susan Rankin. See (among their other studies) Richard L. Crocker, *An Introduction to Gregorian Chant* (New Haven, CT: Yale University Press, 2000), 22–63; and Susan Rankin, "Carolingian Music," in *Carolingian Culture: Emulation and Innovation*, ed. Rosamund McKitterick (Cambridge: Cambridge University Press, 1994), 274–316.

68. The phrase "directed progression" is Sarah Fuller's. See her "Tendencies and Resolutions: The Directed Progression in Ars Nova Music," *Journal of Music Theory* 36, no. 2 (1992): 229–58. On the progression's grammatical status, see esp. Bent, "The Grammar of Early Music."

69. Under that proposition, the only motet to use the DOMINO II melisma that does *not* pair it with *Mellis stilla* (a piece uniquely transmitted in the fifth fascicle of the Montpellier Codex, *Mal d'amors* (811) / *Dame je* (812) / DOMINO II; it is listed as appendix 2(iv)) would of course represent a later composition than the *Mellis stilla*—DOMINO II pair (though not necessarily later than the composition of *Par une matinee*). That this is the most probable chronology is supported by the observation that the motet appendix 2(iv) shares not only the pitch series but also the unusual rhythmic pattern of the tenor in the *Mellis stilla* motets (but states it in just one *cursus*, where *Mellis stilla* requires two). This precise formal sharing is more likely to have come about by borrowing the tenor of one motet directly from its setting in the other than from two independent acts of creation starting from the same now-lost chant and ending up with the same unusual rhythmic pattern by chance. Philological microhistories of this kind are enjoying an exuberant renaissance in motet scholarship of late, especially in studies by Catherine A. Bradley and Matthew P. Thomson. See, e.g., Catherine A. Bradley, "Choosing a Thirteenth-Century Motet Tenor: From the *Magnus liber organi* to Adam de la Halle," *Journal of the American Musicological Society* 72, no. 2 (2019): 431–92; and Matthew P. Thomson, "Building a Motet."

70. This is to suggest we adopt a skeptical view toward medieval and modern claims about the motet's distinguishing writtenness, and also toward those modes of scholarship that

confidently identify this or that stylistic feature of a motet as evidence of its "oral" creation. *Mellis stilla* gives us reason to be skeptical about arguments that draw poietic conclusions from esthetic musical observations (and the aesthetic judgments that attend them). In formulating matters this way, I wish to acknowledge the deep marks left on my thinking by my late teachers Richard Crocker and Richard Taruskin. See Crocker, "Gregorian Studies," esp. 49–63; and Taruskin, "The Poietic Fallacy."

71. Nor, indeed, must it necessarily have been Arras or nearby areas in the southern Low Countries that have recently gathered needed attention as centers of motet-making beyond Paris, and for new stylistic rapprochements of motet and song forms, in the late thirteenth and early fourteenth centuries. See, e.g., Mark Everist, "Friends and Foals: The Polyphonic Music of Adam de la Halle," in *Musical Culture in the World of Adam de la Halle*, ed. Jennifer Saltzstein (Leiden: Brill, 2019), 311–51, and the studies cited there.

72. For more on this sort of social context for music making, see Blake Wilson, *Music and Merchants: The Laudesi Companies of Republican Florence* (Oxford: Clarendon Press, 1992), esp. 154–57.

73. For a synoptic presentation, see the comparative transcription in Curran, "Vernacular Book Production," 335–42.

74. I report the five theoretical citations identified in Gordon A. Anderson, ed., *Motets of the Manuscript La Clayette*, xxxviii, of which all but one (siglum "Anon Pavia") have a critical edition that may be consulted online at *Thesaurus Musicarum Latinarum* (and to each of which I give a link).

75. This is not in itself a surprise, for notated examples are among the most variably transmitted components of medieval theory treatises. On this, see Christian Thomas Leitmeir, "Klang, Zeichen, Schrift: Zwei Fallstudien zur schriftlichen Vermittlung und Überlieferung im Mittelalter und der Frühen Neuzeit," in *"Übertragungen": Formen und Konzepte von Reproduktion in Mittelalter und Früher Neuzeit*, ed. Albrecht Hausmann et al. (Berlin: Walter de Gruyter, 2005), 43–76; and Christian Thomas Leitmeir, "Types and Transmission of Musical Examples in Franco's *Ars cantus mensurabilis musicae*," in *Citation and Authority in Medieval and Renaissance Culture: Learning from the Learned*, ed. Suzannah Clark and Elizabeth Eva Leach (Woodbridge, UK: Boydell, 2005), 29–44. The Franconian treatises that cite *Mellis stilla* present the added complexity that they are in close textual relationship to one another; further study of their manuscript traditions, not undertaken here, might lead to the conclusion that they represent fewer separate texts (or perhaps more) than I have listed. Conditions of access have made it impracticable to check how *Mellis stilla* is presented in the manuscript witnesses of each treatise, but the variation reported by the examples in the critical editions is, in any case, ample evidence to support the claim about reading I make here.

76. Catherine A. Bradley seems to adopt a position akin to mine when she suggests that certain harmonic features of later thirteenth-century motets "were . . . part of a more universal practice of making vernacular polyphony that was current also in France from at least the 1240s" and that "such a hypothesis might seem to threaten the elite status of the motet genre, one whose roots in the notated liturgical polyphony of the *Magnus liber organi* are typically emphasized by scholars, who have preferred to minimize its dependence on the less elevated and monotextual polyphonic rondeaux." Bradley, "Choosing a Thirteenth-Century Motet Tenor," 487. (For my take on related matters, see Curran, "Vernacular Polyphony.") I welcome the agreement, although I observe that by "vernacular polyphony," Bradley means *polyphonic music with text(s) in a vernacular language*. For reasons that will become clear below, I prefer to maintain a notional distinction between musical and linguistic vernacularities, the better to appreciate the creative richness with which thirteenth-century artists involved them with one another.

77. On grafting as a concept with which thirteenth-century poet-musicians described and reflected on the work of song building, see Ardis Butterfield, "The Language of Medieval Music: Two Thirteenth-Century Motets," *Plainsong and Medieval Music* 2 (1993): 1–16; Butterfield, "*Enté*; and Peraino, *Giving Voice to Love*, esp. 208–13.

78. See Samuel N. Rosenberg, "The *envoi* in Trouvère Lyric, with Particular Attention to the Songs of Gace Brulé," *Romance Philology* 58 (2004): 51–67; and Chantal Phan, "La tornada et l'envoi: Functions structurelles et poïétiques," *Cahiers de civilisation médiévale (Xe–XIIe siècles)* 34 (1991): 57–61.

79. On the lyric *je*, the classic study is Kevin Brownlee, "Transformation of the Lyric 'Je': The Example of Guillaume de Machaut," *L'Esprit Créateur* 18, no. 1 (1978): 5–18.

80. These two measures qualify as a moment of "monaurality" as I have delineated the concept elsewhere. See Curran, "Writing, Performance, and Devotion," 217; and Curran, "Hockets Broken and Integrated," 87.

81. For more on the possible vernacularity of Latin, see Christopher Cannon, "Vernacular Latin," *Speculum* 90, no. 3 (2015): 641–53; and for a musicological perspective on the registrations that produce vernacularity in musical cultures, see Michael Long, "The Expressive Vernacular," in *Beautiful Monsters: Imagining the Classic in Musical Media* (Berkeley: University of California Press, 2008), 11–43.

CHAPTER EIGHT

“Where the *Sì* Sounds”

Dante’s Dissonant Vernaculars and Their Sensual Signs

Alison Cornish

At the bottom of Hell, Dante’s interview with Count Ugolino ends not with the awfully ambiguous line, “Then fasting did more than grief could do,” but with the sound of his teeth hitting hard against the skull of his enemy:

> “Poscia, più che ’l dolor, poté ’l digiuno.”
> Quand’ ebbe detto ciò, con li occhi torti
> riprese ’l teschio misero co’ denti,
> che furo a l’osso, come d’un can, forti.
>
> [“Then fasting did more than grief could do.” When he had said this, with twisted eyes he took the skull in his teeth again, which were loud against the bone, like those of a dog. (*Inferno* 33.75–78).][1]

The whole episode pivots around speaking and silence—what is possible to say and what is unspeakable. Speech is offered in return for other speech. In the lowest parts of Hell the promise of personal fame that worked well in higher levels is a less attractive bargaining chip among the most depraved. So Dante cannily offers not fame but infamy for the person for whom Ugolino shows such hatred by means of the "bestial sign" of devouring his head. He promises, if this miserable sinner's complaint is just, to tell the world above about the crimes of the person he is gnawing on, if that with which Dante speaks does not dry up.[2]

What *is* that feminine thing (*quella*) with which Dante speaks? Is it his mouth (*bocca*), like Ugolino's mouth that he has to wipe fastidiously on the hair of the skull that he has wasted from behind before responding? Or is it his voice? By which I mean not just the articulate sound he could once make with his anatomical equipment but the written trace of that voice, the "sign of the voice that survives the voice once it falls silent."[3] Or might that durable medium be poetry itself, the art that "lasts the longest" precisely because of its detachability from its original voice, accent, ink, or parchment, even from its original idiom, since some poetry, like Dante's, actually does survive translation?[4] What the traveler encounters at the bottom of Hell is the reduction of speech to noise, the sound of jaws crushing flesh and bone. The horrific episode pointedly recalls Dante's unfinished treatise on the eloquence of the vernacular, where he gamely went on a virtual "listening tour" of the Italian peninsula in search of an elusive "illustrious" vernacular. The political purpose of such a linguistic quest is to find an idiom that could make populations separated by geography (even those relatively proximate) to be more comprehensible, more eloquent, and more persuasive to each other. The ambition was to provide a common linguistic instrument to the inhabitants of the peninsula that, unlike the technical artificial language of Latin, would retain the naturalness and hence, according to Dante, the nobility of the indigenous vernacular tongue that sounds so different in different regions. The episode of Ugolino shows that it is not a unification of sound that is needed to unite Italy, or indeed even the closest of physical neighbors, but a commonality of spirit, without which voice becomes mere instrument and, ultimately, mere noise, a brutal gnashing of teeth, a zero-sum game of all-against-all. What matters to Dante by the time he comes to write the *Inferno* is less the particular sound of the vernacular in which he chooses to write—which will be and was subject to modification, regional adaptation, modernization, and translation—than what resounds in the soul however differently it gets sounded out. Ultimately, the relation of authentic, local, natural, and audible speech to what can survive it is an issue for Dante's whole poetic project: his choice for the vernacular and his bid for transcendence.

What Ugolino hears in that voice of Dante's—which now, for us, has fallen silent—is his specific regional accent. It tells him where this visitor is from. He says, "I don't know who you are nor how you have come down here; but you seem Florentine to me when I hear you."[5] The count does not know, nor does he ask, who this person is or how he might have gotten to the bottom of Hell with the hope of still getting out—an extraordinary thing, indeed, not an everyday occurrence. The fact that Dante is Florentine and still living, with still-functioning speaking equipment, is important because he can go back to Tuscany and "sow" infamy for Ruggieri, who is of the powerful Ubaldini family, who controlled the valley of the Mugello just outside Florence. Upon lifting his mouth from his savage meal and daintily wiping it on the hair of his victim's head, Ugolino declares that to speak in response to Dante's request will renew "desperate" grief, sorrow, and pain (*dolor*) but that it will be worth it to inflict this additional suffering on himself so long as his words might be seeds that could grow into the fruit of infamy for the traitor whom he hates.[6] The comparison of words to seeds clearly echoes the parable of the sower in Matthew 13, which also has to do with hearing, thereby underscoring that he is requesting a sonic transmission of these words in the world above.[7] It reminds us that there is another dimension to the written word, another layer of meaning transmitted by something the writing cannot capture: the particular sound, accent, or voice to which the writing alludes. For a traitorous partisan like the count, this localization of language is key.

At the other end of the interview, as I have already mentioned, Ugolino's speaking is once again silenced by his eating, when he returns to the wretched skull with his teeth, which were hard, or loud, against the bone, like those of a dog. It is the moment where words end but noise persists. In response, Dante-pilgrim makes no comment and utters no sound. It is, rather, the voice of the poet that reacts with a great general invective against the whole city of Pisa: "Ahi Pisa, vituperio de le genti del bel paese là dove 'l sì suona" (Ah, Pisa, shame of the people of the beautiful country where the *sì* sounds [*Inferno* 33.79–80]). This linguistic designation of the Italian peninsula as the land where *sì* sounds is an echo of Dante's treatise on the eloquence of the vernacular, *De vulgari eloquentia*, where the "triform idiom" of what we might call Romance languages is subdivided by the sound used to express the affirmative—*oil*, *oc*, and *sì*—an affirmative that stands out as particularly ironic in the sheer negation that is nether Hell. The word *vituperio* itself, used in apposition to *Pisa*, suggests that the whole city is a kind of speech act, a disgrace, the opposite of praise. Pisa is an opprobrium, an expression of condemnation, on all the people joined by a particular sound, the sound they make for the affirmative: *sì*, a sound that both crosses linguistic boundaries within the peninsula and marks it off, uniting the discordant cities and regions it contains in a commonality of sound. In the context of treachery, lowest subset of fraud, populated by Tuscans, who certainly did not follow the biblical prescription to "let your yes be yes," this *sì* becomes the empty sibilant signifying the larger geographical region of a city that stands as a kind of curse upon the rest.[8]

It is the vernacular, even when written, that is intimately linked with sound. We associate Dante with the literary origins of the *lingua volgare*, which was still in his day essentially written sound, not yet a fixed language with accepted spellings and grammar. Yet Dante's awareness of the multiplicity, variability, and fragility of the spoken word meant that he could not and perhaps would not care to guarantee the sound of his writing—that is, how his writing would sound over time. In the treatise on language, he offers written poetic examples, primarily his own, to help construct an "illustrious" vernacular out of the sounds of speech heard on the peninsula that could be used by all. He is, in fact, offering the people who live there an instrument that, if they make it their own, would become a powerful voice and could perhaps form the curia, or royal court, that in divided Italy is sorely lacking.[9]

The subject, the noble subject, of Dante's treatise on the eloquence of the vulgar tongue is explicitly sonic. Humans require a rational, sensual sign in order to communicate with each other. "This sign," Dante says, "is the noble subject about which we speak; for it is sensual insofar as it is sound, but rational insofar as it can be seen to signify something at will."[10] Sound is the sensual medium without which the vaunted rationality of humans could not travel, could not transit to the rationality of other humans.[11] The vernacular, as opposed to the grammatical language, is the one that children learn by imitating the voices of their nurses. It is the language used by the whole world, albeit with different pronunciations.[12] Although some scholars have understood *prolationes* as "endings" (*desinenze*), as in verb- or noun-endings, Enrico Fenzi musters an array of sources to make clear that this word indicates the "sensual" aspect of every word-act "insofar as it is sound," citing ancient sources that define *verborum prolatio* as the sound articulated by mouth, lips, and teeth, in order to form voice into words, as in the sounding out of Scripture demanded by devotional reading[13]

Sound seems to be an essential criterion in the winnowing search for an illustrious vernacular among the spoken tongues of the Italian peninsula. Dante, in fact, compares this elusive language to a panther whose perfume is everywhere but whose lair is nowhere. But this fragrance, this redolence, is really the *sound* of the panther's voice, as is clear from the medieval bestiaries from which Dante draws such panther lore: "If the panther arises from his sleep on the third day (like our Savior) . . . he roars out in a loud voice and many a pleasant fragrance issues from his voice. Those who are far away and those who are near, hearing his voice, follow its pleasant fragrance."[14] So language, particularly the language that is the "noble subject" of the treatise on the vernacular, is transmitted by sound and distinguished by sound. Dante says that the Italian *volgare* is "dissonant" in its many varieties, which is to say that the ways in which it is spoken in various geographical locations differ in sound.[15] *Dissonant*, the opposite of *consonant*, obviously suggests a Dantesque political critique. Lacking harmony, Italy is discordant, irreconcilable, clashing, disagreeing, cacophonous, irregular. Indeed, this seems to be the case from what Dante reports from his "listening tour" of the peninsula in the treatise on language. The people of Aquileia and Istria "belch forth with a brutal intonation" (*crudeliter accentuando eructuant*). And the pronounced accent of mountain people like those of Casentino and Fratta always seems to clash (*accentus enormitate dissonare*) with that of the city dwellers. Some pronunciations make women sound like men and men sound like women even if they try to speak in a virile manner (*si viriliter sonet*).[16]

My point is that these are all *sounds*. The criticisms are not about pedigree, or sophistication of constructs, or proximity to Latin. Indeed, one of Dante's most perplexing claims is that the vernacular of the Sardinians resembles Latin *too* closely, in fact, identically. He uses this phrase as an example: *domus nova et dominus meus*. Therefore, Dante says, they seem uniquely to lack their own *volgare*.[17] The defect of their language is precisely that they have not made it proper to themselves. This underlines the sense that a necessary feature of a vernacular is that it be one's own, not a borrowed instrument. Dante, very unkindly, compares the Latin-sounding Sardinians to apes, for this imitative quality. But they could also be compared to magpies, who entered into the discussion early on as a possible example of talking animals, because of an episode in Ovid's *Metamorphoses* where it would seem birds speak.

> Moreover, if anyone finds a contrary argument in what Ovid, in the fifth book of the Metamorphoses, says about talking magpies, I reply that this is said figuratively and means something else. And if it be claimed that, to this day, magpies and other birds do indeed speak, I say that this is not so; for their act is that they try to imitate us insofar as we make a noise, but not insofar as we speak. So that, if to someone who said "*pica*" aloud the bird were to return the word "*pica*," this would only be a reproduction or imitation of the sound made by the person who uttered the word first.[18]

This is not speaking, Dante says, only sounding, an imitation of the sound of the human voice. The Sardinians are similar to magpies insofar as they are capable only of repeating back what has been said to them.

The grammarians distinguished between sounds that could and could not be written, as well as between meaningful (articulate) and nonmeaningful ones, which is sometimes taken as the human-animal boundary and the privilege humans arrogate only to themselves.[19] Yet in the *De vulgari eloquentia*, the ability to speak (or write) by no means places human beings at the summit of creation. Not only are all men beneath the immense category of angels; it is very clear that men require language because of their *deficiencies* with respect to *both* angels and animals: "only to them was it *necessary*." As Enrico Fenzi observes in his commentary: it's not that man *can* speak; it's that he *has* to.[20]

Angels, moreover, when they want to speak, can use animals, because animals have something angels don't have: sound. Thus the ass who spoke to Balaam and the serpent who spoke to Eve had their vocal organs manipulated by spiritual beings who lack their own voice.[21] Even God makes use of instruments in order to speak after the fashion of humans, moving the air "to produce the sounds of words, made articulate by Him": "Adam may well have answered a question from God; nor, on that account, need God have spoken using what we would call language. For who doubts that everything that exists obeys a sign from God . . . ? Therefore, if the air can be moved, at the command of the lesser nature which is God's servant and creation, to transformations so profound that thunderbolts crash, lightning flashes, waters rage, snow falls, and hailstones fly, can it not also, at God's command, so be moved as to make the sound of words?"[22]

Making sound by means of instruments, however intelligent or divine a being you are, is not the same as speaking; and it is not the same as using your own voice, which animals also do. We see this in Thomas Aquinas's commentary on Aristotle's *Politics*: "Now there is a difference between language and mere voice. Voice is a sign of pain and pleasure and consequently of the other passions, such as anger and fear, which are all ordered to pleasure and pain. . . . Thus voice is given to the other animals, whose nature attains the level where they sense their pleasures and pains, and they signify this to one another by means of certain natural sounds of the voice, as a lion by his roar and a dog by his bark, in the place of which we use interjections."[23] Interjections, which humans use, are like the voice of an animal, a raw and natural expression of a present experience. When, in search of eloquence, Dante virtually arrives in Sicily, he is reduced to an incoherent outburst: *racha*! *racha*! This Hebrew word, what he calls "vain speech," is a bestial sign of fratricidal anger, explicitly condemned by Jesus in the Sermon on the Mount.[24] Augustine identifies *racha* among the Hebrew words of the Bible that cannot be translated into another tongue, not because of their more sacred authority (as in the case of *Amen* and

Alleluia) but because they are interjections, "which are words that express an emotion of the mind rather than any part of a thought we have in our mind." *Rachà*, he goes on to say, expresses "the cry of an angry man."[25]

Sicily brings out this passionate exclamation because of the lost real connection between the imperial court and the eloquent poetry called Sicilian, which has given and will give its name forever to "all poetry written by Italians." Yet that illustrious vernacular, known through writing, seems to bear no resemblance to what sounds in the mouth of the average inhabitant of the island today. This linguistic degradation is due to political decline, because unlike the Emperor Frederick and his "well-born" son Manfred (patrons of the Sicilian school of lyric poetry), the rulers of present-day Italy live in a bestial manner. As a result, instead of a stable of poets, these rulers use a variety of noisemakers—wind and percussion instruments: "*Racha, racha!* What is the noise made now by the trumpet of the latest Frederick, or the bells of the second Charles, or the horns of the powerful marquises Giovanni and Azzo, or the pipes of the other warlords? Only 'Come, you butchers! Come, you traitors! Come, you devotees of greed!' "[26] This list of musical instruments suggests that these present-day political regimes do not speak with an authentic voice, as did the poets of the Federician court, or even as Dante does in his incoherent, untranslatable, irrational, and surely uncharitable, but fully natural, cry of anger. Naturalness is the primary characteristic that distinguishes the vernacular from Latin and other grammatical languages.

Scholars have doubted Dante's aural familiarity with all these dialects and have in some cases demonstrated that he gets many of his examples from books—in particular from manuscript *canzonieri* (songbooks or anthologies of vernacular poetry). As Justin Steinberg points out, the second book of the treatise refers explicitly to the material circulation of texts, in particular to the preservation of *canzoni* in written form, as might be observed by those who frequent books (*visitantibus libros*).[27] Sarah Kay has shown how Dante's knowledge of Occitan poetry, his citation of first lines, is heavily mediated by treatises on Occitan and biographical genres, in a tradition of quotation from written text.[28]

So it could well be that the "everyday speech" recorded from the different regions of Italy comes from written sources. All spoken dialects of the peninsula (with the possible exception of Bologna) are rejected as models for the illustrious, courtly vernacular Dante thinks people need. The rest of the unfinished treatise deals with poetry. The suggestion seems to be that these written and writerly texts can be models for the spoken and written eloquence of the Italians more generally. This is the whole problem of the quest for the illustrious vernacular: to be *vernacular*, it has to be natural, authentic to a place and its inhabitants, and associated with oral speech; to be *illustrious*, it might have to be learned through art, that is, artificially, through writing.

Dante of course abandoned the whole project of the *De vulgari eloquentia*, the Latin prescriptive treatise on the vernacular, and, at some point, turned to his *magnum opus*, the *Commedia*. In some sense, and to simplify greatly, he finally did accomplish that original goal of giving the Italians a language. Yet it warrants some reflection that, because of the early transmission history of the poem, the particular form of this language is not totally certain. Not only do we have no autograph, no original in Dante's hand; we also have no manuscripts at all between the earliest attestations of the existence of *Inferno* and *Purgatorio*, around 1314, and the earliest surviving manuscripts that are from 1336 or 1337, fifteen years after the poet's death and more than twenty years, at least, after it began to circulate. What happened to the *Commedia*, which is described by philologists in catastrophic terms (pollution, contamination, devastation, gravely compromised) happened because of its huge success, a frenzy of copying. What is at stake in this philological concern is not so much *what* Dante said—since the interlocking triple-rhyme scheme of the *Commedia* is, in fact, a kind of security system, difficult to break open in order to stuff in interpolated materials—but *how* he said it. To reduce a complicated and indeed inconclusive stemma to its main outlines: there are two branches—one Tuscan and one "Northern." Which one speaks with the voice of Dante, who was—we know—Florentine but spent the last decades of his life outside Florence and, indeed, in Northern Italy? How long does it take to acquire an accent? The reason we cannot know is that both branches are characterized by their copyists—*scrittori volgari* as they were disparagingly called even in the 1330s—who, as Enrico Malato says, even if attentive to lexicon, that is, to getting the words right, were generally less attentive, even completely oblivious, to the linguistic forms of the exemplar from which they were copying, giving free rein to their own linguistic use, their own way of speaking.[29]

The linguist Roger Wright has a theory about the multiplicity of the spoken Romance vernaculars in relation to written Latin texts. His thesis in *Late Latin and Early Romance* is that there were different ways of pronouncing written Latin already in the late Roman Empire, so the same spelling did not prevent people from pronouncing things very differently when reading aloud. The relationship of sound to writing was not at all fixed, as the "constant phonetic and morphological evolution of Latin-Romance had brought an increasing separation between writing and speech." The attempt to standardize pronunciation, where every written letter was sounded out, was an innovation and an imposition of the Carolingian Renaissance, when the training of scribes was systemized at Tours. Wright explains: "Once the reformed pronunciation was introduced, the services stopped being intelligible to the congregation. They were no longer the collective celebrations of all the community; the congregation were uncomprehending spectators. The texts to be used were fixed. Their manner of performance was fixed."[30] This is the reason for the famous decree in 813, often taken as the birth certificate of Romance languages, that sermons should be transferred into *rusticam Romanam linguam* so that people could understand what was being said. Rather than prescribing translation into the *other* language, the common speech of uneducated people, Wright argues that it simply meant that clerics should go back to the old practice of *pronouncing* the written text in a way that people listening could understand.

Because the vernacular was unfixed, Dante could not have had even the ambition to control tightly how the words he wrote would be sounded out. He makes a key distinction in the second book of the treatise on language between the person who composes a song and the person who sings, or performs, it. *Cantio*, he says, or *canzone* (song), has a double meaning:

> One usage refers to something created by an author, so that there is action—and this is the sense in which Virgil uses the word in the first book of the *Aeneid*, when he writes "arma virumque cano"; the other refers to the occasions on which this creation is performed, either by the author or by someone else, whoever it may be, with or without a musical accompaniment—and in this sense it is passive. . . . The proof of this is the fact that we never say "That's Peter's song" when referring to something Peter has performed, but only to something he has written.[31]

The difference, for Dante, is that the writer *acts* upon the song; whereas the song *acts* upon the singer. Although a canzone is "an act of singing" (*ipse canendi*), it is prior to and independent of any audible performance of it.[32] In a performance, the canzone becomes the agent, and the singer becomes its passive instrument. His voice merely parrots or channels the voice of the songwriter. He becomes a human instrument or, as Guido d'Arezzo would say, a beast. In the opening of his *Regulae*, this eleventh-century founder of modern musical notation declares: "Between musicians and singers there is a vast distance: the latter perform; the former know what music comprises. For he who does what he does not understand is termed a beast."[33] The singer of a song is a beast of burden, an instrument for someone else. Dante, for his part, seems to describe the illustrious vernacular as both an instrument and an instrumental animal when he says that "language is nothing other than the vehicle indispensable [*necessarium instrumentum*] to our thinking, as a horse is to a knight."[34]

So which is it? Is the subject of the *De vulgari eloquentia* natural or artificial? Is it the speech we take in with our nurse's milk, or is it a tool we can learn from its best literary practitioners? Dante suggests that the illustrious vernacular emerges from the simply natural one: "That it is sublime in learning is clear when we see it emerge, so outstanding, so lucid, so perfect and so civilised, from among so many ugly words used by Italians, so many convoluted constructions, so many defective formations, and so many barbarous pronunciations—as Cino da Pistoia and his friend show us in their canzoni."[35] But would those who learn an illustrious vernacular from this treatise be mere apes of or mouthpieces for Cino and his friend, Dante? The hope of the *De vulgari eloquentia*, where the author recommends his songs as examples of the still-to-be-invented illustrious vernacular, is that songs can act upon their singers. Language can confer immense power. "And what greater power could there be than that which can melt the hearts of human beings, so as to make the unwilling willing and the willing unwilling, as it has done and still does."[36] But to be *vernacular*, which is, as the treatise polemically states at the outset, *nobler*, it has to be one's own voice, not just a sounding instrument. That is why this new, powerful, *written* language has to come *out* of the actual ugly words used by Italians. What matters is not just the message but also the medium—the sound produced by your particular body—that rings with the accent of the place that you are from or to which you have immigrated.

Even though Dante, like Guido d'Arezzo, seems to disparage the singer, the mere performer, in favor of the writer or composer ("we would never say that it is Peter's song"), there is also the possibility that in sounding out again the songs of others, we find our own voice and make the story our own. This is what Cassiodorus claims about the Psalms: "Whoever recites the words of a psalm seems to be repeating his *own* words, to be singing in solitude words composed by himself; it does not seem to be another speaking or explaining what he takes up and reads. It is as though he were speaking from his own person, such is the nature of the words he utters."[37]

Dante's promise to Ugolino to broadcast his complaint against the archbishop in the world above, so long as that with which he speaks does not "dry up," has been read as an oath, pact, or vow guaranteed by the pilgrim's willingness to have his tongue dry up in his mouth if he does not maintain it. In that way, it has been observed to recall a particular Psalm (136): "By the rivers of Babylon," in the verse: "Let my tongue cleave to my jaws, if I do not remember thee" (*Adhaereat lingua mea faucibus meis, si non meminero tui*). This allusion calls attention to the physical sounding equipment of the mouth and how it ought to be used (to "remember thee"). Ugolino will pull his mouth off the head of Ruggieri only if speaking will serve the same purpose as his eternal eating: to feed his hunger for revenge. In the tower, Ugolino quieted himself and closed his mouth in dreadful silence when his children offered their own bodies as food because they innocently misinterpreted his desperate gesture of biting his hands as a "desire to eat." The children are Ugolino's own flesh and blood; he sees himself reflected in their four small faces. He can find nothing to say to them as the excruciating hours and days of hunger tick off, and his sons succumb to death, one by one. The horror is unspeakable, and he has nothing to say; his tongue cleaves to his jaws as he turns, at some point, whether only in Hell or already in the ghastly tower, to eating human flesh, "as bread is eaten for hunger."

The miserable Ugolino recognizes Dante's voice as useful for the damage it can do, now, to his enemy among a specific audience in a specific region of the world above, a subset of the land identified by the particular kind of "yes" that sounds there. The geographical specificity of the vernacular always distinguishes itself by sound. That thing with which Dante sounded out his immediately recognizable idiom, his physical, anatomical sonic equipment, and even the Florentine vernacular as it was then may have long ago dried up, but the sound of his voice continues to be heard not just because of his elaboration of his spoken vernacular into written eloquence but because of what he has to say.

NOTES

1. Quotations from Dante's *Inferno*, *Purgatorio*, and *Paradiso* are from *La Commedia secondo l'antica vulgata*, ed. Giorgio Petrocchi, 4 vols. (Milan: Mondadori, 1966–67). Translations are mine.

2. *Inferno* 32.133–39:

"O tu che mostri per sì bestial segno
odio sovra colui che tu ti mangi,
dimmi 'l perché," diss' io, "per tal convegno,
che se tu a ragion di lui ti piangi,
sappiendo chi voi siete e la sua pecca,
nel mondo suso ancora io te ne cangi,
se quella con ch'io parlo non si secca."

3. Stephen Nichols, "Augustine and the Troubadour Lyric," in *Vox intexta: Orality and Textuality in the Middle Ages*, ed. Carol Braun Pasternack and Alger Nicolaus Doane (Madison: University of Wisconsin Press, 1991), 137–61, 152.

4. Dante's Statius introduces himself as a poet, which he defines as the "name that lasts longest and confers most honor." *Purgatorio* 21.85–87: "'col nome che più dura e più onora / era io di là,' rispuose quello spirto."

5. *Inferno* 33.10–12: "Io non so chi tu se' né per che modo / venuto se' qua giù; ma fiorentino / mi sembri veramente quand' io t'odo."

6. *Inferno* 33.1–9:

La bocca sollevò dal fiero pasto
quel peccator, forbendola a' capelli
del capo ch'elli avea di retro guasto.
Poi cominciò: "Tu vuo' ch'io rinovelli
disperato dolor che 'l cor mi preme
già pur pensando, pria ch'io ne favelli.
Ma se le mie parole esser dien seme
che frutti infamia al traditor ch'i' rodo,
parlar e lagrimar vedrai insieme."

7. Matthew 13:20: "Qui autem super petrosa seminatus est, hic est qui verbum audit, et continuo cum gaudio accipit illud" (And he that received the seed upon stony ground, is he that heareth the word, and immediately receiveth it with joy). Quotations of the Bible are from the Vulgate and Douay-Rheims versions, available online at http://drbo.org.

8. Dante, *De vulgari eloquentia* I.viii.5, ed. Enrico Fenzi, in Dante, *Le opere*, vol. 3 (Rome: Salerno, 2012): "Nam alii oc, alii si, alii vero dicunt oil." *La rettorica di Brunetto Latini*, ed. Francesco Maggini (Florence: Le Monnier, 1968), 57: "Dimostrativo è quello che ssi reca in laude o in vituperio d'una certa persona."

9. Dante defines *illustrious* by the light indicated by the word itself. But he goes on to say that it will stand out from the "barbarous pronunciations" of the present Italians. Because Italy has no royal court, "Our illustrious vernacular wanders around like a homeless stranger, finding hospitality in more humble homes." *De vulgari eloquentia* I.xviii.2: "nostrum illustre velut acola peregrinatur et in humilibus hospitatur asilis." Translations are from Dante, *De vulgari eloquentia*, trans. Steven Botterill (Cambridge: Cambridge University Press, 1996).

10. *De vulgari eloquentia* I.i.4: "Harum quoque duarum nobilior est vulgaris: tum quia prima fuit humano generi usitata; tum quia totus orbis ipsa perfruitur, licet in diversas prolationes et vocabula sit divisa; tum quia naturalis est nobis, cum illa potius artificialis existat. Et de hac nobiliori nostra est intentio pertractare."

11. *De vulgari eloquentia* I.iii.2–3: "Quare, si tantum rationale esset, pertransire non posset. . . . Hoc equidem signum est ipsum subiectum nobile de quo loquimur: nam sensuale quid est in quantum sonus est; rationale vero in quantum aliquid significare videtur ad placitum."

12. *De vulgari eloquentia* I.i.2, 4: "Quod vulgarem locutionem asserimus eam qua infantes assuefiunt ab assistentibus cum primitus distinguere voces incipiunt. . . . Totus orbis ipsa perfruitur, licet in diversas prolationes." Katharine Breen calls attention to Dante's distinction between the "assuefaction" of the vernacular, "to which infants become accustomed from those around them," and the deliberate *habitus* of learning Latin, to which "we can only become regulated and indoctrinated by over a long period of time and through diligent study." Katharine Breen, *Imagining an English Reading Public* (Cambridge: Cambridge University Press, 2010), 1–2.

13. *De vulgari eloquentia*, 13n–14n.

14. *Physiologus: A Medieval Book of Nature Lore*, ed. Michael J. Curley (Chicago: University of Chicago Press, 2009), 42. See *Bestiari medievali*, ed. Luigina Morini (Turin: Einaudi, 1987), 55, 449. *De vulgari eloquentia* I.xvi.1: "Postquam venati saltus et pascua sumus Ytalie, nec pan-

theram quam sequimur adinvenimus, ut ipsam reperire possimus rationabilius investigemus de illa ut, solerti studio, redolentem ubique et necubi apparentem nostris penitus irretiamus tenticulis." The description of sound as smell might be related to the reality, understood in the Middle Ages, that both odor and sound propagate themselves "as if in circles, like circles formed by casting a stone into a pool of quiet water." See Robert A. Pratt, "Albertus Magnus and the Problem of Sound and Odor in the Summoner's Tale," *Philological Quarterly* 57, no. 2 (Spring 1978): 267–68, 267.

15. *De vulgari eloquentia* I.xi.1: "Quam multis varietatibus latio dissonante vulgari decentiorem atque illustrem Ytalie venemur loquelam."

16. *De vulgari eloquentia* I.xi.6 and I.xiv.2–4. Fenzi points out (81n) that there is also a positive connotation of *eructare*, finding that Jerome talks about *eructuare sermonem bonum, verbum bonum laudes Dei* "indicando una parola che erompe dal profondo del cuore" (to burp a good sermon, a good word in praise of God, "indicating a word that erupts from the bottom of one's heart").

17. *De vulgari eloquentia* I.xi.7: "Sardos etiam, qui non Latii sunt sed Latiis associandi videntur, eiciamus, quoniam soli sine proprio vulgari esse videntur, gramaticam tanquam simie homines imitantes: nam domus nova et dominus meus locuntur."

18. *De vulgari eloquentia* I.ii.7: "Si vero contra argumentetur quis de eo quod Ovidius dicit in quinto Metamorfoseos de picis loquentibus, dicimus quod hoc figurate dicit, aliud intelligens. Et si dicatur quod pice adhuc et alie aves locuntur, dicimus quod falsum est; quia talis actus locutio non est, sed quedam imitatio soni nostre vocis; vel quod nituntur imitari nos in quantum sonamus, sed non in quantum loquimur. Unde si expresse dicenti 'Pica' resonaret etiam 'Pica,' non esset hoc nisi representatio vel imitatio soni illius qui prius dixisset."

19. As Sarah Kay writes: "The effect of this second distinction between articulate and inarticulate voice is to privilege all human sounds over all sounds voiced by other sources. The two categories of human voice—whether they can be notated (*vox distincta*) or not (*vox confusa*)—are alone credited with conveying meaning and thus deemed expressive. Animal sounds, even if they are writable, are by definition inarticulate or meaningless. At their lowest, in an extreme manifestation of their own closedness, they cannot even be written down, like the chattering of a jay or the croaking of a frog." Sarah Kay, "The Soundscape of Troubadour Lyric, or, How Human Is Song?" *Speculum* 91, no. 4 (2016): 1002–15, 1006.

20. *De vulgari eloquentia* I.ii.1: "Nam eorum que sunt omnium soli homini datum est loqui, cum solum sibi necessarium fuerit." Fenzi comments that it is not that man speaks because he has reason but because he needs to speak, and to possess the instrument of speech, in order to make an adequate *prolatio*, by means of material signs produced by the body.

21. *De vulgari eloquentia* I.ii.6: "Et si obiciatur de serpente loquente ad primam mulierem, vel de asina Balaam, quod locuti sint, ad hoc respondemus quod angelus in illa et diabolus in illo taliter operati sunt quod ipsa animalia moverunt organa sua, sic ut vox inde resultavit distincta tanquam vera locutio: non quod aliud esset asine illud quam rudere, nec quam sibilare serpenti."

22. *De vulgari eloquentia* I.iv.6. "Ad quod quidem dicimus quod bene potuit respondisse Deo interrogante, nec propter hoc Deus locutus est ipsa quam dicimus locutionem. Quis enim dubitat quicquid est ad Dei nutum esse flexibile . . . ? Igitur cum ad tantas alterationes moveatur aer imperio nature inferioris, que ministra et factura Dei est, ut tonitrua personet, ignem fulgoret, aquam gemat, spargat nivem, grandines lancinet, nonne imperio Dei movebitur ad quedam sonare verba?" Hildegard of Bingen also meditates on the notion that it is the *sound* of God's Word that "awakened all creatures and called them to itself." She compares this to a human person's enunciation of a "word hidden in his heart." *Liber divinorum operum* 1.4.105, ed. Peter Dronke and Albert Derolez, CCCM 92 (Turnhout: Brepols, 1996): "Et quare dicitur

uerbum? Quia cum sonante uoce omnes creaturas suscitauit et eas ad se uocauit. Nam quod Deus in uerbo dictauit, hoc uerbum sonando iussit; et quod uerbum iussit, hoc Deus in uerbo dictauit . . . et uerbum sonuit et omnes creaturas produxit. . . . Cum uerbum Dei sonuit, omnem creaturam, que ante euum in Deo preordinata et disposita fuit, ad se uocauit, et per uocem eius omnia ad uitam suscitata sunt; sicut etiam in homine designauit, qui uerbum in corde suo occulte dictat antequam illud emittat, quod in emissione se cum est. . . . Quando enim uerbum Dei sonuit, idem uerbum in omni creatura apparuit et idem sonus in omni creatura uita fuit." For English translation, see Hildegard of Bingen, *Book of Divine Works, with Letters and Songs*, ed. Matthew Fox, trans. Robert Cunningham et al. (Santa Fe: Bear, 1987), I.4, 247.

23. Thomas Aquinas, "Commentary on Aristotle's Politics," book 1, lesson 1 [i.1.1252a1–2, 1253a38], trans. Ernest Fortin and Peter O'Neill, in *Medieval Political Philosophy: A Sourcebook*, ed. Ralph Lerner (New York: Free Press of Glencoe, 1963), 310.

24. Matthew 5:22: "But I say to you, that whosoever is angry with his brother, shall be in danger of the judgment. And whosoever shall say to his brother, Raca, shall be in danger of the council. And whosoever shall say, Thou Fool, shall be in danger of hell fire."

25. Augustine, *On Christian Doctrine* II.11, trans. D. W. Robertson (Indianapolis: Bobbs-Merrill, 1958), 515.

26. *De vulgari eloquentia* I.xii.2–5: "Quicquid nostri predecessores vulgariter protulerunt, sicilianum vocetur"; "Fredericus Cesar et benegenitus eius Manfredus"; "Racha, racha! Quid nunc personat tuba novissimi Frederici, quid tintinabulum secundi Karoli, quid cornua Iohannis et Azonis marchionum potentum, quid aliorum magnatum tibie, nisi 'Venite carnifices, venite altriplices, venite avaritie sectatores?' "

27. Justin Steinberg, *Accounting for Dante* (Notre Dame, IN: Notre Dame University Press, 2007), 95.

28. Sarah Kay, *Parrots and Nightingales: Troubadour Quotations and the Development of European Poetry* (Philadelphia: University of Pennsylvania Press, 2013).

29. Enrico Malato, "La tradizione del testo della *Commedia*," *Libri et Documenti* 40–41, no. 2 (Milan: Castello Sforzesco, 2014–15), 143–51. The problem of the critical edition of the *Commedia*, as reignited by the much-discussed 2001 edition by Federico Sanguineti—*Dantis Alagherii Comedia*, ed. crit. Federico Sanguineti (Florence: Sismel Edizioni del Galluzzo, 2001)—has been fully discussed in English by Prue Shaw in Dante Alighieri, *Commedia: A Digital Edition*, ed. Prue Shaw, 2nd ed., www.dantecommedia.it (Sismel per la Fondazione Ezio Franceschini and Inkless Editions, 2021).

30. Roger Wright, *Late Latin and Early Romance in Spain and Carolingian France* (Liverpool: F. Cairns, 1982), 118–20.

31. *De vulgari eloquentia* II.viii.4: "uno modo secundum quod fabricatur ab autore suo, et sic est actio—et secundum istum modum Virgilius primo Eneidorum dicit 'Arma virumque cano'—; alio modo secundum quod fabricata profertur vel ab autore vel ab alio quicunque sit, sive cum soni modulatione proferatur, sive non: et sic est passio. . . . Signum autem huius est quod nunquam dicimus 'Hec est cantio Petri' eo quod ipsam proferat, sed eo quod fabricaverit illam."

32. *De vulgari eloquentia* II.viii.3: "Est enim cantio, secundum verum nominis significatum, ipse canendi actus vel passio, sicut lectio passio vel actus legendi." On this passage, see Albert Ascoli, "Performing Salvation in Dante's *Commedia*," *Dante Studies* 135 (2017): 74–106; and Thomas E. Peterson, "From Casella to Cacciaguida: A Musical Progression toward Innocence," *Bibliotheca Dantesca: Annual Journal of Research Studies* 1 (2018): article12, https://repository.upenn.edu/bibdant/vol1/iss1/12.

33. Guido d'Arezzo, *Regulae rhythmicae* 1–3, ed. Angelo Rusconi (Florence: Galluzzo, 2005), 89: "Musicorum et cantorum magna est distancia / Isti dicunt illi sciunt que componit musica /

Nam qui facit quod non sapit diffinitur bestia." Elizabeth Eva Leach, *Sung Birds: Music, Nature, and Poetry in the Later Middle Ages* (Ithaca, NY: Cornell University Press, 2018), 43.

34. *De vulgari eloquentia* II.i.8: "Loquela non aliter sit necessarium instrumentum nostre conceptionis quam equus militis."

35. *De vulgari eloquentia* I.xvii.3: "Magistratu quidem sublimatum videtur, cum de tot rudibus Latinorum vocabulis, de tot perplexis constructionibus, de tot defectivis prolationibus, de tot rusticanis accentibus, tam egregium, tam extricatum, tam perfectum et tam urbanum videamus electum ut Cynus Pistoriensis et amicus eius ostendunt in cantionibus suis."

36. *De vulgari eloquentia* I.xvii.4: "Et quid maioris potestatis est quam quod humana corda versare potest, ita ut nolentem volentem et volentem nolentem faciat, velut ipsum et fecit et facit?"

37. Cassiodorus, *Explanation of the Psalms*, trans. P. G. Walsh, vol. 1 (Mahwah: Paulist Press, 1990), 41.

CHAPTER NINE

The Phenomenology of *-e*

Christopher Cannon

The phenomenon that interests me here is what the grammarians who have written the history of Middle English usually describe as "final *-e*." It is, as a sound or phoneme, sometimes described as a *schwa*, and as a grammatical form or morpheme, it is understood to represent a reduction of Old English case endings that were themselves much more substantive phenomena: *-u* or *-an* or *-um* at the ends of words. Chaucer does not tackle this issue overtly in *The House of Fame*, although his definition of *speech* specifies it in the very form of its statement:

Soun is noght* but air ybroken*, — nothing/broken
And every speche that is spoken,
Loud or privee*, foul or faire, — hidden
In his substaunce is but aire.[1]

This concise summary of the medieval understanding of the physics of sound, derived from Donatus and Priscian among many others, contains at its spatial center the sound whose reverberations I want to consider: the *-e* at the end of "speche."[2] What might be at stake in such a consideration is the decision between a reading that sounds the *-e* as a schwa—so "speech-*uh*"—and a reading that would interpret that *-e* as a graphic marker with no sound at all. A reader who sounds or imagines sounding this *-e* when reading this line avoids the unpleasant clash of adjacent stresses on "speche" and "that," while a reader who does not sound that *-e* embraces that unusual double thump (unusual because stressed syllables in Chaucer's verse usually alternate with unstressed syllables) or softens those thumps by inserting a pause or caesura between these words. Whether final *-e* has substance or is so much inconsequential "aire," as Chaucer would put it, is, then, not only a question of phonology and grammar but also of aesthetics: what sound will render this line, and all the many like it in Chaucer's poetry, "foul" or "faire" to any particular reader?

The status of such final *-e*'s in Chaucer's verse is complicated by a number of other factors. First, this *-e* was being further reduced phonologically in Chaucer's day, so, while the *-e* at the end of many words was sounded, many others were on their way to the reduction that eventually gave us nothing but Modern English "speech." Second, whatever *-e*'s Chaucer may have expected to be written at the end of any given word in his poems, the scribes who copied them often heard a given word differently, or did not think the final *-e*'s in the text they were copying were important to preserve, and also felt free to add *-e*'s wherever they thought a word needed them. The result is that there are both "genuine Chaucerian *e*'s" and those that can be described as "phantoms" added to a word without grammatical authority.[3]

Grammarians allow for a third complicating factor: Chaucer may have relied on final *-e*'s that were already obsolescent or at least archaic in the speech of his day in order to make a line metrical. So an adverb like *yliche* (similar, equal) might be used by Chaucer in a position where a final *-e* is unnecessary (or conflicts with) regular meter:

> For sothe, **ylich** they suffred tho[4] (*BOOK OF THE DUCHESS* 1292)

Or it might be used where meter made sounding the final *-e* necessary:

> Our joy was ever **yliche** newe (*BOOK OF THE DUCHESS* 1288)

Grammarians have always been firm about the limits of such possibilities. Certain forms, such as an adverb, it is thought, allow for this flexibility, but other forms do not—a third-person preterit, for example. The following line might be allowable if "knewe" can be construed as a third person subjunctive (which takes an *-e*):

> And how she **knewe** first your thought (*BOOK OF THE DUCHESS* 1113)

But if it is a preterit, the line should be:

And how she **knew** first your thought,

with the *-e* unpronounced and two adjacent stresses on "knew" and "first" making the line irregular. It should not be possible to pronounce the final *-e* on the preterit form "spake" in the following line:

And grete him, but he **spake** noght (*BOOK OF THE DUCHESS* 503)

According to the grammarians, this line has to be

And grete him, but he **spak** noght.

The principle competing with grammar in the case of all of the final *-e*'s I have so far mentioned is, then, meter or, more particularly, the regular alternation of unstressed and stressed syllables that we now call iambic rhythm. Editors and scholars who insist on the regularity of such meter in all or most of Chaucer's lines will worry about these final *-e*'s for a different reason than do grammarians. Since those *-e*'s are so nearly ubiquitous, it is usually possible to ensure that Chaucer's lines are iambic by insisting that particular *-e*'s are sounded or even adding them where the meter seems to require them, even though they cannot be found in the manuscripts preserving Chaucer's texts. F. N. Robinson, whose edition of Chaucer was the standard text for all scholarship and teaching from the 1930s until the 1980s, described a process of what he called "metrical rectification," whereby he provided what he called "necessary" final *-e*'s—that is, *-e*'s not in any manuscript but essential to the meter or the poetry's *sound*.[5] But that process has also seemed radical enough, even to the editors who fix Chaucer's text in this way, that they almost never acknowledge that they have employed it. Walter William Skeat, who edited the definitive edition of Chaucer used before Robinson's, rectified metrically quite extensively, although his long discussion of "versification" uses his own emended text for his examples without mentioning that he has altered them.[6] The standard edition until now, the *Riverside Chaucer* is also instrumentally silent about this practice: since it represents itself as a "revised" version of Robinson's edition, it absorbs his emendations without noting them.

Metrical imperatives and the rules of grammarians are, then, generally, if quietly, at war in this matter. Both perspectives engage in something philosophers call "saving the phenomena," whereby a theory is constructed in order to preserve what you are certain you see or perceive instead of acknowledging that the theory is incapable of accounting for all instances and must be complicated or abandoned.[7] I include myself among the metricists invested in saving any final *-e* that results in regular meter, so, returning to my last example, I have added an *-e* to "spake" in the edition of Chaucer I have recently edited with James Simpson to produce the necessary iambs. Eleanor Hammond, writing in 1908, denounced such regularity: "Even among modern students there is the tendency to reason in a circle, to start from the assumption that Chaucer is 'impeccable,' and, after constructing a body of texts on that hypothesis, by eliminating or altering whatever seems incompatible, to deduce from them the original assumption of the impeccability of Chaucer."[8]

But the grammatical position has tended to proceed by a similar circularity. Take for example, the noun *bliss*, which has no final *-e* in Old English but requires it metrically in Chaucer in a line like this:

> That ye have thus your **blisse** lore. (*BOOK OF THE DUCHESS* 748)

The word does not, however, require final *-e* in a line like this:

> Of al the **bliss** that ever was maked . . . (*BOOK OF THE DUCHESS* 578)

Of this particular phenomenon, E. T. Donaldson says that "alternate forms play an important part in the history of the language," so *bliss* and *blisse* "may . . . deriv[e] from the nominative and oblique cases respectively."[9] A metricist such as Ian Robinson, however, is quick to note that such reasoning is self-confirming: "with so widely permissive a 'rule' there is, in fact, *no* rule about final *-e*'s in general or in particular."[10] The circularity of both positions is usually harmonized in practice—or each is allowed to provide hermeneutic cover for the other—so for more than a century, the general understanding of both Chaucer's meter and his grammar has traced the virtuous circle neatly described by Stephen Barney: "It is simply inconceivable . . . that the various traditional findings about Chaucer's final *-e* which underlie any premise about meter, are generally wrong: the historical evidence . . . and the metrical evidence simply concur too often to admit any other hypothesis. The argument is not circular: it is an argument in which reasonable hypotheses about grammar and reasonable hypotheses about meter reinforce each other so firmly that contrary hypotheses become incredible."[11]

If, on its face, this circle-squaring does seem to save the phenomenon of Chaucer's final *-e*, it actually preserves nothing because the result must be that any final *-e* in Chaucer can be rejected or accepted on metrical or grammatical grounds (the one swooping in when the other does not help), with the result that final *-e*'s in Robinson's edition or in Skeat's, or indeed any modern edition of Chaucer, may be printed or sounded or silent or expunged without explanation or conformity to any stateable pattern. Since it is, in fact, impossible to have an edition of Chaucer that is perfectly regular metrically *and* grammatically in historical terms, just as it is impossible to have an edition of Chaucer that is perfectly grammatical but also metrically regular, eclecticism has seemed to be the only editorial option. In this sense—and in ways Chaucerians have been reluctant to acknowledge—the phenomenon of final *-e* finally cannot be saved.

It is a paradox that the sound raising the stakes this high—on which the very possibility of reading Chaucer accurately depends—is so aurally trivial: sometimes also called "mute *-e*," it is as near to a nonsound as phonology might specify. To those who will never edit Chaucer nor describe his grammar, or for any reader willing to forgive Chaucer an unsatisfactory line, the issue is trivial, too. Yet the debate has been, at times, fiery, particularly in a series of exchanges between Donaldson and James Southworth in *PMLA* in the 1940s.[12] To read through their remarks is to see, on the one hand, the coiled aggression of the Yale professor (Donaldson, that is) looking down on the philological naïf and, on the other hand, the sputtering and confused but nonetheless fiercely passionate outsider (Southworth had a position at the University of Toledo, but he construes himself at all times as in opposition to philological authority) struggling in vain to land a single blow. The substance of the exchange is equally uneven: against a method Donaldson describes as "scientific" and the "rational study of Middle English linguistics," Southworth offers only a plangent appeal to attend to what he calls Chaucer's "delicate rhythms."[13] Although Southworth marshals pages of evidence, Donaldson systematically discounts all of it on grammatical grounds: "historical grammar is difficult to prove wrong," he says, "except on its own terms, and its generalizations may be discredited only when one has examined all the bases upon which they depend."[14] Such debate has had a significant afterlife in recent exchanges about a figure usually called the "Ellesmere editor," a "myth" (as Jill Mann has termed it) devised by John Manly and Edith Rickert in order to insist that the excellent manuscript of the *Tales*, conventionally called "Ellesmere," had to be the result of emendations by a scribe since, in the textual history of the *Canterbury Tales* they had spent thirty years devising, that text had to be at least one remove from Chaucer's original.[15] The argument about the existence of this editor did not always turn on final *-e*, but it was always about meter, and final *-e* featured prominently in the examples marshaled. The passion these issues had excited in Southworth and Donaldson remained visible in the number of prominent Chaucerians who waded into the argument about the existence of the "Ellesmere" editor and in the number of books, articles, and chapters devoted to it.[16] The paradoxes that had been inherent to such passions were also still visible in this subsidiary debate to the extent that the very excellence of Chaucer's meter in the Ellesmere text (not least as the disposition of its final *-e*'s consistently made it more regular) has routinely been taken as clear evidence of its departure from Chaucer's intentions.[17]

In the main, however, explicit discussion of Chaucer's meter has worked to ignore these logical fallacies and to sublimate such passions. Rather than acknowledge their own emotionalism, grammarians have tended to describe the metricists as championing a "mechanically regular syllable count."[18] Metricists, for their part, have used the same term to characterize the grammarians as "mechanical" because of their insistence on "rules" even as they provide long lists of exceptions.[19] As the uneven matchup between Donaldson and Southworth predicts, the grammarians have almost always won the argument, not least because, unlike the metricists, and as Donaldson was already pointing out, the grammarians have always had access to Big Data (what Donaldson describes as "countless descriptive analyses . . . of the various branches of Chaucer's language and of that of his contemporaries, his predecessors and his followers" to be found in "a vast array" of studies).[20] All the metricists have to put against this vast array are the sounds they hear individually and the effects they attribute to them.

Another way to think about this debate, however, is that the metricists' phenomenology is particularly vulnerable—no match for science—because it insists that Chaucer's final *-e*'s have *meaning*. This is, in fact, exactly how Ian Robinson put it in 1971: "the sounded *-e*'s are effective," he says, "because of the phrase-rhythms they control," and "the reason for sounding some *-e*'s is that to do so helps the expressiveness of Chaucer's poetry."[21] We are in the realm of what Norman Eliason called, in 1972, "auditory delight," a quality of Chaucer's verse that (it is said) is only accessible when the claims of science and reason are dismissed, where the "auditory satisfaction" of "sounds or sound-patterns" is "inexplicable," where "there is no linguistic evidence applicable to the problem, for even the most delicate acoustic experiments which linguists have been able to devise cannot account for the phenomenon."[22] In the phenomenology of such satisfactions, the appeal is not to the mind but to the senses; it is not what we are reading—as Alan Gaylord put it—"but what [we] should be hearing," effects that are not only "abundant" but "sweet to the *taste*."[23] Such subjectivism breeds the passion with which it is embraced, and that passion is also this phenomenology's rationale. But the metricists' position has also always been weak because, while insisting that Chaucer's sounds mean something, none of them have ever specified exactly what Chaucer's final *-e*'s express. In the remainder of this essay, I will attempt such a specification, sparing a few words and some thought for delicate rhythms and poetic delight, an epiphenomenon that I would like to save. It may be that *delight* is not the best nor only term to describe this effect, and what I will ultimately claim Chaucer's final *-e*'s express may well be understood as trivial too. But the intensity of this passion in those who embrace it relative to the triviality of this sound is itself a phenomenon worthy of interest, suggesting—perhaps above all—that the metricists' position demands more than compassion.

One thing metricists and grammarians do seem to agree on is that Chaucer's verse rhythms are governed by "rhetoric." Southworth says, for example, that the rhythms he favors emerge by way of a "rhetorical reading," and Pearsall, speaking for the grammarians, sees attention to the "rhetorical and syntactical impetus of the verse" as the very antidote to the metricists' "mechanically regular syllable count."[24] Such references are meant, in both cases, to refer Chaucer's verse back to its aural roots in speech. As Pearsall puts it, it is the "natural speech-rhythms" that attention to the rhetorical impetus preserves.[25] For Southworth, Chaucer's verse will "take on the qualities of conversational prose" when read according to his understanding of final *-e*.[26] And, for Ian Robinson, attention to speech is the best way to attend directly to the "expressiveness" of Chaucer's verse, since it was in its contact with the "spoken language" that this verse became what he also described as "speech heightened."[27] As both metricists and grammarians use rhetoric to bring Chaucer's verse rhythms back to the spoken, they are also returning them to the discipline in which we have most usually attended to the alliance of sound in writing. If, for Quintilian, what rhetoric teaches is "good speech" [bona oratio] or the "science of speaking well" [bene dicendi scientia], he is also clear that "speaking well and writing well are one and the same thing" [unum atque idem videtur bene dicere ac bene scribere].[28]

Such a mode of analysis goes back as far as Skeat, who, in describing Chaucer's verse rhythms as "speech waves," was already beginning to develop something of a phenomenology of their sound.[29] By way of just such a phenomenology, James Porter understands Nietzsche's forceful refashioning of rhetoric as a discipline whereby "the ever-elusive sources of meaning" are located, not only in contents but "in the materiality of an utterance."[30] When Nietzsche says in his late writings that "the most intelligible factor in language is not the word itself, but the tone, strength, modulation, tempo, with which a sequence of words is spoken," he is drawing on his early lectures on rhetoric, where he understood "the whole of ancient literature" to be "rhetorical in the root sense of the term (speech-oriented) because its focus is the ear, in order to captivate it."[31] This is also, I think, what Shane Butler has called a text's "vocal claim"—that is, the extent to which a text may be said "not just to represent a voice but, in a sense, to have one."[32] Porter's winning formulation for this move in Nietzsche is to say that he has reread Aristotle so as to "introduce a category mistake into [his] notion of conditions of possibility."[33] Rather than allowing "delivery to be viewed not as essential but only accidental," as Aristotle did, and the rhetorical to be formal rather than material, as Aristotle also did, Nietzsche insists on the "physical presence" of the rhetorical voice and thus—like Skeat, Southworth, Robinson, and Pearsall—also insists that sequenced speech, rhetorical speech, metrical speech, however written in its transmitted form, must be understood as sound.[34]

If what we must analyze, then, is *how* Chaucer's verse makes sound, or in what form, it could also be said that what is at stake in describing (and understanding) the role of Chaucer's final *-e* (that which may or may not lengthen a word and a line of verse with an additional sound) is its duration. In his study of meter, Christopher Hasty has argued that this aspect of sound differs markedly from all its other qualities ("a particular timbre . . . pitch, a certain degree of loudness, a particular density or 'texture,' or a special resonance") because these other aspects exist in a network of associations with all the sounds one has heard in the past.[35] Duration can neither change nor create associations with any other sound, for it is neither "fixed" nor "determinate" while a sound is occurring: it is impossible to *hear* (or know) a duration until a sound ceases.[36] Duration is, therefore—in a term Hasty borrows from Whitehead—always a "becoming," so rhythm or any sequence of durations is also unlike any other quality of sound because it cannot be caught up in the past or even the anticipation of a future. It is always just happening. So whereas other qualities of a given sound exist in the light of other previously heard sounds, for Hasty, duration is an attribute of sound that consists of a "novel immediacy": like the rhythm it produces, it is—and this is the key word—an *experience*.[37]

Hasty's insistence that rhythm is subjective has a familiar component, for just like the grammarians and the metricists who write about Chaucer's verse, he is arguing against the idea that meter is mechanical. In collapsing meter into rhythm, moreover, he also wants to insist that meter as rhythm is, in his words, "expressive" and internal to our "intuitions" and "feelings," a demand for a form of attention, an imperative to listen.[38] Shane Butler has also written about the ways that we are inclined (in this case, he says, by the "linguistic turn" in our criticism) to ignore the sounds of our texts and that when a text insists that we "listen" to it, among the key things it is therefore offering to us—and this is also Butler's word—is an "experience."[39] This very term is also, as it happens, internal to Chaucer's understanding of the physics of sound:

Now hennesforth I wol thee teche,
How every speche, or noise, or soun,
Through his* multiplicacioun,   its
Thogh it were piped* of a mouse,   the squeak
Moot need* come to Fames House.   most necessarily
I preve* it thus—tak hede now—   prove
Be* experience   by
(*THE HOUSE OF FAME* 782–88)

The voice here, as in the definition with which I began, belongs to the Eagle in book 2 of *The House of Fame*, a kind of pedagogic figure—pedantic but also passionate about his subject—most concerned to situate a narrator called "Geoffrey" in the dream-world that is the setting for this poem's explorations of fame. He is not incidentally a chatterbox. As an outpouring of the very "speech" that he says sound is, he is *himself* a vocal claim for Chaucer's verse, a figure describing the experience of speech who also provides that experience.

Both grammarians and metricists have come close to recognizing such a claim in Chaucer's verse when they have understood its sound as a function of rhetoric, but metricists have come closer still when they describe Chaucer's verse as "conversational." Robinson's view that such verse is best understood as heightened speech provides an odd sort of guidance about which final *-e*'s in Chaucer's verse a reader should pronounce: "I have myself read Chaucer to an audience of academics in such a way," he says, "that some thought they heard sounded final *-e*'s which others thought were silent."[40] But, if this sounds less like a method than a form of divination, it is also to insist in a different way that Chaucer's final *-e*'s are a subjective quality of his verse, a series of phonological events structured not by metrical or grammatical rule but by the feelings they produce. In the particular contours of what he calls "pieces of speech" in Chaucer's verse, Robinson says, it is possible to "find . . . wonderful things . . . invisible" to the grammarians, a "feeling that Chaucer is speaking to us" that is itself "no illusion," a "process of familiarization" a "getting to know . . . its rhythms" that "makes traditional phonological considerations seem rather trivial."[41] By driving feeling into sound the metricists insist that the sound of Chaucer's poetry is not only more than its content but also more than its *sound*, not only verse rhythm but, as a consequence of that rhythm, the lived experience of being spoken to.

"Pieces of speech" is a phrase Robinson borrows from Marjorie Daunt, who argued that ideas of "poetic metre" have "distorted" much that we understand about Old English versification by letting us forget how firmly its patterns were rooted in the "spoken language."[42] The "five types" of half-lines in Old English poetry identified by Eduard Sievers in the nineteenth century were not, Daunt insisted, "metrical patterns" but "language patterns," each of which derived from common syntactic groupings (noun as subject or object followed by a finite verb, for example, or a finite verb with a prepositional phrase).[43] Old English verse was, therefore, "a tidied form of spoken language" whose patterns were fundamentally determined by "natural language shapes."[44] Daunt's views have support from more recent linguistic investigation, where it has also seemed that the "Germanic foot" derives from a certain "metrical coherence" in Old English grammar.[45] The phenomenon seems to be translingual, since similar claims have been made about Old French, whose grammar can be seen as "emergent" from, rather than a determinant of, poetic form, so that meter in Old French poetry is not a structure imposed on language but an absorption of "parallel phenomena in naturally occurring discourse."[46] The phenomenon also seems to be transhistorical, since however different the underlying grammars of Old and Middle English may be, Daunt insisted in a short coda that Sievers's types persisted in Chaucer. And she went further still, arguing that Sievers's rhythmic types shape Modern English, surviving as "the mould . . . in which we . . . still largely . . . cast our speech."[47]

As I noted above, the tendency has been for grammarians to explain any final *-e* in Chaucer's verse that eludes traditional paradigms as a departure from his own spoken language. Because Chaucer "made use of inflexional *-e* in a way that was already becoming archaic in its own day," this explanation goes, the sounding or silence of any individual *-e*'s must be explained by the history of the language, not as a version of contemporaneous speech.[48] As M. L. Samuels put the point, Chaucer the poet was "conservative" in his usage, reviving older speech patterns that therefore could not derive from "the colloquial register of his time."[49] This makes perfect sense if "meter is constantly falling behind the spoken language," as Eric Weiskott has argued.[50] And, since "Chaucer's knowledge of where *-e* belonged is not something he could have learned from historical grammar such as is available today," we might assume that he acquired his knowledge of older grammatical forms "first hand from speakers who still pronounced the *-e*" either from the "upper class" or "elderly" or both.[51] But the question begged by all such explanations is how Chaucer's contemporaries could have been expected to read his poetry accurately if Chaucer had to do such historical work to shape it. More to the point, how could any modern theory of either grammar or meter devised *after* Chaucer's day know with any authority whether to sound any particular *-e* if Chaucer's language was only occasionally transhistorical, always both in and out of its time?

This circle can be squared if we insist, in the ways the grammarians do, that what Chaucer was capturing was, indeed, pieces of speech but also insist, in the way the metricists do, that such grammatical speech, in the conversational sense, was metrically regular. Nietzsche is useful again here because he begins a lecture on the "rhythm of discourse" with Cicero's observation (in an uncanny prediction of Daunt's argument) that "we often make verses unintentionally in delivering a speech . . . for our speech consists largely of iambi."[52] Cicero is, of course, making a claim about Latin, but it still has great purchase on English. There is, even now, "a tendency towards an alternation of stressed and unstressed syllables" in the language, readily visible to us in the stress patterns we find in polysyllabic words.[53] Among the principles governing such an understanding of Modern English is that a single principle, often called "iambic reversal," creates "the essential form that rhythmic stress shift assumes in English."[54] Our constant tendency is to avoid the "clash" of adjacent stresses by altering either syntax or pronunciation as necessary "to eliminate these adjacencies," thereby producing a more "desirable" alternation of stresses.[55] It is probably also useful to note that this is work we perform automatically, not because we are thinking in terms of rules (alarmed to find, say, that we are setting ourselves up for an impermissible trochee)—but unconsciously (in the loosest sense of that term).

Underlying any such theory of metrical desire is the general principle that "the kind of foot required by a language's morphological system is the same as that required by its stress system."[56] Although such work has only occasionally informed discussions of Chaucer's meter, it has, in fact, long been clear to linguists that final *-e* was a phenomenon obeying metrical rather than grammatical rules in Middle English even before Chaucer was born.[57] The most useful evidence here is provided by Orm's *Ormulum* (ca. 1180), a poem famous for its poet's insistence on syllabic regularity (he wrote in septenaries or seven-foot lines of exactly fifteen syllables in every case). Orm's text only survives in one copy, in his hand, where his habit of careful correction, and the unswerving regularity of the syllabic count in every line, means that every *-e* we see in the text *had* to be pronounced. Yet, "since nouns, adjectives and adverbs appear with and without final *-e* in identical conditions," it is equally clear that "*-e* was no longer interpreted as a grammatical sign."[58] It is also true that, since final *-e* was already optional for Orm, he used it at the end of words where it was wholly unnecessary grammatically, "inorganic" because it did not derive from Old English inflectional endings.[59] For example, the *Ormulum*'s syllable count requires that *lar* (which meant teaching and gave us Modern English *lore*), which historically should not end in *-e*, acquires it at the end of the following passage:

> & Godd Allmahhtiȝ ȝife uss mahht & lusst & witt & wille
> To follȝhenn thiss Ennglisshe boc Thatt al iss haliȝ lar**e**.
>
> [And God Almighty gave us power and desire and intelligence and will,
> To follow this English book that is entirely holy teaching.]
> (*THE ORMULUM*, "DEDICATION," 315–16)[60]

So, too, does *spaech* acquire an *-e* only to satisfy the poem's meter in this example:

> Forr Crist wass all soth Godess witt & all hiss daerne spaech**e**.
>
> [Because Christ was truly God's intelligence and all his mysterious speech.]
> (*THE ORMULUM*, 18499–500)

Linguists have used such evidence to argue that the behavior of final *-e* in Middle English was a prosodic phenomenon. The point can be put in statistical terms: "the prosodic principle of avoidance of two successive stressed syllables" alone explains "the bulk of the data."[61] But it does so only if one *wants* to avoid stressed syllables in succession, which is itself a function of feeling. As Erik Björkman put it in 1913: "Orm wrote, not as he spoke, but he wrote as he thought he spoke."[62] Another name, then, for the principle or rule dictating whether a particular final *-e* survived or was eliminated or was added to the end of words in Middle English, is *desire*: Orm and Chaucer, as well as all those readers they relied on to experience the rhythm of their poems, sounded final *-e* where they wished to.

An account of Chaucer's verse attentive to the importance of affect in its shaping would not be the first of its kind in criticism. I. A. Richards insisted that "the way in which the rhythm of words is received is not independent of the emotional response which their sense excites."[63] For him, a truly practical criticism would elicit the connection between the sounds we feel in prosody and the rhythm of our own mental activity (the patterns of our own "sense and feeling").[64] Attending to the affect that shaped and is in turn produced by Chaucer's meter also brings me back to where I began, Chaucer's *speche*. The form of this word—its need (which is to say Chaucer's need) for it to end with an *-e* in line 766 of *The House of Fame*—just as the phenomenon that word names, identifies exactly what it was Chaucer wanted when he wrote a line that insisted on the sounding of a final -*e* (or one that insisted such an -*e* remain silent). He wanted to preserve the sound of his *own* speech. That is, what Chaucer's final -*e*'s express, and what metricists and grammarians—and indeed all of us—experience when we attend to them as Chaucer wished us to, is not just what Chaucer said but *how* he said it. Conversely, Chaucer's verse rhythms (as opposed to a verse's contents) only express something when the phenomenon of final -*e* is allowed to produce the pattern of iambs Chaucer wanted English (which is, in every such case, then, "his" English) to have.

If the phenomenology of -*e* must finally be an account of desire, it is perhaps not so surprising that this issue has elicited such passion from its commentators. The vitriol in the pages of *PMLA* in 1948 may seem particularly remarkable with some historical distance, but Donaldson's and Southworth's debate is a consequence of firmly staked positions, each with a perceived rectitude (and secure evidence) on its side and, therefore, no possibility of compromise or accommodation. In that sense, no explanation, theory, or set of observations about Chaucer's final -*e* could ever quell such strong feeling. Indeed, if I am right in attempting to correct grammatical history with metrical prosody, I should also, by definition, enrage everyone who still cares about this issue. This is also to suggest that any phenomenology of Chaucer's final -*e*, however dispassionate in itself, will always stir up rather than calm passions. Yet in the face of such inevitabilities, what I also want to assert here is that the sound of Chaucer's writing, the phenomenology of his -*e*'s, has the profound ability to diagnose the very problem it seems to pose. Those -*e*'s do not ask us to find the rule that explains them; they tell us, if we have ears to hear, that their sound is the only rule we need.

NOTES

1. *The House of Fame*, in Geoffrey Chaucer, *The Oxford Chaucer*, ed. Christopher Cannon and James Simpson (Oxford: Oxford University Press, 2023), lines 765–68. All subsequent quotations from Chaucer are from this edition.

2. On Chaucer's sources here see Martin Irvine, "Medieval Grammatical Theory and Chaucer's *House of Fame*," *Speculum* 60 (1985): 850–76, 862–64.

3. E. Talbot Donaldson, "Chaucer's Final -*E*," *PMLA* 63 (1948): 1101–24, 1108.

4. The text from which *The Book of the Duchess* is commonly edited, Oxford, Bodleian Library, MS Fairfax 16, has "yliche" here, a reading adopted in most modern editions (see, e.g., *The Book of the Duchess*, 330–46, in *The Riverside Chaucer*, ed. Larry D. Benson et al. [Cambridge: Houghton Mifflin, 1987], line 1292). Oxford, Bodleian Library, MS Tanner 346 (another important witness for the text of this poem) has "yilch," the reading adopted in the *Oxford Chaucer*. For the manuscript readings, see *A Parallel-Text Edition of Chaucer's Minor Poems*,

ed. F. J. Furnivall, Chaucer Society, 1st series, vols. 21, 57–58 (London: Trübner, 1871–79), 21:37. Subsequent variants will be cited from these transcriptions of the primary medieval witnesses to this text.

5. See Geoffrey Chaucer, *The Complete Works of Geoffrey Chaucer*, ed. F. N. Robinson (Boston: Houghton Mifflin, 1933), xxxvi ("metrical") and xxxix ("necessary").

6. Walter W. Skeat, ed., *The Complete Works of Geoffrey Chaucer, Edited, from Numerous Manuscripts*, 7 vols. (Oxford: Clarendon Press, 1894–97), 6:lxxii–xcvii.

7. See Bernard R. Goldstein, "Saving the Phenomena: The Background to Ptolemy's Planetary Theory," *Journal of the History of Astronomy* 28 (1997): 1–12, esp. 7–8.

8. Eleanor Prescott Hammond, *Chaucer: A Bibliographical Manual* (New York: Macmillan, 1908), 481.

9. Donaldson, "Chaucer's Final *-E*," 1115n43.

10. Ian Robinson, *Chaucer's Prosody: A Study of the Middle English Verse Tradition* (Cambridge: Cambridge University Press, 1971), 91.

11. Stephen A. Barney, *Studies in "Troilus": Chaucer's Text, Meter, and Diction* (East Lansing, MI: Colleagues Press, 1993), 164.

12. James Southworth, "Chaucer's Final *-E* in Rhyme," *PMLA* 62 (1947): 910–35; Donaldson, "Chaucer's Final *-E*"; James G. Southworth and E. T. Donaldson, "Chaucer's Final *-E*," *PMLA* 64 (1949): 601–10.

13. Donaldson, "Chaucer's Final *-E*," 1122 ("scientific") and "rational" (1124); Southworth, "Chaucer's Final *-E* in Rhyme," 935.

14. Donaldson, "Chaucer's Final *-E*," 1120.

15. Jill Mann, "Chaucer's Meter and the Myth of the Ellesmere Editor of the *Canterbury Tales*," *SAC* 23 (2001): 71–107, 77, citing *The Text of the Canterbury Tales: Studied on the Basis of All Known Manuscripts*, ed. John M. Manly and Edith Rickert, 8 vols. (Chicago: University of Chicago Press, 1940), 1:150, and following George Kane, "John M. Manly (1865–1940) and Edith Rickert (1871–1938)," in *Editing Chaucer: The Great Tradition*, ed. Paul G. Ruggiers [Norman, OK: Pilgrim Books, 1984), 207–29, 214. The full shelfmark of the "Ellesmere MS" is San Marino, CA, Huntington Library, MS El 26 C 9.

16. For examples central to the debate turning on the disposition of final *-e*, see Mann, "Chaucer's Meter," 91, 94–95. For Norman Blake's "vigorous campaign" on this matter, see Mann, 73nn10–11. For a summary of Derek Pearsall's important advocacy for the Ellesmere editor, see Mann, 95nn56–58. For an equally vigorous attempt to dispel the myth prior to Mann's, see Ralph Hanna III, "(The) Editing (of) the Ellesmere Text," in *The Ellesmere Chaucer: Essays in Interpretation*, ed. Martin Stevens and Daniel Woodward (San Marino: Huntington Library, 1995), 225–44. George Kane said that Manly and Rickert's invention of the Ellesmere editor was "emotionally based" (Kane, "John M. Manly," 220).

17. The most concise formulation of this enduring paradox appears in Manly and Rickert, who suggest, on the one hand, that the Ellesmere editor had access to "changes made by Chaucer himself" in a copy of a text now lost but that this circumstance "would be entirely consistent with the presence in [Ellesmere] . . . of emendations . . . due to the scribe or his supervisor [i.e., the 'Ellesmere editor']." Manly and Rickert, *The Text of the Canterbury Tales*, 3:439 (cited in Mann, "Chaucer's Meter," 76–77).

18. Derek Pearsall, "Chaucer's Meter: The Evidence of the Manuscripts," in *Essays on the Art of Chaucer's Verse*, ed. Alan T. Gaylord (New York: Routledge, 2001), 139.

19. Robinson, *Chaucer's Prosody*, 90.

20. Donaldson, "Chaucer's Final *-E*," 1119.

21. Robinson, *Chaucer's Prosody*, 107.

22. Norman Eliason, *The Language of Chaucer's Poetry: An Appraisal of the Verse, Style, and Structure* (Copenhagen: Rosenkilde and Bagger, 1972), 12.

23. Alan Gaylord, "Scanning the Prosodists: An Essay in Metacriticism," *Chaucer Review* 11, no. 1 (1976): 22–82, 76–77 (emphasis mine).

24. James Southworth, *Verses of Cadence: An Introduction to the Prosody of Chaucer and His Followers* (Oxford: Blackwell, 1954), 63; Pearsall, "Chaucer's Meter," 139.

25. Pearsall, "Chaucer's Meter," 139.

26. Southworth, *Verses of Cadence*, 63.

27. Ian Robinson, *Chaucer's Prosody*, 91 ("there is no") and 172 ("speech"). Robinson claims that "speech heightened is 'Hopkins's phrase,' " but he seems to have misremembered a passage in one of Hopkins's letters to Robert Bridges: "the poetical language of an age should be the current language heightened," in *The Letters of Gerard Manley Hopkins to Robert Bridges*, ed. Claude Colleer Abbott (Oxford: Oxford University Press, 1955), 89.

28. Quintilian, *The Orator's Education*, ed. and trans. Donald A. Russell, 5 vols. (Cambridge: MA: Harvard University Press, 2001), 1:350–51 (2.14 ["bona" and "bene"]) and 5:308–9 (12.10 ["unum"]).

29. Skeat, *Complete Works of Geoffrey Chaucer*, 6:lxxxiv.

30. James I. Porter, "Nietzsche, Rhetoric, Philology," in *Philology and Its Histories*, ed. Sean Gurd (Columbus: Ohio State University Press, 2010), 164–91, 169.

31. The first quotation from Nietzsche is Porter's translation taken from "Nietzsche, Rhetoric, Philology," 167. It is, in the original, "Das Verständlichste an der Sprache ist nicht das Wort selber, sondern Ton, Stärke, Modulation, Tempo, mit denen eine Reihe von Worten gesprochen werden." Friedrich Nietzsche, "Nachgelassene Fragmente," in *Sämtliche Werke: Kritische Studienausgabe*, ed. Giorgio Colli and Mazzino Montinari, 15 vols. (Berlin: De Gruyter, 1980), 10:89. Porter describes and quotes the second passage (in "Nietzsche, Rhetoric, Philology," 172–73) from *Friedrich Nietzsche on Rhetoric and Language*, ed. and trans. Sander L. Gilman, Carole Blair, and David J. Parent (Oxford: Oxford University Press, 1989), 20–21.

32. Shane Butler, "Principles of Sound Reading," in *Sound and the Ancient Senses*, ed. Shane Butler and Sarah Nooter (New York: Routledge, 2019), 233–55, 238.

33. Porter, "Nietzsche, Rhetoric, Philology," 187.

34. The phrase from Nietzsche is a translation adapted by Porter ("Nietzsche, Rhetoric, Philology," 185) from Gilman, Blair, and Parent, *Friedrich Nietzsche on Rhetoric and Language*, 10–11 (the original in this edition is "den Vortrag nicht als essentiell, sondern nur als Accidens betrachtet wissen" and "sinnliche Erscheinen" for "physical presence").

35. Christopher Hasty, *Meter as Rhythm* (Oxford: Oxford University Press, 1997), 93.

36. Hasty, 93.

37. Alfred North Whitehead, *Process and Reality* (New York: Free Press, 1978), 137 (cited in Hasty, *Meter and Rhythm*, 65; see also the elaboration of the term on 93).

38. Hasty, *Meter as Rhythm*, 5.

39. Butler, "Principles of Sound Reading," 250 ("The poem offers something far harder to come by: experience"); see also p. 255 on the effect of the "linguistic turn" on our experience of texts.

40. Robinson, *Chaucer's Prosody*, 100.

41. Robinson, 156 ("pieces") 172 ("find . . . feeling . . . process").

42. Marjorie Daunt, "Old English Verse and English Speech Rhythm," *Transactions of the Philological Society* 45 (1946): 56–72, 56.

43. Daunt, 59. For the five types, see Eduard Sievers, "Zur Rhythmik der germanischen Alliterationsverses," *Beiträge zur Geschichte der deutschen Sprache und Literatur* 10 (1885): 209–314, 451–545; and 12 (1887): 454–82.

44. Daunt, "Old English Verse," 69.

45. B. Elan Dresher and Aditi Lahiri, "The Germanic Foot: Metrical Coherence in Old English," *Linguistic Inquiry* 22 (1991): 251–86, 283.

46. Suzanne Fleischman, "Philology, Linguistics and the Discourse of the Medieval Text," *Speculum* 65 (1990): 19–37, 23 ("parallel") and 28 ("emergent"). Fleischman derives the view of grammar as emergent from Paul Hopper, who explains his proposal thus: "in place of forms with contexts . . . we will have texts with forms, and contextuality will be replaced by textuality. Structure and grammar in general, instead of being seen as present *a priori*, will emerge out of quite concrete repetitions in discourse." Paul J. Hopper, "Discourse Analysis: Grammar and Critical Theory in the 1980s," *Profession* 88 (1988): 18–24, 22 (cited by Fleischman, 28–29).

47. At the foundation of the historical study of English grammar, Otto Jespersen also claimed that "rhythm undoubtedly plays a great part in ordinary language." See Otto Jespersen, *Growth and Structure of the English Language*, 9th ed. (1905; Oxford: Basil Blackwell, 1952), 220.

48. Derek Pearsall, *John Lydgate* (Charlottesville: University Press of Virginia, 1970), 61.

49. M. L. Samuels, "Chaucerian Final '-E,'" *Notes and Queries* 217 (1972): 445–48, 447.

50. Eric Weiskott, "Phantom Syllables in the English Alliterative Tradition," *Modern Philology* 110 (2013): 441–58, 455, but see also 447–49.

51. Eliason, *Language of Chaucer's Poetry*, 30.

52. "Versus saepe in orationem imprudentiam dicimus . . . magnam enim partem ex iambis nostra constat oratio," §189 (464–65), in Cicero, *Orator*, ed. H. M. Hubbell, in Cicero, *Brutus; Orator* (Cambridge, MA: Harvard University Press, 1939; rev. 1962), 297–509, cited in Gilman, Blair, and Parent, *Friedrich Nietzsche on Rhetoric and Language*, 82–85.

53. See Derek Attridge, *Moving Words: Forms of English Poetry* (Oxford: Oxford University Press, 2013), 124.

54. See Richard Hogg and C. B. McCully, *Metrical Phonology: A Coursebook* (Cambridge: Cambridge University Press, 1987), 132. For careful attention to the variation within such norms, see Meredith Martin's essay in this collection (137–44).

55. Mark Liberman and Alan Prince, "On Stress and Linguistic Rhythm," *Linguistic Inquiry* 8 (1977): 249–336, 334. The rhythms Daunt identified in Old English were generally falling rhythms, trochaic structures where stressed syllables regularly preceded unstressed syllables, but these rhythms could just as easily have been produced by iambic reversal, since, as in Modern and Middle English, they rely on a constant alternation of stressed and unstressed syllables.

56. Bruce Hayes, *Metrical Stress Theory: Principles and Case Studies* (Chicago: University of Chicago Press, 1995), 47.

57. Stephen Barney has made the most use of this work, observing that the preservation or loss of final *-e*'s in English was not a grammatical issue but a matter of "euphony and rhythm." Barney, *Studies in "Troilus,"* 78n1. Barney bases his observation on "a series of articles by Donka Minkova," citing her "The Prosodic Character of Early Schwa Deletion in English," in *Papers from the 7th International Conference on Historical Linguistics*, ed. A. G. Ramat et al. (Philadelphia: Benjamins, 1987), 445–57, "which refers to her earlier work."

58. Donka Minkova, "Unstressed Final *-E* in the *Ormulum*," in *English Studies: Articles on English and American Literature and the English Language* (Sofia: Kliment of Ohrida University, 1981), 162–80, 167. For the poem, see Orm, *The Ormulum*, ed. Robert Holt, notes and glossary by R. M. White, 2 vols. (Oxford: Clarendon Press, 1878). On Orm's rigorous, if unending, program of correction, see Christopher Cannon, "Right Writing: The *Ormulum*," in *The Grounds of English Literature* (Oxford: Oxford University Press, 2004), 82–110.

59. "It is metrical considerations that decide the fate of the final *-e* in the text." Minkova, "Unstressed Final *-E*," 174.

60. I derive this and the next example from Minkova, "Unstressed Final *-E*," 169.

61. Donka Minkova, *The History of Final Vowels in English: The Sound of Muting* (Berlin: De Gruyter Mouton, 1991), 177–78.

62. "Orm schrieb nicht wie er sprach . . . sondern er schrieb wie er zu sprechen glaubte." Erik Björkman, "Orrms Doppelkonsonanten," *Anglia* 37 (1913): 351–82, 381 (cited in Minkova, "Unstressed Final -*E*," 164).

63. I. A. Richards, *Practical Criticism: A Study of Literary Judgment* (Edinburgh: Edingurgh Press, 1929), 58.

64. Richards, 229.

CHAPTER TEN

Writing Reading Rhythm

Christopher Hasty

Sound and Sense and Rhythm

"The sound of writing" has a provocatively jarring sound in reading, a sound that might give us pause. But as writing, it would seem to make no sound. At most, we might say that it represents a sound that can be read. As a verb, *writing* is customarily understood as making visible, tangible marks that silently carry sonic information to be retrieved later. As a noun, *writing* is those marks themselves, inscriptions that, repeatable as such, stay the same and thus defy the decay of sound and memory by bringing back the original sound or, at least, a sound close enough to the original to constitute the same message or meaning, a same thing, a "what" that can be said again and again in different ways or manners. Thus, writing would seem to have little say in the "how" of saying, the rhythmic character or manner of speech-sound, its tempo, intonation, pacing—all those features described in theories of prosody and, doubtless, features yet to be named. I will say more about rhythm later, but suffice it for now to say that the word will refer very broadly to a characterful and engaging course of events (for language, a manner or way of saying), including but not limited to the timing of events and their more or less regular recurrence. That course is always particular and never precisely repeatable. Everything runs its own course.

I will argue in this essay that such particularity and unrepeatability in rhythmic saying is the necessary condition for its propagation in writing. I argue that language is sounding, even in its writing, and that variety in sounding (saying and hearing) is not necessarily an impediment to communication but rather a necessity that with goodwill and good fortune can enhance communicating and promote learning. I will prefer *sounding* to *sound*, as I will prefer the verb *writing* to the noun *writing*. These verbal forms speak of the complexity of ongoing processes, activities that run their courses in the formation of events. Since I don't propose to dispense with the word, I will ask that *sound* be hearable as noun and verb, as something active, happening, something emerging, coming out or eventuating (*evenire*) into a larger world, born into that world—an event that is necessarily situated in the world it comes out into. In their comings out of and into the world, events bear the complexities of the world they are born into. Speech-sound bears the complexities of an actual cultural-historical world, a world that, moreover, includes all the senses, all working together. Although rooted in the sense of hearing, speech-sound is always involved in other senses—above all, the tactile-kinesthetic world of speaking and the visual world of seeing (reading) other people speak and seeing (reading) symbols that can speak. In the activity of language, senses work with or against one another in changing foci to create a course of ongoing events, events more or less rhythmic to the degree differences in character or manner intensify feeling or experience. Here, intensity will be figured as rhythmicity, something akin to what Gertrude Stein means by "insistence" as a creative alternative to the deadening conservatism she calls "repetition."

My essay of this argument will be an attempt to think freshly about sound (sounding) and writing by thinking broadly about rhythm, not as form or as an abstractable component of speech but as activity, the ongoing activity of bodies individual and social. Motivating my argument is a concern that sound and rhythm are often marginalized in literary studies and pedagogy in part because they seem indescribable as objects of discourse, "musical," perhaps, but in a sense of *musical* peripheral to content or meaning and thus on the periphery of the properly linguistic, exiled to the "paralinguistic." This judgment has a long speculative history that I will barely touch on. But to value sound and rhythm will require a different sort of speculation and a questioning of conventional terminologies. I will attempt a specifically temporalizing approach to rethinking a few central terms: principally, *sounding* or *speaking, writing, the written*, and *rhythm*. In this approach, I draw on various strands of process thinking—principally, that of William James, Henri Bergson, Alfred North Whitehead, Giles Deleuze, Eugene Gendlin, and Jason W. Brown. Against this speculative background, I will attempt to develop a flexible and engaging method for reading free verse or "artistic prose" in a theoretical environment that would be open to a wide variety of poetic practices. I have chosen as my single example an excerpt of Gertrude Stein's writing, a brief passage that crowns the ending of the first half of her essay "Portraits and Repetition." This excerpt will serve as a sort of laboratory for testing my proposed method or way (*hodos*) of reading. It is a fitting example in that Stein was a subtle process thinker (and never far from the laboratory); moreover, she was a student of James and a friend and admirer of Whitehead.[1]

My writing of this attempt will proceed through a series of connected vignettes in preparation for a close reading/hearing of Stein, a reading/hearing that is necessarily rhythmic. Choosing *how to say* this passage is how we will make sense of the writing as we read; it is the way we read and make sense. Variability in saying will in some sensible way (however small) contribute to the variability of the senses we can make. Rhythm and sound and sense all work together. But in what way?

For much reading, and especially "silent" or subvocal reading, the properly sonic rhythm of speaking is, let's say, subsidiary to a focus on the unfolding of idea, image, or story that, as unfolding, has its apparently own rhythm. Yet the two rhythms, subsidiary and focal, are inseparable in their creation of meaning. Rather than two discrete, fixed, spatialized levels, imagine a vectoral or directional difference, a temporal, rhythmic interaction in the activity of attending *from* one *to* the other, *from* sound *to* an apparently higher sense, a "making sense" that can involve all the senses, sound included. The paired terms *subsidiary* and *focal* come from Michael Polanyi's theory of tacit knowing in which knowing as activity or fait accomplissant replaces knowledge as fait accompli.[2] An example of the subsidiary/focal distinction from the tactile domain is the skilled use of a cane to guide your steps if you are deprived of sight. The feeling of the cane in your hand is not the focus of your attention; that focus is the feeling of the ground at the tip of the cane (say, a break in the pavement). If you shift your attention to your palm, you lose a feeling of the ground, a feeling that is the purpose and the meaning of your use of the cane and, moreover, part of a making-sense that involves all your senses working together (otherwise, you'd fall). Or, in terms of language, think of feeling braille.

It is important to note that for Polanyi, *subsidiary* and *focal* name a difference of kind in attention, *not* a difference of degree or importance. Both working together are required for the production of meaning. In language, sound is often subsidiary to a focus on sense; and if rhythm is restricted to strict isochrony, such sense can seem arrhythmic. Moreover, if the larger view of *sense* as sense-making (with all its verbal adventure and uncertainty) is detemporalized, made a noun, *sense* can come to be seen simply as a persisting, renewed, and renewing idea or image or story that can endure as an afterimage, long after sound's last echo. Such a "sense-made" as a fait accompli, as something held on to (*concepere*), can seem to escape the sequential time of language and thus to persist as an apparently all-at-once and enduring "content," an endlessly describable, paraphrasable, external "meaning" (what the words are *about*) that might magically encompass all ways of saying all at once. Yet, in the actual, "real-time" *sense-making* of language, sound and rhythm are essential.[3]

In speech, a familiar example of making focal what was subsidiary is the well-documented phenomenon of "semantic satiation," in which holding on to a word in repetition leads to a new focus on sound and the loss of a prior focus on sematic meaning. Here, decontextualization (deterritorialization) is revealed through the experimental artifice or apparatus of repeating. But rather than see this process only in the direction of loss, as the destruction of meaning, imagine repeating as an opportunity for recontextualization (reterritorialization), as an opening for creation of new meaning. In the art or technology of poetry, repetition enhances opportunities for sound and sense to work together in a lively play of perspectival difference, where shifts in focal awareness or changes in balance allow sound and image to come in and out of focus in an engaging, "meaningful" rhythm that requires both working together—without engagement, no rhythm. Though it can seem a visible threat to sound, if writing complicates the rhythm of language, then writing is inseparable from sound and sense, all three working together.[4]

Sound and Sounding

The conjunction of writing and sound can quickly conjure a set of contrasts: eye and ear, inanimate and animate, fixed and changing, lasting and ephemeral, one text and many soundings or readings of that text. Sound can seem unreliable and perhaps dispensable if writing is thought sufficient for "conveying" meaning. What is lost of the vivid immediacy of sound would thus seem made up for in the stability of the written. Indeed, how valuable is the immediacy of sound if it leads to the babel of countless tongues? But how valuable, indeed, is the medium of a writing that could hold all possible readings.

The last of the contrasts listed above suggests replacing *sound* by *sounding* or *speaking* (or as Stein prefers, "talking")—that is, specifying an abstract noun by reference to living, acting, and enduring human beings with all their histories and hopes. This substitution of *sounding* for *sound* has the virtue of eliminating the contrast of the ephemeral and changing with the fixed and lasting and, thus, of putting sound on an equal temporal footing with writing: both endure. Indeed, if we wish to relate the two, it will help to find a common ground. *Sound* can imply ephemerality in the quick passage of sensation or in the attenuation of amplitude in an articulated sound, the fading of echo and the perpetual dying, dying away of sound. *Sounding* as coordinated actions of speaking and hearing (talking and listening) allows sound to continue or to last by repeating and changing. If change as vibration is the hallmark of acoustical sound (and, indeed, of rhythm), sounding amplifies change by entering bodies and changing them—from the movement of air to ear to nerve to whole body and, however subtly, changing that acting and hearing body, changing other contemporary bodies and across generations. Rather than the fading of sound, imagine an amplification or growth in resonating. There is, in this sense, no end to sounding.

Rhythm

The process of sounding I have sketched, since it involves repetition and change, implies rhythm, at least in the very broad sense I would suggest. In this sense, *rhythm* characterizes actual, ongoing experience. It therefore needs to be conceived very broadly as the manner (way, how) in which events emerge and succeed one another and come to shape one another in characterful and meaningful ways. Most succinctly, *rhythm is the manner of moving* (flowing, changing, becoming).[5]

The ways or manners of rhythm involve everything that can come into play in shaping the course of sounding.[6] Studies in interactional prosody show the remarkable, highly nuanced interdependencies of all prosodic domains in interactive speech, including such complex things as the gestured cueing of turn-taking opportunities among participants.[7] Indeed, studies across disciplines suggest that complexities of speech and body rhythm, across many modalities and levels of duration, can communicate far more meaning(s) than the properly (exclusively) lexical. Interactional prosody studies rely on the technologies of audio and video recording instruments and the development of a sophisticated and widely shared system for notating prosodic features. Because of the repeatability of a sonic/visual record, outside observers can analyze in minute detail the activity of their subjects and discover subtleties ("subsidiaries") and interdependencies hidden from the participants, whose attention is directed solely toward acting and interacting. Thus observed, the language of everyday conversation displays remarkable skill. The artful and skillful language of poetry can intensify, bring into focus, and play with the rhythmicity of everyday speech.

In informal social interaction there is no time for rhythm to become focal. A lot is going on, and things move quickly. But reading and hearing written poetry can slow things down enough to make rhythm focal, not for an outside observer but for an acting reader/hearer working to make sense of an artifact that has been precisely designed for play with sound and a play that with practice can be very quick indeed. The technology of writing makes poems easily repeatable and can thus enable a reader to make repeated (slowed, paused) experiments in reading/hearing—when and at whatever pace the reader chooses. These experiments, all this reading and rereading, constitute the practice of written poetry. Although the repetition of rereading is never the same, it can be more or less the same, more or less intense, more or less engaging, and more or less challenging. Imagine a scale from tedious sameness and lack of novelty to an opaqueness that asks for work to find meaning in (or rather, *as*) meaningful *ways* of actually saying, hearing, listening. When we turn to the verse of Stein we can see the virtues of opaqueness, or in temporal terms, virtues of a holding up saying that asks for repetition, for trying again, for practice.

Conceived in this way, rhythm challenges description. How do we describe change in the course of changing, an "again" that is always and essentially different? And in the case of language, what are the terms of change, the various namable parts and dimensions of change that in rhythm are so interwoven? How would we judge a rhythmicity that is precisely variable? And as outside observers, how would we gauge the intricacy of a situated saying and an attentiveness that shape the rhythm we would merely observe? But why privilege a description from outside and make rhythm purely an object?

As an alternative, I suggest describing (writing about) rhythm as a process, something we could enter into as an activity and experiment with. In the case of written poetry, we could experiment saying, again and again, to test to see what's involved. This would be to follow the path of an engaged reading of poetry and to ask about skill and opportunities for learning. Rather than aim for a proper reading, we might experiment with potentials for reading and see what questions and problems or provocations emerge.

Since the sound of language is speech-sound, let's consider the rhythm of speaking. The words come. They come slowly or quickly, with more or less effort, haltingly or fluently; and they come out with all sorts of valuations or feelings. When you stop speaking, new words may come before you start speaking again. In calm and reflective mode, you might faintly hear them before you speak; and with more attention their sound can become more palpable. These are things that "come to you." This coming could be from outside-in, say, via a muse or genius or the mechanistic and deterministic wheels of cultural history. But let's imagine a coming inside-out. Let's say that speaking comes out of incipient, imagining/imagined sound and out of a yet prior silence of thought/feeling/inspiration.[8] If, for whatever reason, you need to hold on to the new words that come out and to stop the influx of more new words, you can repeat or rehearse them. With attention, as you continue repeating your words, they can become quite vivid with intonation and a rhythm you might eventually be able to tap your foot to. In conversation, you can switch off your inner speech to listen, though you may hear yourself silently interjecting (rather than interrupting) or planning and rehearsing your eventual coming-out response. From these observations, it seems clear that "inner" and "outer" speech are continuous. This continuity has been extensively interrogated in studies of "subvocalization," with its sometimes surprising findings—for example, that even speed reading cannot escape minute movements of larynx and associated musculature. Speed readers are sometimes encouraged to bite their tongues in a futile attempt to escape the retarding effect their very bodies impose in resistance to the ideal of a machine speed.

Inner speech, for all its power, can be viewed as a pale copy of outer speech, a memory or residual habit acquired in the imitation of countless overlearned outer speech acts. In this picture, inner is derived from outer. This may not be wrong, but if inner and outer work together and need one another equally, there can be a sense in which outer also derives from inner. Imagine beginning with the silence of thought/feeling as inner and moving outward to inner speech and thence to outer speech. Think of inner speech as an intermediary stage of speaking, on the way from the silence of thought to the actual production of acoustic sound, which requires an expulsion of inner air that sets outer air in motion (breathing in and out, and perhaps holding). Imagine the sounding of language as a *way* of thinking, a way of thinking through the medium of a language-sound that, pictured perhaps as an intricately patterned environment or as a dense or viscous (sticky) medium, perplexes thinking, slowing it down and holding it up. By repeating or rehearsing, we intensify this slowing/holding, and in doing so, we can attempt to hold thinking up in a faithful repetition of the same. Or instead, we can go with the flow (or ride the wave) and hold on to a thinking that admits change in the construction of new events of thinking/feeling, a holding that is also a moving.[9] However the negotiations of preservation and change might play out, in this scenario an incipient, un-sighted, unheard pre-speech would be understood as an intricate *potential* for speaking, full of possibilities for patterning. Keats's "viewless [and, let's say, soundless] wings of Poesy" might then be an ethereal, quick, and yet-to-be fully embodied thought that perplexed and retarded by tongue and hand can turn into verse.[10] "Poesy" here names a gift and a skill for the making of poems—traditionally, a gift of inspiration in the figure of a spirit or genius or muse or tradition that precedes and guides the tongue's skilled telling. But if inside and outside are one, this gift is not other than an encultured body's rhythmic course of thinking/feeling, here and now. Of course, thinking need not be retarded in talking much less in the retardations of writing and reading. Although the encultured body is never without language, thinking can move too fast to be held up in language, especially when urgent action is required; but perhaps thinking can move very fast, too, when simply witnessing the world without commenting, a goal of some meditative practices.

Writing and the Written

But what about the rhythm of writing? Writing, like speaking, crystallizes out of the imagined, incipient sound of silent or implicit or not-yet speech. In writing, the words still come with the speed of speech but must be held up to be written down and repeated or rehearsed before or while writing. Writing takes time. Writing slows or holds up speaking in the time it takes to write the words down. But slowing and holding can have benefits. Holding up / slowing down can be an opportunity for change and growth, for thinking further, or "farther ahead," having more time. And although the rhythm of writing/speaking/thinking is in part the choice of the writer, the physical action of writing imposes its own "external" constraints. The technology of writing requires instruments of the hearing-speaking body. Various writing instruments—pen, typewriter, word processor—bring their own time constraints to writing and thus variously shape the act of writing and its product, the written. Some present-day writers prefer the writing body of the pen or the typewriter to that of the word processor because of the virtues of slowness.[11] Indeed, neurological studies show "improved" brain activity and quality of writing with the medium of pen and paper.[12] What was the rhythm of writing with quill and ink? Imagine the writing constraints that challenged the blind Milton in his composing and dictating (and doubtless editing) *Paradise Lost* with the daily help of his word-"milking" staff?

Although it does shape writing (and thence the reading of that writing), the slowing caused by writing instruments is the means, not the aim, of writing; the aim is for a more general slowing and pausing. Writing is a technology for recording and repeating speech-sound in a written artifact that can be returned to as needed and reread. Reading is speaking (out loud or sotto voce), and that speaking can be continued in further writing. Think of the experience of writing: trying to hold on to the thought lest you lose it; trying out several sayings; rereading and revising, rewriting, coming back to that thought and working with it or rejecting it but, in any case, being haunted by what you've written. All of this working may eventuate in a final product, an opus or work (however grand or slight) when your speaking stops writing. Of course, writing need not be published; it can be just for the writer, a way to explore thought and feeling (you don't have to send that letter that you wrote and read and reread).

The medium of the work of writing is the written artifact, an object and a sort of "outer" memory; it is something manufactured by human hands but endowed with speech, an object that has been domesticated by its making and marking, becoming almost a member of the family. Written objects are often cherished and carefully preserved, and this is part of their having their own pampered lives as objects. Because artifacts/writings belong to the human world, they age together with people or peoples but at different rates; for example, a papyrus might have lasted more than four thousand years. In this difference of speed, the legibility of the writing can be lost over time, or it can be renewed and changed. As instruments used for thinking and remembering, writings are always on the move, making new reading and writing (*poesis*). Yet the artifact can seem relatively permanent. It can seem that speech-sound is fragile, ephemeral, passing without a trace and that the written artifact endures more or less secure, changeless, its characters carved in stone. In fact, it is sounding that sustains the written, the soundings of those able and willing to read. And since sounding continues to change, it is the written artifacts that are vulnerable and that suffer a loss of legibility, even if the markings are not degraded. Writing is a fragile instrument, an artifact that fades in sound as it ages unless it is reanimated by changing speech. Indeed, written artifacts are kept alive by changing—changing by copying (and miscopying), by translating, by generating commentary, by leading to new writing, new reading, changing precisely by repeating. If the artifact finally becomes mute, it loses its animacy and becomes an ordinary object. Yet, seen as an artifact, even a mute object can have a nostalgic or speculative value or "voice," as, for example, a clay of Linear A imbued with a sniff of ancient romance and the challenge of deciphering. But even in death, if totally forgotten, the *writing* of an artifact endures in whatever changes it made that continue to matter, to make a difference, however slight, to a following course of speaking and hearing and to further reading and writing.

Rhythm and Poetry

But what of the sound of all that speaking and hearing, writing and reading? Since we are talking about language, it is all the sounding of speech. Let's say this all is not a collection of speech sounds or a set of features such as pitch, contour, and stress. It is all these things and many more (how many dimensions of sounding might we propose, how many sets and subsets and set classes?). Let's say, too, that this many is not composed of separate individuals but is rather the many sounding together as the "composition" or putting-together of whatever features or factors we might wish to name, all working together in concert in a speaking event that is an actual course and manner of sounding. This complexity of factors working together in changing ways is *rhythm*—at least I know no better word. In language, the rhythm of sounding-speaking is always involved with ideational meaning because such meaning is always involved in the language one speaks. But this involvement is variable. In rapid inner reading, sound, and thus sound's vivid rhythm, can be highly attenuated. Or in slow and repeated reading, such as poetry can invite, rhythmic sound can take center stage.

Slow and rewardingly complex, especially when said again, this might be a definition of the speech (writing) we call poetry.[13] In poetry, and especially "sung" poetry, rhythmic sound can become focal, and image can become, if not precisely subsidiary then at least significantly altered, saturated by sound to become an emotional, moving, and evolving Sense in which all contributing factors are felt and evaluated. Remember that the distinction of *focal* and *subsidiary* is not a difference of importance; the two need one another equally. It is rather a difference of function in the composition of whole and part. To animate Polanyi's distinction of "subsidiary and focal," think of them as varying or differing in intensity in a lively changing of focus; also understand *composition* as a verb, a putting-together that is an always complex process involving changes of focus among a multitude of factors and their intensities. Might we not then say that such changes or movements are a sort of vibration of whole and part together (to borrow from Stein, "the two in one and the one in two"). And if there is difference and oscillation, to-and from or between, then this would be a kind of rhythm, a movement or changing that in poetry can be felt viscerally as a kind of vibrancy or liveliness.

Reading Writing

There are two rhythms of writing: the rhythm in the writing (in the process of actually creating the written, through cycles of listening and speaking held up in episodes of writing down) and the rhythm in the written (in how the result of that process might now be read). The first rhythm is actual; it eventuates in an actual written. The second is a *potential* for rhythm, not actual rhythm; in this sense, strange as it may sound, there is no *actual* artwork. The writer had to hear into this potential in order to write it and, by writing, make it something definite, a *beginning* of something new that can be repeated. And the reader must hear into that definite and changing potential to make actual speech. The rhythms of writing and reading can't be separated. The potential for reading was shaped by the labor of the writing of the work. One evidence of this potential from the writer's standpoint is an eventual diminishing of returns in the writing. A way of knowing that the work is completed is sensing that nothing more can be done to create more potential, that your revising is now becoming destructive: you've reached your limits; time to stop. But this does not mean that a reader must be so limited nor, indeed, that you might not later return to the writing and make productive changes. If writing in its incarnation as the written is potential, it must be a variable and changing potential for reading, varying from person to person and changing from time to time. This variability can raise anxiety by asking for some sort of judgment of adequacy in reading and by raising questions of skill or competence, or even gift, in a reading that would make the most of the poesis or making of poetry.

Who Can Say?

Because the recorded work is a vessel not of an encoded message but of an exquisite potential, a vehicle or instrument for thinking/feeling, the work's author(s), though expert and practiced in reading the work through all its stages of writing, cannot know how the work might be taken. Polanyi's message that we know more than we can say holds also in inversion for writers, who always say more than they can know. This is the creative imprecision or the depth of language. The particular openness of potential in a written work is a wager that that potential can power engaged readings that can make the most of the work in the making of new readings, new meanings that keep the work alive.

If the work intends an outer-spoken reading, a skilled actor would seem an ideal reader. In an age in which reading out loud (or even slow, repeated inner reading) is no longer widely practiced, audiobooks can provide beautifully nuanced rhythmic readings to a grateful audience spared the labor of reading out loud. These are labor-saving devices that can also have the great virtue of allowing for the comparison of multiple readings or actualizations (materializations) of the same text. Recordings of works of literature are like recordings of musical works, and they speak similarly of specialization—a professionalization of reading. But they do not allow for the experience of discovery that an amateur reader can enjoy. Reading, performing (if only for oneself) is challenging; it can invite repetition and discovery in the service of learning. To perform (*per-formare*) is to actually, really form or shape. This shaping is, I would suggest, the point of poetry, its poesis. This activity of shaping with its implication of skill and spontaneity is the antithesis of an anesthetic transmission of information. And if the poesis of poetry is continuous invention, then acknowledging the infinitely various potential for saying that a writing offers should not be dispiriting. It can be interesting to experiment with ways of saying to test various constraints or resistances in the writing and to see what differences in saying can reveal and what questions they can raise. Abundance can be a virtue.

Reading Rhythm

Poetry is an art that uses repetition and pattern precisely to make rhythms that are nothing if not precisely sayable; thus, poems offer especially promising laboratories for experimenting with sounding/saying the written. Compared to a written prose that is open to a great variety of sayings and that can move very quickly, so quickly that one may have little time to attend to the complexities of sound, poetry can slow things down and offer a security in saying through the sensing of repeated patterns. Sensing opportunities for a rhythmic saying and working with them is all that can be asked of a reader. In an out-loud reading culture, a proper reading is one that sounds right. The right sounding of poetry is a measure of skill in poetry. It is learned early in nursery rhymes and developed in reading grown-up poetry. But since there are gaps in education and because grown-up poetry is so various and challenging and disputable, there can be a need for a pedagogy to help develop an ear for a poetry that doesn't yet sound right when read.[14] Traditional poetic prosody is an effective pedagogical device for ear training (otherwise it wouldn't have lasted so long). As an elementary device for learning to hear, and not as the truth of poetry, it serves as a scaffolding that is no longer needed once it has served its initiatory purpose. As a specialized science of verse, it can be subjected to endless elaboration by theorists and theoretically minded poets. But even at its most precise, it can't quite tell us *how* to say. Reading *Paradise Lost*, for all its putative iambic pentameter regularity, is extraordinarily challenging: every line is different, and this changing contextual difference is the rhythm of the poem. Moreover, these lines are embedded in all the lines Milton heard and, indirectly, in lines his ancestors heard. Although the repetitions of poetic "form" (the items of prosody) do point to poetic craft, they can hardly touch a poetic crafting (and craftiness) that involves all poetic domains and that can invent new rules as it goes. Were it not for an intrinsic complexity that allows such openness, poetic forms would be useless. But if they are intrinsically complex, poetic forms cannot be simply described. In the following, I will mean by *form* a complex and changing system of constraints, a "forming system," rather than a fixed set of constraints.

The survival in English-language poetry of what is called "iambic pentameter" is a testament to the opportunities a sufficiently engaging form can offer for the growth of a tradition.[15] Departing from such forms is a risky move. Without the expectation of, for example, four or five beats and between nine and eleven syllables per line and all the subtle patterning and weighting that make the line sound properly "iambic pentameter," free verse was a daring move, comparable to music's early twentieth-century move to "free tonality." Could the poet's written voice be powerful enough to make its potential for being spoken known to a reader deprived of traditional cues? This movement in poetry was a source of anxiety for writer and reader alike. But at least a crucial ingredient was left intact—the written. In free verse, the notation of turns is retained in lineation. To make up for the loss of the ear-form of lines formed of accentual/syllabic repetition, modernist free-versers turned to the page. The display of characters on the page takes on a new level of importance as a system of cues for saying and in support of a proper saying that would take everything available into account to make the most of an elusive poetic potential. To the extent that free verse draws on notation to help secure a proper saying, it is high writing, a writing that intensifies the graphic in an advancement and promotion of notation. An alternative was to let go of lineation and to rely more on hearing. Modernist "prose poetry" or "poetic prose" relies on the minimal orthography of prose (upper or lower case, punctuation symbols, paragraph indentation) and the maximal hearing of rhythm. It asks for an unaccustomed slowing of what looks to be made for quick saying. In her fearless prose-poetic experiments Gertrude Stein engages vocabularies of "everyday speech" only to throw numerous monkey-wrenches into a quick and easy reading.

Writing Reading Stein's Rhythm

I have argued that the activity of writing crucially involves the activities of listening and speaking and is itself rhythmic. In the following passage from her essay "Portraits and Repetition," Stein writes of a process of writing in which *listening and talking* (rather than my formal "speaking") always work together, the two in one and the one in two. The "Repetition" of Stein's title is unredeemed habit and a distraction from intense living. Leery of the attempt to redeem this word from an anesthetic return of the same, she names intense, creative repetition "insistence." Thus, *Do you, do you, do you* . . . is insistence, not repetition (though it is sort of a pun here). To begin working with this text, I would ask you to try saying it a few times, insistently rather than repetitively, either out loud or subvocally, and to find a comfortable pace, not too fast; take your time and experiment using your time; and as you speak, listen:

> I say I never repeat when I am writing because when I am writing I am most completely, and that is if you like being a genius, I am most entirely and completely listening and talking, the two in one and the one in two and that is having completely its own time and it has in it no element of repetition. Therefore, there is in it no element of confusion, therefore there is in it no element of repetition. Do you, do you, do you really understand.
>
> And does it make any difference to you if you do understand. It makes an awful lot of difference to me. It is very exciting to have all this be.[16]

Stein said that as a child her favorite thing was diagraming sentences, and it shows.[17] Syntax is the rhythmic, bodily formation of speech events and their combination, and in this passage, it is the first thing to hold us up, slow us down, and make us repeat. Stein's vocabulary is commonplace and, in the fractured speech events she constructs, disarmingly colloquial. Something seems clearly wrong here but maybe intriguingly right. This is a highly arresting writing that aims to hold us, her attentive readers, up but that in return offers us the opportunity to ask new questions born of a perplexity that slows reading in repetition, repetition now in the constructive (redeemed, intensified) sense of trying again, saying again with the aim of trying out, ex-perimenting with, asking ab-out in an intensification or insistence of reading.

The first rhythmic-syntactic glitch is marked with the first comma. In her writings, Stein uses only two marks of punctuation, comma and period, and she uses them strategically. The parenthetical *that is* (a favorite Steinian device) leaves *completely* hanging. You can begin again after the next comma and resume *I am most entirely and completely* . . . , but then the parenthesis makes no sense and the nonsense might give you pause. There is a way of saying that would make good sense, though by altering a likely first pass born of habit. If the focus is on *am* rather than *I* (*I* ***am*** *most completely,* I most completely am), the sentence is closed and the parenthesis clicks into place: being who I truly am is like being a genius, and perhaps being the genius I like to be, that I find exciting and fulfilling to be (see the end of the passage). This is a paraphrase that would not lead outside the writing but rather would point to a particular rhythmic reading, a performance of this juncture of the writing that can have all sorts of repercussions.

Indeed, this first insistence on a careful saying/sounding can lure us into further experimentation, as far as we care to go. As we read on in this passage, we're not let off the hook; more and more problems arise, not just uncomfortable glitches but curious changes of diction, sudden changes in the logic or the direction of thought, changes in speed. Eventually, all this might seem like too much work and incline us to move quickly on. But if sufficiently lured by curiosity, we might pause in this passage and thus hold on to or stay with a complexity that promises to reveal something of value—maybe there's really something to all this complex patterning, a something the rhythmic precision of our saying can reveal. A willingness to work with this abundance of meaning is a matter of taste—and of hunger.

If we do stay with this writing, eventually everything may be up in the air. In the semantic-syntactic domain, *it* and *that is* (i.e., "that is to say," or "that is"?) are puzzling, as they always are in Stein's writing where they point to an insistent givenness that invites but resists naming yet can be explored through a practice of insistent repetition, not-letting-go as a creative act. Puzzling indeed are all the repetitions. Instead of a repetition of line, there is a repetition (difference) that spreads through the whole text, repetitions of words, phrases, grammatical constructions, diction. Although there is virtue in the puzzlement such unaccustomed repetition/difference can inspire, the poetic aim is to find a solution in an actual rhythmic saying; poetry asks for saying/hearing.

A rhythmic saying will require repetition and difference, both together (also two in one and one in two) because both are required for event formation—one event after and together with an other-one. In example 1, I have enumerated a succession of thirteen sentential or "verse" events in this passage, thirteen turns of speech or taking turns in play. But how can we be certain that these are events? By performing them. I think there is little room for disagreement here. Example 1's enumeration is presented to facilitate reference. I might instead have presented thirteen lines of verse, but this intervention would be destructive of Stein's intricate, polyphonic rhythm. This nonlineated free verse requires a robust patterning to generate a confident and caring saying. But its nonlineation also creates opportunities for intricate saying that would be lost in a lineation. The course of these verse events, the way they form together, is the rhythm of the passage.

> Example 1
>
> [1] I say I never repeat when I am writing [2] because when I am writing I am most completely, [3] and that is if you like being a genius, [4] I am most entirely and completely listening and talking, [5] the two in one and the one in two [6] and that is having completely its own time [7] and it has in it no element of repetition. [8] Therefore, there is in it no element of confusion, [9] therefore there is in it no element of repetition. [10] Do you, do you, do you really understand.
>
> [11] And does it make any difference to you if you do understand. [12] It makes an awful lot of difference to me. [13] It is very exciting to have all this be.

Coming out of the parenthetical [3], [4] takes up where [2] more or less abruptly left off and releases into a long and fluid gesture if *am* need no longer be so held; in this way, the verse moves quickly and decisively to *listening and talking*. Phrase event [5] is something new, a change of diction to high apodictic;[18] [5] is also the shortest most "regular" verse, triple and rather singsong, nine syllables in two-times-two beats—*two, one; one, two*. From here, verses get longer and begin to form larger continuous events, first through the concatenations of *and* in [6] and [7], and then through the repetition of *therefore* (like *and* but more intense), and also through the near repetition of [7], [8], and [9]. Notice the complex overlappings of these three events and the challenges for saying in a way that would make sense, that would sound right. Diction changes with [7], [8], and [9], returning to the ecclesiastical mood of [5] but now the King James Version. Next, [10] breaks with all this and closes the notated paragraph or stanza with a suddenly insistent call to the reader in a new kind of rhythm. The second and concluding stanza beginning again with *And* ([11]) overlaps with and expands on the first stanza; this *And* is "the same" conjunction ("and") but initiates a new event on a larger scale. Phrase [12] repeats and expands on [11] and changes from *you* back to *me*. Finally, [13] closes this passage (and the first half of the essay) in a rhyming couplet (*be*) with a new, lilting and very familiar measure (anapestic tetrameter). Note that [12] and [13] are each twelve syllables long.

This quick tour of a syntax or rhythm of combining verses (a rhythm of breathing and thinking together) has barely touched on the quicker work of tongue and mouth. Yet, without a precise feeling for these more immediate and urgent rhythms-events, the more dilated rhythms-events cannot be said. This is the level of syllables and feet. Indeed, all contemporaneous events work together as we heard in a decision to make *am* focal in the second event. Example 2 introduces a notation for identifying "foot" events.[19] Think here of footfalls and a movement of mouth assemblages (or ensembles of movements) that, slowed, could be played out at the same time in walking or dancing or in arm motions—that is, with larger muscle groups. Vertical marks (|) indicate beginnings of the durations or "endurings" or "lastings" of actual speech events that take time to become and that once they come to be, can also be for succeeding events, informing the events that follow. These viscerally felt events are full of action and balance in their working together, as are footsteps (otherwise, you'd fall down). A step lasts until the next step begins. Here, beginning will be understood as an entrance or opening, a step into a new being or coming to be, a becoming that takes time, that has, or rather is, duration. Imagine *duration* as a verb (like *action*), from *durare* (to harden or solidify). Thus, I would emphasize that "|" marks a durational quantity, not an instant, and not a quality attached to an instant (such as "stress" or "accent" marking a state). Instants are fictions, as your walking will tell you.

Any thing/event that happens in this marked event-duration is a continuation of this present, ongoing, emerging, evolving event; any articulation that does not end the event continues it. Thus, I make the fundamental distinction in my notation of beginning or opening (|) and continuing (\ or /) that opening in an event both begun and becoming. Thus, a slanted mark (\ or /) indicates continuation. The two marks of continuation also make a fundamental distinction that takes into account the succession of events: (1) Continuing can remain in the thrall of the promise of the event's beginning, playing out that potential for the creation of this new event (new because now, actually going on); this function is marked with a backward-slanting line (\). (2) Continuing can at some point (generally, late in the duration) change from maintaining to preparing for a new event, not for the new now event that is now becoming but for an event to come, a possibility that is now pressing on the present with more or less urgency (what next!). This is a moment of preparation, a movement toward an upcoming event; this distinction is marked with a forward-slanting line (/). Think again of walking or dancing (or conducting), of follow-through and preparation.[20] Prosodies have long recognized these functions as arsic and anacrustic, falling (\) and rising (/). In example 2, beginnings and continuations are variously distributed. The notations labeled (a), (b), (c), and (d) mark progressively "faster" and less highly differentiated sayings of the "verse" event given below them, each one less attentive to detail than the example below it (though it must be said that a high degree of attentiveness can also be brought to quicker sayings, such as might be demanded in drama).

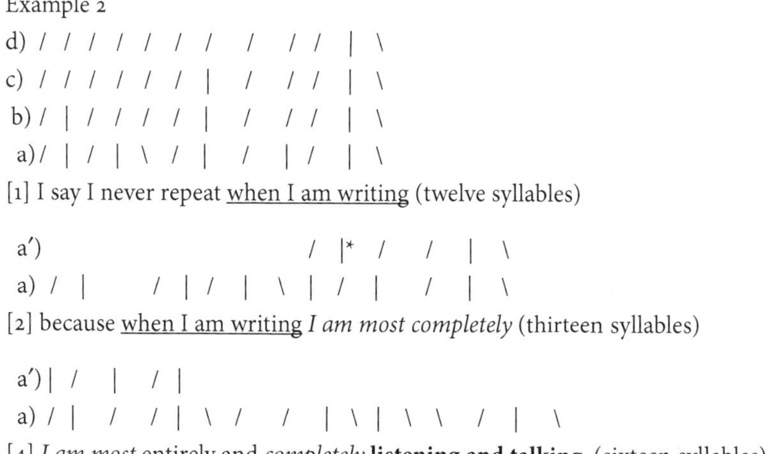

Try saying the line [1] quite slowly at first to experiment with the markings shown in [1] (a). As with the numbering of verses in example 1, I believe there will likely be little disagreement with this labeling given a moderately slow speed of saying and with the understanding that "timing" or "how long" is not specified in these diagrams. Such decisions will be made in the course of experimenting with saying. I wish to call these "prosodic" decisions for saying also "syntactic" (syntax as an art of composing or putting together) but working at a different scale from the "sentential" syntax exhibited by the thirteen events shown in example 1. To make the distinction, we might call this faster component of speaking the "microsyntactic."[21] The two scales can work together, as can be seen in [2] (a) and (a′), where the difference matters to both scales. Experiment moving between the two sayings; as you say the difference, listen to the rhythm of the whole phrase.

In the course of experimenting with saying [1], you may find that a variety of emphases and changes of tempo or speed suggest themselves. It should be possible to play with these and to ask why they might come about and what they might accomplish in the larger context of saying, what *difference* they might make to you. As this line is said faster, emphases can emerge more clearly and eventually drain most syllables of functional distinctions.[22] The diagrams [1] (a)–(d) (slow to fast) show a progressive winnowing of differences with increasing speed. At high speed, speech turns from a detailed patterning to patter or a repetition that minimizes difference. These higher levels of simplicity (and thus lower levels of intensity or insistence) are, however, sensitive to larger contexts within the line and among lines. In the case of [1], no larger context is given. Level (b) emphasizes the verbs.

At (c) an emphasis of *say* would likely promise a compound sentence beginning with *but*, a counterfactual. The choice for (d) would be between *repeat* and *writing*; here, I assume a default in *writing*, as I imagine Stein would.

But in example 2 [2], there is now the context created by the now past event [1]. This context can color anything or everything in [2].[23] Here, consider the word-repetition, *when I am writing*—the end of [1] and the beginning of [2], following an anacrustic *because*. The repetition can (in my reading) repeat the focus on *writing*. And if *am* is an auxiliary, as in [2] (a), *writing* can stand, and the resulting five continuations in a row will ask for quick reading. But if, as in [2] (a′), *am* is a main or lexical verb, *writing* will fade, and reading will slow. But again, this latter interpretation is likely to come to light only after encountering the parenthetical and interruptive [3]; thus, rereading—the asterisk in [2] (a′)—signals a reinterpretation in light of a later context (that is, later in the text). In [4], *am* can slide back into what might have been its initial promise as an auxiliary in [2] (feeling an actual shift from lexical to auxiliary would be an interesting refinement in performance).

Notice the expansion from [1] to [2] to [4]. Each builds on its predecessor(s): [2] on [1], and [4] on [2] and [1]. Together they build a sentence—without the stutters, *when I am writing I am most completely listening and talking*. The expansion is also an acceleration to a crowning *listening and talking*; but I confess, I have something invested in "listening and talking" (investment is part of rhythmic engagement). From the lexical domain, notice that the *repeat* we start with in [1] has been quite thoroughly replaced by *complete*. The theme of completion prevails with something of an apotheosis in [5] and [6]. But *repetition* (now the noun) bringing *confusion* returns with a properly biblical vengeance, eventuating in the cry of the prophet—*Do you, do you, do you really understand*. (This is all very dramatic.) To experiment without my direct interference, try saying "Do you really understand?" in as unaffected a way as you can, and then say Stein's [10] a few times in context.[24] Notice the changes. Working with Stein, what sounds right? What are the alternatives? Speculate on why you might have made your choices (some might be fairly personal).

But back to the diagrams. There is something very misleading about the levels drawn in example 2 [1]. It's the all-at-onceness of the image and the lineation of levels. Could (d) learn something from (a), and could (a) learn something from (d)? After all, it is the pleasure and promise of learning, using and gaining skill, that is the point of reading and rereading as poetic practice. The zigzag motion in my analysis has been a modest attempt to point to the working together of various *kinds* of difference. Of course, there are "levels," too, of kinds of concepts. Within the concept of "duration" example 2 [1] shows four kinds. But there is only one saying, and that saying, depending on how complex it is, can involve all these differences of kind in the moment, in momentary and changing ways; and this changing itself could be called rhythmic.

The new stanza in example 1 is a second event, a second beginning and the climax, a moment of great intensity and a crucial turn. In the enjambment of the two stanzas with the concluding [10] and the beginning [11], it is as if [10] were an anacrusis to the second stanza. The new event begins with a very important *And* (outdoing even those two anxious *therefores*) that succeeds, at the end of this two-stanza event, in moving the topic to *difference* and into a resounding victory over *repetition*. But back to the tongue. Note that [11] is long (seventeen syllables, the longest line of the passage), and it can be both challenging and exciting to say. But just try saying, and see what comes out. Because of its complexity, this is a good verse for experimenting.

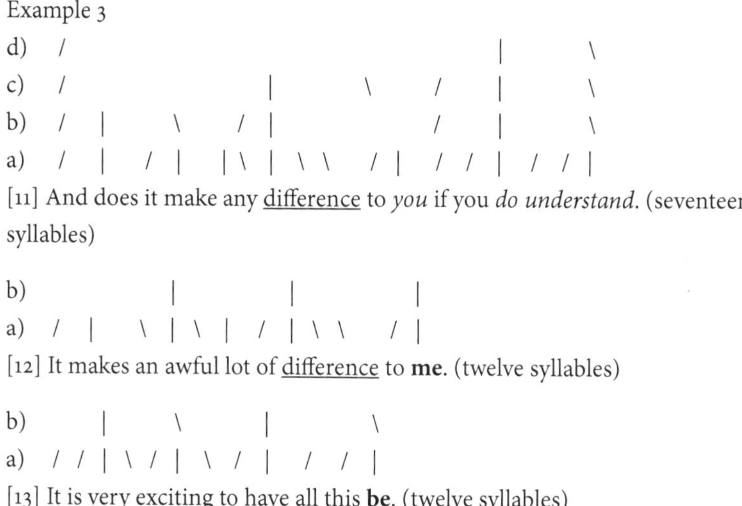

Example 3 [11] (b)–(d) shows three larger events. (Here, I have omitted some marks of continuation to make reading easier.) Here, [11] (b) celebrates the three "*d*'s" (*does*, *difference*, and *do*) headed to *understand*; [11] (d) is a relatively unstructured anacrusis to *do understand*. All three sayings respond to the intensifications of the *do you* repetitions in [10] with an expanded second question finally answered in [12] with an emphatic *awful* and *difference* and *me*. Next, [13] "re-forms" and calms down [12], which comes to work now as the first verse of the concluding couplet that signals the end of the thought in dancing celebration. All the energy of the fiery and personal [12] turns to play and music (isochrony, doubling). The ending rhyme *me-be* can heighten interest and attention, which are here rewarded with the sudden, cooling move from *difference* and *me* to *all* and *be*.

And since we are at the end, we can take a deep breath, hear the echo of all this sounding/feeling, and reflect without speech in a moment of fullness or completeness not interrupted by sound.[25] In such a moment, the final and, let's say, focal *all be* might ring with the now subsidiary sounds we began with, *am completely*. But such resonance at the end would involve much more than this; it would involve many fluid subsidiaries working together. Even if we were to focus on something like "achieving a fullness of being in writing," such an idea, however vaguely or sharply envisioned, would be involved with all the other countless meanings that grow together in the saying and thus together have come to shape this last celebratory phrase. In this way, the truth of "fullness of being" (or whatever we might call the end of the poem) would be a fullness that exceeds the naming of themes. Yet excess was never a foe of naming; indeed, fullness or abundance in opportunities for connection is a powerful inspiration for naming. If as Polanyi says, "we know more than we can say," the possibilities for naming are endless.

But I've argued that we can also say/write more than we can know (a more that Stein calls "genius") and that writing is nothing if not creative of new saying. This excess of Stein's writing is full justification for naming or writing about her work but only if our writing-about aims for new sayings. If suggestions for saying can be tried out, they will have done their service and can be either rejected or simply let go and forgotten as we continue practicing with the passage. And for the sake of freshness, it's good to have a range of plausible suggestions lest a focus on one or another interfere with creative, iterative reading. Along the way, we might pause to ask why different sayings emerge and what difference they can possibly make. This could lead to all sorts of other questions. Some questions might then ask for new repetition, sayings again that can help develop our skills of saying Stein, and perhaps other writers. With practice, we might become good sight readers and take a lot in on a first reading. Or if we are slow-moving theorists, questions could give us pause and, thus, an opportunity to broaden and test our thinking. In either case, we can use this and other written artifacts of passage in an attempt to speak or write further as we would use an instrument or apparatus for productive exploration and discovery of a world. In a world of literary artifacts, institutions, and practices, "the sound of writing" can be heard as a reminder of the rhythmic energy and fluidity of sounding and resounding waves of writing and perhaps be heard, too, as a call for new ways of describing such processes in general and in particular.

NOTES

1. Alfred North Whitehead turns up most prominently at the beginning of Stein's *Autobiography of Alice B. Toklas*: "The three geniuses of whom I wish to speak are Gertrude Stein, Pablo Picasso and Alfred Whitehead. I have met many important people, several great people but I have only known three first class geniuses and in each case on sight within me something rang. . . . In this way my new full life began." Gertrude Stein, *The Autobiography of Alice B.* Toklas (London: Penguin, 1966), 9. But of course, this is Alice's way of speaking of her journey. In "Portraits and Repetition," Stein speaks of genius in far less exclusive terms. For Stein's connections to James, Whitehead, and other process thinkers, see Steven Meyer, *Irresistible Dictation: Gertrude Stein and the Correlations of Writing and Science* (Stanford, CA: Stanford University Press, 2001). At the end of his study, Meyer presents an analysis of intonational contour in Stein's 1935 readings of excerpts from *The Making of Americans*, an analysis that has clear relevance for a description of rhythm.

2. A scientist and philosopher, Polanyi is best known for his concept of "tacit knowledge"—we always know more than we can say. I suggest that that *more* can be held in the saying or writing as a *potential* for meanings beyond the sayer's or writer's, in the meanings made by hearers and the sayings made by readers. Although Polanyi does not explicitly discuss rhythm, rhythm is implicit (tacit) in his theory of discovery and learning. For a compelling introduction to Polanyi's theory, see the essays "Knowing and Being" and "The Logic of Tacit Inference" in Michael Polanyi, *Knowing and Being*, ed. Marjorie Grene (Chicago: University of Chicago Press, 1969), 123–58.

3. This actual, "real time" happening is focally or explicitly here-and-now and also situated in and inseparable from a much larger world constituted of other times and other places. Reciprocally, here-and-now sounding can be said to situate and bring to life a larger world of sedimented meaning.

4. In *The Ancient Phonograph*, Shane Butler argues for the survival, in certain kinds of written language, of *phōnē* as "voice" conceived as a nonlinguistic or extralinguistic speech-sound that can be captured in writing (*graphē*); see Shane Butler, *The Ancient Phonograph* (Brooklyn, NY: Zone, 2015). "Voice" inhabits an interstitial realm between musical sound and linguistic sense as a sort of remainder or excess (see, e.g., the discussion of "Heraclean" voice, 156). As Butler writes, "Centuries of literary texts are filled with—and at least partly defined by—phonic features that cannot be reduced to a function that is, properly speaking, linguistic, even though we might be inclined to call them 'expressive' or 'communicative.' It will be the contention of this book that the ensemble of such features, *added to writing's linguistic work*, long constituted what we should identify as a phonographic claim" (13–14, my italics). For Butler, such features, heard as "sound effects," are constituted primarily by phonic repetitions or alliterations, rhythms of distinctive features. Butler's illustrations are wide-ranging and subtly read, and his narrative is fascinating. Yet I find his restriction of the linguistic to the categories of scientific linguistics too great a limitation. Lost are the fully temporal and rhythmic complexities of active and material tongues and lungs of human beings working throughout human history and, indeed, working within a larger, fully temporal and rhythmic environment that forever exceeds the human.

5. "*Rhuthmos*, meaning literally 'the particular manner of flowing,' describes 'dispositions' or 'configurations' without fixation or natural necessity arising from an arrangement which is always subject to change." Emile Benveniste, *Problems of General Linguistics*, trans. Mary Elizabeth Meek (Coral Gables, FL: University of Miami Press, 1971), 286.

6. This "everything" in the case of writing necessarily includes the manner or mode of

hearing and the manner or mode of seeing. For the present essay, vision will be largely taken for granted as we share an "unlineated" passage from Stein where the visual lines give us no clue of how to say. But we are, of course, reading. Moreover, my suggestions for reading Stein will require visual, diagrammatic examples that themselves must be read and so add another layer of writing, one that would say how to speak.

7. See, e.g., Peter Auer, Elizabeth Couper-Kuhlen, and Frank Muller, *Language in Time: The Rhythm and Tempo of Spoken Interaction* (New York: Oxford University Press, 1999).

8. For an account of "the implicit" at work in linguistic expression, which might support and flesh out this hypothesis, see Eugene Gendlin, "How Philosophy Cannot Appeal to Experience and How It Can," in *Language after Postmodernism: Saying and Thinking in Gendlin's Philosophy*, ed. David Michael Levin (Evanston, IL: Northwestern University Press, 1997), 3–41. For a neurologically based account of the unfolding of mental content inside-out, from "depth" to "surface," see Jason W. Brown, *Self and Process: Brain States and the Conscious Present* (New York: Springer, 1991).

9. For a discussion of "holding" and "moving," see Christopher Hasty, "Rhythmusexperimente—Halt und Bewegung," in *Rhythmus—Balance—Metrum: Formen raumzeitlicher Organisation in den Künsten*, ed. Christian Grüny and Matteo Nanni (Bielefeld: Transcript, 2014), 155–207. This essay also contains close readings of several passages from Stein's *Tender Buttons.*

10. John Keats, "Ode to a Nightingale," in *Complete Poems*, ed. Jack Stillinger (Cambridge, MA: Harvard University Press, 1982), 279–81, line 33.

11. As Will Self explains in conversation with Christopher Tayler, "Writing on a manual makes you slower in a good way, I think. You don't revise as much, you just think more, because you know you're going to have to retype the entire fucking thing. Which is a big stop on just slapping anything down and playing with it." Christopher Tayler, "Smoking Gun," The *Guardian* (US edition), March 21, 2008, www.theguardian.com/books/2008/mar/22/fiction.willself.

12. See, e.g., Eve Ose Askvik, F. R. (Ruud) van der Weel, and Audrey L. H. van der Meer, "The Importance of Cursive Handwriting over Typewriting for Learning in the Classroom: A High-Density EEG Study of 12-Year-Old Children and Young Adults," *Frontiers in Psychology* 11 (July 28, 2020): https://doi.org/10.3389/fpsyg.2020.01810.

13. The "slow/fast" distinction here would have to be developed to take into account that speed can be a virtue, a mark of virtuosity. Suffice it to say that the price of such speed is intense repetition and attention to detail as the way of getting *up* to speed.

14. Derek Attridge has contributed two books that eloquently revise and revive prosodic pedagogy: *Poetic Rhythm: An Introduction* (Cambridge: Cambridge University Press, 1995); and, with Thomas Carper, *Meter and Meaning in Poetry: An Introduction to Rhythm in Poetry* (New York: Routledge, 2003).

15. For a discussion of iambic pentameter, see Christopher Hasty, "Complexity and Passage: Experimenting with Poetic Rhythm," in *The Philosophy of Rhythm*, ed. Peter Cheyne, Andy Hamilton, and Max Paddison (New York: Oxford University Press, 2019), 233–54. This essay, which focuses on Keats's "Hymn to Pan" from *Endymion*, also engages the dimension of phonic rhythm

16. Gertrude Stein, "Portraits and Repetition," in *Lectures in America* (New York: Random House, 1935), 180–81. This passage comes at the midpoint of the text as a summary and conclusion of the first of two parts. The topics of repetition and hearing/talking have been turned over again and again, together with the topic of insistence. To provide some context, here is the end of the preceding paragraph in which the topic of time is first broached:

> Intelligent people although they talk as if they knew something are really confusing, because they are so to speak keeping two times going at once, the repetition time of remem-

> bering and the actual time of talking but, and as they are rarely talking and listening, that is the talking being listening and the listening being talking, although they are clearly saying something they are not clearly creating something, because they are because they always are remembering, they are not at the same time talking and listening. Do you understand. Do you any or all of you understand. Anyway that is the way it is. And you hear it even if you do not say it in the way I say it as I hear it and say it. (180)

The topic of genius was raised only once before: "One may really indeed say that that is the essence of genius, of being most intensely alive, that is being one who is at the same time talking and listening. It is really that that makes one a genius" (170). Here, genius seems generic, a kind and not a degree as it is in *The Autobiography of Alice B. Toklas*, where Alice speaks of "three high class geniuses" she has known (see note 1 above).

17. See Gertrude Stein, "Poetry and Syntax," in *Lectures in America* (New York: Random House, 1935), 209.

18. I suspect that Gilbert Rorison's popular Anglican hymn "Three in One, and One in Three" (1849) was something of a commonplace in Stein's anglophone social and literary world.

19. For a detailed account of this notation and its motivations, see Hasty, "Complexity and Passage."

20. I would warn here that walking and dancing can be misleading examples of rhythm to the extent they imply precise regularity or isochrony. In your experiments saying these "lines," don't seek a beat; instead, try out variations in speed. This experimentation will likely reveal a more intricate regularity (a free "beat"), one ruled by countless factors that come into play in improvisatory saying. Of course, real dancings and walkings are quite complicated, too, in their play with regularity.

21. Think of each "|" as a new turn or new line, a new event. On this durational/scalar analogy, anacrusis would be enjambment, a decision against closure (| \ ) in favor of opening (/ |).

22. Notice that if, instead, you progressively slow your speech, lengthening vowels, you will eventually find yourself singing pitches.

23. I call this inheritance from past to present "projection." As in Polanyi's implicit/explicit, from/to, "inside-out" model, both terms work together. In "projection," past and present work together, goaded or at least further unsettled by future. See Christopher Hasty, *Meter as Rhythm* (New York: Oxford University Press, 2020).

24. Rereading the immediately preceding passage shown in note 15 will give you more to go on and perhaps lead to heightened intensity or insistence in your saying [10]. In context, this intensity might be told as a story of "exasperation" reaching its limit and provoking "acceptance" in [11]–[13]. In your reading, you might try such feelings out. Imagine that a reading is an acting, a performing that is a *poesis*.

25. A kind of holding in the ending of an event can occur also at other time scales, even the sentential ("verses") and the phrasal (| \).

Contributors

Christopher Cannon is Bloomberg Distinguished Professor of English and Classics at Johns Hopkins University. He is the coeditor (with James Simpson) of *The Oxford Chaucer* (Oxford University Press, 2023) and the author of *From Literacy to Literature: England, 1300–1400* (Oxford University Press, 2016).

Ian Cornelius is Associate Professor of English at Loyola University Chicago. He is author of *Reconstructing Alliterative Verse: The Pursuit of a Medieval Meter* (Cambridge University Press, 2017) and of essays and articles on medieval English literature.

Alison Cornish is Professor and Chair of Italian Studies at NYU and current president of the Dante Society of America. She is the author of *Reading Dante's Stars* (Yale University Press, 2000); *Vernacular Translation in Dante's Italy: Illiterate Literature* (Cambridge University Press, 2011); a commentary on Dante's *Paradiso*, translated by Stanley Lombardo (Hackett, 2017); and a number of essays on Dante, Petrarch, Boccaccio, and the culture of translation in which they flourished. Her latest book is *Believing in Dante: Truth in Fiction* (Cambridge University Press, 2022).

Sean Curran is Fellow and College Lecturer in Music and English at Trinity College, Cambridge. In 2018, he was the recipient of both the Jerome Roche Prize of the Royal Musical Association and the Alfred Einstein Award of the American Musicological Society.

Christopher Hasty is the Walter W. Naumburg Professor of Music Emeritus at Harvard University, where he taught music theory.

Steven Justice is Professor Emeritus of English at the University of California, Berkeley.

Sarah Kay has taught medieval French and Occitan at several universities, including Cambridge, Princeton, and most recently New York University, where she is now Professor Emerita. Her latest book, *Medieval Song from Aristotle to Opera*, with an accompanying website of recordings and other documentation, was published by Cornell University Press in 2022.

Meredith Martin is a professor of English at Princeton University, where she also directs the Center for Digital Humanities. Since 2007, she has been the principal investigator on an ongoing digital humanities project called the Princeton Prosody Archive.

Sarah Nooter is Professor at the University of Chicago in Classics and in Theater and Performance Studies. She is the author of *When Heroes Sing: Sophocles and the Shifting Soundscape of Tragedy* (Cambridge University Press, 2012); and *The Mortal Voice in the Tragedies of Aeschylus* (Cambridge University Press, 2017). She is coeditor (with Shane Butler) of *Sound and the Ancient Senses* (Routledge, 2018); and editor of the journal *Classical Philology*. Her most recent monograph is *Greek Poetry in the Age of Ephemerality* (Cambridge University Press, 2023).

Jennifer Richards is the English (2001) Chair in the Faculty of English, University of Cambridge, UK. She is the author of *Rhetoric and Courtliness in Early Modern Literature* (Cambridge University Press, 2003); *Rhetoric: The New Critical Idiom* (Routledge, 2007); and *Voices and Books in the English Renaissance: A New History of Reading* (Oxford University Press, 2019), winner of the 2020 ESSE Book Prize. With Virginia Cox she is coediting volume 3 of *The Cambridge History of Rhetoric* (Cambridge University Press, forthcoming). She is the lead of the AHRC-funded Thomas Nashe Project, editing the works of Thomas Nashe for Oxford University Press. She has recently been awarded a Leverhulme Trust Project Grant for a new project, working with scientists on the emotions of bees, titled "Bee-ing Human: An Interactive Bee Book for the Twenty-First Century."

Emily V. Thornbury is Associate Professor of English at Yale University. She specializes in the aesthetics of Old English and medieval Latin verse and is currently completing a monograph on ornament and its valences in pre-Conquest England.

Index

Illustrations and appendices are indicated by italicized page numbers.